QUOTING IN PARLIAMENTARY QUESTION TIME

Why do recordings of speakers engaging in reported speech at British Prime Minister's Questions from the 1970s–80s sound so distant to us? This cutting-edge study explores how the practices of quoting have changed at parliamentary question time in light of changing conventions and an evolving media landscape. Comparing data from authentic audio and video recordings from 1978 to 1988 and 2003 to 2013, it provides evidence for qualitative and quantitative changes at the micro level (e.g., grammaticalisation processes in the reporting clause) and in more global structures (e.g., rhetorical patterns, and activities). These analytic findings contribute to the theoretical modelling of evidentiality in English, our understanding of constructions, interaction, and change, and of PMQs as an evolving community of practice. One of the first large-scale studies of recent change in an interactional genre of English, this ground-breaking monograph offers a framework for a diachronic interactional sociolinguistic research programme.

ELISABETH REBER is a senior lecturer, University of Würzburg, and currently a replacement professor in English Linguistics, University of Heidelberg. Her work focuses on Interactional (Socio-)Linguistics, Construction Grammar, and Multimodality. She has published the monograph *Affectivity in Interaction* (2012), numerous co-edited volumes, book chapters, and peer-reviewed journal articles.

STUDIES IN ENGLISH LANGUAGE

General Editor
Merja Kytö (Uppsala University)

Editorial Board
Bas Aarts (University College London),
John Algeo (University of Georgia),
Susan Fitzmaurice (University of Sheffield),
Christian Mair (University of Freiburg),
Charles F. Meyer (University of Massachusetts)

The aim of this series is to provide a framework for original studies of English, both present-day and past. All books are based securely on empirical research, and represent theoretical and descriptive contributions to our knowledge of national and international varieties of English, both written and spoken. The series covers a broad range of topics and approaches, including syntax, phonology, grammar, vocabulary, discourse, pragmatics and sociolinguistics, and is aimed at an international readership.

Already published in this series

Haruko Momma: *From Philology to English Studies: Language and Culture in the Nineteenth Century*
Raymond Hickey (ed.): *Standards of English: Codified Varieties around the World*
Benedikt Szmrecsanyi: *Grammatical Variation in British English Dialects: A Study in Corpus-Based Dialectometry*
Daniel Schreier and Marianne Hundt (eds.): *English as a Contact Language*
Bas Aarts, Joanne Close, Geoffrey Leech and Sean Wallis (eds.): *The Verb Phrase in English: Investigating Recent Language Change with Corpora*
Martin Hilpert: *Constructional Change in English: Developments in Allomorphy, Word Formation, and Syntax*
Jakob R. E. Leimgruber: *Singapore English: Structure, Variation, and Usage*
Christoph Rühlemann: *Narrative in English Conversation: A Corpus Analysis of Storytelling*
Dagmar Deuber: *English in the Caribbean: Variation, Style and Standards in Jamaica and Trinidad*
Eva Berlage: *Noun Phrase Complexity in English*
Nicole Dehé: *Parentheticals in Spoken English: The Syntax-Prosody Relation*
Jock O. Wong: *The Culture of Singapore English*
Marianne Hundt (ed.): *Late Modern English Syntax*
Irma Taavitsainen, Merja Kytö, Claudia Claridge and Jeremy Smith (eds.): *Developments in English: Expanding Electronic Evidence*
Arne Lohmann: *English Coordinate Constructions: A Processing Perspective on Constituent Order*

Nuria Yáñez-Bouza: *Grammar, Rhetoric and Usage in English: Preposition Placement 1500–1900*

Anita Auer, Daniel Schreier and Richard J. Watts (eds.): *Letter Writing and Language Change*

John Flowerdew and Richard W. Forest: *Signalling Nouns in English: A Corpus-Based Discourse Approach*

Jeffrey P. Williams, Edgar W. Schneider, Peter Trudgill and Daniel Schreier (eds.): *Further Studies in the Lesser-Known Varieties of English*

Jack Grieve: *Regional Variation in Written American English*

Douglas Biber and Bethany Gray: *Grammatical Complexity in Academic English: Linguistics Change in Writing*

Gjertrud Flermoen Stenbrenden: *Long-Vowel Shifts in English, c. 1050–1700: Evidence from Spelling*

Zoya G. Proshina and Anna A. Eddy (eds.): *Russian English: History, Functions, and Features*

Raymond Hickey (ed.): *Listening to the Past: Audio Records of Accents of English*

Phillip Wallage: *Negation in Early English: Grammatical and Functional Change*

Marianne Hundt, Sandra Mollin and Simone E. Pfenninger (eds.): *The Changing English Language: Psycholinguistic Perspectives*

Joanna Kopaczyk and Hans Sauer (eds.): *Binomials in the History of English: Fixed and Flexible*

Alexander Haselow: *Spontaneous Spoken English: An Integrated Approach to the Emergent Grammar of Speech*

Christina Sanchez-Stockhammer: *English Compounds and Their Spelling*

David West Brown: *English and Empire: Language History, Dialect, and the Digital Archive*

Paula Rodríguez-Puente: *The English Phrasal Verb, 1650–present: History, Stylistic Drifts, and Lexicalisation*

Erik. R. Thomas (ed.): *Mexican American English: Substrate Influence and the Birth of an Ethnolect*

Thomas Hoffmann: *English Comparative Correlatives: Diachronic and Synchronic Variation at the Lexicon-Syntax Interface*

Nuria Yáñez-Bouza, Emma Moore, Linda van Bergen and Willem B. Hollmann (eds.): *Categories, Constructions, and Change in English Syntax*

Raymond Hickey (ed.): *English in the German-speaking World*

Axel Bohmann: *Variation in English World-wide: Registers and Global Varieties*

Raymond Hickey (ed.): *English in Multilingual South Africa: The Linguistics of Contact and Change*

Jeremy J. Smith: *Transforming Early English: The Reinvention of Early English and Older Scots*

Tobias Bernaisch: *Gender in World Englishes*

Lorena Pérez-Hernández: *Speech Acts in English: From Research to Instruction and Textbook Development*

Earlier titles not listed are also available

QUOTING IN PARLIAMENTARY QUESTION TIME

Exploring Recent Change

ELISABETH REBER

University of Würzburg, Germany

Shaftesbury Road, Cambridge CB2 8EA, United Kingdom

One Liberty Plaza, 20th Floor, New York, NY 10006, USA

477 Williamstown Road, Port Melbourne, VIC 3207, Australia

314–321, 3rd Floor, Plot 3, Splendor Forum, Jasola District Centre, New Delhi – 110025, India

103 Penang Road, #05–06/07, Visioncrest Commercial, Singapore 238467

Cambridge University Press is part of Cambridge University Press & Assessment, a department of the University of Cambridge.

We share the University's mission to contribute to society through the pursuit of education, learning and research at the highest international levels of excellence.

www.cambridge.org
Information on this title: www.cambridge.org/9781108799041

DOI: 10.1017/9781108869898

© Elisabeth Reber 2021

This publication is in copyright. Subject to statutory exception and to the provisions of relevant collective licensing agreements, no reproduction of any part may take place without the written permission of Cambridge University Press & Assessment.

First published 2021
First paperback edition 2025

A catalogue record for this publication is available from the British Library

Library of Congress Cataloging-in-Publication data
NAMES: Reber, Elisabeth, author.
TITLE: Quoting in parliamentary question time: exploring recent change / Elisabeth Reber.
DESCRIPTION: Cambridge, UK; New York: Cambridge University Press, 2021. | Series: Studies in English language | Includes bibliographical references and index.
IDENTIFIERS: LCCN 2021001527 (print) | LCCN 2021001528 (ebook) | ISBN 9781108835978 (hardback) | ISBN 9781108799041 (paperback) | ISBN 9781108869898 (ebook)
SUBJECTS: LCSH: English language – Indirect discourse. | Linguistic change – Great Britain. | Legislators – Great Britain – Language. | Prime ministers – Great Britain – Language.
CLASSIFICATION: LCC PE1444.5 .R43 2021 (print) | LCC PE1444.5 (ebook) | DDC 417/.7–dc23
LC record available at https://lccn.loc.gov/2021001527
LC ebook record available at https://lccn.loc.gov/2021001528

ISBN   978-1-108-83597-8   Hardback
ISBN   978-1-108-79904-1   Paperback

Cambridge University Press & Assessment has no responsibility for the persistence or accuracy of URLs for external or third-party internet websites referred to in this publication and does not guarantee that any content on such websites is, or will remain, accurate or appropriate.

Contents

List of Figures	*page* x
List of Tables	xiii
Acknowledgements	xvii
List of Abbreviations	xix

1 Introduction 1
  1.1 Background 4
    1.1.1 Quoting as an Evidential Practice 5
    1.1.2 Constructions, Interaction, and Change 6
    1.1.3 The House of Commons as a Community of Practice 7
    1.1.4 A Proposal for a Diachronic Interactional (Socio-) Linguistic Research Programme 8
  1.2 Outline of Chapters 9
    1.2.1 Literature Review 9
    1.2.2 Analytic Study 9

2 Reported Speech and Evidentiality 12
  2.1 Reported Speech as a Grammatical Construction 12
  2.2 Reported Speech as an Evidential Practice 15
  2.3 Reported Speech in Parliamentary Interaction 18
  2.4 Reported Speech and Authorship 22
  2.5 Summary and Conclusions 24

3 Prime Minister's Questions 26
  3.1 History of Prime Minister's Questions 26
  3.2 Spatial Arrangements 30
  3.3 Institutional Procedure 31
  3.4 Participation Framework and Turn-taking System 33
  3.5 Question and Answer Sequences 35
  3.6 Summary and Conclusions 37

4 Data, Transcription, and Methodology 38
  4.1 Database for the Study 38
    4.1.1 Compilation 38

	4.1.2	Composition of Participation and Calculation of Frequencies	42
4.2	Transcription		46
4.3	Basic Methodological Assumptions		47
4.4	Analytic Questions and Procedure		51

5 Reporting Clauses 53
- 5.1 Past Research 54
  - 5.1.1 Reporting Clauses as a Locus for Reference 54
  - 5.1.2 Reporting Clauses with *Say* and Grammaticalisation 56
- 5.2 Subjects 58
  - 5.2.1 Nominal Subjects 60
  - 5.2.2 Pronominal Subjects 76
- 5.3 Verbs 85
- 5.4 Indirect Objects 91
- 5.5 Adverbials 96
- 5.6 Entering Grammaticalisation? The Case of HE SAID 103
- 5.7 Entering Grammaticalisation? The Case of [Temporal adverbial + THE PRIME MINISTER + SAY + quotation] 117
- 5.8 Summary and Conclusions 120
  - 5.8.1 Reporting Clauses as Constructions 121
  - 5.8.2 General Tendencies 123

6 Reported Clauses 125
- 6.1 Past Research 126
- 6.2 Indirect Speech 129
- 6.3 'In Between' 143
- 6.4 Direct Speech 150
- 6.5 Repackaging Quotations (2003–2013) 178
- 6.6 The Formula (AND) I QUOTE (2003–2013) 185
- 6.7 Summary and Conclusions 190
  - 6.7.1 Contextualisations of Reported Clauses in Public Speaking in Parliament over Time 191
  - 6.7.2 General Tendencies 193

7 Reported Speech and Rhetorical Structures 195
- 7.1 Past Research 195
- 7.2 Lists 199
- 7.3 Contrast 202
- 7.4 Combined Structures (2003–2013) 207
  - 7.4.1 Combined List, Contrast, and Puzzle–Solution 207
  - 7.4.2 Puzzle–Solution 211
- 7.5 Summary and Conclusions 216
  - 7.5.1 Rhetorical Structures as a Resource for Public, Mediated Speaking in Parliament 217
  - 7.5.2 General Tendencies 218

8	Reported Speech in Recurrent Courses of Action	219
	8.1 Past Research	220
	8.2 The Enticing Sequence (2003–2013)	225
	8.3 Trading-Quotes Sequences	245
	8.4 Summary and Conclusions	292
	8.4.1 Building Sequences with Quotations: Enticing and Trading-quotes Sequences	292
	8.4.2 General Tendencies	294
9	Summary and Conclusions	296
	9.1 Summary of Findings	296
	9.2 Conclusions	299
	9.2.1 Evidentiality in English	299
	9.2.2 Constructions, Interaction, and Change	302
	9.2.3 The House of Commons as a Community of Practice in Change – PMQs as an Activity in Change	303
	9.2.4 Diachronic Interactional (Socio-)Linguistics	305

Appendix A   307
   GAT 2 Transcription Conventions   307
   Conventions for Multimodal Transcription   311
   Audience Responses   311
Appendix B   312
References   325
Index   343

Figures

3.1	Ecology of space of the House of Commons Chamber.	*page* 30
3.2	Positions of cameras, microphones, and clock.	32
3.3	Addressees and audiences targeted by parliamentary speakers.	34
4.1	Distribution of turn types and speaker roles in 1978–1988.	44
4.2	Distribution of turn types and speaker roles in 2003–2010.	44
4.3	Distribution of turn types and speaker roles in 2010–2013.	45
5.1	1978–1988 exemplar cloud of reporting clauses.	121
5.2	2003–2013 exemplar cloud of reporting clauses.	122
6.1	The Leader of the Liberal Democrats displays visual orientation towards the PM.	139
6.2	The Leader of the Liberal Democrats orients down to his notes, tracing the point where he has written down the quotation with his left thumb.	139
6.3	The Leader of the Liberal Democrats glances towards the PM.	140
6.4	The Leader of the Liberal Democrats sustains a downward gaze at his notes.	140
6.5	The Leader of the Liberal Democrats displays visual orientation towards the PM.	141
6.6	The Leader of the Liberal Democrats is midway into the production of the reporting clause without consulting his notes, orienting towards the opposition benches.	142
6.7	The Leader of the Liberal Democrats sustains a gaze at the opposition benches towards the end of the quotation.	143
6.8	The LO shows repeated visual engagement with his notes during the production of the quotation.	149
6.9	The PM is holding the page midway.	157
6.10	The PM has turned the page completely.	158
6.11	The PM rests on the dispatch box and leans forward.	159
6.12	The PM looks up from his notes.	160
6.13	The PM is positioned at the onset of the reporting clause.	163

List of Figures

6.14	The PM readjusts his posture at the initial boundary of the quotation.	163
6.15	The PM looks down at the final boundary of the quotation.	164
6.16	The LO shifts his visual orientation towards the PM.	165
6.17	The PM looks towards the opposition benches before engaging with his notes.	167
6.18	The PM is touching the notes in synchrony with the proper name of the source, *jock STIRrup*.	168
6.19	The PM is tracing the direct quotation as written in the orator's notes.	169
6.20	The PM shows visual orientation to his notes.	169
6.21	The PM displays visual disengagement from his notes.	170
6.22	The LO looks at the Speaker during the reporting clause.	172
6.23	The LO sustains his gaze, beginning the quotation.	173
6.24	The LO reorients his gaze towards the PM and government benches.	173
6.25	The PM orients his gesture and gaze towards the Speaker and the government benches.	175
6.26	The PM indexes the ascribed source gesturally and verbally while showing no orientation to his notes.	176
6.27	The PM maintains his bodily alignment during the quotation.	176
6.28	The PM has readopted his original posture of head position and gesture.	177
6.29	The PM marks the source, while gazing towards the Speaker and gesturally referring to the author of the source, the LO sitting on the opposite bench.	180
6.30	The PM gesturally references the author of the source.	181
6.31	The PM shows kinetic, manual engagement with notes, searching for the quotation in his folder.	181
6.32	The PM rips out the page from his folder.	182
6.33	The PM displays full engagement with his notes before resuming with a restart of the quotation.	183
6.34	The PM performs a 'literalised' quotation.	183
6.35	On completion of the quotation, the PM puts the paper back down on the dispatch box.	184
8.1	The LO displays visual disengagement from his notes and orientation towards the PM.	233
8.2	The LO thanks the Prime Minister, accompanied by the opposition MPs' audible laughter.	234

List of Figures

8.3	The LO displays an orientation to his notes to read out the quotation.	235
8.4	The LO sustains a gaze onto his notes.	236
8.5	The LO looks up towards the government benches post-completion of the quotation.	237
8.6	The PM looks towards the S, showing disengagement from his notes.	240
8.7	The PM displays visual engagement with his notes.	241
8.8	The PM takes his notes, preparing for a visual presentation of his sources.	262
8.9	The PM reorients his gaze towards his notes.	262
8.10	The PM disengages from his notes to look towards the opposition benches.	263
8.11	The PM taps on his notes with his open hand.	265
8.12	The LO displays visual engagement with his notes.	268
8.13	The LO again displays visual engagement with his notes.	269
8.14	The PM shows haptic and visual engagement with his notes.	273
8.15	The LO rests on the dispatch box.	276
8.16	The LO displays haptic and visual engagement with his notes.	277
8.17	The LO disengages his visual orientation from his notes.	277
8.18	The PM sustains a gaze towards the opposition benches.	280
8.19	The PM sustains a gaze oriented towards the opposition benches.	280
8.20	The LO places his notes on the dispatch box.	284
8.21	The LO produces more written evidence while the PM consults his notes.	285
8.22	The LO prepares to quote.	285
8.23	The LO delivers 'literalised' indirect speech.	286
8.24	The LO points at his evidence in coordination with the key word in the quotation.	287
8.25	The LO produces direct speech in the question component without visually recruiting his sources.	288
8.26	The PM produces the quotation, showing multiple orientations towards the opposition benches.	291
8.27	The PM continues to produce the quotation, showing multiple orientations towards the opposition benches.	291

Tables

2.1	The grammatical form of reported speech	page 25
3.1	Historical outline of Prime Minister's Questions	28
4.1	Speakers at the dispatch box in the 1978–1988 data set	40
4.2	Speakers at the dispatch box in the 2003–2013 data set	41
4.3	Number of substantial questions (1978–1988 and 2003–2013)	43
5.1	Relative frequencies of heavy and light noun phrases over turn types and speaker roles in subjects of finite reporting clauses (1978–1989)	313
5.2	Absolute distribution of noun phrases in 1978–1988 subjects in finite reporting clauses	62
5.3a	Relative frequencies of noun phrases in subject position of finite reporting clauses across question turns (MPs, LOs) and answer turns (PMs, 2003–2013)	314
5.3b	Relative frequencies of noun phrases in subject position of finite reporting clauses in question–answer sequences between the Leader of the Liberal Democrats and the PM (2003–2010)	315
5.4	Absolute distribution of light and heavy NPs over subjects in finite reporting clauses (2003–2013)	69
5.5	Absolute distribution of personal and relative pronouns in subjects of finite reporting clauses (1978–1988)	77
5.6	Absolute distribution of pronominal subjects in finite reporting clauses (1978–1988)	78
5.7	Absolute distribution of pronominal subjects in finite reporting clauses (2003–2013)	80
5.8	Absolute distribution of personal pronouns in subjects of finite reporting clauses (2003–2013)	81
5.9	Relative frequency of verb forms across turns types and speaker roles (1978–1988)	316

5.10a	Relative frequencies of verb forms across turns types and speaker roles (LOs, MPs and PMs, 2003–2013)	317
5.10b	Relative frequencies of verb forms in the sequences between the Leader of the Liberal Democrats and the PM (2003–2010)	318
5.11	Relative frequency of indirect objects across turns types and speaker roles (1978–1988)	319
5.12a	Relative frequency of indirect objects across turns types and speaker roles (LOs, MPs and PMs, 2003–2013)	319
5.12b	Relative frequency of indirect objects in question–answer sequences between the Leader of the Liberal Democrats and the PM (2003–2010)	319
5.13	Relative frequency of circumstantial adverbials in finite reporting clauses relative to number of question and answer turns, defined by speaker role (1978–1988)	320
5.14	Absolute syntactic and semantic distribution of adverbials in finite reporting clauses (1978–1988)	97
5.15a	Relative frequency of circumstantial adverbials in finite reporting clauses across turn types and speaker roles (MPs, LOs, PMs, 2003–2013)	321
5.15b	Relative frequency of circumstantial adverbials in finite reporting clauses in question–answer sequences between the Leader of the Liberal Democrats and the PM (2003–2010)	321
5.16	Syntactic and semantic distribution of circumstantial adverbials in finite clauses (2003–2013)	99
5.17	Frequency of candidates for formulaic constructions relative to number of question and answer turns, defined by speaker role (1978–1988)	322
5.18	Absolute distribution of I SAID in finite reporting clauses (1978–1988)	104
5.19a	Relative frequencies of candidates for formulaic constructions across turn types and speaker roles (2003–2013)	323
5.19b	Relative frequencies of candidates for formulaic constructions across turn types and speaker roles (2003–2013)	324
5.20	Absolute distribution of [pronominal subject + SAY in simple aspect + bare reported clause] and other formats	105
5.21	Absolute distribution of candidates for 'formulaic' constructions in reporting clauses (2003–2013)	105

List of Tables

5.22	Correlation between subject THE PRIME MINISTER and temporal adverbials in finite reporting clauses (1978–1988, 2003–2013)	118
6.1	Relative frequencies of indirect speech across turn types and speaker roles (1978–1988)	130
6.2a	Relative frequencies of indirect speech across turn types and speaker roles (MPs, LOs, and PMs, 2003–2013)	135
6.2b	Relative frequencies of indirect speech in question–answer sequences between the Leader of the Liberal Democrats and the PM (2003–2010)	135
6.3	Relative frequencies of grammatically ambiguous speech across turn types and speaker roles (1978–1988)	144
6.4a	Relative frequencies of grammatically ambiguous speech across turn types and speaker roles (MPs, LOs, PMs, 2003–2013)	146
6.4b	Relative frequencies of grammatically ambiguous speech in question–answer sequences between the Leader of the Liberal Democrats and the PM (2003–2010)	147
6.5	Frequencies of direct speech relative to number of question and answer turns defined by speaker roles (1978–1988)	150
6.6a	Relative frequencies of direct speech across turn types and speaker roles (MPs, LOs, PMs, 2003–2013)	156
6.6b	Relative frequencies of direct speech in question–answer sequences between the Leader of the Liberal Democrats and the PM (2003–2010)	156
6.7a	Relative frequencies of (AND) I QUOTE across turn types and speaker roles (MPs, LOs, PMs, 2003–2013)	189
6.7b	Relative frequencies of (AND) I QUOTE in question–answer sequences between the Leader of the Liberal Democrats and the PM (2003–2010)	190
7.1a	Absolute distribution of puzzle–solution structures in the question–answer sequences between the LO or MPs and the PM (2003–2013)	211
7.1b	Absolute distribution of puzzle–solution structures in the question–answer sequences between the LLD and the PM (2003–2010)	211
8.1	The sequence of enticing a challengeable	222
8.2	Dimensions of questioning	223
8.3	Collection of enticing sequences (2003–2013)	226

8.4	Absolute distribution of initial, simple questions	226
8.5	Distribution of verbs of communication with quotative function in prefaces of second question turns	226
8.6	Trading-quotes sequences in the 2003–2013 sample	254
8.7	Absolute distribution of interrogatives in first, simple question turns in trading-quotes sequences	254
8.8	Distribution of SAY and other quotative markers in the first three turns of the trading-quotes sequence	255

Acknowledgements

This monograph represents a slightly revised version of my *Habilitationsschrift* (post-doctoral thesis), accepted by the Faculty of Arts, University of Potsdam, in December 2018.

My post-doctoral thesis project was partially supported by a research fellowship awarded by the Deutsche Forschungsgemeinschaft (DFG, German Research Foundation) to conduct the project 'Quoting as an evidential practice in Prime Minister's Question Time' as a visiting scholar at the Department of Sociology, University of California at Santa Barbara (UCSB), 1 March–15 July 2016 (reference number RE 2824/3–1) and by a grant (DFG) for the scientific network 'Multimodality and embodied interaction' (directors: Cornelia Gerhardt and Elisabeth Reber) between 2012 and 2019 (reference number: GE 1137/4–1).

No project like this can be undertaken without the tremendous help from a wide range of individuals, and I would like to thank the following: my referees Dagmar Barth-Weingarten, Elizabeth Couper-Kuhlen, and Andreas H. Jucker, for their inspiring mentorship and belief in me. The chair of my Habilitation committee, Margret Selting, for her unwavering support and motivation. My faculty sponsor, Geoffrey Raymond, and Sandra A. Thompson, for being so generous with their time and expertise, during my research stay at UCSB, and the members of the Language, Interaction, and Social Organization unit (LISO). Stephen Bates and Alison Sealey for sharing their data and insights of PMQs with me on a lecture trip to the Universities of Birmingham and Lancaster. Carolin Biewer, Anita Fetzer, and Oliver Traxel, for their help and advice. Hans Sauer for valuable discussions and encouragement. Cornelia Gerhardt and the members and guests of the scientific network 'Multimodality and embodied interaction' for exploring embodiments of evidential practices with me. My colleagues at the Universities of Erlangen-Nürnberg, Potsdam, and Würzburg for their helpful feedback and support during various stages of this project. The Cambridge University Press series editor, Merja Kytö, and an anonymous reviewer for their thorough comments and helpful suggestions. The commissioning editor Helen Barton and editorial assistant Isabel Collins, for guiding me with a sure hand. Allison Adelman and Gordon Lee for their outstanding, meticulous copyediting. My friends for pushing me to keep going throughout this long journey, and first and foremost my family, especially Felizia, Jonathan, and Sebastian for their love, enthusiasm, and joy.

Abbreviations

BBC	British Broadcasting Corporation
C	challenger
C. difficile	*Clostridium difficile*
CGEL	*Comprehensive Grammar of the English Language*
Con	Conservative Party
CTP	complement-taking predicate
DepPM	deputy Prime Minister
DS	direct speech
HC	House of Commons
HMRC	HM Revenue and Customs
IDS	indirect speech
Lab	Labour Party
LD	Liberal Democrats
Lib	Liberal Party
LLD	Leader of the Liberal Party (until 1988)/Liberal Democrats (from 1989)
LO	Leader of the Opposition
MP(s)	Member(s) of Parliament
MRSA	Methicillin-resistant *Staphylococcus aureus*
NHS	National Health Service
NP	noun phrase
OED	Oxford English Dictionary
PM	Prime Minister
PMQs	Prime Minister's Questions
PP	prepositional phrase
RAF	Royal Air Force

RST	Rhetorical Structure Theory
S	Speaker of the House of Commons
SDP	Social Democratic Party
SNP	Scottish National Party
T	target
VAT	Value Added Tax

CHAPTER I

Introduction

The general interest which drives this study is to explore why audio recordings of speakers engaging in reported speech at Prime Minister's Questions (PMQs) from the late 1970s and 1980s sound so distant to us today. PMQs is a parliamentary question time in the British House of Commons where the Prime Minister (PM) takes questions from backbench Members of Parliament (MPs), the Leader of the Opposition (LO), and other leaders of opposition parties. Taking a real-time approach, the study analyses how practices of quoting have emerged in the rapidly evolving 'community of practice' of the House of Commons (Lave and Wenger 1991; see also Harris 2001; Jucker and Kopaczyk 2013; Wenger 1998), comparing its uses based on authentic audio and video recordings from two periods (1978–1988, i.e., before television cameras were allowed into the House and PMQs was broadcast on radio, and 2003–2013, for which we have television footage). These two periods span 36 years, that is, 'one or two generations' (Weinreich *et al.* 1968: 103), a timeframe across which change can be observed.[1]

To get a first glimpse into how reported speech has changed at PMQs, consider Exx. (1) and (2). Ex. (1) is drawn from audio recordings of the 1978–1988 data set. Here quotations are typically performed in the MPs' question turns. The excerpt has two quotations (lines 3–4 and 6–9).[2]

---

[1] In a later publication, Labov defines the suitable time span as 'a minimum of a half generation to a maximum of two' (Labov 1981: 177).
[2] See Appendix A for the transcription conventions.

(1)   PMQs 01 Nov. 1979
MP: William Hamilton (Lab); PM: Margaret Thatcher (Con); S: George Thomas

```
1    S:           HAmilton-
2    MP:          will the right honourable lady take: tIme this afternoon to
                  reread (.) the manifesto on which she was eLECted;
3          ->     uh in which it said that it WASn't the intention of the tory
           ->     government;
4          ->     to reDUCE expenditure on the national hEAlth service;
5                 will she Also take time to READ,
6          ->     a recent debate on the national health service when (.) HER party
           ->     was in opposition and the present leader;
7          ->     the present SPOKESman;
8          ->     the present minister for the health service said that the NURses;
9          ->     needed as GOOD treatment as the: polIce and the armed fOrces;
10                will shE: seek to: implement BOTH those prOmises;
11                (2.0)
12   PM:          ((takes turn))
```

In what is typical of this period, the quotations at PMQs are produced in indirect speech with the complementiser *that* (*in which it said that it WASn't the intention of the tory government to reDUCE expenditure (...)*, lines 3–4; *(...) the present minister for the health service said that the NURses needed as GOOD treatment as the: polIce and the armed fOrces*, lines 6–9) and are prefaced by interrogative structures (*will the right honourable lady take: tIme this afternoon (...)*, line 2; *will she Also take time to READ (...)*, lines 5–6).

This contrasts with what we find in the 2003–2013 data set where there is not only a general increase of reported speech but also that quotations are most frequently performed in question turns by the LO. Ex. (2) illustrates such a case. The quotations are in lines 3–8.

(2)   PMQs 16 July 2003
PM: Tony Blair (Lab); LO: Iain Duncan Smith (Con); S: Michael Martin

```
1    S:              Iain dUncan SM |°[ITH-]
2    MPs:                           |°[h h]*[h h h hh hh h °] [h h  h h]*
     cam         >> medium close-up of PM|extreme long shot --->
     loW                            °walks towards dispatch box°
     loG                                 *places notes onto dispatch box*
3    LO:    ->                      [(1.54)] [(1.15)] □+[the ↑FOReign
     loP                                          □rests on dispatch
     loH                                          +gaze down onto
     LO:    -> affairs select committee chairman|*has sAId;]+=
```

```
        cam                              -->| medium close-up
        loP     box -->
        loH     notes                                -->+
        loG                              *holds notes in right hand -->
4    LO:  -> +=<<p>then I QUOTE;>+=
     loH     +gaze towards PM     +
5    LO:  -> =<<rall>+it's MOST unlIkely>,=
     loH             +gaze down onto notes --->
6    LO:  -> =that dOctor kelly was the prIme source for the story +about
     loH                                                        -->+ gaze
     LO:  -> the government's + manipu[lation of inTELLigence;]+
7    MPs:                     [<<pp> mur mur mur mur>    ]=
     loH        towards PM     + down to notes                  +
8    LO:  -> +°h [↑AND that he has been + pOorly treated by the
9    MPs:        [<<pp> mur mur mur mur mur mur mur mur mur mur
     loH     +gaze towards PM       + down to notes -->
     LO:     gOvernment;]+
     MPs:    mur mur>   ]=
     loH                 -->+
10   LO:     +[°h will the ↑PRIME minister□*now apOlogise;]□*|
11   MPs:    =[<<pp> mur mur mur mur mur mur mur mur mur>    ]=
     cam                                              -->  |
     loP                              -->□straightens himself□
     loH     +gaze towards PM --->>
     loG                              *picks up notes       *
12   LO:     |□§‡ (0.21) [(0.46) ] [(1.17)] □§
13   MPs              [mur mur]  [1 1 1]  [j j j j]
     cam     |long shot --->>
     loP     □sitting down              □
     pmP        §standing up            §
     pmH        ‡downward gaze -->>
```

Although forms of indirect speech with the complementiser *that* dominate (*↑AND that he has been pOorly treated by the gOvernment*, line 8), the use of *that* is increasingly absent in the years of 2003–2013. Speakers more often enact what Rumsey (1992) calls 'literalized' direct speech (*it's MOST unlikely that dOctor kelly was the prIme source (. . .)*, lines 5–6), producing the verbal routine (AND) I QUOTE (line 4) to claim direct access to the original wording of the evidence, and visually recruiting their sources.[3] Finally, it has become more common for MPs to produce orchestrated,

---

[3] I use capital letters when making generic reference to all possible forms – phonetic-prosodic, morphosyntactic – of a linguistic expression in my data.

collective audience responses. All in all, the conduct of question time has become more interactional, which seems to have fostered processes of grammaticalisation in the quotative clauses.

As illustrated in the two excerpts, the analytic focus of the study is on reported speech with the quotative SAY. What triggered this choice was the observation that claims of evidential access, in particular in the form of reported speech with SAY, are pervasive in the question–answer sequences at today's PMQs. In linking changes in the use of reported speech, that is, a differentiation of forms and an overall increased frequency, with a changed composition of participation in the interaction as well as a changed mediation of PMQs between 1978 and 2013, the study identifies grammaticalisation processes in the reporting clause HE SAID (Chapter 5); changes in the forms, frequencies, and distribution of reported clauses, that is, of quotations across participant roles (Chapter 6); changes in the performances of rhetorical structures (e.g., lists, contrasts, puzzle–solutions) in which reported speech is organised (Chapter 7); and changes in the practices of how quotations are deployed as building blocks for action formation in the question–answer sequences at PMQs, leading to the evolution of recurrent courses of action (Chapter 8). Based on these findings, this monograph contributes to our theoretical understanding of evidentiality in English as a (seemingly) non-evidential language (cf. Aikhenvald 2004; Diewald and Smirnova 2010a); and to our understanding of PMQs as a changing activity performed by an evolving community of practice. Selected findings are discussed with respect to constructions, interaction, and change (e.g., Bybee 2013; Hopper 1987, 1998; Mulder and Thompson 2008). The book makes a proposal for a diachronic interactional (socio)linguistic research programme.

In what follows, I will present the previous research background of the study (1.1) as well as outline the subsequent chapters (1.2).

1.1 Background

Language change in contemporary English represents a burgeoning field and has primarily been studied from a corpus-linguistic perspective since the mid-1990s (e.g., Hundt and Mair 1999; Leech *et al.* 2009; Mair 2006; Mair and Leech 2006). Despite relevant article-length investigations on historical recordings from the perspectives of Historical Pragmatics (Jucker and Landert 2015) and Conversation Analysis (Clayman and Heritage 2002a; Clayman *et al.* 2006, 2007; Heritage and Clayman 2013), as well as the acknowledgement of the need for historical spoken corpora in Interactional Linguistics (e.g., Barth-Weingarten 2014; Couper-Kuhlen

2011), questions of recent change in interactional English have nevertheless remained under-researched to date. Because of the lack of suitable recordings, the historical study of recent change in spoken English was not considered to be a methodologically feasible research direction even during the mid-2000s (e.g., Mair 2006: 21). Against this backdrop, the present study breaks new ground in analysing evolving practices in spoken English (here forms of reported speech) based on authentic recordings from different periods.[4] In what represents a novel approach, the observed changes are correlated with and interpreted in terms of the evolution of the parliamentary community of practice, which engages in interaction at PMQs, facing changing institutional conditions and an evolving media landscape (from radio to TV/internet broadcasts) during the 36 years spanned by the data under study.

This means that the objective of the study is to examine the actual use of reported speech in parliamentary interaction in and over time, but it does not intend to offer a critical analysis of British politics.

1.1.1 Quoting as an Evidential Practice

Claims of evidential access are pervasive to the question–answer sequences at PMQs, where they serve as important building blocks for action formation and courses of action as well as for the social construction of authority and credibility (Reber 2014a). While there is a plethora of literature on quotations and reported speech in spoken and written English (see, e.g., Buchstaller 2017; Holt 2009 for an overview, and the contributions to Arendholz *et al.* 2015; Buchstaller and van Alphen 2012; Holt and Clift 2010), little research has been done on reported speech in British parliamentary interaction. Antaki and Leudar (2001) – based on material taken from Hansard, the official written record of parliamentary debates, from the 1990s – show how MPs use literal quotations from political opponents as a rhetorical device to build hostile actions in parliamentary debates. Their work is seminal in demonstrating the evidential function of verbatim quotations in parliamentary discourse. Some of the most recent research has revealed a new style of quoting by Jeremy Corbyn, when he became the Labour Leader of the Opposition in 2015 (Bull and Waddle 2019; Fetzer and Bull 2019; Fetzer and Weizman 2018), in that he quotes ordinary people rather than the government (1978–1988) or political and public authorities in

---

[4] At the time of writing, the London–Lund Corpus 2 of spoken British English (LLC 2) had just been launched, and the Spoken British National Corpus 2014 (Love *et al.* 2017) had been publicly available for only a few years, suggesting a greater interest in Linguistics and an increased possibility of doing this research compared to ten years before.

general (2003–2013) as shown by this study. While this recent work is relevant in confirming the observation made in this study that changes in practices are tied to changes in the participation framework, it focuses on written transcripts rather than taking PMQs for what it is – *embodied, oral* performances of interactional power talk for a public audience.

To return to the notion of quoting as an evidential practice, note that the adjective 'evidential' can have two meanings (see also Anderson 1986: 274), both of which will be relevant in the study. In its more vernacular use, it means 'providing or relating to evidence'.[5] This is how Antaki and Leudar (2001: 479, 481) use it, and this function of reported speech is central at PMQs. The corresponding noun is 'evidence'.[6] I will show that in serving this function, performances of reported speech are interactionally relevant and have emerged as patterned building blocks for action formation in the question–answer sequences in general but also, in particular, recently in recurrent courses of action between the LO and the PM.

As a linguistic term, 'evidential' refers to the expressions providing or relating to 'the speaker's/writer's basis of knowledge as something seen, heard, inferred, or told' (Bednarek 2006: 636). This understanding formed the starting point of my study. Here related forms are 'evidential' or 'evidentiality'. Typologically, a distinction has been made between languages where evidentiality forms a linguistic category, for example, in smaller South American languages or Russian, and those where this is not the case, such as English (Aikhenvald 2004).

However, based on the observation that reporting clauses come in formulaic chunks which have been emergent in and over time and can even enter processes of grammaticalisation at PMQs, I will suggest that the relation of evidential and non-evidential languages should not be conceived of as dichotomous but as more dynamic than has been previously suggested (see also Diewald and Smirnova 2010a, for German).

1.1.2 Constructions, Interaction, and Change

With respect to grammatical theory, the study draws on Emergent Grammar (Hopper 1987, 1998) and usage-based approaches (e.g., Bybee 2003, 2006, 2011; Bybee and Thompson 1997). According to Emergent Grammar, grammatical structure not only stems from but also forms context-specific language use over

---

[5] https://dictionary.cambridge.org/dictionary/english/evidential
[6] Evidence is defined as 'objects, documents, official statements, etc. that are used to prove something is true or not true, especially for legal or insurance purposes' (https://dictionary.cambridge.org/dictionary/english/evidence).

time and in the real time of social interaction (Hopper 1987: 142). Language is 'pre-patterned, pre-fabricated' (Hopper 1987: 145), that is, made up of 'formulaic' expressions (Hopper 1987: 146), but at the same time always emergent historically and in the in situ production of talk. Because of its functional perspective on linguistic patterns in conversation, Emergent Grammar has been welcomed by students of spoken interaction in a shared enterprise to offer a historical, theoretical account of spoken language use which is empirically grounded in the analysis of emergent structures in naturally occurring interaction (e.g., Barth-Weingarten 2014; Couper-Kuhlen 2011). Moreover, I show that the principles put forward in terms of frequency and change in usage-based grammar theory are interrelated with social change. In an attempt to model the findings theoretically, I use Bybee's exemplar model (Bybee 2013; Bybee and Eddington 2006) to depict constructional change.

1.1.3 The House of Commons as a Community of Practice

Data from PMQs present the rare opportunity to have access to authentic recordings of spoken English which span several decades, that is, since the first year that it was radio broadcast (1978) up to today's television programmes and webcasts. Prior research (Harris 2001: 453–454; Shaw 2000: 402) has conceptualised the House of Commons, where PMQs takes place, as a community of practice, a view which is adopted in the present study. First and foremost, such a perspective allows us to:

> take into account the historical continuity of Prime Minister's Question Time, the sense in which, as an activity, it represents discourse practices that have evolved over a long period of time and are still evolving [...] (Harris 2001: 454)

From this perspective, the locations where linguistic practices are developed, deployed, and changed again to achieve specific communicative goals, are social activities – genres – which members of a community engage in (see Jucker and Kopaczyk 2013 for discussion). Communities of practice and the wider speech community are treated as 'complementary' notions (Eckert 2006: 685). In proposing 'how social practice and individual "place" in the community interconnect' (Eckert and McConnell 1992a: 464), the notion of communities of practice explains how members of a speech community form smaller 'sub-communities' (Eckert and McConnell 1992a: 464) where they 'develop linguistic patterns as they engage in activity in the various communities in which they participate' (Eckert and McConnell 1992b: 96; see also Eckert and

McConnell 1992a: 473; Eckert 2006: 683). In this view, the emergence (and loss) of linguistic structures is achieved locally in communities of practice in social interaction, two processes which can spread across greater parts of the speech community.

1.1.4 A Proposal for a Diachronic Interactional (Socio-)Linguistic Research Programme

Although grammaticalisation has been one of the core interests of interactional-linguistic research, diachronic study designs exploring change and variation in interactional English have been completely absent. Earlier interactional-linguistic studies on grammaticalisation have taken a synchronic perspective, although the need for diachronic research has been identified (e.g., Barth-Weingarten 2014; Couper-Kuhlen 2011). Previous related work in Conversation Analysis (Clayman and Heritage 2002a; Clayman et al. 2006, 2007; Heritage and Clayman 2013) has centred on the description of action formation rather than linguistic structures. Despite calls for the integration of corpus-linguistic and discourse-analytic methodology to analyse change in spoken genres (Mair 2013), studies following this path have been scarce (e.g., Seggewiß 2013).

In line with the interactional-linguistic research programme, the present study treats the authentic recordings – rather than written transcripts – as the primary database, and takes an inductive approach to examine the phonetic-prosodic realisation of reported speech, as well as its morphosyntactic and lexico-semantic dimensions, in meticulous detail. In two of the four analytic chapters, a detailed study of the bodily movements and manipulation of objects in reported speech is provided (Chapters 6 and 8). I mix qualitative with quantitative methods, which also means to correlate genre-specific, social changes (i.e., a heightened prominence of the Leader of the Opposition over the years) with interactionally driven linguistic quantitative and qualitative changes. In this vein, a diachronic interactional perspective means examining practices in contextualised, situated ways from a participant's perspective, that is, in light of the evolving community of practice and possibly changing participation in the interaction. Moreover, a diachronic interactional approach means examining not only changes in structures on the micro level, but also their organisation in larger rhetorical structures and their role for implementing recurrent courses of action, shedding light on how more global patterns come into being.

1.2 Outline of Chapters

Chapters 2–3 prepare the ground for the analytic study, presenting a literature review of past relevant research. Chapters 4–8 comprise the analytical study, and Chapter 9 summarises and concludes it.

1.2.1 Literature Review

Chapter 2 offers a literature review of reported speech and evidentiality and introduces reported speech in its canonical grammatical form as an object of study. In contrast to everyday interaction, participants in parliamentary debates make use of written sources, which they may quote verbatim, a practice which has also been referred to 'literalised' direct speech (Rumsey 1992). In spite of this, the authenticity of direct quotations may be secondary in political oratory, in serving as an involvement strategy similar to mundane talk. The functions of quotations in political discourse very much depend on the sources recruited (self, other, and third party), which warrants the perspective of reported speech as an evidential resource at PMQs.

I propose that evidentiality be understood as the study of practices through which speakers display claims of how they came to know. Finally, the functions of evidential practices with respect to the construction of authority, credibility, and truth in the social processes of political discourse are explained.

Chapter 3 characterises PMQs as an institutionalised, parliamentary activity in which members of the House of Commons have engaged as a community of practice since 1961. A review of the past literature suggests that although its location, the House of Commons Chamber, and the organisation of the activity in question–answer sequences have largely remained the same, the introduction of radio and television broadcasts and the increased prominence of the LO as a questioner may have influenced the forms and distribution of actions performed at PMQs, a development that had not yet been explored from an interactional perspective.

1.2.2 Analytic Study

Chapter 4 describes the datasets for the study and discusses the language-external processes that have contributed to the changes in interaction at PMQs between 1978 and 2013 and that provide the backdrop against which the evolution of reported speech is analysed in the study. The chapter presents the methodology and its implications as well as the transcription conventions and procedure followed.

Chapter 5 represents the first of four empirical chapters constituted by complementary short-time diachronic studies on reporting clauses built with the quotative verb SAY at PMQs. The chapter examines how reporting clauses are emergent constructions. To this end, it compares reporting clauses built with the quotative verb SAY in a qualitative and quantitative study of the 1978–1988 and 2003–2013 data sets. It examines the forms, semantics, and aspects of use and function in a detailed study of the elements of the clause: the subject, which gives the evidential source, the verb, which conveys the act of saying and serves as a quotative, and the optional indirect object (recipient) as well as the circumstance adverbials. Based on further frequency counts, the conventionalisation and grammaticalisation of two specific clausal patterns are explored in detail.

In Chapter 6, the contextualisation patterns of reported clauses, that is, the quotations, are described from the perspective of listeners (1978–1988 audio) and viewers (2003–2013 video). The analysis of phonetic-prosodic, and lexico-syntactic cues as well as audio-visual signals, that is, for example, the crackling of paper notes in the audio data and bodily movements together with the manipulation of objects in the video data, revealed patterned productions of quotations: various types of indirect, direct, and 'in between' speech, showing different distributions between the two data sets. In two case studies it is discussed how the 2003–2013 participants show the tendency towards a more interactional construction of categories, allowing a 'repackaging' in real time, and towards an increased 'literalisation' of quotations, which is also displayed by the emergent use of the construction (AND) I QUOTE.

Chapter 7 studies the organisation of reported speech in rhetorical structures, which densely packages the positions claimed in a way that gets straight to the point. The 1978–1988 and 2003–2013 data sets have both lists and contrasts, while the latter also shows combined list and contrast patterns as well as puzzle–solution structures. This development is indicative of a densification and incisiveness but also a 'popularisation' (Biber 2003) in the delivery of messages.

Chapter 8 investigates the use of reported speech as an evidential practice in the interaction between the LO and PM, where reported speech is most frequently used in the 2003–2013 data set. I analyse how quotations are constitutive of two emergent, recurrent courses of action, enticing sequences and trading-quotes sequences. In both sequence types, reported speech is deployed to build adversarial action formats. Enticing sequences, which are initiated by simple questions, are only documented in the 2003–2013 sample. The practice of trading quotes, on the other hand, has already been known and implemented in the 1978–1988 data but only emerges as a building block for patterned, recurrent courses of action in the 2003–2013 sample. The construction [IF + 3rd person reference to a co-present party + V] is discussed as evidence that the procedural knowledge of the practice of trading quotes has been constructionalised in a linguistic expression.

The study ends with a summary and conclusions which address its implications for our understanding of evidentiality in English, for constructions, interaction, and change, for PMQs as a community of practice, and for Diachronic Interactional (Socio-)Linguistics as an emerging strand of research.

CHAPTER 2

Reported Speech and Evidentiality

In this chapter, I present a general literature review on reported speech and evidentiality relevant to the present study. This discussion is continued in the empirical chapters, 5–6, where past research pertinent to the specific research questions addressed in each of these chapters is reviewed.

In a recent article, Buchstaller describes quotations as a multimodal practice, which are indexed by a quotative verb:

> [R]eported speech – or quotation – [...] involves the recreation of speech, thoughts, sounds or gestures that were originally produced by someone else or by ourselves at a different time (t_{-1}) from the interactive now (t_0). In most speech communities, speakers use *verba dicendi*, such as English *say* and *think* [...] for the reporting of speech and thought processes. (Buchstaller 2017: 399)

Broadly speaking, this is the understanding of reported speech which is used in the study. In this chapter, the initial focus is on quotations as a grammatical construction (2.1; but see Chapters 5–6 for a wider discussion). Next, I discuss reported speech as an evidential practice (2.2), and reported speech in parliamentary interaction (2.3). Finally, I examine questions of authorship in reported speech, in particular with respect to political discourse (2.4). The chapter ends with a summary and conclusions (2.5). Due to the analytic interest of the study, a focus is placed on accounts made for English.

2.1 Reported Speech as a Grammatical Construction

Grammatically, reported speech is composed of what the *Comprehensive Grammar of the English Language* (CGEL) calls a 'reporting clause' and a 'reported clause' (Quirk *et al.* 1985: 1020). The reporting clause includes information about the source and the act of communication, as well as potentially the addressee(s), the manner of speaking, and circumstantial aspects of the utterance.¹ The reported clause represents the quotation, and can traditionally be formatted as direct or indirect speech. According to Quirk *et al.* (1985), the syntactic format of the direct speech can be analysed as either a subordinated clause or a main clause. Ex. (3) illustrates direct speech as a subordinated clause.

(3)   Direct speech (Quirk *et al.* 1985: 1022)
       Dorothy said, *'My mother's on the phone.'*

The CGEL argues that since the direct speech can form a response to a *what*-question, the subordinate clause functions as a direct object, shown in Ex. (4).

(4)   Direct speech as a direct object (Quirk *et al.* 1985: 1022)
       A: What did Dorothy actually say?
       B: 'My mother's on the phone.'

In examples where the direct speech has an interrogative or imperative form, it is argued that these act like main clauses:

(5)   Direct speech as a main clause (Quirk *et al.* 1985: 1023)
       Dorothy said, 'Is my mother on the phone?'
       Dorothy said, 'Tell my mother I'll be over soon.'

Unfortunately, the CGEL does not give a detailed explanation of how they arrive at this syntactic categorisation of direct speech, which for this reason does not seem very convincing. I discuss this problem further in Chapter 5 and present empirical findings from PMQs which warrant an alternative description of the relation between the reporting clause and reported clause. Direct speech can also be produced as the subject complement in pseudo-cleft constructions (Ex. 6):

(6)   Direct speech in pseudo-cleft constructions (Quirk *et al.* 1985: 1022)
       What Dorothy said was *'My mother's on the phone.'*

Pseudo-cleft constructions generally feature a given-new structure, with the complement providing the 'climax' (Quirk *et al.* 1985: 1388). According to Hopper (2001), pseudo-cleft constructions are typical of formal speech.

Indirect speech is produced in a nominal *that*-clause, which functions as a direct object (Ex. 7a) and can be extraposed (Ex. 7b); it is also found in subject complements in pseudo-cleft constructions (Ex. 7c).²

---

[1] See also Biber *et al.* (1999: 126) for the term 'reporting clause'.
[2] Nominal clauses are subordinate clauses which can take on functions similar to those of noun phrases (Quirk *et al.* 1985: 1047).

(7) Indirect speech (Quirk *et al.* 1985: 1025)
   a. Neighbours said *that as a teenager he had earned his pocket money by delivering newspapers.*
   b. It was said *that as a teenager Max had earned his pocket money by delivering newspapers.*
   c. What neighbours said was *that as a teenager he had earned his pocket money by delivering newspapers.*

Finally, reported speech can be indexed by *as*-clauses, that is, comment clauses. (e.g., '*As you said*, George is a liar'; Quirk *et al.* 1985: 1116). Notably, it is not made clear if the reported speech indexed by comment clauses should be analysed as direct or indirect speech.

Another form of reported speech relevant to the present study are so-called 'mixed quotations'. Here, 'an utterance is directly and indirectly quoted concurrently' (Cappelen and Lepore 1997: 429). In written discourse, the direct portion is indexed by quotation marks. This is exemplified by Ex. (8).

(8) Mixed quotation (Cappelen and Lepore 1997: 429)
   Alice said that life 'is difficult to understand'.

Here the first part of the quotation (*life*) is marked as indirect by the complementiser *that*. The quotation marks frame '*is difficult to understand*' as a direct quotation.

More recently, reported speech has been described as a construction, that is, a form-meaning pairing, defined as 'a routinized sequence of words used together to express a certain meaning, in this case reportativity' (Buchstaller (2014: 15). When SAY is deployed as a quotative, it consists of a 'NOUN PHRASE + TRANSITIVE VERB OF REPORTING + QUOTE' (Buchstaller 2014: 15, emphasis in the original).

From a typological perspective, Aikhenvald states that the meaning of reported speech in English, ascribed to others or third parties, is comparable to grammaticalised reported and quotative evidentials (Aikhenvald 2004: 105) in that the utterance reported is non-first-hand: using reported speech, speakers 'indicate that the information was acquired from someone else' (Aikhenvald 2004: 135). She further points out that reported speech can undergo grammaticalisation, which leads to the creation of new grammatical evidentials. Two processes are named: a change in status of the reported clause from a subordinate to a main clause, and the reanalysis of the quotative verb, for example, *say* (Aikhenvald 2004: 140–141; see also Deutscher 2011). The topic of grammaticalisation is further expanded on in Chapter 5.

This review has shown that reported speech is traditionally divided into direct and indirect speech but can come in diverse grammatical forms, which can have fixed form–meaning pairings and enter processes of grammaticalisation; this is worth considering from the short-term diachronic perspective taken in the study. As far as the analytic focus of the forms of reported speech at PMQs is concerned, I examine the spoken forms of reported speech as exemplified by (3), (5), (7a), (7b), and (8). I further provide evidence for forms 'in between' direct and indirect speech in the embodied interaction at PMQs.

Sealey and Bates (2016) have suggested that self-quotations by the PM are frequently built as comment clauses. For reasons of time and space, a more detailed analysis of reported speech formatted in pseudo-cleft constructions and comment clauses at PMQs must be left to future research. Furthermore, past research has been concerned with the vocal and visual features of reported speech in discourse. These findings are reviewed in Chapter 6.

2.2 Reported Speech as an Evidential Practice

Historically, research on evidentiality originates from an interest in the description of grammatical categories of the verb across languages (see also de Haan 2012 for a historical outline). In his study of Native American languages, Franz Boas was among the first scholars to observe that there are languages which require verbal marking for source of information (Boas 1911a: 496). Exemplifying this point with the sentence 'The man is sick' in Kwakiutl, he states: '[I]n case the speaker had not seen the sick person himself, he would have to express whether he knows by hearsay or by evidence that the person is sick, or whether he has dreamed it' (Boas 1911b: 43). Jakobson later introduces 'evidential' as a technical term in order to label this grammatical category of the verb in Russian: 'EVIDENTIAL is a tentative label for the verbal category which takes into account three events – a narrated event, a speech event and a narrated speech event [. . .]' (Jakobson 1990: 392, emphasis in the original).

Aikhenvald's widely cited definition, which defines evidentiality as 'a linguistic category whose primary meaning is source of information' (Aikhenvald 2004: 3), stands in this historical tradition. Her influential, typological work centres on the languages where the speaker's source of information is expressed through morphosyntactic markers, such as 'affixes, clitics or particles, or special verb forms' (Aikhenvald 2004: 67). In such languages, 'marking how one knows something is a must' (Aikhenvald 2004: 6). This contrasts with languages such as English and German where evidential marking is optional in the sense that it is not grammatically obligatory like, for instance, the expression of tense in verb forms. Hence, she argues that English has no evidentiality (Aikhenvald 2004: 10). The present study suggests that the divide between evidential and non-evidential languages is fluid and can change over time and shows that this dichotomy between languages with and without evidentiality as a linguistic category cannot be maintained.

Chafe and Nichols (1986) paved the way for a second strand of research, which takes a 'broad' approach, involving the study of 'any linguistic expression of attitudes toward knowledge' (Chafe 1986: 271). This approach opens the field for the study of languages where evidentiality is not a grammatical category but is expressed through lexical items, and additionally broadens the scope to epistemology, including not only expressions through which speakers claim how they came to know (evidentiality) but also how confident they are about their knowledge (epistemic modality) or if the new knowledge is unexpected (mirativity; see, e.g., Bednarek 2006, for a more recent example of this broad approach).[3]

Recent findings from text linguistic, pragmatic, and interactional perspectives have cut across both narrow and broad approaches to evidentiality (e.g., the contributions to Diewald and Smirnova 2010b; Fetzer and Oishi 2014; Nuckolls and Michael 2012).

One controversial issue in the theory of evidentiality is that three different positions regarding the relation between epistemic modality and evidentiality can be found: (1) exclusion, (2) overlap, and (3) inclusion (see Boye 2010: 14; Cornillie 2009 for a general review of the relation between evidentiality and epistemic modality; cf. Portner 2009: 167–172 for the relation between evidentials and epistemic modals).

1 In the most radical view, evidentiality and epistemic modality are each considered to be grammatical categories in their own right (Aikhenvald 2004; de Haan 1999; Reber 2014a).
2 A more moderate approach assumes what Aijmer calls 'mixed systems' (Aijmer 2009: 66), that is, that epistemic modality is distinct from evidentiality but the two categories may overlap (see also Palmer 1986).
3 At the other end of the spectrum, evidentiality is regarded as a subcategory of epistemic modality (e.g., Boye 2010: 11). Related to this

---

[3] Lexical items used for evidential expressions in English include, for instance, adverbs (*obviously, clearly*; Ernst 2009), linking adverbials (*so*; Reber 2012), verbs (*must*, Cornillie 2009; *seem, appear*, Fetzer 2014a; *see*, Reber 2014a; *see, look, hear, sound, feel*, etc., Whitt 2010); cf. also Fox 2001 for a list of expressions for illustration. It has been suggested that the evidential meaning of perception verbs is linked to particular complementation patterns (Aijmer 2004; Whitt 2010).

discussion about the link between epistemic modality and evidentiality is the analysis of evidential expressions as markers of subjectivity (see Nuyts 2001).

The study of evidentiality in social interaction and political discourse is still only in its beginnings. It is generally acknowledged that speaker choices in terms of evidential expressions may be constrained by discourse types, conversational activities, and sequential position as well as social factors, and these choices are functional in stance-taking and positioning (e.g., Aikhenvald 2006; Clift 2006; Fox 2001; Hara 2008; Mushin 2001; Reber 2012, 2014a, 2014b, 2014c; Sidnell 2012; Whitt 2010).

Crucially, evidentiality is concerned with linguistic claims of how speakers came to know something. Along these lines, Hanks argues that '[t]he term "knowledge" seems preferable to "information", because it is the speaker's access to the information, and not the information per se, that is in play' (Hanks 2012: 172), terminology which is adopted in this study. Along these lines, research informed by Conversation Analysis has approached issues of evidentiality from the perspective of knowledge management (Stivers *et al.* 2011), generally subsuming evidentiality as a resource for doing epistemics (e.g., Heritage 2013; Raymond and Heritage 2006).[4] Nevertheless, early work by Fox (2001) shows explicitly that evidentiality and epistemics are independent but interrelated domains in social interaction: she demonstrates that claims of how a speaker knows in epistemic displays may be used to index the social relationship between speakers, a finding which is also evidenced in my study of reported speech at PMQs. She points out that function-based research on knowledge management has been shaped by assuming an asymmetry between the epistemic rights of participants, resulting in a use of evidential claims which reflects tacit considerations of 'entitlement', 'responsibility', or 'authority' over the knowledge displayed (Fox 2001: 176). Fox makes reference to Du Bois's (1986) discussion of evidentiality in relation to authority, which is also relevant to the present analysis:

> The problem of evidence is clarified if I first draw a distinction between providing evidence for a statement and providing authority for it. I propose as an initial principle that NO UTTERANCE IS ACCEPTED WITHOUT AUTHORITY. In a large subset of cases, the authority provided will be that of visual evidence, inferential evidence, and so on. But providing evidence is simply a special case of providing authority. This formulation forces us to

---

[4] Epistemics is the study of the 'knowledge claims that interactants assert, contest and defend in and through turns-at-talk and sequences of interaction' (Heritage 2013: 370).

take seriously two questions. First, what is the domain of applicability of evidentiality? Second, what alternative sources of authority are there besides evidence? (Du Bois 1986: 322, emphasis in the original)

Note that Du Bois's concern is about the authority of speakers in ritual speech (in the context of religious, spiritual ceremonies) which is 'self-evident' (Fox 2001: 173), that is, they do not need to back up their claims using evidence. It can be concluded that if the authority of an utterance is (maybe only tacitly) disputed or attacked, speakers will draw on evidential practices to construct authority. As Anderson puts it: 'Evidentials express the kinds of evidence a person has for making factual claims' (Anderson 1986: 273). In light of this past research, I use the notion of evidential authority as shorthand for the authority gained through the presentation of evidence through evidential practices, such as reported speech. In this understanding, authority is a social concept that is interactionally (de)constructed. Van Dijk (2014), concerned with knowledge and political discourse, links the use of evidential expressions with the construction of credibility, reliability, and authority:

> [E]videntials of different kinds as well as other epistemic strategies are used in order to establish, confirm or enhance the credibility of speakers, their reliability as a source of knowledge and as an authority who has or had access to the events reported or to a reliable source who did have such access. (van Dijk 2014: 269–270)

In this sense, speakers' own experiential access, or access to reliable sources having that access, represents a specific resource to construct authority, reliability, and credibility in political discourse. I use the term 'evidential access' as shorthand for this kind of access.[5] In political discourse in particular, knowledge is managed and even manipulated for reasons of power (van Dijk 2014: 166) by the politicians who (seem to) provide it.

Similar to authority, credibility is understood as a social notion which is constructed and deconstructed in interactional processes.

2.3 Reported Speech in Parliamentary Interaction

Quoting in the parliamentary interaction at PMQs has recently attracted a great deal of attention; it has generated a range of article-length investigations that share an interest in the linguistic forms and discursive

---

[5] Related to this, the experiential access of the speaker towards an event (or the lack of it) may further upgrade or downgrade the force of claims and assessments (Heritage and Raymond 2005).

2.3 Reported Speech in Parliamentary Interaction

functions of quotations in question time. What makes this work markedly different from the present study is that it primarily draws on Hansard and/or the linguistic interaction of PMQs in its written form.

Returning to Antaki and Leudar (2001), the quoting of the political opponent's own words as unchallengeable and impartial moves in parliament is particularly suitable for building hostile actions. Prime-ministerial self-quotations are heard as reiterations of past positions in order to rebut attacks on the PM's authority at PMQs (Sealey and Bates 2016: 28). In this sense, self-quotations are associated with responsive rather than first actions.

Moreover, Sealey and Bates (2016) provide evidence for patterned discourse chunks in action formation at PMQs: they find that three of the most frequent verbal patterns with first-person singular pronominal subjects (*I*) in answer turns by the PM are verbs of cognition (*think, understand*) and of communication (*say*). The formal, corpus-linguistic analysis reveals frequently recurrent, formulaic lexico-syntactic patterns. Functionally, these indicate a presentation of self which 'attempts to project not only authority and command within and beyond the Chamber but also empathy and representativeness' (Sealey and Bates 2016: 29). For instance, *say* often occurs in comment clauses (e.g., *as I have said / as I said earlier*), where PMs refer to their previous speech, repeating their position to rebut challenges of their authority (Sealey and Bates 2016: 28). As such, the authors conclude that these patterned uses of self-referential utterances are reflexive of 'argumentation, face management and the norms of this political institution, as well as those of the wider society' (Sealey and Bates 2016: 29).

Other research, conducted mainly within the field of Discourse Analysis, has centred on the construction of ordinariness through quotations in the questions by the then newly elected Leader of the Labour Party, and Leader of the Opposition Jeremy Corbyn, in 2015 (Bull and Waddle 2019; Fetzer and Weizman 2018) and in comparison to the practices by his predecessor Ed Miliband (Fetzer and Bull 2019). In particular, Fetzer and Bull (2019; see also Fetzer and Weizman 2018) demonstrate that Jeremy Corbyn introduced a new style of quoting, by quoting ordinary people rather than official authorities, which had constituted the prior default practice. This work, which is concerned with a period which goes beyond the time span examined in the present study, corroborates my findings that quoting practices are in a constant state of flux. It is interesting to see what results come out of the analysis of even more recent developments of various kinds, for example, PMQs in a 'virtual' parliament, which marks an arrangement due to the coronavirus pandemic since April 2020, and the so-called 'People's Prime Minister's Questions' on Facebook, undertaken by PM Boris Johnson in a vlog since autumn 2019.

The work by Fetzer and colleagues is also noteworthy in that it describes types of quotations which in part differ from the classification made in the present study: direct quotations, indirect quotations, hypothetical quotations, mixed quotations, and mixed types of quotation, as well as focussing quotations, which were identified as specific to PMQs (Fetzer 2020; Fetzer and Bull 2019). These differences from my work might be due to an analytic focus on written transcripts rather than audio and video recordings; they might also be due to a wider database which includes other forms of quoting than just those indexed by the quotative verb *say*.

Although quoting in parliamentary discourse has become a thriving strand of research, it is only in its preliminary stages. In what follows, I therefore review previous research on quoting in other areas of political research or political speech in general which is relevant to the present study.

In English news interviews, Clayman finds that the shift in footing involved in journalists' use of reported speech functions to maintain neutrality, a stance expected of their professional role. 'By virtue of these practices, interviewers are able to give voice to controversial points of view without going on record as endorsing such views' (Clayman 1992: 196).

Dickerson complements Clayman's study by examining how quotations, and here the attribution of cited others in particular, function in the rhetoric of interviewees' turns (on American and British English TV shows) to support their own position.

> [P]oliticians cite others not so much to achieve neutrality but rather to orientate to sceptical readings of their own utterances, [...] cited others are constructed as providing apolitical, expert or counter-interest warrants, and [...] the process of citing others forms just one move in an ongoing rhetorical struggle. (Dickerson 1997: 36)[6]

In this rhetoric, the naming of the identity of the quoted source is an essential component. I show that quoting counter-interest positions, that is, positions which seem to oppose the current speaker's interests, represents a common rhetorical resource at PMQs. This is corroborated by the observation that 'a counter-interest claim, such as criticizing the political

---

[6] Further parties cited are members of the studio audience and others 'to highlight an inconsistency (between past and present claims of political opponents)' (Dickerson 1997: 37).

party to whom one belongs, has more rhetorical efficacy than an interest-consistent claim, such as criticizing one's political opponents' (Dickerson 1997: 46).

To summarise, while self-quotations are deployed by politicians to reassert their credibility and authority in responsive, adversarial action formats, news interviewers use quotations of others to maintain neutralism, while in politicians' rhetoric they serve to frame quoted positions as being apolitical, expert, or counter to the speaker's interest. Here quotations ascribed to the interlocutor constitute particularly hostile acts.

Tannen's work on constructed dialogue in political oratory is also relevant here. She identifies three functions of constructed dialogue: authorising claims (Tannen 2007: 171), pre-empting objections (Tannen 2007: 172), and 'emotional identification' (Tannen 2007: 186). Crucially, the strategies deployed in political oratory are 'the same linguistic strategies that create involvement and make understanding possible in everyday conversation' (Tannen 2007: 186).

In written English, the use of direct speech has been interpreted as indicative of an oral style. I shortly review a study by Mair in what follows, since it is – to my knowledge – the only work which examines reported speech from a short-time diachronic perspective. In a comparative study on the use of SAY as a quotative in British and American newspapers and science texts, Mair (2006) identifies an increased frequency of SAY in the former but not the latter between two corpora from the 1960s and 1990s:

> Press texts of the 1990s (F-LOB and Frown) contain far more quotations and – real or fabricated – passages of direct speech than those of the 1960s (LOB and Brown). The intended stylistic effect is to make the texts appear more dramatic, interesting, and accessible and, presumably, also to involve the reader emotionally. (Mair 2006: 188)

This change of style is exemplary for processes of what Mair calls 'colloquialisation' on the macro level (as opposed to the micro level of syntactic structures, e.g., contracted forms). The concept of colloquialisation seeks to capture 'a significant stylistic shift' observed for the written norms of English of the twentieth century, which comprises a tendency towards 'spoken usage' as well as 'informality' or even 'anti-formality' (Mair 2006: 187).

To sum up, constructed dialogue is described as a strategy typical for mundane, spoken English to create emotional involvement and epistemic access, which is also made use of by speakers in political oratory. Its use in written text types is interpreted as a normative shift towards a more oral, informal style.

2.4 Reported Speech and Authorship

Quotations of others (Vološinov 1986) involve what Goffman (1979) calls a shift of footing: '[W]hen we shift from saying something ourselves to reporting what someone else said, we are changing our footing' (Goffman 1979: 22).[7] In other words, speakers only serve as 'the talking machine' (Goffman 1979: 17), that is, as what Goffman calls 'animators' of the current talk. If speakers summarise past speech as an indirect quotation, they are the 'authors', that is, the party responsible for the wording of what is said, but not the 'principals', that is, the party whose position and beliefs have been displayed (Goffman 1979: 17). In verbatim quotations, the current speaker is the animator but not the author or principal. In the analysis presented, I largely use 'source' with respect to the person/organisation/document to whom/which the quoted utterance is ascribed – in Goffman's (1979) words, the 'principle' of the quoted utterance.

Recall that verbatim quotations are commonly associated with the grammatical format of direct speech. Here, the question of authorship has been a burning topic. Essentially, the question is whether direct speech represents a verbatim rendering of the quoted speech. For everyday interaction, this position has been discarded – for political discourse, there are varied positions.

To begin with mundane conversation, Holt makes the point that while direct reported speech has often been treated as a verbatim rendering of past speech, at least in everyday conversation it often is not, because past speech simply cannot be easily memorised (Holt 1996: 226). This is corroborated by Mathis and Yule, who speak of direct speech more as a 'construction of the reporter than a verbatim record of any reportée's actual speech' (Mathis and Yule 1994: 63; see also Mayes 1990; Rumsey 1992, for discussion).

This contrasts with contexts such as the British House of Commons, where interactions are recorded in the House and made available through Hansard, the official public record of parliamentary proceedings (Antaki and Leudar 2001). This allows MPs to recruit literal quotations of what

---

[7] Generally, a change in footing is associated with a change in alignment: 'A change in footing implies a change in the alignment we take up to ourselves and the others present as expressed in the way we manage the production or reception of an utterance' (Goffman 1979: 5).

2.4 Reported Speech and Authorship

political opponents have said in past parliamentary debates from Hansard and to use these previous utterances against them. In other words, written sources are used as a basis for building hostile actions. Here '[l]iteral recruitment works to provide an unchallengeable, impartial, and counter-intuitive source for the speaker's position' (Antaki and Leudar 2001: 486). The present study corroborates these findings, yet has discovered slightly different practices of delivering verbatim reported speech which have developed between the 1978–1988 and 2003–2013 data sets.

Rumsey's observations on the use of direct speech in courtroom interaction are relevant here. Referring to direct speech, he states that:

> a grammatical category whose erstwhile function is to signal that some (largely unspecified) encoding features of the reported utterance are being imported from another speech situation, now becomes 'literalized' in such a way as to specify that the reported utterance reproduces *all* lexico-grammatical features of the original, at just the level of delicacy that is captured by our graphemic writing system [...] (Rumsey 1992: 356, italics in the original)

Rumsey (1992: 356) points out that such normative constraints to reproduce past speech as verbatim are widespread but specific to certain text types, such as academic writing. At the same time, they are symptomatic of what Linell (2005) has called a 'written language bias' (Rumsey 1992: Fn 2). In Reber (2020b), I argue that while parliamentary speakers claim to present 'literalised' quotations at PMQs, the recipients do not have evidence that these quotations are in fact verbatim versions of past speech. To indicate this, I put the term 'literalisation' in single quotation marks in what follows.

Tannen proposes the notion of 'constructed dialogue' (Tannen 2007: 112) instead of direct speech, direct quotation, or direct discourse because there are cases where what is presented as constructed dialogue was 'not actually spoken by the person to whom it is attributed' (Tannen 2007: 112). She concedes, however, that constructed dialogue may not necessarily be fictitious in the sense that it was not actually produced by the person to whom it is ascribed. Rather, it represents a '[creative and enlivening] act of transforming others' words into one's own discourse' (Tannen 2007: 112). She points out that stretches of speech taken from one situation, produced for a specific communicative goal, are used as constructed dialogue in another, deployed for purposes which may be completely different from the original context (Tannen 2007: 107). Because of this ability for transformation, constructed dialogue constitutes a powerful tool in argumentative rhetoric. Tannen notes that when criticism is implemented through reported speech, commonly the 'literal truth of the report is not questioned' (Tannen 2007: 108) (nor do Americans consider what the interactional goals of the reporter might be, which can be exploited by speakers). Constructed dialogue can take a variety of forms, including, for example, what Tannen (2007: 112–119 calls 'dialogue representing what wasn't said', 'summarising dialogue', 'choral dialogue', and 'fadeout, fadein', where indirect and direct quotation are formally blurred.

To summarise, in contrast to everyday contexts, participants in parliamentary interaction have access to a written record of past debates. Verbatim quotations from these written sources can be exploited as a rhetorical weapon and used against political opponents in what comes off as unchallengeable, impartial moves. Here direct speech becomes – or is at least presented as – 'literalised'. Tannen takes this point further by arguing that direct speech, presented as constructed dialogue, does not even have to have an evidential basis in order to be functional as an unchallengeable rhetorical resource for doing criticism.

2.5 Summary and Conclusions

In this chapter, I have demonstrated that the present study treats reported speech as an evidential practice. In evidentiality, there is a growing body of research seeking to bridge what has traditionally been called narrow and broad approaches. In the same vein, this study is located at the crossroads of a narrow and broad approach, in examining reported speech as a practice of expressing how the reporting speaker came to know in English, a language where evidentiality seems to be primarily indexed through lexical resources. I have argued that evidential expressions mark speakers' access to knowledge ('evidential access') and that knowledge (management) relates to authority, credibility, and power. Thus, the term 'evidential authority' is used to refer to the authority interactionally constructed and deconstructed through evidential practices, such as reported speech.

Reported speech comes in grammatically diverse structures. The analytic starting point of this study is reported speech in its canonical form, as described by the CGEL illustrated in Table 2.1.

I have shown that past research on quoting in parliamentary question time has been largely concerned with the authorship of quoted speech and its functions in discourse and is based on written transcripts. Parliamentary debates seem to be a context where the 'literalisation' of direct speech is normatively constrained and, moreover, possible (due to the availability of written records of sources recruited). The notion of constructed dialogue,

2.5 Summary and Conclusions

Table 2.1 *The grammatical form of reported speech*

Reported speech	Reporting clause	Reported clause
Direct speech	The MP says,	*'The university in my constituency is at risk.'*
Indirect speech	The MP said	that the university in her constituency was at risk.

on the other hand, suggests that in successful political oratory direct speech does not have to be an authentic version of the past speech it claims to quote. Rather, the framing of assertions as direct speech makes these be heard as truthful and authentic; it creates emotive involvement with and epistemic access to what is said on the part of the audience. Relating to the notion of direct speech as an involvement strategy, its more frequent use in written texts is taken as an indicator of decreasing formality and increasing orality in style.

The ascribed source of quotations is relevant to their discourse functions in political discourse. Self-quotations of politicians in adversarial, responsive actions come off as repetition of past positions to reassert credibility and authority. Quotations of others in politicians' speech are produced in order to support the current speaker's positions, in drawing on 'apolitical, expert or counter-interest' (Dickerson 1997: 36) authorities; such quotations display the politicians' orientation towards a potential lack in the credibility of their speech. Finally, quotations ascribed to the interlocutor are functional in building hostile actions.

Although political discourse has been mediated through radio and television broadcasts through much of the twentieth century up to today, and there are thus recordings of reported speech which date back to decades ago, the development of reported speech in this setting has not yet been described. Moreover, this literature review has illustrated that while the function of reported speech for claim-backing and action formation is tightly connected to the choice of sources, reported speech has not much been analysed as an evidential resource in parliamentary interaction.[8]

---

[8] For reported speech as an evidential resource in non-political interaction see, e.g., Clift (2006), Couper-Kuhlen (2007), Galatolo (2007), Holt (1996).

CHAPTER 3

Prime Minister's Questions

PMQs is the name of an institutionalised, parliamentary multi-party activity which has been performed in the House of Commons Chamber of the British Parliament every week during parliamentary sitting days since 1961. According to Harris (2001), this history as a community which shares a joint enterprise and includes senior representatives as well as novices who are still learning the practices of how things are done is what characterises the members of the House of Commons as a 'community of practice'.[1] In line with this, PMQs can be described as an activity shared by this community of practice, and reported speech as a practice 'evolved' and 'still evolving' (Harris 2001: 454) over time: 'A practice is a way of doing things, as grounded in and shared by a community' (Eckert and Wenger 2005: 583). To give an understanding of what PMQs involves, this chapter presents a review of past research which describes the history of Question Time (3.1), the spatial arrangements of the House of Commons Chamber (3.2), the institutional procedures of PMQs as an activity performed by the members of the House of Commons (3.3), the participation framework and turn-taking system (3.4), and the organisation of PMQs in question and answer sequences (3.5). The chapter wraps up with a summary and conclusions (3.6).

3.1 History of Prime Minister's Questions

The questioning of the government has a long history in the British Parliament. Sources vary as to when it began: Wilson gives a precise year

---

[1] The notion of communities of practice, first introduced by Lave and Wenger (1991), is based on the assumption that the interactional engagement with others and the world is a process of constant learning. Crucially, Wenger states:
   Over time, this collective learning results in practices that reflect both the pursuit of our enterprises and the attendant social relations. These practices are thus the property of a kind of community created over time by the sustained pursuit of a shared enterprise. It makes sense, therefore, to call these kinds of communities *communities of practice*. (Wenger 1998: 45, italics in the original)

3.1 History of Prime Minister's Questions

('in 1721', Wilson 1990: 144); Chilton is vaguer ('since the late seventeenth or early eighteenth century', Chilton 2007: 92). Jones describes the practice of how the PM was first questioned along with other government ministers before questions to the PM were scheduled at the end of the question time under the premiership of William Ewart Gladstone. This development eventually led to the 1961 institutionalisation of PMQs as we know it today (see also Chilton 2007: 92):

> Questions to the prime minister have not always had the unique place in Parliamentary proceedings that they have today. Before the 1880s questions to the prime minister were treated no differently from questions to other ministers. They were asked, without notice, on any day when ministers were present to answer, normally Mondays, Tuesdays, Thursdays and Fridays, and in whatever order members rose to ask them. And questions had to be completed before public business proper could begin, which was a boon to obstructionists. There was a departure from this arrangement in 1881, when as a courtesy to Mr Gladstone, then aged 72, questions to the prime minister were placed last on the day's list to allow him to come in late. (Jones 1972/1973: 260)

Institutionalised as a separated session, PMQs was first scheduled as two weekly fifteen-minute sessions on Tuesdays and Thursdays in 1961. When Tony Blair came into office in 1997, the two sessions were combined into one single thirty-minute session on Wednesdays at noon, a practice which has been maintained until today (see Coe and Kelly 2009 for a detailed historical account).

The proceedings of PMQs have been traditionally reported in Hansard, the official record of the House of Commons and the House of Lords.[2] It was not until 1978 that PMQs was first broadcast live on the radio. In 1989, the first television broadcast took place. In 2002, internet broadcasting of PMQs (and other parliamentary sessions) was introduced (House of Commons Information Office 2010). Table 3.1 gives an outline of the history of PMQs.

Note that the press began reporting on the parliamentary proceedings long before Question Time was institutionalised in the House. Before 1803, representatives of the press sat in the Commons Chamber. Subsequently, they were moved to the Public Gallery, where parts were reserved for the press.[3]

---

[2] For more information on the history and making of PMQs, as well as access to Hansard, see Vice and Farrell (n.d.), https://hansard.parliament.uk and https://bit.ly/3ra5glt
[3] https://pressgallery.org.uk

Table 3.1 *Historical outline of Prime Minister's Questions*

Year	Event
1869	Formal recognition of Question Time as a parliamentary institution
1881	Questions to the Prime Minister placed last on the day's list
1961	Institutionalisation of PMQs: two weekly 15-minute sessions on Tuesdays and Thursdays
1978	First live broadcast on BBC Radio
1989	First live broadcast on TV
1997	Tony Blair elected into office: one single weekly 30-minute session on Wednesdays
2002	Introduction of internet broadcasting

PMQs has undergone two major changes since it was institutionalised as a separate parliamentary session in 1961: (1) mediation and mediatisation, and (2) merging and a more prominent role for the LO.

1. Mediation and mediatisation Although the debates in the House of Commons have been put down in written form and also published in the press since the late eighteenth century as well as officially recorded in Hansard since the early nineteenth century (Vice and Farrell, n.d.), the introduction of radio and later television and internet broadcasts have marked turning points in providing a non-present public audience with auditive and visual access to the unfolding debates in parliament in real time.

There is – to my knowledge – no systematic study of how the broadcasting has affected PMQs, but it is implied in various reports that PMQs, as we know it today, constitutes a media event which enjoys wide public attention and is watched and critically assessed by a global audience.[4] As such, it has been pointed out that PMQs is not a setting where the different policies of the different parties are examined in the best, most objective way possible as part of the democratic process:

> Reporting of the event nearly always talks in terms of a victory for either the PM, or the Opposition leader, and broadcast media concentrate on soundbites that are about confrontation rather than explanation. The event is often very rowdy, with frequent interruptions, adding to the impression of a battle rather than a calm debate. (Beard 2000: 105–106)

---

[4] For instance, PMQs is broadcast live on C-SPAN, a US television network: www.c-span.org

3.1 History of Prime Minister's Questions

Lovenduski (2014a) confirms this impression:

> Performance is evaluated in terms of competitive success framed in the way that the discourse of sporting competitions, races or wars are framed. (Did David Cameron win over Ed Miliband during PMQs today?) Commentary, if often amusing and erudite, is rarely framed in terms of the contribution to policy made in the contributions to the debate.

In his chapter on 'quotability', Atkinson (1984) gives a detailed account of the mechanisms behind how excerpts from political speeches are selected by the mass media. It is safe to assume that these mechanisms apply similarly to PMQs and, moreover, that speakers seek and are trained to play to the mass media in their performances in order to get selected for media coverage. According to Hjarvard (2008), it is a defining feature of the mediatisation process that social institutions accommodate to the logic of media. It can thus be hypothesised that the House of Commons Chamber has been a mediatised arena for political debate ever since the debates have been covered by the press, but that participants at PMQs have adapted their performances even further to the new conditions of radio and television/internet coverage.

2. *Merging and a more prominent role for the LO* Bates *et al.* (2014) explore how the composition of actions per speaker role has changed at PMQs from the premiership of Margaret Thatcher to that of David Cameron. The authors analyse data from Hansard comprising an equal amount of question time from the beginnings of each premiership (1979–2010), that is, roughly the period covered by the present study. Crucially, their sample shows that the total number of questions per session has decreased since 1979, while the number of interruptions and the speaking time of the PM and LO have increased (Bates *et al.* 2014: 264). Bates *et al.* report that John Smith, who became Labour Leader after his party lost the election and the Conservative John Major became PM in July 1992, was actually the first LO to ask six questions a week, that is, to use the full amount of allotted question slots, a change in practice which – after a sharp decrease – has led to a consistently smaller proportion of MPs' questions at PMQs up to today (Bates *et al.* 2014: Fn 11). In other words, due to the LO's longer questioning, the profile of the institutional role of the LO is heightened at the cost of that of MPs, who are generally allocated only one question each, and whose questioning time is thus correspondingly diminished. When the two weekly fifteen-minute sessions were combined into one single thirty-minute session following Tony Blair's election as PM in 1997, this happened against the recommendations made by the Procedure Committee in

1995, which suggested that PMQs be '[extended] to two sessions of 30 min. each to accommodate more backbench questions' (Bates *et al.* 2014: 272). In the light of this, the merging of sessions seems to have furthered the decline of MPs' questioning and increased the roles of the LO (and PM).

3.2 Spatial Arrangements

In order to understand how PMQs is set up as an activity in which relations of opposition between two major parties, that is, Her Majesty's Government and the Opposition, are verbally, vocally, and also physically enacted, it is necessary to examine the spatial arrangements of the House of Commons Chamber. Reber (2019) illustrates how the House of Commons Chamber provides a physical setting where relations of opposition and agreement are made visible in its ecology of space: the government and opposition MPs face each other on opposite benches, with the Speaker of the House of Commons located on the Speaker's Chair in between, at the far end of the Chamber. The PM and members of the government sit on the front bench (to the right from the Speaker's perspective), opposite the LO and members of his shadow cabinet. When speaking, they are not permitted to cross the red line on the floor in front of them, allegedly to prevent physical contact (House of Commons Information Office 2012; Fig. 3.1).

Figure 3.1 Ecology of space of the House of Commons Chamber.[5]

---

[5] All photographs are courtesy of the UK Parliament.

Hall (1969) has cited these spatial arrangements as a poignant example of fixed-feature space:

> The important point about fixed-feature space is that it is the mold into which a great deal of behavior is cast. It was this feature of space that the late Winston Churchill referred to when he said: 'We shape our buildings and they shape us.' During the debate on restoring the House of Commons after the war, Churchill feared that departure from the intimate spatial pattern of the House, where opponents face each other across a narrow aisle, would seriously alter the patterns of government. (Hall 1969: 106–107)

Note that a comparison between the more recent recordings in my corpus and those of the first televised PMQs (28 November 1989) suggests that the spatial arrangements of the Chamber have not been altered between the premierships of Thatcher (from which the majority of the 1978–1988 data set comes) and of Cameron (the last PM in the 2003–2013 sample), that is, there is a general continuity of the physical setting where the reported speech is performed in the two data sets, at least with respect to the seating of members.[6]

In terms of the technical equipment, the Chamber has, however, been gradually adapted: the circles in Figure 3.2 illustrate the position of one of the cameras installed in the late 1980s to televise the proceedings in the Chamber, one of the many microphones which allow audio recordings, and one of the two clocks on either side which show the time.

3.3 Institutional Procedure

The procedure of posing questions at PMQs is a highly formalised one: by the rules of the institution laid out in Erskine May (1989), MPs who intend to pose a question have to submit (i.e., to table) their question in writing to the Table Office no later than three days in advance in order to allow for the preparation of answers. Since there are always more MPs than time to allow for all tabled questions to be asked, questions are put to the ballot and randomly selected. Questions successful in the ballot are printed on what is called the Order Paper (House of Commons Information Office 2013: 3).

---

[6] I have not been able to find drawings of what the House of Commons looked like before TV cameras were installed in the House.

Figure 3.2 Positions of cameras, microphones, and clock.

Having asked their tabled question at PMQs, MPs may be given the floor to ask a so-called supplementary question on the same topic, which does not have to be submitted beforehand.

The right to ask a supplementary rather than a tabled question is highly important in terms of issues of knowledge management. Tabled questions are known to PMs when they enter Question Time, while supplementary questions are not. Supplementary questions thus represent a useful weapon for probing PMs with respect to their factual knowledge and credibility, as they may take them by surprise.

In an effort to find a way around the existing rules, MPs increasingly began to table so-called 'open' questions, which allowed them to ask a subsequent non-tabled supplementary question: 'Since the latter half of the 1970s, the standard open question has been the 'engagements' question, asking the Prime Minister to list his engagements for the day' (Norton 1996: n.p.; quoted in Coe and Kelly 2009: 4).

When Tony Blair entered office in May 1997, MPs who had tabled open (i.e., engagements) questions were requested to 'only ask their supplementary question' (Coe and Kelly 2009: 5), as had been recommended by the Procedure Committee on 'Prime Minister's Questions' in 1995. As is evidenced by Chilton's (2007: 101) analysis of an excerpt taken from PMQs in July 1999, the engagements question subsequently evolved into the ritual question asked in the opening of PMQs and simply referred to as (question) number one.

MPs' questions have been criticised as not always being free but often 'syndicated', that is, they are provided by the parties and do not stem from a genuine concern of the MPs (Bates *et al*. 2014; Giddings and Irwin 2005). This means that MPs do not speak for themselves, as it were, in their own voice, but ask questions on behalf of their parties.

In contrast to MPs, LOs are generally entitled to ask six supplementary questions per week, that is, up to three questions in each of the fifteen-minute sessions and up to six in the thirty-minute sessions (House of Commons Information Office 2013: 4). As mentioned above, LOs did not make use of their right to ask all six questions until 1992, which has led to a decrease of MPs' questions at PMQs that remains today (Bates *et al*. 2014: Fn 11).

The Leaders of the Liberal Democrats (LLDs), who traditionally represent the second largest opposition party in the House of Commons, are generally allocated two supplementary questions. Unfortunately, Bates *et al*. (2014) do not consider their role in their count but the House of Commons Information Office (2013: 4) states that after the Liberal Democrats entered a coalition government with the Conservatives in 2010, this practice was not continued with smaller opposition parties (although members of such parties can still be called to ask supplementary questions).

3.4 Participation Framework and Turn-taking System

PMQs is chaired and moderated by the Speaker of the House of Commons who allocates the rights to the floor by summoning the next speaker. In this way, the interaction is mediated through the Speaker. The Speaker further sanctions deviations from the question–answer format and other types of misconduct. The LO and PM are allocated the floor in each session. Backbenchers may signal that they wish to pose a question by rising to their feet. They can make their agreement or disagreement publicly heard through (collective) audience responses. As is characteristic of formal interaction, action design and types are reflective of institutional speaker roles (Atkinson 1982: 91); at the same time, the institution allocates specific action types to institutional speaker roles.[7] In this sense, PMQs shares typical features of formal multi-party activities: 'turn pre-allocation', 'turn-type pre-allocation', and 'turn mediation' (Atkinson 1982: 102–103).

---

[7] See Komter (2013), who points out for courtroom interaction: 'The participants' institutional identities are manifested in the kinds of actions that questions and answers are seen to perform' (Komter 2013: 628).

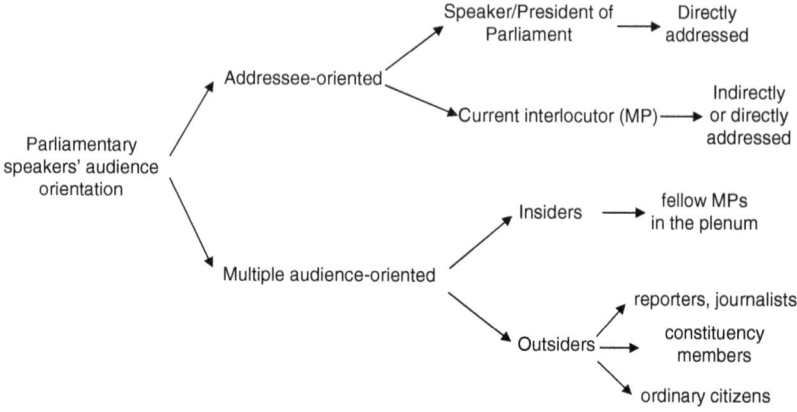

Figure 3.3 Addressees and audiences targeted by parliamentary speakers.[8]

The Speaker addresses participants by their common names (MPs) or title (Prime Minister). In return, participants address the Speaker directly by title (Mr Speaker), that is, through second-person address (Ilie 2010a: 67). In contrast, parliamentary speakers can only address each other indirectly through the Speaker, using third-person address. The convention of third-party address has been described as 'deferential and distance-marking' (Ilie 2010b: 896) as well as one of the 'mitigating techniques' deployed on both sides to soften face-threatening acts (Bull and Wells 2012: 43).

The participation framework of PMQs is typical of parliamentary interaction found elsewhere, involving several kinds of addressees and audiences (Ilie 2010a, see Fig. 3.3). Note that the participation framework at PMQs is slightly more complex than the way it is depicted in the figure. Current interlocutors and insiders not only include MPs, but of course also the PM, the LO, and the Leaders of smaller opposition parties. Also, the outsiders can be differentiated between these sitting in the galleries of the House of Commons Chamber and – once radio broadcasts were introduced – those who represent non-co-present, mediated audiences.

While the third-person address system has not changed since the beginnings of PMQs, there are signs in the data that the ways in which it is deployed have evolved. The present study also suggests that not only the mediated audiences have changed but also the ways in which parliamentary speakers deal with them.

[8] Reproduced from Ilie (2010a: 66) with kind permission by John Benjamins Publishing Company.

3.5 Question and Answer Sequences

The former LO Ed Miliband remarked in an exchange with the then PM David Cameron, 'it is Prime Minister's questions. The clue is in the name. I ask the questions and he is supposed to answer them' (Hansard, HC, vol. 543, col. 313, 18 April 2012). However, despite the labels used by the institution for the actions allocated to the MPs and PMs, questions and answers, the literature largely agrees that what is formally required by the institution is exploited for other kind of actions. I come back to this point later.

From the interactional perspective taken in the study, I propose that the mediated question–answer sequences 'embody' (Levinson 2013: 121) courses of action which – in their sum – are components of a larger, multi-party activity. I understand activities as coherent courses of action in which participants engage, sharing a joint goal and/or topic (see also Gerhardt and Reber 2019). This notion is informed by Heritage and Sorjonen (1994) who use:

> the term activity [...] to characterize the work that is achieved across a sequence or series of sequences of a unit or course of action – meaning by this a relatively sustained topically coherent and/or goal-coherent course of action. (Heritage and Sorjonen 1994: 4)

The form and content of the courses of action are constrained by the rules and procedures established by the institutional body (see Chilton 2007: 94–95, for more details). It has been noted that action formation in parliamentary question time resembles news interviews (Jucker 1986; Clayman and Heritage 2002b; see, for instance, Wilson 1990, on the forms and functions of parliamentary questioning compared to news interviews).

Past research has focused on the adversarial nature of PMQs and highlighted the role of face-threatening acts in building questions. For instance, Bull and Wells (2012) offer a classification of the types of action components and dimensions where face-threatening acts occur in question turns and strategies for dealing with them in responses, analysing the interaction between the LO and PM recorded in 18 sessions from April to November 2007.[9] Notably, the classification indicates that question

---

[9] I use the terms 'question turns' and 'answer turns' to describe the turn type required by the institutional constraints on sequence organisation. Through this terminology, on the one hand, I seek to highlight that question and answer turns can have different turn-internal organisations, as, for instance, indicated by Clayman and Heritage's (2002b) distinction between simple and prefaced questions (see Chapter 8). On the other, I wish to suggest that on the action level, what happens in question–answer sequences is not necessarily questioning and answering but, for example, attacking and counter-attacking.

turn slots are a locus not just for questioning but, crucially, to attack the PM. Likewise, the PM's responsive actions can embody multiple strategies, not just one dealing with such attacks. Bull and Wells further name 'mitigating techniques' deployed on both sides to soften face-threatening acts: these include quotations ascribed to the interlocutor (prepared and done on the fly) through which the interlocutors' own words are used against them (cf. also Harris 2001; Bates *et al.* 2014; Waddle *et al.* 2019; cf. also Robles 2011, on the British House of Lords). The highly confrontational nature of PMQs has been criticised as 'institutionalised masculinity' (Lovenduski 2014a), which marginalises women MPs as equal participants. It represents an institutional environment that privileges a white, male culture and is hostile to those who do not conform to these gendered norms (Lovenduski 2014a, 2014b). This is instantiated by the fact that female politicians are trained to speak in a lower-pitched voice, most notably Margaret Thatcher.[10] Ilie (2013) shows how terms of reference and address are deployed by male MPs (but notably also female MPs) in British and Swedish Question Time as what Ås (1978) calls master suppression techniques to undermine the authority of MPs of the opposite sex.

To my knowledge, Reber (2014a, 2014b, 2019) is the first to take a truly interactional perspective examining larger sequences of action in a systematic fashion (but see Chilton 2007, for single case analyses). In a study on action formation and knowledge management in the question and answer sequences between the LO and the PM at PMQs, Reber (2014b) examines third-positioned follow-ups (Sinclair and Coulthard 1975), which I describe as Janus-faced action components situated in the LO's question turns. Here follow-ups ratify or challenge the prior response of the PM. Ratifying follow-up actions project a local sequence-closing, acknowledging the evidential claims made by the PM and treating his response as a preferred action. Challenging follow-up actions, on the other hand, represent a more complex picture: these are functional in doing mock ratifications, providing the answer solicited but not produced by the PM, or contradicting the evidential claim by the PM. They are sequence-expanding, projecting and accounting for further challenging actions (cf. further Ilie 2015; Fetzer 2015).

Reber (2019) analyses recurrent courses of action as an embodied performance in a physical context which features oppositeness. Here the LO and the PM perform adversariality through embodied claims of epistemic

---

[10] Videos contrasting Thatcher before and after she consulted a speech coach exist online (see also Ilie 2013: 504).

and evidential access, which are deployed for mutual claims of power and authority/dominance. Specifically, it is found that the 'index-up gesture' (Streeck 2008) is coordinated with the first accusation, with almost all LOs across party lines performing the gesture to claim superior epistemic and evidential access as a resource for claims of power, dominance, and authority.

3.6 Summary and Conclusions

The foregoing literature review has demonstrated that PMQs, institutionalised in 1961, shows a relative continuity with regard to the spatial arrangements of the House of Commons Chamber, the use of the third-person address system, and its organisation in terms of question–answer sequences mediated by the Speaker of the House of Commons. However, there are indications that PMQs has been undergoing change concerning several aspects. The mediation through radio and television broadcasts, as well as webcasts, has brought microphones and cameras into the Chamber and seems to have led to an increasing mediatisation. The LOs' making use of the total number of allocated turn slots has resulted in a more prominent role for the LO and a diminishment of MPs' roles at PMQs. The change of institutional procedure for questioners not to ask their (open) 'engagements' question but only their supplementary question has led to the emergence of a ritualised opening question ('number one').

This suggests that PMQs has been undergoing rapid change with respect to the practices, actions, and courses of action participants engage in, as well as in terms of the mass media which mediate the activity to a public audience. On the other hand, what could be regarded as the institutional backbone of the activity, that is, the physical set-up of the Chamber, and the question–answer sequences performed by participants defined by their institutional role and moderated by the Speaker, has remained largely the same, which warrants a comparative perspective on the 1978–1988 and 2003–2013 data sets as representatives of the same activity in different times.

CHAPTER 4

Data, Transcription, and Methodology

This study represents a first in taking a diachronic, interactional perspective on authentic recordings of parliamentary question time. Such an approach involves the compilation of a balanced corpus, meticulous transcription, and the development of a new methodology, drawing on principles from linguistic and sociological qualitative and quantitative analysis. In this chapter, I present the database for the study (4.1), discuss the transcription of recordings as a process of data constitution (4.2), and present the basic methodological assumptions made in this study (4.3).

4.1 Database for the Study

I first critically discuss the compilation of the database. Next, I show how the composition of participation has changed during the 36 years spanned by the database and explain how the relative frequencies of reported speech are calculated as a basis for numerical comparison.

4.1.1 Compilation

The first radio broadcast of PMQs was aired in 1978, before video footage of PMQs was televised in 1989 (and made available for online access in 2002). Because of these continuous audio and video recordings, the analysis of PMQs allows a unique insight into recent and short-term diachronic change in a mediated social activity. The database for the study consists of two sets of recordings (1978–1988, 2003–2013), which amounts to a period of 36 years (1978–2013). In addition, it includes corresponding files from Hansard, the official record of the parliamentary proceedings in the House of Commons.

These main considerations mark the compilation of this database:

1 It was composed such that it spans from one to two generations, making it suitable for an analysis of real-time change in Labov's (1981) sense.[1]
2 The older data set (1978–1988) contains the entire time span during which PMQs was radio broadcast in order to have the best possible representation of this period from which only audio recordings are available. The more recent data set (2003–2013), all video footage, is taken from the televised era. To make the two data sets as comparable as possible, the latter also extends across 11 years.
3 At the same time, the two data sets stand for the two parliamentary formats PMQs has had following its institutionalisation in 1961: as outlined in Chapter 3, PMQs first took place in two fifteen-minute sessions on Tuesday and Thursday afternoons during sitting time. When Tony Blair took office in 1997, the two sessions were integrated into a single half-hour Wednesday session.
4 Although the analysis takes a core interest in the actual performance of PMQs as mediated political interaction, Hansard provides an initial access to the wording and contents of the speech produced, which facilitated the analytic process. Moreover, Hansard constitutes – along similar lines as the audio and video recordings – a mediated representation of PMQs saved for posterity. Having access to and knowledge of this representation allowed me to have a fuller picture of PMQs and to be able to relate to prior research on parliamentary interaction, which is – as has been outlined in previous chapters – often grounded in the written record.

To illustrate how the data sets are compiled, Table 4.1 shows the composition of the 1978–1988 data set, which contains the audio recordings of twenty-two sessions, each fifteen minutes long (i.e., approximately 5.5 hours in total). To have a balanced sample, the first Tuesday sessions in May and the first Thursday sessions in November of each year were chosen.

Table 4.1 gives an overview of the Prime Ministers and Leaders of the Opposition in office during 1978–1988. Con stands for Conservative Party, and Lab for Labour Party. The inclusion of some recordings with an acting PM and LO was intentional to study variant cases of how these respective roles can be performed.

---

[1] Labov distinguishes between the study of (1) 'change in apparent time: that is, the distribution of linguistic variables across age levels' (Labov 1994: 45–46) and (2) change 'in real-time, that is, to observe a speech community at two discrete points in time' (Labov 1994: 73).

40 Data, Transcription, and Methodology

Table 4.1 *Speakers at the dispatch box in the 1978–1988 data set*

Date	Prime Minister	Leader of the Opposition
02 May 1978	James Callaghan (Lab)	Margaret Thatcher (Con)
09 Nov. 1978	James Callaghan (Lab)	Margaret Thatcher (Con)
22 May 1979	Margaret Thatcher (Con)	James Callaghan (Lab)
01 Nov. 1979	Margaret Thatcher (Con)	James Callaghan (Lab)
06 May 1980	Margaret Thatcher (Con)	James Callaghan (Lab)
06 Nov. 1980	Margaret Thatcher (Con)	Michael Foot (Lab)
05 May 1981	Margaret Thatcher (Con)	Michael Foot (Lab)
12 Nov. 1981	Margaret Thatcher (Con)	Michael Foot (Lab)
04 May 1982	Margaret Thatcher (Con)	Michael Foot (Lab)
11 Nov. 1982	Margaret Thatcher (Con)	Michael Foot (Lab)
03 May 1983	Margaret Thatcher (Con)	Michael Foot (Lab)
03 Nov. 1983	Margaret Thatcher (Con)	Neil Kinnock (Lab)
01 May 1984	Margaret Thatcher (Con)	Neil Kinnock (Lab)
15 Nov. 1984	Margaret Thatcher (Con)	Neil Kinnock (Lab)
07 May 1985	Margaret Thatcher (Con)	Neil Kinnock (Lab)
14 Nov. 1985	Margaret Thatcher (Con)	Neil Kinnock (Lab)
06 May 1986	The Lord Privy Seal and Leader of the House of Commons (Mr John Biffen, Con) acting for Margaret Thatcher	Neil Kinnock (Lab)
06 Nov. 1986	Margaret Thatcher (Con)	Neil Kinnock (Lab)
05 May 1987	Margaret Thatcher (Con)	Neil Kinnock (Lab)
05 Nov. 1987	Margaret Thatcher (Con)	Neil Kinnock (Lab)
03 May 1988	Margaret Thatcher	Roy Hattersley (Lab, deputy Leader of the Opposition, acting for Neil Kinnock)
10 Nov. 1988[2]	Margaret Thatcher (Con)	Neil Kinnock (Lab)

Table 4.2 gives an overview of the more recent sample (2003–2013). Since the television footage was far easier and less expensive to access, it is considerably larger, consisting of forty-four video recordings (thirty minutes each, all in all approximately twenty-two hours). Again, an attempt was made to have a balanced sample, and acting PMs and LOs were included. As Leech *et al.* point out, 'the ideal of complete

---

[2] The session on 10 November 1988 was selected instead of the first Thursday session in November 1988, which was not taken by Mrs Thatcher but by the Leader of the House of Commons.

4.1 Database for the Study

Table 4.2 *Speakers at the dispatch box in the 2003–2013 data set*

Date	Prime Minister	Leader of the Opposition
15 Jan. 2003	Tony Blair (Lab)	Ian Duncan Smith (Con)
02 April 2003	Tony Blair	Ian Duncan Smith (Con)
16 July 2003	Tony Blair (Lab)	Ian Duncan Smith (Con)
03 Dec. 2003	Tony Blair (Lab)	Michael Howard (Con)
14 Jan. 2004	Tony Blair (Lab)	Michael Howard (Con)
21 April 2004	Tony Blair (Lab)	Michael Howard (Con)
14 July 2004	Tony Blair (Lab)	Michael Howard (Con)
13 Oct. 2004	Tony Blair (Lab)	Michael Howard (Con)
08 June 2005	Tony Blair (Lab)	Michael Howard (Con)
22 June 2005	Tony Blair (Lab)	Michael Howard (Con)
16 Nov. 2005	Tony Blair (Lab)	Michael Howard (Con)
07 Dec. 2005	Tony Blair (Lab)	David Cameron (Con)
01 Feb. 2006	Tony Blair (Lab)	David Cameron (Con)
24 May 2006	Tony Blair (Lab)	David Cameron (Con)
11 Oct. 2006	Tony Blair (Lab)	David Cameron (Con)
01 Nov. 2006	Tony Blair (Lab)	David Cameron (Con)
23 May 2007	Tony Blair (Lab)	David Cameron (Con)
27 June 2007	Tony Blair (Lab)	David Cameron (Con)
11 July 2007	Gordon Brown (Lab)	David Cameron (Con)
17 Oct. 2007	Gordon Brown (Lab)	David Cameron (Con)
09 Jan. 2008	Gordon Brown (Lab)	David Cameron (Con)
06 Feb. 2008	Gordon Brown (Lab)	David Cameron (Con)
27 Feb. 2008	Gordon Brown (Lab)	David Cameron (Con)
02 July 2008	Gordon Brown (Lab)	David Cameron (Con)
14 Jan. 2009	Gordon Brown (Lab)	David Cameron (Con)
11 March 2009	Gordon Brown (Lab)	David Cameron (Con)
10 June 2009	Gordon Brown (Lab)	David Cameron (Con)
16 Dec. 2009	Harriet Harman (Lab, acting)	William Hague (Con, acting)
14 July 2010	David Cameron (Con)	Harriet Harman (Lab, acting)
03 Nov. 2010	David Cameron (Con)	Ed Miliband (Lab)
01 Dec. 2010	David Cameron (Con)	Ed Miliband (Lab)
08 Dec. 2010	David Cameron (Con)	Ed Miliband (Lab)
19 Jan. 2011	David Cameron (Con)	Ed Miliband (Lab)
30 March 2011	David Cameron (Con)	Ed Miliband (Lab)
27 April 2011	David Cameron (Con)	Ed Miliband (Lab)
11 May 2011	David Cameron (Con)	Ed Miliband (Lab)
11 Jan. 2012	David Cameron (Con)	Ed Miliband (Lab)
18 April 2012	David Cameron (Con)	Ed Miliband (Lab)
11 July 2012	David Cameron (Con)	Ed Miliband (Lab)
17 Oct. 2012	David Cameron (Con)	Ed Miliband (Lab)
09 Jan. 2013	David Cameron (Con)	Ed Miliband (Lab)
24 April 2013	David Cameron (Con)	Ed Miliband (Lab)
17 July 2013	David Cameron (Con)	Ed Miliband (Lab)
16 Oct. 2013	David Cameron (Con)	Ed Miliband (Lab)

comparability' (Leech *et al.* 2009: 28) can never be reached, since deviations in size and make-up between corresponding subcorpora are hard to avoid.³

It has been a methodological principle in Conversation Analysis and Interactional Linguistics to use only recordings which provide the analyst with the same situated communicative cues as are available to the interactants in a social encounter. For this reason, a major bulk of conversation analytic research was grounded in audio recordings of telephone interaction (where participants exclusively deploy auditive cues to base their understanding on), until video cameras became cheap enough to capture face-to-face interaction on a larger scale. The data for this study thus deviate from this principle in two ways: on the one hand, the 1978–1988 data offer only an audio impression of the face-to-face interaction at PMQs. On the other, while the 2003–2013 data set comprises videos, my analytic access is constrained by the scene editing, camera direction, and orchestrated use of microphones in the video recordings, constraints that are typical of media broadcasts.⁴ The wider implications of such data as an analytic basis are discussed in Section 4.3.

4.1.2 Composition of Participation and Calculation of Frequencies

In Chapter 3, I identified two global processes which have affected PMQs during the 36 years I am examining:

1 Mediation and mediatisation, and
2 Merging and a more prominent role for the LO.

In what follows, I want to take up the latter factor, the LO's more prominent role, in more detail and discuss how over the years, this has changed the composition of participation in the activity at PMQs, which provides the backdrop of reported speech as an emergent construction.

As outlined before, Bates *et al.* (2014) have found that the composition of participation has changed during the premierships of Margaret Thatcher to David Cameron. Their study, based on data taken from Hansard, comprises an equal number of PMQs sessions from the beginnings of

---

[3] The audio recordings were purchased through the Parliamentary Recording Unit and the British Film Institute. The video recordings were acquired from the Parliamentary Recording Unit as well as downloaded free of charge – but at lower quality – from the online archive of the US television network C-SPAN (www.c-span.org).

[4] The problem of 'visibility' as a methodological problem is being increasingly discussed in terms of video data in general (see, e.g., Mondada 2019b).

Table 4.3 *Number of substantial questions (1978–1988 and 2003–2013)*

Number of sessions per data set	Total number of substantial questions	Average number of substantial questions per week	Average number of substantial questions by LOs per week
1978–1988 (n=22; two 15-minute sessions per week)	331	30	4 (i.e., 2 per session)
2003–2013 (n=44; one 30-minute session per week)	1159	26	6 (i.e., 6 per session)

each premiership (1979–2010), that is, roughly the period covered by my study. Importantly, their sample shows that the total number of questions per session has decreased, while the number of interruptions and the speaking time of the PM and LO have increased at the cost of MPs' question time and power (Bates *et al.* 2014: 264). My counts based on the 1978–1988 and 2003–2013 data sets roughly match Bates *et al.*'s results, with the average number of question turns having declined during the 36 years between 1978–2013 (Table 4.3). Recall that there is a distinction between engagements questions which are only matters of ritual (see Chapter 3) and substantial questions (which may contain quotations). Because of the focus of the study, I only calculated the numerical development of substantial questions.

Table 4.3 shows that the average number of substantial questions has dropped from 30 to 26 per week between the two data sets, while the number of such questions asked by the LO has increased from a weekly 4 to 6. Bates *et al.* (2014: 262–264) do not give information on the basis for their calculation. Their average numbers – at 35.7, slightly higher for the Thatcher years (roughly corresponding to the 1978–1988 subset), and at 25–26, roughly the same for the Blair, Brown, and Cameron premierships (the approximate equivalent of the 2003–2013 period) – suggest, however, that engagements questions were included, considering that the number of engagements questions has been restricted to one only per week since the Blair period.

Figures 4.1 and 4.2 show the distribution during 1978–1988 and 2003–2010, when the Liberal Democrats were the second largest opposition party and entitled to up to two question turns per week. After the 2010 national election, when the Liberal Democrats formed a coalition government with the Conservatives, this right was not transferred to other parties.

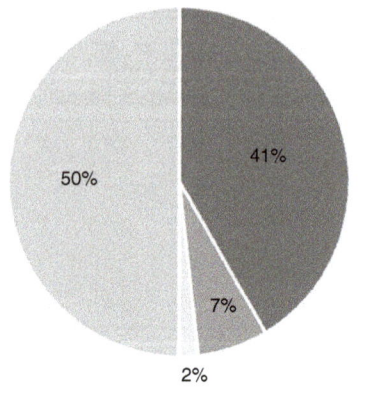

Figure 4.1 Distribution of turn types and speaker roles in 1978–1988.

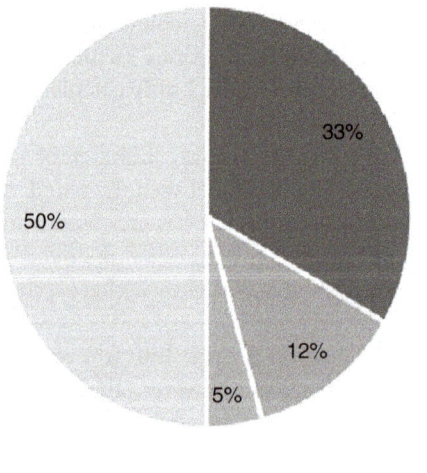

Figure 4.2 Distribution of turn types and speaker roles in 2003–2010.

4.1 Database for the Study

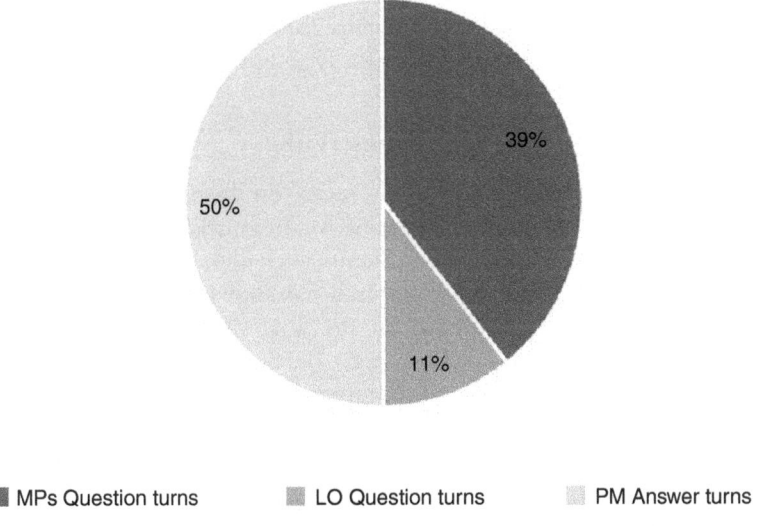

Figure 4.3 Distribution of turn types and speaker roles in 2010–2013.

Fig. 4.3 shows the post-election distribution (2010–2013).
The comparison reveals that the percentage of questions by the LO increased from 7 per cent (1978–1988) to a peak of 12 per cent (2003–2010). With the number of questions by the Liberal Democrats almost doubling (2 per cent compared to 5 per cent), the percentage of MPs' question turns dropped from 41 per cent to 33 per cent. When the Liberal Democrats are in power, the proportion of MPs' question turns almost returns to its original value (39 per cent), with LO's question turns only seeing a slight decline (11 per cent).

To compare both data sets in terms of turn types and speaker roles, I first counted all turn types by speaker role, distinguishing between question turns by the MPs, LOs, and the Leader of the Liberal Party/SDP (Social Democratic Party) or Liberal Democrats, respectively, and answer turns by the PMs.[5] Again, since engagements questions are only matters of ritual and do not contain quotations, I deducted these from the total sum of question turns before calculating the distribution, turn types, and speaker

---

[5] The Liberal Party and the SDP formed the SDP–Liberal electoral Alliance (in June 1981), before merging as the Liberal Democrats in March 1988 (www.liberalhistory.org.uk/history/formation-of-the-sdp).

roles as depicted. This also means that I did not include answers to engagements questions in the calculations. This calculation of question turns was also used as a point of reference for the calculation of the average frequencies of reported speech per turn type and speaker role.

4.2 Transcription

Although prior research has often relied on Hansard in analyses of PMQs, the shortcomings of Hansard for linguistic analysis have been widely illustrated (Mollin 2007; Slembrouck 1992) and acknowledged (Sealey and Bates 2016). Prior research has shown what can be gained from a microanalytic approach to the analysis of grammatical constructions in spoken interaction (e.g., Barth-Weingarten 2006, 2009, 2014; Barth-Weingarten and Couper-Kuhlen 2002, 2011). This requires a fine-grained transcription of the vocal, verbal, and – where videos are available – bodily comportment of participants. To this end, I transcribed all examples using GAT (Couper-Kuhlen and Barth-Weingarten 2011) and – when visual cues were considered – Mondada's (2019a, 2019b) 'Conventions for multimodal transcription'. With respect to the audio files in the 1978–1988 data set, this meant that I created transcripts by repeatedly listening to the recordings. For an embodied analysis, I first created additional audio files from the edited videos to transcribe verbal and vocal detail, before transcribing the camera work as well as the bodily conduct and kinetic manipulation of objects relevant to the performance of reported speech. This follows an understanding that to be able to describe bodily and kinetic conduct and how it is coordinated with verbal and vocal resources, it is important to analyse whether and how such conduct is made visible to in-house participants and the television and online audience (Streeck 1993: 293).[6] To complete transcripts with bodily representations, I synchronised the vocal and verbal transcript with the visual one: for instance, I based my decision of whether to place pauses at the end or the beginning of the next transcript line on the trajectory of concurrent visual actions. The whole procedure was supported by the use of the software *QuickTime Pro* and *Praat*. Appendix A has a complete overview of the transcription conventions used.

---

[6] Camera work also constitutes a tool for the mediatised representation of PMQs, an aspect which is not included in the analysis.

4.3 Basic Methodological Assumptions

In this study, I embrace a combined approach to the short-term diachronic study of reported speech at PMQs, which integrates a qualitative with a quantitative analysis. In this vein, the methodology employed in the study is fundamentally informed by Interactional Linguistics, Conversation Analysis, and Emergent Grammar, and draws on Variationist Sociolinguistics, usage-based grammar, and Historical Pragmatics to accommodate the short-term diachronic approach to reported speech at PMQs. It has been designed with respect to the following assumptions:

1. *Naturally occurring social interaction*

The analysis of reported speech is based on authentic video and audio recordings (rather than Hansard) because they give the best possible picture of the performance of participants at PMQs (cf. Mazeland 2003; Streeck 2008). What underlies this interest in the actual performance is a general interest in the study of language in its home, social interaction.

2. *Community of practice*

A view of social interaction as the home of language is compatible with a view of language as emergent in social activities in which members of communities of practice engage. These communities of practice – and along with them the social activities and practices they deploy – have evolved over time. Practices – or ways of doing things – can involve the use of linguistic structures, voice, bodily movements, and the manipulation of objects. As such the community-of-practice view allows us to account for why the 1978–1988 and 2003–2013 data are similar enough to be suitable for comparison but also different enough to be used as a window into the uses of emergent reported speech as an evidential practice at PMQs over time. Finally, the concept of communities of practice has been acknowledged as a sociolinguistic method to provide fine-grained, contextualised detail to our understanding of variation and change in more global linguistic communities.

3. *Language as emergent in and over time*

An interactional-linguistic perspective on the analysis of spoken language means describing structures as they unfold – emerge – in the real time of social interaction and as they incrementally build on prior talk as well as project what is to come (Couper-Kuhlen and Selting 1996, 2001, 2018). The use of linguistic structures in the here and now is only a snapshot of emergent structures which are always potentially adapted, lost, and newly created in spoken interaction in and over time.

4. Linguistic structures as conventionalised, formulaic constructions

In line with Emergent Grammar and a general, usage-based grammar view on language, linguistic structures are assumed to be stored as more or less conventionalised chunks, ranging between fully fixed formulaic fragments and more schematic constructions stored as exemplar representations (e.g., Bybee 2013; Fox and Thompson 2007; Thompson 2002).

5. Frequency as a concomitant of language change and variation

Going hand in hand with this usage-based view is the assumption that frequency is concomitant with grammaticalisation (Bybee 2003). The work by Clayman *et al.* (2006, 2007) further shows that frequency also constitutes a methodological tool for understanding processes on a more global discourse level, that is, what participants treat as appropriate linguistic structures for action formation in social interaction. The present study seeks to integrate these assumptions in calculating the relative frequencies of reported speech with respect to turn types and participant role. In addition, I calculated the average proportion of turns per speaker role across the sample. This approach is also informed by the participant perspective taken in the study.

6. The participants' perspective

A primary methodological principle of Conversation Analysis and Interactional Linguistics is that the data are analysed from the participants' perspective, which is implemented through 'next turn proof procedure' (Sacks *et al.* 1974: 728–729). The basic assumption is that participants signal their understanding of and orientation to the current linguistic action in their next turn (Sacks *et al.* 1974: 728). Based on the shape and sequential positioning of these next turns, analysts can reconstruct an action analysis from the participants' perspective (Sacks *et al.* 1974: 729). The following problems and implications are connected to the data analysis from the participants' perspective in the study:

6a. Mediated interaction

The data taken from PMQs present us with several problems when applying next-turn-proof procedure. PMQs is a mediated setting with professional orators performing (commonly rehearsed and scripted) actions predefined by their institutional roles in a split participation framework, involving participants and audiences co-present in the House as well as listeners and viewers of the broadcast. These considerations and the above-mentioned constraints on the recordings have the implications that the analyst's access and participants' perspective are those of the public media

4.3 Basic Methodological Assumptions

audience rather than the participants present in the House of Commons Chamber. In this sense the analytic perspective taken is a mediated participants' perspective. The two data sets are taken for what they are, recordings as products to be broadcast via different mass media (radio, television, internet), available to and consumed by the public (cf. Gerhardt 2006, for a literature review on mass media audiences). These different media settings are taken into consideration in the analysis (by incorporating an analysis of visual resources and camera work in the TV data, for instance) where warranted by the research questions. When relevant to the analysis, the ways in which political agents potentially orient to these diverse mediated settings in their performance are also considered.

6b. *Opacity of next speakers' understanding*
Another methodological problem is that interlocutors in their institutional roles put on their game faces such that their understanding of the prior action is often methodically not displayed (as is assumed to be done, e.g., in mundane conversation between family and friends, see Clayman and Heritage 2002b: 242; Robles 2011: 151, for discussion). Clayman and Heritage state:

> A more fundamental difficulty is the fact that the participants' understandings are not always transparent, and they may at times be designedly opaque. Consider that when interviewees sidestep a question, they may strive to conceal that fact in an effort both to avoid prompting a hostile follow-up question and to forestall negative inferences from the viewing audience. Correspondingly, even if interviewers recognize that an evasion has occurred, they may decide to 'let it pass' in the interest of moving the interview forward. (Clayman and Heritage 2002b: 242)

Nevertheless, Clayman and Heritage decide to label actions according to how they are treated by recipients. The present study adopts this approach as well as drawing on co-participant, that is, audience, responses as evidence in the analysis. Audience responses are particularly valuable in the analysis of answer turns to MPs' questions, to which the questioning MP cannot follow up.

6c. *Multi-unit turns*
Another problem is that PMQs is characterised by lengthy multi-unit turns, which bear traits of political oratory and implement multiple and/or complex actions, whose single components cannot exclusively be analysed through next-turn proof procedure. To analyse single turn units and action components from the participants' perspective, I make use of participants' displays of understanding in multiple ways: (1) Audience

responses are analysed as evidence for points of possible completion during and/or positioning towards the orator's ongoing speech. These audience responses may be forthcoming in a seemingly spontaneous fashion but are also visibly solicited by the current speaker, for example, when rallying members of their own party behind them. (2) What is typical of multi-unit turns in general – but also shows in-house participants' orientation to a split audience in particular – is that current speakers make their actions recognisable in very explicit ways. Projected by conventionalised, ritualised practices, these discrete components are recognisable from early on and make the speaker's understanding and planning of their own project visible. In as much as these practices guide participants' understanding of the current speaker's enterprise, they guide the study's analysis from a public participant's perspective.[7]

6d. *Empirical grounding of analytic categories*
In a more general sense, the participants' perspective also means that analytic categories are derived inductively from the data, as made relevant by the speakers who use them. This corresponds to a speaker-centred, usage-based perspective, which argues for 'the importance of looking at the recurrent patterns in everyday interactions in order to know what constructions speakers are using and storing' (Thompson and Hopper 2001). Moreover, this calls for a methodological procedure where the categories used for the calculation of frequencies are established on the back of qualitative analysis rather than being based on a priori concepts.

7. *Deviant cases*
Deviant cases are a powerful methodological tool in Conversation Analysis because they expose 'participant's own orientations to the normative structures most clearly' (Sidnell 2013: 80). This means that deviant cases can give an insight into normative patterns in the data. Thus, the study of low-frequency structures allows an insight into the larger picture (Schegloff 1968).

Based on these assumptions, the study applies a methodological framework which is flexible enough to account for both reported speech as an evidential practice in a mediated institutional setting and reported speech as an emergent construction during the period of 36 years in which PMQs has been evolving.

---

[7] The formal design of the participation framework further puts heavy constraints on rights to the floor, action types and design, and the vocal, verbal, and visual choices made by participants, as shown in the analysis.

4.4 Analytic Questions and Procedure

I began the study with a first survey of the 2003–2013 data set, where I found that SAY constitutes the most frequent verb of communication. Following this very first finding, I built a collection of all occurrences of the verb irrespective of context in the 2003–2013 set. To this end, I first searched the Hansard files for instances of SAY before checking the video recordings to verify the accuracy and authenticity of my initial findings. The analysis generated this functional distribution of the verb SAY:[8]

1. as a quotative verb, indicating reported speech (e.g., *IN: afghanistan on mOnday; the PRIME minister said; BRITtish troops; could start coming home from afGHANistan; (–) as EArly as next YEAR*);
2. as a full verb (e.g., *i agree with every word the prime minister has just said about zimBABwe*, or *bEAring in mind what the MEdia is saying*);
3. as part of 'metapragmatic' (Caffi 2006) constructions (e.g., *but i must sAy to the prime minister that he is in danger of sounding ex↑trEmely com↑PLACent*); and
(4) to build indirect questions (e.g., *and can he say how many oTHer local authorities across the country (...)*).[9]

Among these functions, SAY is most commonly used as a quotative, where it was mainly found in the following grammatical structures:

1. comment clauses (e.g., *°h their fIght in afghAnistan is not just about the stability °h of !THAT! country; <<all,p> but as the PRIME minister has said;> °h about kEEping OUr strEEts sAfe HERE; (-) in BRItain*);
2. pseudo-cleft clauses (e.g., *<<f>whAt we SAID> in the september dossier, was that THIS was the intelligence that we have recEived.*); and
3. reporting clauses (e.g., *and his ↑OWN labour mEmber of the commIttee Actually says; °h that the ↑CIvil servant has been used as a fAll guy by the government*).

The analysis of SAY as a quotative verb revealed that it represents the most frequent grammatical choice across turn types and participant roles in reporting clauses. For this reason, a decision was made to place the focus on this grammatical structure, and specifically on constructions with SAY in reporting clauses. Recall that this study seeks to take a combined

---

[8] All examples are taken from the recordings from the 1978–1988 and 2003–2013 data sets.
[9] Jucker (1986) calls what I call indirect questions 'prefaced questions'.

methodological approach, analysing reported speech as an emergent, evidential construction at PMQs, using qualitative and quantitative methods to compare two data sets spanning 36 years. To this end, I conducted four smaller studies, examining the uses of reporting and reported clauses (Chapters 5 and 6) as well as the organisation of reported speech with respect to other rhetorical structures (Chapter 7) and recurrent courses of action (Chapter 8).

CHAPTER 5

Reporting Clauses

This chapter is concerned with the analysis of reporting clauses, comparing their use as a changing construction between the 1978–1988 and 2003–2013 data sets. The two research questions addressed are:

1. How are the reporting clauses composed in terms of their form, meaning, and function in the two data sets?
2. Can these reporting clauses be described as conventionalised constructions undergoing processes of change?

To answer these questions, I analysed the forms and meanings of the elements of reporting clauses. On the basis of the categories established, I calculated their relative frequencies across participant roles and turn types. I compared the findings from both data sets and did additional interactional analyses to illustrate the evolving uses and functions. Based on further frequency counts, I explored possible grammaticalisation processes and the emergence of conventionalised constructions in the uses of reporting clauses.

It is shown that there is a steep increase in the 2003–2013 use of reporting clauses and that the construction of reporting clauses is undergoing change on multiple levels; Some of these changes are specific to the contextual constraints of PMQs, and some are indicative of larger processes in English.

The chapter is organised as follows: after a review of relevant past research (5.1), the forms and functions of the elements of reporting clauses, that is, the subject (5.2), verb (5.3), optional indirect object (5.4), and circumstantial adverbials (5.5), are studied in a comparative analysis between the 1978–1988 and 2003–2013 samples. The implications of some of the findings are discussed in two case studies in which it is argued that the clause HE SAID has entered a path of grammaticalisation (5.6), and that the serial production of the construction [Temporal adverbial + THE PRIME MINISTER + SAY+ quotation] has evolved into a recurrent pattern (5.7), showing signs of formulaicity. The chapter wraps up with a summary and conclusions (5.8).

5.1 Past Research

In this section, I prepare the ground for a comparative analysis of 1978–1988 and 2003–2013 reporting clauses. Reporting clauses (see also Chapter 2) provide an evidential grounding for the reported clause by making reference to the ascribed source (expressed by the subject), the mode of communication (verb), and potentially to the recipient(s) (indirect object), as well as to the circumstances of what was said (circumstantial adverbials). The linguistic means to provide reference have been studied from various relevant perspectives. Section 5.1.1 summarises this past research. As was suggested in Chapter 2, reporting clauses with *say* tend to be grammaticalised as an evidential marker across languages. Section 5.1.2 continues this discussion, providing a literature review on *say* in reporting clauses and grammaticalisation.

5.1.1 *Reporting Clauses as a Locus for Reference*

Reference in conversation analytic research has been studied most thoroughly with respect to person, but some research has focused on place and time reference.

In terms of the formulation of person reference in English, Sacks and Schegloff (2007: 24) first proposed two basic principles of preference organisation: recognition and minimisation (see also Schegloff 1996a). Summarising how these two principles have been expanded in follow-up research, Enfield puts forward the following list:

> Summary of 'preference' type principles for reference to persons
>
> (i) Design the expression for the recipient
>   a. achieve recognition
>   b. invoke or display relationship proximity/type
> (ii) Minimize the expressive means
>   a. use a single referring expression
>   b. use a name rather than a description
>   c. use only one name from a binomial if possible
> (iii) Fit the expressive format to the action being performed
> (iv) Observe local cultural/institutional constraints
> (v) Associate the referent explicitly with one of the speech participants
>
> (Enfield 2013: 443)

This suggests that reference is generally organised in terms of recipient design, minimisation, the ongoing action format, cultural and institutional constraints, and in association with speech participants. These principles are echoed in studies on reference in political settings.

In his analysis of a political speech, Mazeland finds that person reference and categorisation is selective and recipient-designed, functioning to 'accomplish some kind of social-structural mapping of the parties involved' (Mazeland 2003: 96). Holly argues that, in this way, referential expressions are a highly strategic resource for political propaganda:

> There is a nearly universal principle in political language. Any utterance ought to be formulated, any expression ought to be chosen such that it conveys as much additional material as possible for propaganda purposes. The most effective place for this material is not in the official focus of an utterance, nor in the obvious speech act or in the central predication, but in less obvious positions: for example referential expressions, presuppositions and implications. (Holly 1989: 124)

In other words, participants portray people they talk about such that they can be recognised, in ways that are both relevant to and coherent with the activity described, as well as recipient designed to achieve situated communicative goals contingent on the ongoing interaction. In political discourse in particular, referential expressions are designed such that they serve politicians' propaganda campaigns and political agendas.

These findings are corroborated by investigations of written texts. In a study on chain compounds (e.g., 'systemloss-of-data failure', 'in-the-field complaints') in English engineering journals, Varantola suggests that the linguistic packaging of referencing can have a communicative function. She notes:

> These forms are generally self-explanatory, and may serve to disambiguate and condense information. In contrast to chain compounds used in other fields, such as advertising, engineering chain compounds appear to serve a special communicative purpose of clarifying and differentiating where a shorter term could be ambiguous. (Varantola 1984: 94)

Complementing these findings, dense information packaging has been associated with the constraints of time and space under which certain types of texts are produced (Fox 1987). As regards short-term diachronic change, Leech *et al.* identify 'densification' as a driving force for change in contemporary English (see, e.g., Leech *et al.* 2009: 249–252).

In terms of who is referred to as a source of quotation, a source's authority is key: Jucker on newspaper discourse states that high-ranking politicians (and officials) – in contrast to ordinary members of the public – are considered elite news sources who have a 'perceived authority' (Jucker 1996: 376). It can be inferred that the more elite the source, the more it is understood to be authoritative. Elite sources further:

> may be newsworthy because of what they say, while non-elite people only become newsworthy through their actions (e.g., criminals or accused), or when something happens to them (e.g., as victims of a crime or a natural catastrophe). (Jucker 1996: 375)

Similarly, Johnstone (1987) notes in her analysis of authority narratives in everyday conversation that story tellers construct the characters in reported dialogues on a continuum between what she calls 'authority' and 'non-authority' figures through lexical choices.

Schegloff (1972) observes that three dimensions are oriented to the production of place reference: location, membership, and topic analysis. This means that speakers and recipients display an orientation towards their own and the interlocutor's current location(s), towards the social status of the interlocutor and recognisability, and towards the topic or goals of the activity under way when producing or hearing place formulations (cf. also Atkinson and Drew 1979). According to Enfield, this three-dimensional analysis of place reference is also relevant to time reference (Enfield 2013: 437–438). Moreover, Schegloff observes that 'place terms can be used to formulate objects other than place' (Schegloff 1972: 81), for example, 'occupation' (*I work inna driving school*), 'stage of life' (*When I was in Junior High School*), and 'activities' (*What's Jim doing? Oh, he's at the ballpark*; labels and examples from Schegloff 1972: 81–82). Linguistically, these uses can be conceptualised as 'a figurative extension' (Quirk *et al.* 1985: 479) of spatial adverbials.

This literature review has shown that the design of referential choices is functional in securing maximum recognition at minimal cost, which becomes apparent in dense information packaging. Referential expressions are reflective of their discourse context and communicative aims and display membership categorisation, which may serve the purpose of political propaganda. We can expect that these patterns are at work in references to the source (and circumstantial details) in reporting clauses as well.

5.1.2 *Reporting Clauses with* Say *and Grammaticalisation*

Say constitutes a high-frequency verb of communication across contexts (e.g., M. Goodwin 1990; Sealey and Bates 2016; Quirk *et al.*

1985: 1024; Wooffitt and Alistone 2008). Due to this frequency, reported speech with the quotative *say* has attracted a great deal of attention in the literature.

Although it is agreed that *say* is a transitive verb, there is an equally common understanding that it is not a prototypical member of its class: it does not passivise easily and its complement clause, when formatted as direct speech, does not behave as a regular object (e.g., Buchstaller 2014: 39–41; Munro 1982; Quirk *et al.* 1985: 1022–1023; Vandelanotte and Davidse 2009). Thompson (2002) argues that this behaviour is typical of epistemic, evidential, and evaluative complement-taking predicates (CTPs; Noonan 1985) in spoken English. In line with Hopper (1991), her research shows that a high frequency of epistemic CTPs correlates with the reanalysis of epistemic formulaic fragments as epistemic phrases (Thompson and Mulac 1991a: 319; see also Bybee 2011). Thompson concedes that she 'did not include any complements with the CTP *say* since reported speech raises special issues beyond the grammar of complementation, which deserve their own study' (Thompson 2002: Fn 3). However, Kärkkäinen (2003) suggests with respect to American English that '*s/he said* [...] is grammaticizing into an epistemic phrase' (Kärkkäinen 2003: 43) because of the frequency in her corpus. Holt's study on direct reported speech in British and American English informal conversation seems to corroborate Kärkkäinen's hypothesis: 'Reported speech is generally preceded by a pronoun, such as *I/he/she/they*, plus a speech verb which is usually "said" but can be "says", "goes", "thought", etc. [...]' (Holt 1996: 224). Although the cognitive foundation of grammar is not Holt's concern, her observations suggest that reporting clauses with *say* projecting direct quotations could be formulaic. Vandelanotte and Davidse (2009) propose that the reporting clause is dependent on the reported clause rather than vice versa, since the former is incomplete without the latter but not the other way round.

There is evidence from other languages that the quotative *say* can undergo grammaticalisation (see also Chapter 2) and occurs in conventionalised constructions (Imo 2007, 2009). Here Deutscher points out the relation between the frequency and formulaicity of quotative constructions:

> Few things occur as frequently in natural speech as the reporting of speech itself. The extreme frequency of reported speech constructions in discourse, coupled with their formulaic nature, makes them a prototypical locus for grammaticalization. (Deutscher 2011: 646)

For instance, the Akkadian quotative clause *enma X* ('this is what X said') has grammaticalised into an obligatory, syntactically dependent, redundant quotative particle, through gradual processes of phonological and morphological change, semantic bleaching, and loss of syntactic independence (Deutscher 2011). Following another quotative clause, the particle prefaces the quotation in the reported speech (cf. also Keevallik 2008 on the grammaticalisation of the Estonian complementiser *et* into an evidential particle).

In sum, this review demonstrates that *say* is a highly frequent quotative verb which tends to enter patterned constructions and undergo grammaticalisation across languages and discourse contexts. I show that similar processes can be observed in the PMQs data.

5.2 Subjects

As pointed out earlier, the linguistic form of ascribed sources, realised as the subject in reporting clauses, is highly indexical of its context and tightly connected to its meaning and function. For this reason, the following analysis characterises the subjects in reporting clauses in terms of their syntactic, semantic, and functional aspects. I illustrate that syntactically, the subject of the reporting clause can be nominal or pronominal, that is, the noun phrases (NPs) serving as subjects can have nouns or pronouns as heads. Semantically, the subject generally refers to the ascribed source of the quotation. However, it is also shown that subjects can serve as forms of address. Functionally, speakers' choices of subjects display institutional and interactional contingencies shaped by their assumptions about the local, ongoing interaction.

To describe the forms of NPs serving as subjects, we need to make the following distinctions: in his seminal paper, Aarts (1971) distinguishes between 'light' and 'heavy' types of noun phrases. Light noun phrases comprise '(1) pronouns, (2) names, (3) nouns, neither pre- nor postmodified, (4) nouns, premodified by determiners only' (Aarts 1971: 281). Heavy noun phrases, on the other hand, include:

a. All other premodified noun-phrases, that is, those premodified by (1) adjective(s), (2) genitive, (3) noun, (4) adjective + noun, (5) genitive+ noun
b. All postmodified noun-phrases, that is, those postmodified by (1) prepositional phrase(s), (2) prepositional phrase(s) + clause, (3) prepositional phrase + non-finite clause, (4) non-finite clause, (5) relative clause. (Aarts 1971: 282)

5.2 Subjects

Based on Aarts, Quirk *et al.* (1985) differentiate between simple and complex noun phrase structures:

> 'Simple' is here defined as nouns without modification, that is, simple noun phrases (e.g., *John, she, the man*). In view of their numerical and distributional importance, pronouns and names are distinguished as a subclass of 'simple'. 'Complex' embraces all other noun phrases, but a subclass is distinguished comprising those having multiple modification (more than merely a single adjective premodifier or prepositional phrase postmodifier). (Quirk *et al.* 1985: 1350; cf. Jucker 1992 for a critical discussion)

I adopt Aarts' terminology because he offers a more detailed description of what the categories involve, which makes it easier to apply.

Further formal realisations of subject noun phrases in the data are appositions and coordinated noun phrases. According to Jucker, 'appositions consist of two coreferential noun phrases which fulfil basically the same syntactic role within one single clause' (Jucker 1992: 77; see also Quirk *et al.* 1985: 1300–1321). The concept of full apposition (as opposed to partial apposition) where 'either of the two appositives can be deleted, and the resultant sentence is still grammatical' (Jucker 1992: 77) is relevant to the following description of the data. Exx. (9a)–(9c) illustrate this. The italicised apposition is in (9a). As a deletion test, (9b) and (9c) show that each of the appositives (*Mr Simpson, The vicar of Barnston*) can serve as subjects in grammatical clauses.

(9)   Full apposition (Jucker 1992: 78)
    a. *Mr Simpson, the vicar of Barnston*, said last night: . . .
    b. *Mr Simpson* said last night: . . .
    c. *The vicar of Barnston* said last night: . . .

Jucker's examples, taken from a corpus of newspaper texts, also nicely evidence the use of such appositive structures as subjects in reporting clauses with *say* across discourse contexts.

Subjects which consist 'of two or more noun phrases (or clauses) coordinated by *and*' (Quirk *et al.* 1985: 759) and agree with a plural verb, are called coordinated subjects (Ex. 10).

(10) Coordinated subjects (Quirk *et al.* 1985: 759)
    Tom and Alice *are* now ready. ['Tom is now ready and Alice is now ready']

The example shows that the coordinated subject matches the coordinated clausal structure in square brackets, which represents a way of testing coordinated subjects.

This outline has illustrated that nominal subjects can come in a variety of forms. Crucially they can range between light- and heavy-headed structures. Against the backdrop of this terminology, I now turn to the data analysis of 1978–1988 and 2003–2013 nominal subjects.

5.2.1 *Nominal Subjects*

I begin with the analysis of 1978–1988 nominal subjects before comparing the findings with those of the 2003–2013 sample.

1978–1988
In total, most noun phrases in subject position of finite reporting clauses are light-headed, that is, they have pronouns or simple nouns as heads. The latter (simple nouns as heads) are in the clear minority. Table 5.1 (Appendix B) gives an overview of the relative frequencies with respect to the number of question and answer turns across speaker roles. Ex. (11) is an example of such a rare, light nominal NP:

(11)   PMQs 03 May 1988
MP: Harry Greenway (Con); PM: Margaret Thatcher (Con); S: Bernard Weatherill

```
1 PM: -> °h thAt report SAID; ((quotation))
```

The noun phrase consists of a determiner, the demonstrative determiner *that*, and the head, the noun *report*, with no modifiers, and is thus considered light.

In general, nominal NPs are heavy-headed. Here half of them represent compounds; the Prime Minister is a typical example (see Ex. (12), line 1):[1]

(12)   PMQs 03 May 1988
MP: Ernie Ross (Lab); PM: Margaret Thatcher (Con); S: Bernard Weatherill

```
1   MP:    -> [the prIme minister has said toDAY,]
2   MPs:      [mur mur mur mur mur mur mur mur  ]

3   MP:       [(.) and last THURSday;] ((quotation))
4   MPs:      [mur mur mur mur mur   ]
```

---

[1] I have based the distinction between phrases and compound nouns on the question of whether an example is listed in the OED. If the item in question represented an entry in the OED, I classified it as compound noun.

5.2 Subjects

The data also contain heavy phrasal constructions with one premodifier and one postmodifier. Ex. (13) which represents a shorter version of Ex. (1) is an example.

(13)   PMQs 01 Nov. 1979
MP: William Hamilton (Lab); PM: Margaret Thatcher (Con); S: George Thomas

```
1   MP:      will she also take time to READ,
2            a recent debate on the national health service when (.) HER
             party was in opposition and the present leader;
3            the present SPOKESman;
4         -> the present minister for the health service sAid that the
             NURses;
5            needed (.) as ↑GOOD treatment as the: polIce and the armed
             fOrces;
```

Following self-repair (*and the present leader; the present SPOKESman;* in lines 2–3), the MP produces *the present minister for the health service* (line 4) as the subject of the reporting clause. The head *minister* is determined by the definite article *the*, and has the adjective phrase *present* as premodifier and the prepositional phrase *for the health service* as postmodifier. Ex. (14) illustrates the only apposition in the sample:

(14)   PMQs 07 May 1985
LO: Neil Kinnock (Lab); PM: Margaret Thatcher (Con); S: Bernard Weatherill

```
1   PM:       (0.51) i NOtice [that he SAID,]
2   MPs:                      [1 1 1 1 1 1][1 1 1  ] [sh sh sh sh sh sh sh sh
3   PM:   ->                               [(0.56)] [that my RIGHT honourable
    MPs:   sh sh sh sh sh sh sh sh sh sh sh ]
    PM:    friend the secretary of energy sAid,] ((quotation))
```

The subject is composed of two subsequent complex NPs, *my RIGHT honourable friend* plus *the secretary of energy* (line 3). They form a full apposition in that both appositive NPs could each serve as the subject of *sAid*.

This shows that when considering pronominal and nominal subjects together, light-headed NPs dominate. When focusing on nominal heads only, the sample shows a preference for subjects with heavy-headed noun phrases. The other way round, when the subject has a nominal (rather than a pronominal) head, it tends to be heavy. Table 5.2 shows this 1978–1988 preference for heavy (rather than light) nominal noun phrases in the subject position of finite reporting clauses.

Table 5.2 *Absolute distribution of noun phrases in 1978–1988 subjects in finite reporting clauses*

(n=20)	Light NPs: pronominal heads	Light NPs: nominal heads	Heavy NPs	Other
Subjects in finite reporting clauses	50% (10)	10% (2)	40% (8)	0% (0)

The foregoing analysis has shown that although light-headed NPs dominate, there is a tendency towards heavy-headed NPs if the head is a noun (rather than a pronoun). This suggests that quotative subjects are a locus for dense information packaging, showing an orientation towards making the labels used for quotative subjects both differentiating and self-explanatory.

Semantically, the subjects in reporting clauses overwhelmingly make reference to elite sources, which fall into two types: human, named by their titles (e.g., *the prIme minister, the present minister for the health service, my right honourable friend*), and inanimate, specifically, official documents (e.g., *thAt report, the FIRST=uh (.) communiqué, (-) uh aBOUT the sinking; from the: (.) ARgentine sIde*).[2] These choices show an orientation to the institutional character of the interaction at PMQs, signalling the rank and status of the source, which is a resource for constructing its (evidential) authority. To illustrate an uncommon case, Ex. (15), taken from the question turn of an MP, exemplifies the use of an inanimate source.

(15)   PMQs 04 May 1982

MP1: Anthony Kershaw (Con); PM: Margaret Thatcher (Con); S: George Thomas

```
1   MP1:    [°hh and° (0.25) WILL my right honourable friend also bear in
2   MPs:    [mur mur mur mur mur mur mur mur mur mur mur mur mur mur mur
```

---

[2] The use of 'My Right Honourable Friend' can be explained as follows:

> 'Right Honourable' is a form of address used within the House of Commons, for members of the Privy Council. Members of the person's own party will refer to him as 'My Right Honourable Friend, the member for [constituency]'. Members of other parties will refer to him as 'The Right Honourable Gentleman, the member for [constituency]'. The Privy Council consists of, among others, Cabinet ministers and a number of junior ministers as well as former office holders.(www.theyworkforyou.com/glossary/?gl=214)

```
        MP1:      mInd;[(0.70)]
        MP2:            [(.) NO;]
        MPs:      mur mur mur    ]

 3  MP1:  -> [that the FIRST_uh (.) communiqué,]
 4  MPs:     [mur mur mur mur mur mur mur mur  ]

 5  MP1:  -> [(.) uh' aBOUT the sinking;]
 6  MPs:     [mur mur mur mur mur mur mur]

 7  MP1   -> [from the: (.) ARgentine sIde;]
 8  MPs:     [mur mur mur mur mur mur mur  ]

 9  MP1:     [(0.33) uh said that the ship was All RIGHT,]
10  MPs:     [mur mur mur mur mur mur mur mur mur mur mur]

11  MP1:     [≪all>except dAmage to its STEEring>;]
12  MPs:     [mur mur mur mur mur mur mur mur mur  ]
```

The source recruited is an official document: *the FIRST_uh communiqué, uh aBOUT the sinking; from the: ARgentine sIde;* (lines 3, 5, 7). Produced as the subject of the quotative *said* (line 9), it is personified as a person having a voice. (Note that inanimate sources are not always personified in the data.) Personification is a classical rhetorical figure in political speech where 'human qualities are ascribed to non-human entities' (Charteris-Black 2014: 47).

Marking a stark contrast to the 2003–2013 data set, references to human elite sources are almost exclusively recruited from single members of the government, both in question and answer turns. In the question turns, it is the Prime Minister who is most widely cited, as in Ex. (16).

(16)   PMQs 03 May 1988
MP1: Ernie Ross (Lab); PM: Margaret Thatcher (Con); S: Bernard Weatherill

```
 1  MP:   -> [the prIme minister has said toDAY,]
 2  MPs:     [mur mur mur mur mur mur mur mur mur]

 3  MP:      [(.) and last THURSday;  ]
 4  MPs:     [mur mur mur mur mur mur]

 5  MP:      [that she expects the SAME level of sErvice;]
 6  MPs:     [mur mur mur mur mur mur mur mur mur]

 7  MP:      delivered at the sAme STANDard of service-
 8           ((click)) °h with uh: and (thus) resulting in the SAME community
             charge (xxx xxx xxx length and breadth xxx) the united kIngdom;
 9  MP:   -> (.) does the prime minister not underSTAND; ((turn continues))
```

In the reporting clause *the prIme minister has said toDAY, (...)* (lines 1, 3), the NP *the prIme minister* is in subject position. The speaker in Ex. (16) uses a disambiguating label to refer to the head of state, which shows deference to her rank and authority, rather than 'the right honourable lady', which would technically also be possible. This is illustrated in Ex. (17), which is taken from a question turn by the LO.

(17)   PMQs 05 May 1987

LO: Neil Kinnock (Lab); PM: Margaret Thatcher (Con); S: Bernard Weatherill

```
1    S:            «pp>mister> KINnock-
2                  (0.24)
3    LO:           [SPEAker-]
4    MPs:          [h h h h ]
5    LO:           [(.) does the:_uh (3.90)]
6    MPs:          [h h h h h h h h h h h ]
7    LO:     ->    DOES the right honourable lAdy; (0.28)
8                  REalise that she's gonna have dIfficulty explaining why
                   manufacturing investment in this country is twenty per cent
                   lower than it was in [nineteen seventy nIne, (1.12)]
9    MPs:                               [h h h h h h h h h h h h h  ]
```

The data only show uses of *the right honourable lAdy;* (line 7) (or my honourable friend, used for members of the same parties) as a form of reference for the Prime Minister in an environment other than the subject position of reporting clauses. The fact that this referential form is not used in reporting clauses suggests a preference for the differentiating and self-explanatory label 'The Prime Minister' for source referencing, which goes hand in hand with displays of claimed deference. Ex. (18) is an example from an answer turn, where a member of government is quoted. Here the more general form *my right honourable friend* (line 4) is used in subject position.

(18)   PMQs 07 May 1985

MP: David Alton (LD); PM: Margaret Thatcher; S: Bernard Weatherill

```
1    PM:    [i notice also that he refers to the speech of my]
2    MPs:   [sh sh sh sh sh sh sh sh sh sh sh sh sh sh sh]
     PM:    [rIght honourable friend the secretary of state for ENergy-
     MPs:   [chu chu chu chu chu chu chu chu chu chu chu chu chu chu
     PM:    (0.27)]
```

```
3   MPs:         h h h ]
4   PM:     ->   [with regArd to unemployment i notice that my right honourable
5   MPs:         [chu chu chu chu chu chu chu chu chu chu chu chu chu chu chu
    PM:          friend SAID;] ((quotation))
    MPs:         chu chu chu ]
```

Here the speaker labels the source using a generic, honorific title in a metapragmatic expression *i notice that my right honourable friend SAID;* (line 4). Note, however, that the referent has been fully identified in an appositive structure in terms of his professional role in government in prior talk (*i notice also that he refers to the speech of my rIght honourable friend the secretary of state for ENergy*- line 1). The example is further indicative of a more general preference pattern in the sample: the analysis of the situated formatting of sources as the turn emerges in time reveals that the formatting of nominal reference to human as well as inanimate referents is organised following 'preference' type principles. This is shown in Exx. (19) and (20).

(19)   PMQs 12 Nov. 1981

MP: Christopher Price (Lab); PM: Margaret Thatcher (Con); S: George Thomas

```
1    MP:          [((clears throat)) could (.) ↑could the prime minister (0.42)
2    MPs:         [mur mur mur mur mur mur mur mur mur mur mur mur mur mur mur
     MP:          clear up (0.51) one: disCREPancy.]
     MPs:         mur mur mur mur mur mur mur mur ]
3    MP:          [(0.48) which (.) stands between HER statement (0.26) about
4    MPs:         [mur mur mur mur mur mur mur mur mur mur mur mur mur mur
     MP:          mister leo lOng's espionage actIvities,]
     MPs:         mur mur mur mur mur mur mur mur mur mur]
5    MP:     ->   [˚h and that of the attorney GENeral.   (0.48)]
6    MPs:         [mur mur mur mur mur mur mur mur mur mur mur]
7    MP:          [where ↑SHE said; (0.43)]
8    MPs:         [mur mur mur mur mur mur]
9    MP:          [that there was ONE other indivIdual; (0.33)]
10   MPs:         [mur mur mur mur mur (h h h h h h h h h h h) ]
11   MP:          [to whom: inducements: had been GIven; (0.42)]
12   MPs:         [(h h h h h h h h h h h h h h h h h h h h)]
13   MP:     ->   and the at↑TORney said, (0.32)
14                there were a ↑FEW other individuals.
```

There are two reporting clauses in the example: one with a pronominal subject (*where* ↑*SHE said;* line 7), and the other with a nominal subject (*and the at*↑*TORney said,* line 13). The analytic focus is on the nominal subject. The referent of *the at*↑*TORney* is first introduced through a compound *the attorney GENeral;* (line 5), a complex noun phrase, which is treated by the speaker as achieving recognition (but note that this is not the full title, which is *Her Majesty's Attorney General for England and Wales*).[3] When the referent is recycled in the reporting clause, *and the at*↑*TORney said,* it is produced in a simple NP, having a simple noun as the head. This more minimal form shows that the information is treated as given, while still displaying the current speaker's formal relational distance towards the referent and invoking his elite status as an authority. A similar strategy can be observed in Ex. (20), which exemplifies a noun phrase with an inanimate head.

(20)   PMQs 03 May 1988
MP: Harry Greenway; PM: Margaret Thatcher; S: Bernard Weatherill

```
1   PM:   ->  if i might quOte (.) from the report of the interdepartmental
                committee on the lAw. of conTEMPT, (0.35)
2             <<all>as it affects> tribUnals of inQUIry, (0.25)
3             chaired by lord ↑SALMon,
4         ->  °h thAt report [SAID; (0.56)]
5   MPs:                     [mur mur mur ]
6   PM:       One would ↑NOT wish to sEe in this cOuntry;
7             °h the hOrror of trIal by PRESS-
8             °h tElevision and [RAdio. (0.61)]
9   MPs:                        [h h h h h h h ]
```

The nominal subject of the reporting clause *°h thAt report SAID;* (line 4) has been evoked through its full official title in prior speech (*the report of the interdepartmental committee on the lAw: of conTEMPT;≪all≫ as it affects> tribUnals of inQUIry,* lines 1–2), which is postmodified by an -ed participle clause (*chaired by lord* ↑*SALMon,* line 3). This is treated as securing recognition by the audience and invokes the report as a formal, authoritative document relevant to the situated argument during the ongoing institutional interaction.

---

[3] The Attorney General also serves as the Attorney General for Northern Ireland. Since the criminal activities in question allegedly took place in the England, it is inferred that the full reference in this context would have been Her Majesty's Attorney General for England and Wales.
    Since 'Attorney General' is a compound, I argue that the noun phrase is more complex than an NP with the simplex 'Attorney' as head.

5.2 Subjects

When it is recycled in the reporting clause, the speaker orients to the principle of minimalisation, producing a light noun phrase, *thAt report*. Here the demonstrative determiner that makes anaphoric reference to the first naming of the report, evoking recognition and authority.

In contrast to elite sources, which can be first named in the subject position of reporting clauses, the few examples of non-elite sources illustrate that the relevance of non-elite sources must first be accounted for through a description of their past actions. Consider Ex. (21).

(21) PMQs 03 May 1988

MP: Timothy Devlin (Con); PM: Margaret Thatcher (Con); S: Bernard Weatherill

```
1   MP:         dOes my right honourable frIend (.) recall mEeting mister eric
                FLETcher.
2               the thirty five year old mIddlesbrough man [during her tOur
3   MPs:                                                   [mur mur mur mur
    MP:         of TEEsside; (0.39)]
    MPs:        mur mur mur mur mur]
4   MP:     ->  [who THREW;]
5   MPs:        [sh sh sh  ]
6   MP:     ->  [(0.30) who THREW at her one thousand jOb applications saying
7   MPs:        [≪p>mur mur mur mur mur mur mur mur mur mur mur mur mur mur>
    MP:         he hadn't got a JOB; (0.64)]
    MPs:        sh sh sh sh sh sh sh sh sh ]
8   MP:         [and would (1.46) and (0.94) and (.) was (.) was she
9   MPs:        [sh sh sh sh sh sh sh sh sh sh sh sh sh sh sh sh sh
    MP:         ((turn continues))
```

The source is first referenced in an appositive structure *mister eric FLETcher. the thirty five year old mIddlesbrough man;* (lines 1–2), in which his full name (first appositive) and age and hometown (second appositive) are named. This serves as the antecedent of the pronominal subject of a postmodifying relative clause (*who THREW at her one thousand jOb applications;* line 6), which further specifies the source through a memorable past action. This heavy NP forms the implicit subject of a nonfinite quotative verb form (*saying*, line 6).

In Ex. (22), the relevance of a non-elite source is again constructed through past actions. This time, however, these past actions are conveyed in a phrasal structure.

(22)   PMQs 03 Nov. 1983
MP: Syd Bidwell (Lab); PM: Margaret Thatcher (Con); S: Bernard Weatherill

```
1   MP1:       [does she parTICularly, (0.48)]
2   MPs:       [j j j j j j j j j j j j j]
3   MP1: ->    [look at an interview with One woman demonstrator] [who SAID
4   MPs:       [j j j j j j j j j j j  j j j j j j j j j j j  ] [chu chu
    MP1: ->    that;]
    MPs:       chu ]
5   MP1: ->    [british sOldiers would not FIRE, (0.37)]
    MPs:       [chu chu chu chu chu chu chu chu chu chu]
6   MP1: ->    [but MAYbe; (0.28)]
7   MPs:       [chu chu chu chu ]
8   MP1: ->    [american defEnse sources might FIRE, (.)]
9   MPs:       [chu chu chu chu chu chu chu chu chu ]
```

The relative pronoun *who* serves as the subject in the reporting clause *who SAID* (line 3), and refers back to the antecedent *One woman demonstrator* (line 3). Although an anonymous non-elite member of the public is quoted, note that her authority and newsworthiness is constructed through her categorisation as a *demonstrator*, that is, as someone actively engaged in a conflict between the government and members of the public.

With the caveat that the data set is rather small, it can be concluded that when nominal phrases (rather than pronominal phrases) are deployed in subject position, they tend to be heavy-headed phrases, showing dense information packaging. Semantically, there is preference for animate nouns. Socially, these subjects – animate and non-animate – can generally be classified as elite sources, which are authoritative and self-explanatory. The membership categorisation (government and state) displays an orientation to the institutional setting of the interaction. Notably, these elite sources are exclusively recruited from members and documents of the government and state, which suggests that the opposition between government and opposition parties is less enacted through the recruiting of sources.

The analysis of the wider turn context shows that the construction of reference to sources orients towards general principles of recognition and minimalisation. In a nutshell, the formatting of subject noun phrases exhibits a calibration between institutional constraints, recipient design, and linguistic and interactional principles.

2003–2013

Compared to the 1978–1988 sample, the relative distribution between light- and heavy-headed noun phrases in the total sample remains the same in the 2003–2013 data set. However, the sources in the more recent sample show a diversification with respect to formal and semantic categories. Tables 5.3a, 5.3b (Appendix B) illustrate the relative frequencies of light and heavy NPs in subject position in finite reporting clauses and their distribution over speaker roles and turn types. Given that the percentages of subject NPs are indicative of the general percentages of reported speech across the sample, there is a dramatic increase of reported speech compared to the 1978–1988 sample, especially as regards action turns in the question–answer sequences between the LO – or the LLD – and the PM. This goes hand in hand with the heightened profile of the participant roles of the LO and LLD at PMQs, which is interactionally embodied through more multiple and lengthy question–answer sequences. This contrasts sharply with the 1978–1988 sample, where they play a more marginalised role.

Taken in total, the distribution of NPs in the 2003–2013 data set confirms the general tendencies visible in the 1978–1988 sample: while pronominal subjects dominate the picture, noun phrases are generally complex in finite reporting clauses (Table 5.4).

In contrast to the 1978–1988 data set, however, there is a formal diversification in the subject NPs. Apart from simple nouns (e.g., the chancellor), compounds (e.g., the Prime Minister), multiple modifications (e.g., the former chairman of the British Medical Association), and appositions (e.g., the former head of his delivery unit, Sir Michael Barber), which are also attested in the 1978–1988 sample, the more recent data set has the following forms: names, heads with one premodifier (e.g., the Israeli Government) or one postmodifier (e.g.,

Table 5.4 *Absolute distribution of light and heavy NPs over subjects in finite reporting clauses (2003–2013)*

2003–2013 (n=356)	Light NPs: pronominal heads	Light NPs: nominal heads	Heavy NPs	Other
Subjects in finite reporting clauses	59.3% (211)	6.5% (23)	30.6% (109)	3.7% (13)

the President of France), abbreviations (e.g., the OBR), and coordinated NPs. The names in the sample come in two forms: [first name + last name] (e.g., Tony Blair, Ruud Luubers) and [title + first name + last name] (e.g., Sir John Bourne). The use of coordinated noun phrases deserves a closer look (Ex. 23).

(23)   PMQs 16 Dec. 2009
MP: Andrew Mackay (Con); depPM: Harriet Harman (Lab); S: Michael Martin

```
1   MPs:       [mur mur mur mur mur mur ]
2   depPM:     [i think both the' (0.23)]
3   MPs:       [mur mur mur mur mur mur mur mur mur    ]
4   depPM: -> [both the PRIME minister and the trAns]port secretary has
              sAid- ((quotation))
```

Here *both the PRIME minister and the trAnsport secretary* (line 4) occur in subject position (with the singular verb form *has* appearing ungrammatical). From a discourse point of view, plural noun phrases (*all leaders*) or coordinated noun phrases as in this example functions in what Tannen calls 'choral dialogue', 'instantiating' rather than 'representing' the past speech: 'Since they [the sources, ER] are not likely to have spoken in unison, the wording supplied instantiates rather than represents what [they] said' (Tannen 2007: 115).

As in the 1978–1988 data set, subjects most frequently make reference to authoritative, elite sources, which can have human or inanimate semantics. They are generally labelled in a way that reflects their official capacity and are thus constructed as an authority relevant to the argument and position claimed. In contrast to the older data set, the more recent sample shows a diversification in terms of semantic referent categorisation. Recall that in 1978–1988, speakers generally recruited government sources when quoting. Human elite sources are (generally implicitly) categorised as:

1. members of the government (e.g., the Prime Minister), or the government as a collective (e.g., the last Labour government);
2. members of the opposition (e.g., the shadow Chancellor) or single opposition parties as a collective (e.g., a Conservative party); or
3. independent experts and representatives (e.g., the nurse of the year, who resigned today).

The use of (individual and collective) government vs. opposition sources suggests a tendency for source marking to be deployed in order to polarise the two sides of the House, a practice which is completely absent in the 1978–1988 sample. Moreover, the recruiting of independent authorities, which is almost non-existent in the 1978–1988 data set, also points to a change in the self-presentation of speakers at PMQs: they construct themselves as having access to and relying on expert knowledge for their arguments. Finally, sources can be called by their personal names (e.g., Tom Kelly).

Not surprisingly, the most frequent member of government cited is the Prime Minister. There is a preference for the Prime Minister as a source in question turns. Note that Ex. (23), which I just examined, represents a deviant case in that the Deputy Prime Minister refers to the Prime Minister in an answer turn, using the occupational title when acting in his place at PMQs. This means that, in general, the mere mentioning of the Prime Minister as a source makes the ongoing action format recognisable as a question turn. As in the 1978–1988 data set, the label used for the Prime Minister is 'the Prime Minister'. Ex. (24) illustrates this.

(24) PMQs 08 Dec. 2010

MP1: Richard Ottaway (Con); PM: David Cameron (Con); S: John Bercow

```
1   MP1: IN: afghanistan on mOnday;=
2        =the PRIME minister said;=((quotation))
```

Following two adverbials, *IN: afghanistan on mOnday;=* (line 1), *the PRIME minister* is produced as the subject of the verb *said;* (line 2). In doing so, the speaker makes relevant that the target of the question turn is relevant as a source through his public role as head of government.

The opposition members most quoted are members of the shadow cabinet. Ex. (25) exemplifies this:

(25) PMQs 10 June 2009

MP: Gerald Kaufman (Lab); PM: Gordon Brown (Lab); S: Michael Martin

```
1   PM: -> speCIFically the shadow health secretary s'_sAid this morning;
            ((quotation))
```

Here the PM refers to a member of the shadow cabinet, *the shadow health secretary*, as the ascribed source. In the same way as the 2003–2013 data set shows a preference for referencing and quoting sources from the other political camp, independent experts are recruited for supporting positions. Ex. (26) represents an example of an expert source as the ascribed source of a quotation. NHS (*en aitch es*, line 1) stands for the National Health Service.

(26)   PMQs 01 Nov. 2006
LO: David Cameron (Con); PM: Tony Blair (Lab); S: Michael Martin

```
1    MPs:      [h h h h h h h h h h h h h h h h h h h h h h h h ]
2    LO:       [(0.20) let's ↑HEAR from someone Else in the en aitch Es;]
3         ->   °h the CHAIRman of the british medical association,
4              says that ↑THIS↑ year has seen vItally needed; ((quotation
               continues))
```

In line 2, the LO makes reference to *the CHAIRman of the british medical assOciation*, an organisation which describes itself as 'the trade union and professional body for doctors in the UK'.[4] In line with what Dickerson finds with respect to politicians' rhetoric in television shows, the choice of expert sources may 'orientate to sceptical readings of their own utterances' (Dickerson 1997: 36) and of politicians' statements in general.

To label sources through their personal names rather than occupational role constructs less social distance but also less deference to the authority of their function, which points to a general process of 'personalization' (Conboy 2003: 47). This term – related to colloquialisation – describes the adoption of colloquial features to play to and attract a wider audience. At the same time, it shows that these sources are recognisable by their names on the part of the split audience.[5] Ex. (27) illustrates this:

(27)   PMQs 24 April 2013
MP: Stephen Metcalfe (Con); PM: David Cameron; S: John Bercow

```
1    MPs:        [ch 1 ch 1 ch 1 ch ]
2    PM:         [no WONder; (1.34)]
3    MPs:        [ch sh ch sh ch sh ch sh ch ]
4    PM:    ->   [no ↑wOnder tony BLAIR said;]
5    MPs         [ch sh ch sh ch sh ch sh ch sh ch sh ]
6    PM:         [(.) thEy're fellow travellers not LEAders;]
```

---

[4] www.bma.org.uk/about-us
[5] There are other cases in the sample where the occupational role and function is explained, e.g., in appositional structures. These cases are categorised as 'apposition'.

5.2 Subjects

The reference in the form [first name + last name] evokes a source, the former Prime Minister Blair, which is treated as known not only to the in-house audience but also to the public viewers. This is evidenced by the fact that the speaker only uses his name without describing how he is relevant to the argument through his occupational role (elite source) or actions (non-elite source) to secure recognition. Moreover, Ex. (28) exemplifies that the formatting of sources can show an explicit orientation to the split audience of PMQs to secure recognition:

(28)   PMQs 01 Nov. 2006
LO: David Cameron (Con); PM: Tony Blair (Lab); S: Michael Martin

```
1   LO:  -> the ↑GOvernment's chief medical officer has sAId;
2            (-) evidence from with↑IN the en aitch Es, ((quotation
             continues))
```

The subject comes in the form of a complex noun phrase (*the ↑GOvernment's chief medical officer*, line 1), which names the referee by his official title, Chief Medical Officer. Notice that the nominal reference shows a recipient design directly addressed to the public audience: the premodifier *↑GOvernment's* explicitly frames the ascribed source as a member of the government, a redundant categorisation for the Prime Minister, at whom the LO's talk is targeted (but only indirectly addressed). The primary accent signals that this is the key trait of the source.

Apart from these explicit labels of membership, the 2003–2013 sample shows a use of honorifics in the subject position of reporting clauses which does not allow a context-free categorisation of membership. They are exclusively used in answer turns by Tony Blair, the Prime Minister between 1997–2007, to display agreement as part of an evaluative routine (MY RIGHT HONOURABLE FRIEND IS RIGHT IN SAYING/TO SAY).

When ordinary members of the public are recruited as sources of direct quotations in the 2003–2013 data, their mentioning requires more elaborate accounts as to why their position is relevant to the speaker's action. Consider Ex. (29). The questioning speaker is the MP for Tooting. *EE cee gEe* stands for ECG, *EX rays* for X-rays, and *Ay and Ee* for A&E or Accident and Emergency department.

(29)   PMQs 07 Dec. 2005
MP: Sadiq Khan (Lab); PM: Tony Blair (Lab); S: Michael Martin

```
1   MP:     wOuld my (.) right honourable friend like to cOmment on the
        -> experience of mister CHUTtun,
2       -> a TOOting rEsident;
```

```
3        -> who unFORtunately was sIck on sUnday;
4        -> and had to go to saint GEORGEs;=
5           =he had an EE cee gEe,
6           TWO types of blOod tests,
7           EX rays,
8           vArious BLOOD prEssure tests tAken,
9           and was trEated by the doctors and nurses WONderfully;=
10       -> =↑he SAID;
11          this is the FIRST time i have used the ay and Ee,
12          i was THOroughly impressed by the hospital and the cOnscientious
            stAff;
```

The reporting clause, which pre-empts space for direct speech in the next slot, is produced in line 10 (↑*he SAID,*). The source, referred to by a pronominal subject (↑*he*), is categorised in various forms in the previous context of the turn. First, he is introduced through nominal references which personalise him (*mister CHUTtun*, line 1) and categorise him as the orator's constituent (*a TOOting rEsident*, an apposition, line 2). He is next categorised as a patient of the local hospital (*who unFORtunately was sIck on sUnday; and had to go to saint GEORGEs;=* lines 3–4) in a postmodifying relative clause which prefaces the subsequent narrative (lines 5–12). The reported speech serves as the point of the story (lines 10–12).

The analysis has shown that authorities whose relevance to the orator's argument is obvious through the institutional function named in their titles do not have to be further accounted for as ascribed sources of direct quotations. They may even be only referred to through pronominal deixis. This contrasts with cases (e.g., Ex. 29) where ordinary members of the public are quoted: here their relevance as the source of a quoted position is motivated and accounted for through membership categorisation in a way that is designed to meet local contingencies, that is, a mediated parliamentary interaction, of action formation. Ex. (30) exemplifies a nominal reference to an inanimate source, that is, an official written document.

(30)   PMQs 22 June 2005

LO: Michael Howard (Con); PM: Tony Blair (Lab); S: Michael Martin

```
1  MPs: [h h h h h h h h h h ]
2  LO:  [the ↑CE ai be report] sAYs, ((quotation)
```

The ascribed source is referred to through a nominal subject of the verb SAY (*the* ↑ *CE ai be report sAYs*, line 2). The noun phrase is complex, having a compound head noun composed of the abbreviation ↑ *CE ai be* and the simplex *report*. A look at the prior course of the turn sequence shows that – similar to the 1978–1988 data set – the formatting of the noun phrase is minimised while allowing full recognition: the abbreviation used in the ascribed source is first introduced in what appears to be its full form at the beginning of the LO's first question turn (*citizens advIce service*; not shown here). In his answer turn, the PM abbreviates the noun, using it as part of a compound (*CE ai be service*; not shown here). This is then taken up by the LO, as shown in the excerpt.

As Schegloff (1968) demonstrates, it is the anomalous cases which provide us with an understanding of the regularities of conduct. There are only two examples in the 2003–2013 data set where the quotation is contextualised as past speech to which the orator does not claim direct experiential access. Consider Ex. (31).

(31)   PMQs 16 July 2003
LO: Iain Duncan Smith (Con); PM: Tony Blair (Lab); S: Michael Martin

```
1  LO:   ->  =the ↑TIMES on the [tEnth of juĭlY; ]
2  MPs:                         [1 1 1 1 1 1 h h]
3  LO:   ->  [(0.98) <<f>on the ↑tEnth of july the ↑TIMES>];
4  MPs:      [j j j j j j j j j j j j j j j j j j  ]
5  LO:   ->  [(0.59) <<f>has a ↑QUOTE from number tEn>,  ]
6  MPs:      [j j j j j j j j j j j j j j j j j j j]
7  LO:       [(0.43) <<f>saying that they were] InInety-nine per cent
8  MPs:      [j j j j j j j j j j j j j j j]
9  LO:       con ↑!VINCED!>;
10            that the GILligan source-
11            °h was DAvid kelly;
```

The quotative SAY is produced in a nonfinite form, *saying* (line 7), with the preceding noun phrase *a ↑QUOTE from number tEn* (line 5) as the implied subject. By stemming from the PM's office, the source itself is authoritative. The current speaker, however, does not claim to have directly retrieved it from Number Ten, but to have retrieved and accessed it via a third party [*on the ↑tEnth of july the ↑TIMES>; has a ↑QUOTE from number tEn*, lines 3–5), which frames the quotation as second-hand evidence. Although *The Times* is an upmarket paper with a high reader readership profile (Jucker 1992: 47–58) and thus itself represents an elite source, second-hand evidence may not be viewed as reliable, reducing the credibility of the orator. This accounts for why there are so few examples of second-hand evidence in the data. The MPs' laughter (line 2), in response to the naming of the newspaper, suggests why the quotation was still delivered in the example. The laughter displays that they know the quotation and can anticipate what follows, which makes it interactionally highly involving.

In sum, I have shown that nominal subjects tend to be complex in both the 1978–1988 and 2003–2013 data sets but that the membership categorisation has become more diversified and polarised in the more recent sample. I now turn to pronominal subjects.

5.2.2 *Pronominal Subjects*

The data contain personal and relative pronouns as heads of simple noun phrases in subject position. In contrast to relative pronouns, which are functionally restricted to anaphoric reference, personal (as well as possessive and demonstrative) pronouns can serve as both deictic and anaphoric pronouns (Lyons 1995: 302).[6]

In political discourse, the use of pronominal reference has generally been shown to be a resource for polarisation between (political) groups and camps (Bull and Fetzer 2006; Fetzer 2014b, 2014c). The third-person address system at PMQs in particular, which is reflected in the use of the third-person singular pronouns *he* and *she* over second-person *you*, has been described as a cushion between opposing parties (see Chapter 3). Here the pronominal, third-person subjects may evoke personal deixis, referring to co-present participants as forms of address (like second-person terms of address in everyday conversation; see Wooffitt and Alistone 2008 on *you said* speech markers). At the same time, they can make anaphoric reference to an antecedent in the prior speech.

The use of first-person references (*I, we, me, us*) has been generally described as the manifestation of a 'speaker's involvement with his or her audience' (Chafe 1982: 46), typical of spoken language. As for political speeches, Fetzer and Bull noted that self-referential constructions of the

---

[6] As Lyons (1995) notes, pronouns are 'referring expressions' (Lyons 1995: 302).

> Traditionally, pronouns are thought of as noun-substitutes (as the noun 'pronoun' suggests). But most subclasses of pronouns (other than relative pronouns: 'who', 'which', and, in certain instances, 'that' in English) also have a quite different function, which arguably is more basic than that of standing for an antecedent noun or noun-phrase. This is their **indexical** or **deictic** function.(Lyons 1995: 302, emphasis in the original)

form [first-person singular I + communication verb] are used to claim 'involvement with others' (Fetzer and Bull 2012: 142). This is opposed to such constructions with a first-person plural pronoun, which serve to objectify claims.

Research in Conversation Analysis and Rhetorical Structure Theory has taken a particular interest in how anaphora is patterned, that is, when (and why) a pronominal substitute is chosen over a full nominal form. Pronominal noun-substitution may be subject to 'structural factors' (Fox 1987), that is, constraints with respect to sequential organisation in conversation and rhetorical units in written texts. In conversation, pronominal anaphoric reference displays the speaker's 'understanding that the preceding sequence has not been closed down' (Fox 1987: 18). Uses of nominal reference that deviate from these patterns are explained by what is called 'non-structural factors' (Fox 1987: 62): displays of disagreement and of recognition (specifically in *know+NP* formats), assessment contexts (in particular negative assessments), the marking of a new unit, and the recycling or replacing of a prior action (Fox 1987: 62–76). When there is deviating pronominal reference, that is, 'the first mention' (Fox 1987: 66) of a pronoun without a nominal antecedent, the referent can be inferred from a semantic frame evoked in prior discourse, and the referent identity is not treated as relevant.

1978–1988
In the 1978–1988 data set, pronominal reference is realised through personal and relative pronouns, with the former representing the overwhelming majority (Table 5.5).

Table 5.5 *Absolute distribution of personal and relative pronouns in subjects of finite reporting clauses (1978–1988)*

Subject pronouns	Personal pronouns	Relative pronouns
1978–1988 (n=10)	70% (7)	30% (3)

Ex. (22′) illustrates the use of a relative pronoun.

(22′)   PMQs 03 Nov. 1983

MP: Syd Bidwell (Lab); PM: Margaret Thatcher (Con); S: Bernard Weatherill

```
1  MP1:     [does she parTICularly, (0.48)]
2  MPs:     [j j j j j j j j j j j j j]

3  MP1: -> [look at an interview with One woman demonstrator] [who SAID
4  MPs:     [j j j j j j j j j j j j j j j j j j j j  ] [chu chu
   MP1:     that;]
   MPs:     chu  ]

5  MP1:     [british sOldiers would not FIRE, (0.37) ]
   MPs:     [chu chu chu chu chu chu chu chu chu chu]

6  MP1:     [but MAYbe; (0.28)]
7  MPs:     [chu chu chu chu  ]

8  MP1: -> [american defEnse sources might FIRE, (.)]
9  MPs:     [chu chu chu chu chu chu chu chu chu chu ]
```

The relative pronoun *who* serves as the subject in the reporting clause *who SAID*, and refers back to the antecedent, *One woman demonstrator* (line 3), but does not evoke deictic reference. To turn to personal pronouns, their distribution shows a clear tendency towards animate referents (*I, he, she*; see Table 5.6). Noticeably, there are no plural forms (*we, they*), which would point to collective referents.

The distribution of this small sample does not allow for far-reaching generalisations. Ex. (32) exemplifies the use of a first-person singular pronoun. Self-quotations have been described as reaffirmatory (see also Chapter 8).

Table 5.6 *Absolute distribution of pronominal subjects in finite reporting clauses (1978–1988)*

Personal pronouns	I	WE	YOU (sing.)	YOU (pl.)	HE	SHE	IT	THEY
1978–1988 (n=7)	43% (3)	0% (0)	0% (0)	0% (0)	14% (1)	29% (2)	14% (1)	0% (0)

(32)   PMQs 09 Nov. 1978

PM: James Callaghan (Labour); MP: Neil Kinnock (Labour); S: George Thomas

```
1   PM:     the government is nOt (.) ready to DO that;
2           and i have said MORE than [once;]
3   MPs:                              [h h h]
4   MPs:    [h h h h h h h h h h ]
5   PM:     [and SAY again; (0.20)]
6   MPs:    [h h h h h h h h h h h h h h h h h h h h  ]
7   PM:     [we should take ↑ALL the necessary measures.]
8   MPs:    [h h h ]
9           [(1.06)]
```

In line 1, the PM makes a self-reference as part of an objective collective (*the government*), positioning himself to the topical talk. Objective collectives are a resource for implying the speakers' leadership (Fetzer and Bull 2012: 132). The reporting clause is forthcoming in line 2. In an *and*-prefaced intonation phrase, he next refers to himself as the ascribed source of the quotation (*I have said*). The adverbial of time *MORE than [once;]* indicates that the subsequent quotation constitutes what Tannen calls 'summarizing dialogue', that is, 'the gist rather than the wording of what was said in a single discourse' (Tannen 2007: 114). This is additionally emphasised by line 5 (*and SAY again;*). Summarising dialogue has been described as an involvement strategy. In this example, it serves to solicit an affiliative uptake of a reiterated governmental position: in overlap with the last item, the government MPs respond to the self-referencing quotative construction with audible appreciation, which continues until turn post-completion (lines 3–8; cf. also Clayman 1993 on disaffiliative audience responses).

When third-person pronouns are deployed, anaphoric reference and person deixis become blurred. Ex. (33) illustrates this.

(33)   PMQs 01 May 1984

MP: Dr David Owen (SDP); PM: Margaret Thatcher (Con); S: Bernard Weatherill

```
1   MPs:        [mur mur mur mur mur mur mur mur]
2   MP:   ->    [(is) the prIme minister aWARE;  ]
3   MPs:        [mur mur mur mur mur mur mur mur mur]
4   MP:         [that mEmbers of the FRANKS committee;=  ]
5   MPs:        [mur mur mur mur mur mur mur mur mur mur mur  ]
```

```
 6  MP:     =[let alone members of other privy COUNcillers;]
 7  MPs:    [mur mur mur mur mur mur mur mur mur mur    ]
 8  MP:     [°h i' inQUIries into intelligence matters,]
 9  MPs:    [mur mur mur mur mur mur mur mur mur mur mur mur mur mur]
10  MP: ->  [°h will find it a little hArd to underSTAND how she can sAy;]
11  MPs:    [mur mur mur mur mur mur mur mur mur mur mur mur]
12  MP:     [°h that those inquiries would risk compromising SOURces;]
13  MPs:    [mur mur mur mur mur mur mur mur mur mur mur    ]
14  MP:     [°h and damaging the operational efFECtiveness:;]
15  MPs:    [mur mur mur mur mur mur mur]
16  MP:     [and VAlue of the services?]
```

The target of the action, the Prime Minister, is first referred to with a nominal phrase, that is, her title *the prIme minister* (line 2). The pronominal subject of the reporting clause, *how she can sAy;* (line 10) anaphorically refers to this nominal form. At the same time, it is functional as an indexical pronominal term of address, making the Prime Minister directly accountable for the position quoted, as in *you said* clauses (cf. Wooffitt and Alistone 2008: 421). Importantly, pronominal subjects, as in Ex. (33), always have a nominal antecedent to which they make anaphoric reference. This is not necessarily the case in the 2003–2013 data set, which is shown in what follows.

2003–2013

As in the 1978–1988 data set, personal pronouns dominate in the distribution of pronominal subjects. Relative pronouns form the second largest group, and there is one instance of an indefinite pronoun (Table 5.7).

Compared with the 1978–1988 sample, the 2003–2013 data set shows more diversification of types of pronouns. The first- and third-person plural forms *we* and *they* are added to the stock of singular forms, *I*, *he*, *she*, *it* (Table 5.8). The use of the relative pronoun *that* indicates a trend towards a more informal style.

Table 5.7 *Absolute distribution of pronominal subjects in finite reporting clauses (2003–2013)*

Subject pronouns	Personal pronouns	Relative pronouns	Indefinite Pronoun
2003–2013 (n= 211)	85.8% (181) (I, WE, HE, SHE, IT, THEY)	13.3% (28) (WHO, WHICH, THAT)	0.9% (2) (ONE, SOMEONE)

5.2 *Subjects* 81

Table 5.8 *Absolute distribution of personal pronouns in subjects of finite reporting clauses (2003–2013)*

Personal pronouns	I	WE	YOU (sing.)	YOU (pl.)	HE	SHE	IT	THEY
2003–2013 (n=181)	11.6% (21)	10.5% (19)	0% (0)	0% (0)	58.6% (106)	0.6% (1)	7.2% (13)	11.6% (21)

The new use of the plural pronouns *we* and *they* means that quotations are ascribed to collective groups, and these ascriptions can be exploited to contribute to the polarisation of government and opposition or other groups constructed as opponents. Ex. (34) exemplifies this. It is taken from an answer turn in response to an accusation of the LO, that the Blair government wrongly blamed a civil servant for leaking intelligence information, and a request that the government should apologise.

(34)   PMQs 16 July 2003
PM: Tony Blair (Lab); LO: Iain Duncan Smith (Con); S: Michael Martin

```
1   PM:   ->   °h <<all>WE have said to the ministry of de↑fEnce>,=
2   PM:   ->   =<<all>that we don't KNOW who the source Is<<all>>?
3   PM:   ->   °h bUt the [bee bee ↑CEE?]
4   MPs:               [mur mur mur> ]
5   PM:   ->   [°h are in the position (.) ↑TO know who the source is; ]
6   MPs:       [mur mur mur mur mur mur mur mur mur mur mur mur mur mur ]
7   PM:        [((click)) and they can ↑SAY surely,]
8   MPs:       [mur mur mur mur mur mur mur> ]
9   PM:        [(-) whether this man is that source or ↑NOT;  ]
10  MPs:       [mur mur mur mur mur mur mur mur mur mur mur ]
```

The PM produces a self-quote in lines 1–2, in which it is claimed that they are ignorant of who the source is. The reporting clause contains the source, that is, the personal pronoun *WE*, the quotative SAY in present perfect, and the receiver of the message, the Ministry of Defence (*WE have said to the ministry of de↑fEnce*, line 1). Note that while the referent of the collective *we* includes the PM, it is not specified what group exactly is referred to (He and his office? He and his government?), in a strategy to defer his personal involvement and responsibility (cf. Bull and Fetzer 2006: 30). On the other hand, the use of the collective *we* serves to mark contrast and opposition: the *bUt* in the next line constructs a syndetic, contrastive link to a construction in which the BBC is constructed as knowable (*bUt the bee bee ↑CEE? °h are in the position, (.) ↑TO know who the source is; (...)*, lines 3, 5). Again, the collective reference allows the PM to be vague about the person responsible. Thus, collective references are a useful resource for polarising groups and positions, while also deferring personal involvement and responsibility.

To turn to the topic of anaphoric reference and personal deixis, in the 2003–2013 data set, the referent of third-person pronouns in subject position is not always anaphorically tied to a nominal antecedent, a finding which contrasts with the 1978–1988 data set. The referent can also be evoked through personal deixis only in the 2003–2013 data set. To illustrate this, I begin with an example analogous to Ex. (33), which was from the 1978–1988 sample. Ex. (35), from the more recent data sample, illustrates a case where both anaphoric reference and personal deixis are evoked.

(35)   PMQs 10 June 2009
LO: David Cameron (Con); PM: Gordon Brown (Lab); S: John Bercow

```
1    LO:     NOW; (0.42)
2            ON the issue of public spending, (0.25)
3            <<all>ON the issue of public spending>;
4    ->      °h let's be CLEAR;
5    ->      °h <<len>about the:> ANswers the prime minister has given;
6    ->      hE said LAST week, (0.43)
7            pUblic spEnding is rising every YEAR;
```

The referent of the ascribed source, *the prime minister*, is first named in a metapragmatic construction (*let's be CLEAR; °h <<len>about the:> ANswers the prime minister has given;* lines 4–5), which projects and frames the subsequent quotation as an answer previously given by the PM at PMQs. Next follows a reporting clause (*hE said LAST week*, line 6), with a personal pronoun in third person singular, *hE*, as the subject. The referent of the pronoun is evoked through anaphoric reference to the nominal phrase *the prime minister* (line 5) as well as through person deixis. In this way, the pronominal phrase serves as a form of address for Gordon Brown, the co-present interlocutor and Prime Minister targeted by the question turn.

Note that in contrast to the 1978–1988 data set, the referent of a pronominal subject of reporting clauses is not necessarily explicitly introduced through a full nominal form in the prior speech but can be evoked through person deixis only. Ex. (36) shows such a case.

(36)   PMQs 01 Dec. 2010
LO: Ed Miliband (Lab); PM: David Cameron (Con); S: John Bercow

```
1   S:      E:d MILiband;
2   LO:     <<all>mister SPEAker>;=
3       ->  =<<all>he says> hOw do we get the GROWTH of the economy up,
4           (0.32) Absolutely RIGHT; ((turn continues))
```

This excerpt is taken from the LO's third question turn during a longer question–answer sequence. After the LO answers to the Speaker's summons (*E:d MILiband;* line 1) with a term of address directed at the Speaker (*<<all> mister SPEAker>*; line 2), he produces a reporting clause followed by the quotation (*=<<all> he says> hOw do we get the GROWTH of the economy up,* line 3). The referent of the pronominal subject, formatted in first-person singular masculine, deictically refers to the PM, as the LO 'formulates' (Heritage 1985) a portion of the PM's prior speech in his own words.[7] Ex. (37) represents more evidence from the 2003–2013 data set that the referent of pronominal subjects does not have to be made recognisable by a nominal antecedent in responsive turn formats. Like Ex. (36), it is taken from a follow-up by the LO, this time in the fifth question turn in a sequence of question–answer sequences.

(37)   PMQs 14 July 2010
LO: Harriet Harman (Lab); PM: David Cameron (Con); S: John Bercow

```
1   MPs:    [h h h h h h ]
2   S:      [(1.0) harriet] HARman;
```

---

[7] In contrast to the formulations described by Heritage (1985: 101) for news interviews, however, these do not recycle the interlocutor's prior speech in a neutral fashion but do so to evidence the current orator's position. The following two implications are relevant to the current discussion:
  1. The information conveyed by the evidential formulaic fragment is given in the sense that the contents of the Prime Minister's prior speech is shared by the orator's audience. In this sense who said it is not the new information, only what the gist of it is. This accounts for the prosodic downgrading, that is, unaccented and accelerated production, of the evidential formulaic fragment.
  2. What is formatted as direct speech does not constitute a verbatim rendering of prior speech retrieved from prepared, written sources but is formulated or even fabricated on the fly.

```
 3   LO:    ->   (0.22) ʔum (.) ↑he's tALking about longer tErm (.) SPECulative
                 sAvings,
 4          ->   but he hAsn't Answered (0.30) mY (.) ↑QUEStion;
 5               (0.82)
 6          ->   and it's no good him resorting to his Usual ploy of asking ME
                 questions,
 7               ↑I Asking about the REAL costs;
 8          ->   °h of his reORganisation nExt yEar;
 9               °h the vEry TIME; (0.27)
10          ->   when hE says his priority will be CUTting administration and
                 cutting the dEficit;
11               °h the whIte paper adMITS:;
12               there will be EXtra cost;
13               <<all>because of> LOSS of productivity-
14               °h STAFF relocation-
15               reDUNdancy. (0.56)
16          ->   does he stAnd by what he said just a few MONTHS ago about en
                 aytch es reorganisAtions-=
17          ->   =he SAID-
18               °h the disRUPtion is tErrible;
19               °h <<f>the deMORalisation wOrse>;
20               and the wAste of money (.) inexCUSa[ble;]
21   MPs:                                          [h h ][h h h ]
22   PM:                                                [(1.50)] ((takes turn))
```

There are two reporting clauses with SAY: in the question preface *when hE says (...)* (line 10), and in the question component *=he SAID-* (line 17); both have pronominal subjects.[8] (Although the yes/no-interrogative *does he stAnd by what he said just a few MONTHS ago about en aytch es reorganisAtions-=* (line 16) contains the verb SAY, it is not functional in introducing a quotation and is therefore not analysed as a reporting clause.) These third-person singular masculine pronouns form part of a referential chain (including more personal (*he*, line 4; *him*, line 6; *he*, twice, line 16) and possessive pronouns (*his*, lines 6, 8, 10)), which begins with the first production of the pronoun early in the LO's follow-up move (↑*he's tALking about longer tErm (.) SPECulative sAvings*, line 3). The referent of the pronoun ↑*he*, the Prime Minister David Cameron, is indexically retrieved from the interactional context. At the same time, the items in this referential chain make both anaphoric and deictic reference as the turn evolves.

---

[8] I use question preface in the sense of Clayman and Heritage's (2002b) notion, referring to the material which gives the background to the interrogative question to be asked (see Chapter 8 for a detailed discussion).

These examples of pronominal, nonanaphoric third-person reference are restricted to responsive contexts, where the current speaker refers to in situ prior speech, shared as common ground by participants. Note that from an interactional point of view, the use of the pronominal form of address signals continuation of the sequence (Fox 1987). From the perspective of the sociology of the institution, the use of the pronoun over the nominal referent, 'the Prime Minister', displays a lack of deference and respect for the authority of the interlocutor targeted by the action, a use which comes off as aggressive and hostile.

5.3 Verbs

In this section I present a brief analysis of the verb phrases which form part of the predicate of the reporting clauses. As previous research suggests, the tense of quotatives represents a participant's construct designed for communicative purposes. For instance, Johnstone (1987) finds in her analysis of authority narratives that past-tense quotatives are used to introduce the reported speech of non-authority figures, while the reported speech of authority figures is constructed with marked forms, that is, quotatives in historical present tense or no lexical quotative at all. Blyth *et al.* confirm that the tense of quotatives in narratives serves 'pragmatic purposes' (Blyth *et al.* 1990: 222). They further identify patterned choices in terms of tense, aspect, person, and number between the quotatives *say*, *be like*, and *go* (see also Buchstaller 2002). Here *say* occurs most frequently in past tense, simple aspect, and in third person singular. It is described as 'the most neutral verb' (Blyth *et al.* 1990: 222) in that it can introduce both direct and indirect speech, while *be like* and *go,* only functional as quotatives of direct speech, are used in evaluative and dramatic contexts. This is corroborated by Holt (1996) on English mundane interaction, who suggests that *say* is the neutral choice over more evaluative verbs (e.g., *whisper, moan*): it suffices because prosody allows the speaker to stage how the reported voice sounded (Holt 1996: 224). The use of *say* as a quotative is further associated with authority and high status. An experimental study found that reporters' use of the quotative *say* increased 'when reporting speech of a high status quotee, or when speaking to a high status addressee' (Blackwell and Tree 2012: 1153). Finally, *say* is a typical quotative verb in argumentative interaction, as shown by Wooffitt and Alistone (2008) on *you said* prefaces of direct reported speech in British English, and by M. Goodwin (1990) on *he-said-she-said* constructions deployed by African-American children to implement accusations and denials.

This literature review has shown that the choice of the verb *say* as a quotative is grammatically, semantically, interactionally, and socially constrained: while *say* represents a neutral quotative both in terms of its ability to introduce direct and indirect speech and in terms of its verbal meaning, it is used to construct the quoted source as a high-status authority, depending on the tense in authority narratives. *Say* is further documented as a common quotative in argumentative contexts.

The interaction at PMQs is an argumentative environment where speakers show a preference for recruiting sources who are constructed as high-status and authoritative through the design of the labels used. I now examine further how the quotative SAY is designed to co-construct the reported speech as an authoritative evidential resource. To this end, I first analyse the grammatical form of the verb in terms of tense and aspect, as well as modality and voice. Since questions of person and number were addressed in the previous chapter to some extent, they are excluded here. I then turn to the reporting clauses with SAY in its predominant verb form in the two data sets, simple past, in turn-constructional environments.

1978–1988

The distribution of tense, modality, aspect, and voice in the 1978–1988 data shows a clear preference for finite verb phrases in the simple past (Table 5.9, Appendix B). Overall, verb phrases with simple aspect dominate the picture. The study did not yield any verb phrases in passive voice.

Moreover, verb phrases in simple past tense dominate across speaker roles and turn types. In general, past tense, along with present and future tense, has traditionally been termed 'absolute tense', a notion which – contrary to common understanding – should be taken as 'a tense which includes as part of its meaning the present moment as deictic centre' (Comrie 1985: 36). Specifically, past tense means 'location in time prior to the present moment' (Comrie 1985: 41). Although more detailed analysis is needed, it can be inferred from this and the past research summarised above that simple-past *say* represents the unmarked, neutral choice for introducing reported speech as it simply indicates that something was said at some point prior to the here and now. At the same time, the preference for active constructions depicts the sources as agents relevant to the scenario, as *say* in passive voice is only acceptable in impersonal constructions, for example, *it was said that* (...), where the agent is generally omitted. In what represents a typical example of the 1978–1988 period in general (see Chapter 1), Ex. (1′) illustrates the most frequent case, that is, SAY in the simple past, deployed in the question turn of an MP.

5.3 Verbs

(1′)   PMQs 01 Nov. 1979

MP: William Hamilton (Lab); PM: Margaret Thatcher (Con); S: George Thomas

```
1   S:      HAmilton-
2   MP:     will the right honourable lady take: tIme this afternoon to
            reread (.) the manifesto on which she was eLECted;
3       -> uh in which it said that it WASn't the intention of the tory
            government;
4           to reDUCE expenditure on the national hEAlth service;
5           will she Also take time to READ,
6           a recent debate on the national health service when (.) HER party
            was in opposition and the present leader;
7           the present SPOKESman;
8       -> the present minister for the health service said that the NURses;
9           needed as GOOD treatment as the: polIce and the armed fOrces;
10          will shE: seek to: implement BOTH those prOmises;
11          (2.0)
12  PM:     ((takes turn))
```

This excerpt contains two reporting clauses with SAY in simple past tense: *it said* (line 3), and *the present minister for the health service said* (line 8), used in the question preface of an opposition MP's question turn. He quotes two positions ascribed to government sources: (1) *that it WASn't the intention of the tory government; to reDUCE expenditure on the national hEAlth service;* (lines 3–4); and (2) *that the NURses; needed as GOOD treatment as the: polIce and the armed fOrces;* (lines 8-9). The sources recruited – the manifesto and the minister – are both high status, representing the government. The reference to sources which are independent of the speaker's political party function as a strategy to present a position quoted in a counter-interest and unchallengeable fashion. The choice of SAY in simple past tense as a quotative verb serves as a neutral choice to convey that things were said at some point in the past. Note also that the manifesto is quoted in an impersonal construction *the manifesto (...) in which it said* (lines 2–3) rather than a personal, personified construction, which would also be possible ('the manifesto which said'). In this way, the reporting clause frames the subsequent reported clause in an objectivised manner. This design is particularly powerful in building a hostile action. In terms of turn-internal organisation, the subsequent yes/no-interrogative builds on this objectivised evidence: here the MP asks the PM if she will seek to implement what was stated in the party manifesto and by the minister, two utterances which he calls promises (*will shE: seek to implement*

BOTH those prOmises;, line 10). The implication of the interrogative is that she has not implemented these yet or might not implement them; this constitutes an attack on the credibility and authority of the PM and makes it a hostile action. There is no next-positioned audible audience response. To sum up, simple past-tense SAY can contribute to framing reported speech as an event which happened in the past in an objectivised way, framing the reported speech in a counter-interest and unchallengeable fashion.

Before I turn to the analysis of 2003–2013 verb phrases, I make a short excursus to a deviant case in the sample, a modal expression. Given that many expressions where SAY is used with a modal verb were discarded in preparation for the study because they are not functional in indexing reported speech but as metapragmatic constructions, as in, for example, *and i have to SAY to him*, the result that modal meaning does not figure prominently in quotative uses of the verb phrase may seem circular. On the other hand, the exception to the rule offers us valuable insight into how a reporting clause may contain a modal auxiliary, and on a more theoretical level, how evidentiality and modality relate in English. Consider Ex. (38), which includes the same interaction seen in Ex. (33). It is again taken from a question turn by an opposition MP.

(38)   PMQs 01 May 1984

PM: Margaret Thatcher (Con), MP1: Dr David Owen (SDP); S: Bernard Weatherill

```
1   S:       mister DAvid Owen;
2            (0.76)
3   MPs:     [mur mur mur mur mur mur mur mur ]
4   MP:     [(is) the prIme minister aWARE;]
5   MPs:    [mur mur mur mur mur mur mur mur mur mur]
6   MP:    [that mEmbers of the FRANKS committee;=]
7   MPs:   [mur mur mur mur mur mur mur mur mur mur mur mur]
8   MP:    [=let alone members of other privy COUNcillers;]
9   MPs:   [mur mur mur mur mur mur mur mur mur mur]
10  MP:    [°h i⁷ inQUIries into intelligence matters,]
11  MPs:   [mur mur mur mur mur mur mur mur mur mur mur mur mur mur mur ]
12  MP: -> [°h will find it a little hArd to underSTAND how she can sAy;]
13  MPs:   [mur mur mur mur mur mur mur mur mur mur mur mur mur mur ]
14  MP:    [°h that those inquiries would risk compromising SOURces;]
15  MPs:   [mur mur mur mur mur mur mur mur mur mur mur mur   ]
16  MP    [°h and damaging the operational efFECtiveness:;]
17  MPs:   [mur mur mur mur mur mur mur ]
```

```
18  MP:     [and VAlue of the services?]
19  MPs:    [mur mur mur mur mur mur mur mur mur mur]
20  MP:     [↑If she continues to HOLD this rather;]
21          °h uh: derisory view of ex:TERNal inquiries, ((turn continues))
```

The reported speech is ascribed to the PM (*how she can sAy; °h that (...)*, lines 12, 14, 16, 18). It is embedded in a larger yes/no-interrogative structure, *(is) the prIme minister aWARE; that mEmbers of the FRANKS committee; (...) °h will find it a little hArd to underSTAND; (...)* (lines 4, 6, 8, 10, 12). The reporting clause, which introduces indirect speech with *that* is formatted as a wh-clause *how she can SAY*. Here the verb phrase consists of the modal auxiliary *can* and the lexical verb *SAY*. The modal meaning dimensions of *can* have been described as 'possibility' (very common), 'ability' (common), and 'permission' (less common, quoted from Leech 2004: 74–76). But note that in its interrogative form (*how can she say that...*, which translates into *how can you say that...* with second-person address), the reporting clause comes off as an idiomatic expression of exasperation.[9] In this way, the reporting clause itself is framed in an affect-laden, disaffiliative fashion, attacking the PM, who is referred to and addressed through the pronominal subject she.[10] This suggests that the literal sense of the modal auxiliary is not relevant here in meaning-making, confirming the initial observation that modal expressions are not deployed in the regular construction of reporting clauses at PMQs.

2003–2013
Like in the 1978–1988 sample, the most frequent verb form of SAY in the 2003–2013 verb phrases is simple past active. But note that the range of verb forms in which SAY is used has been diversified compared to the 1978–1988 sample (Tables 5.10a, 5.10b, Appendix B). Moreover, simple-past forms of SAY are most common in the question turns of LOs. Ex. (39) exemplifies this.

---

[9] Idioms are defined according to Fillmore *et al.* (1988):

> We think of a locution or manner of speaking as idiomatic if it is assigned an interpretation by the speech community but if somebody who merely knew the grammar and the vocabulary of the language could not, by virtue of that knowledge alone, know (i) how to say it or (ii) what it means, or (iii) whether it is a conventional thing to say. Put differently, an idiomatic expression or construction is something a language user could fail to know while knowing everything else in the language (Fillmore *et al.* 1988: 504).

[10] This disaffiliative stance towards the PM's past speech is also made explicit in lines 20–21, where the MP labels the PM's position in the quotation as *rather; °h uh: derisory view of ex:TERNal inquiries*.

(39)   PMQs 30 March 2011

LO: Ed Miliband (Lab); PM: David Cameron (Con); S: John Bercow

```
1   MPs:     [1 1 1 1 1 1 1 1 1 1]
2   LO:      [let let ↑me uh: (0.45) ]
3   MPs:     [mur mur mur mur mur mur mur mur mur mur mur mur mur ]
4   LO:      [let let let let ↑me turn to the issue of uh: (0.23)]
5   MPs:     [mur mur mur mur mur mur mur mur mur mur       ]
6   Lo:      [let me let me turn to a different ISsue:,]
7   MPs:     [mur mur mur mur mur ]
8   LO:      [uh? mister SPEAker;]
9   MPs:     [mur mur mur mur mur mur mur mur mur mur mur mur mur ]
10  LO:      [(0.34) which is uh: the issue of (0.42) tuITion fees.]
11  LO:   -> °h the ↑PRIME minister said,
12              that Universities will Only charge nine thousand pound °h
                tuITion fees,
13              in exCEPtional circumstances.
14              °h <<all>↑CAN the prime minister tell the house> of the twenty
                three univErsities;
15              who've anNOUNCED their plans,
16              (.) ↑how MANy are planning to charge nine-thousand pounds.
17  MP:      haha
```

The reporting clause (*the ↑PRIME minister said,* line 11) is built in terms of the subject, which gives the Prime Minister as the source, and the quotative SAY in simple past. Again *the ↑PRIME minister* constitutes a high-status counter-interest source, representative of the government. The simple past in which the quotative is formatted frames the act of saying as an event of the past in a neutral fashion. In this way, the quoted utterance (lines 12–13) is framed in an objectivised manner. It contains the announcement that it will be the exception that universities will charge high tuition fees. The subsequent interrogative builds on this promise (lines 14–16). Here the LO asks if the PM can tell the House how many universities will charge this high sum. It is designed such that it implements a hostile action in light of the reported speech. On the one hand, it challenges the PM with respect to his epistemic access to figures and statistics (*<<all>↑CAN the prime minister tell the house>* (...)). Recall that displays of knowledge are associated with power. On the other hand, in requesting information about the number of universities (*↑how MANy* (...)) charging the highest tuition fees, it attacks the credibility and authority of PM, by implicitly questioning the truthfulness of the announcement that those would be an exception.

To sum up, the grammatical formatting of SAY between the two data sets has remained stable in that simple past forms constitute the most common choice in both. In simply conveying that the act of saying took place at a point located prior to the here and now, simple past-tense SAY – along with its neutral semantics and other devices external to the verb – contributes to constructing the reporting clause such that it provides an objectivised, evidential framing for the reported clause. It is shown in Section 5.6 that the high frequency of the past tense form is also connected to grammaticalisation processes.

5.4 Indirect Objects

The indirect object represents an optional argument of *say*, which points to the low transitivity of the verb (see Hopper and Thompson 1980). Formally, indirect objects in English can be realised in terms of noun phrases or prepositional phrases (prepositional objects), a phenomenon called the 'dative alternation' (e.g., Collins 1995): that is, for many ditransitive verbs, the recipient role, realised as indirect object, can appear in two alternative positions (Thompson and Koide 1987). In contrast, *say* and other verbs of communication, such as *announce*, *report*, etc., 'may take a *to* phrase indicating the addressee (goal) of a communication but [...] do not allow the dative alternation' (Levin 1993: 210, italics in the original). The range of options with *say* is exemplified in Ex. (40).

(40) Properties of *say*-verbs (Levin 1993: 209–210)
 a. Ellen said that melons were selling well.
 b. Ellen said to Helen that melons were selling well.
 c. Ellen said something/a few words to Helen.
 d. *Dative Alternation:
  i. Ellen said something to Helen.
  ii. *Ellen said Helen something.

My research interest is in how the alternation exemplified in Ex. (40a) and (40b) can be accounted for in the reporting clauses at PMQs. According to Biber *et al.*, this constitutes an alternation in the production of what they call 'recipient adverbials' (Biber *et al.* 1999: 781) – rather than a production or non-production of the indirect object – which is similar to other optional circumstance adverbials of *say*, such as adverbials of place or time (see Section 5.5).

To my knowledge, there exists no substantial research on this recipient adverbial alternation. My analysis shows that such recipient adverbials are only infrequently produced in both the 1978–1988 and 2003–2013 samples. When they are used, this is to achieve interactional goals and to construct coherence.

1978–1988

Indirect objects – or recipient adverbials – are practically non-existent in the reporting clauses. Table 5.11 (Appendix B) gives the relative frequency. There is only one example in the 1978–1988 collection, occurring in a finite reporting clause in a question turn by the Leader of the Liberal Party/SDP (LLD). The use of this indirect object is shown in Ex. (41).

(41)   PMQs 09 Nov. 1978

LLD: David Steel (Lib); PM: James Callaghan (Lab); S: George Thomas

```
1    LLD:     the prIme minister told the house last week about the three
              legged (.) STOOL; (0.44)
2         ->  and i thInk he SAID to us;=
3    LLD:     =that if the: [leg of ]
4    MP2:                   [mur mur]
5    LLD:     [If the leg of pay policy were WEAK, (0.47)]
6    MP2:     [mur mur mur mur mur mur mur mur mur mur ]
7    LLD:     the other two would have to be STRENGthened;
```

In this excerpt, the Leader of the Liberal Party first takes up a topic of the prime-ministerial talk from a previous question time (*the prIme minister told the house last week about the three legged (.) STOOL;*, line 1). In the reported speech which follows, this is further specified. The *and*-prefaced reporting clause is qualified through an epistemic marker, *i think*. In addition to the core members of the clause, a prepositional indirect object, *to us*, is produced (*and i thInk he SAID to us;=*, line 2).[11] The indirect object *to us* reformulates the collective audience of the act of communication, first framed as *the house* in line 1. According to Chafe (1982), this indicates a more involved style, emphasising the relevance of the following quotation to the in situ audience, which is typical of leadership speech (Fetzer and Bull 2012). Unfortunately, it is not clear from the recording if

---

[11] Epistemic framings of SAY are noticeably rare in the 1978–1988 data. In fact, this is the only example in the sample.

5.4 Indirect Objects

MP2's soft background speech in overlap (lines 4, 6) forms a response to this. Structurally, on the clause and discourse level, the indirect object *to us* is redundant; if it had not been produced, the speech would still have been coherent. Interactionally, however, it can be hypothesised that the recycling of the recipient adds emphasis to the fact that the subsequent quotation is relevant to the co-present audience as recipients of the message.

2003–2013

As in the 1978–1988 data set, indirect objects are generally not common in the 2003–2013 sample. There is a total relative frequency of under 4 per cent of reporting clauses that occur with an indirect object, realised as a prepositional object with the preposition *to*. This means that the recipients of the communicative act of 'saying' remain largely underspecified. Tables 5.12a, 5.12b (Appendix B) show the relative frequencies distributed over turn types and participant roles.

It was suggested in the 1978–1988 analysis that a possible function of indirect objects may be to create involvement, which is associated with leadership speech. This explanation seems to be corroborated by findings that indirect objects are most frequently produced in the PM's answer turns in 2003–2013. As far as form is concerned, the 2003–2013 data set does not contain examples which directly correspond to the single 1978–1988 instance of an indirect object. Nevertheless, Ex. (42) is similar in the sense that the production of the indirect object creates involvement.

(42)   PMQs 09 Jan 2008
LLD: Nick Clegg; PM: Gordon Brown; S: Michael Martin

```
1    MPs:   [h h h h h h h h h h h h h  ]
2    PM:    [(0.69) <<all>mister SPEAker;>]

3    MPs:   [l l l l l l l l l l l l]
4    PM:    [let let me welcome uh (.)] [the right honourable MEMber; (0.61)]
5    MPs:                                [ch ch ch ch ch ch ch ch ch ch ch  ]

6    PM:    [uh to the:=uh LEAdership of the (.) <<all>lIberal party,>=]
7    MPs:   [mur mur mur mur mur mur mur mur mur mur mur mur mur mur mur]

8    PM:    [=i look FORward; (0.67)]
9    MPs:   [mur mur mur mur mur mur]

10   PM:    [uh? to working WITH him on many of the issues facing the
11   MPs:   [mur mur mur mur mur mur mur mur mur mur mur mur mur mur mur

     PM:    cOuntry,]
     MPs:   mur mur ]
```

```
12  PM:   i've SAID to him in our private conversations that uh'] there's
13  MPs:  [mur mur mur mur mur mur mur mur mur mur mur mur mur ]
    PM:   an open dOor for [hIm- (0.86)]
14  MPs:                   [ch ch ch ch ]
15  PM:   [and we are ready (.)] [to discuss the major issues that affect
16  MPs:  [ch ch ch ch ch ch ch] [mur mur mur mur mur mur mur mur mur mur
    PM:   the COUNtry; (0.49)]
    MPs:  mur mur mur mur mur]
17        [WHERE there is common grOund.] ((turn continues))
18  MPs:  [mur mur mur mur mur mur mur     ]
```

The answer turn in Ex. (42) responds to a question turn in which the LLD attacks the PM for his past actions: he claims that the PM is responsible for four million British families being unable to afford their fuel bills (not shown here), an attack which is especially hostile because it is winter. The PM first welcomes the questioner to the House and claims to be looking forward to working with him (lines 4, 6, 8, 10). Next follows the PM's reported speech, ascribed to himself. In addition to the pronominal subject and the verb, the reporting clause contains an indirect object, referring to the past recipient of the reported speech, and an adverbial providing the speech events where the past speech took place (*i've SAID to him in our private conversations,* line 12). The indirect object is realised as a prepositional phrase, consisting of the preposition *to* and the prepositional complement *him*, referring to the questioner. The adverbial *in our private conversations,* which gives the speech event when the past utterance was produced (see Section 5.5), is in plural form, which frames the indirect quotation (*that uh' there's an open dOor for hIm- (...),* lines 12, 15, 17) as a 'summarizing dialogue' (Tannen 2007: 114). Syntactically and in terms of speech coherence, the indirect object is redundant. Interactionally, however, it seeks to create involvement with the interlocutor, emphasising the point made in the quoted utterance, that the PM is open to collaboration. In this sense, it can be interpreted as a reminder that the PM has offered the Leader of the second-largest opposition party cooperation rather than confrontation. As in the 1987–1988 excerpt shown above, the indirect object is deployed where the past recipient of the quoted position (*to us, to him*) is co-referential with the recipient in the here and now. This pronominal reference adds emphasis to the why-that-now of the reported speech, seeking to create involvement with not only in situ recipients but also – it can be assumed – the mediated audience.

5.4 Indirect Objects

I turn now to an example which illustrates that in addition to creating involvement, indirect objects can also be used to construct discourse coherence (Ex. 43).

(43)   PMQs 01 Dec. 2010

PM: David Cameron (Con); MP: Chris Heaton-Harris; S: John Bercow

```
1   MPs:    [mur mur mur mur mur   ]
2   S:      [↑chris heaton HARris;]
3   MPs:    [mur mur mur mur mur mur   ]
4   MP:     [<<all>thank you SIR;- (0.38)]
5   MP:     um? ↑with the: reNEWED prospect of travel chaos for british
            airways pAssengers,
6           [(0.38) wIll the prime minister conDEMN, (0.52)]
7   MPs:    [j l j l j l j l j l j l j l j l j l j   ]
8   MP:     [<<all>wIll the prime minister condemn> <<f>the leader of
9   MPs:    [j j j j j j j j j j j j j j j j j j j j j j j
    MP:     uNITE'S:? im? imPLIED thrEat to fAmilies,>]
    MPs:    j j j j j j j j j j j j j j j j j j   ]
10  MP: ->  [when he SAID to them- (0.26)]
11  MPs:    [j j j j j j j j j j j j   ]
12  MP:     [<<len>DON'T go on hOliday>;]
13  MPs:    [j j j j j j j j j j j j j   ]
```

The reported speech is produced as part of an interrogative structure, *wIll the prime minister condemn the leader of uNITE'S:? im? imPLIED thrEat to fAmilies*, (line 8), where it occurs in a temporal clause, *when he SAID to them- DON'T go on hOliday* (lines 10, 12). The indirect object is realised as a prepositional object *to them* (line 10), referring to the recipient of the quoted utterance. If it were absent, the speech would not be coherent. In contrast with Exx. (41) and (42) above, the referent is not identical with co-present participants, but the speaker plays to the mediated public audience.

The foregoing analysis has shown that the production of indirect objects can be motivated by interactional functions, that is, to construct an emphatic, involved style as part of a self-presentation of leadership, and by semantic constraints, that is, to create coherence (2003–2013). In using indirect objects, the speaker may appeal to in situ recipients (1978–1988, 2003–2013) as well as play to mediated audiences (2003–2013).

These few examples do not allow the analyst to draw conclusions concerning whether these motivations have undergone change between the two data sets. Nevertheless, the use of indirect objects can be seen as an additional resource for the speaker to create rhetorical involvement, which in the 2003–2013 is also explicitly deployed to play to mediated audiences. This suggests a greater speaker orientation towards the split audience in the 2003–2013 sample.

5.5 Adverbials

Adverbials can come in a variety of forms and functions in English. In terms of the forms, Quirk *et al.* list adverb phrases (closed-class: *then*; open-class: *recently*), noun phrases (*last week*), prepositional phrases (*in the evening*), and clauses (verbless: *though obviously ill*; nonfinite clause: *while waiting for the job*; finite clause: *after she had seen the announcement*) (labels and examples quoted from Quirk *et al.* 1985: 489).

1978–1988
The adverbials deployed in the 1978–1988 data set specify the time (e.g., *toDAY, (.) and last THURSday;*) location (e.g., *in the HOUSE*), and what I call speech event (e.g., *on radio four's aNALysis programme*), that is, a figurative use of spatial adverbials, where the medium or act of communication is further described. The only case of the latter, which I call a speech event adverbial, was found in a nonfinite reporting clause. It is illustrated in Ex. (44).

(44)   PMQs 05 Nov. 1987
MP: Alex Carlile (Lib); PM: Margaret Thatcher Con; S: Bernard Weatherill

```
1   MP:      will the right honourable lady find tIme in her busy SCHEdule;
2        ->  to hear the deputy prime minister say on radio four's aNALysis
             programme tonIght;
3            °h that the government's school OPTout proposals,
4            will be deFEAted in the other plAce;
```

The nonfinite reporting clause contains two circumstantial adverbials, a figurative adverbial of place (*on radio four's aNALysis programme*, line 2), which specifies the speech event, and an adverbial of time (*tonight*, line 2), and introduces a *that*-prefaced quotation (*that the government's school OPTout proposals, will be defeated (...)*, lines 3–4). At the same time, Ex. (44) is the only example of a nonfinite reporting clause with a circumstantial adverbial. For this reason, I turn to finite reporting clauses in what follows.

Only a minority of the finite reporting clauses contain circumstantial adverbials, a finding which explains the low relative frequency across turn types and speaker roles (Table 5.13, Appendix B). Seen the other way

5.5 Adverbials

round, the vast majority of the finite 1978–1988 reporting clauses do not provide circumstantial details of what is framed as past speech. Table 5.14 shows the distribution over forms and semantic roles in finite reporting clauses. (The percentage of the category 'speech event' figures as 0% because the only instance in the sample was found in a nonfinite clause.)

These adverbials do not necessarily have to be integrated with the other elements of the reporting clause in one intonation phrase, but are produced in processes of the online emergence of syntax (Auer 2000, 2005, 2015). In Ex. (45), the time and place of the past speech are detailed.

(45) PMQs 09 Nov. 1978
LO: Margaret Thatcher (Con); PM: James Callaghan (Lab); S: George Thomas

```
1   S:      missus THATcher;
2   LO:     ↑dOEs the prime minister reCALL,
3           -> that the lAst time minimum lending rate went Up in jU:ne to ten
            -> per CENT;
4           -> the <<all>chAncellor of the exchequer> ↑THEN said;
5           -> in the HOUSE;
6           -> that he expected it to come dOwn at mOst (.) within a few WEEKS;
7           <<all>whAt wEnt wrOng THIS tIme;>=
8   MPs:    =[h h h h h h h h ] [mur mur]
9   PM:     [(2.20) yes=sir uhm] [(1.10)] ((turn continues))
```

The *that*-prefaced quotation (*that he expected it to come dOwn (...)*, line 6) is introduced by a reporting clause which incrementally emerges online during three intonation phrases. In the first intonation phrase, the first adverbial of time is produced in the form of a complex noun phrase (*the lAst time minimum lending rate went Up in jU:ne to ten per CENT;*, line 3). In the second intonation phrase, another temporal adverbial occurs as an adverb phrase, positioned between the subject and the verb (*the <<all> chAncellor of the exchequer>*

Table 5.14 *Absolute syntactic and semantic distribution of adverbials in finite reporting clauses (1978–1988)*

Adverbials (n=5)	NP	PP	AdvP	Clause	Total
Time	0% (0)	20% (1)	60% (3)	0% (0)	80% (4)
Space	0% (0)	20% (1)	0% (0)	0% (0)	20% (1)
Speech event	0% (0)	0% (0)	0% (0)	0% (0)	0% (0)
Respect	0% (0)	0% (0)	0% (0)	0% (0)	0% (0)
Manner	0% (0)	0% (0)	0% (0)	0% (0)	0% (0)

↑*THEN said*, line 4). In the third intonation phrase, an adverbial of place follows, formatted as a prepositional phrase (*in the HOUSE;*, line 5).

Recall that reporting clauses as illustrated above constitute the minority in the sample. So how do circumstantial adverbials function in performing reported speech? Since we cannot rely on displays of participant understanding, one way to test their function is to ask what goes missing if we leave them out. Let us return to Ex. (45′), reproduced for convenience below, to illustrate such a hypothetical scenario. The missing chunks are indicated by ((. . .)):

(45′)   PMQs 09 Nov. 1978

LO: Margaret Thatcher (Con); PM: James Callaghan (Lab); S: George Thomas

```
1   S:        mistress THATcher;
2   LO:       ↑dOEs the prime minister reCALL,
3             ((...))
4        ->   that the <<all>chAncellor of the exchequer> ((...)) said;
5             ((...))
6        ->   that he expected it to come dOwn at mOst (.) within a few WEEKS;
7             <<all>whAt wEnt wrOng THIS tIme;>=
8   MPs:      =[h h h h h h h h ] [mur mur]
9   PM:        [(2.20) yes=sir uhm] [(1.10) ] ((turn continues))
```

The fabricated excerpt shows that the time reference, omitted in line 3, constructs coherence: the meaning of *it* (line 6) cannot be retrieved without it. The omission of the adverbials of time and space in lines 4 and 5 does not make the question turn incoherent. However, the additional information and prosodic design, with each bearing primary accents (↑*THEN, in the HOUSE*), add emphasis to the reported speech, creating a dramatic scenario which provides the backdrop for the subsequent wh-interrogative, <<*all> whAt wEnt wrOng THIS tIme;>* =(line 7), which is strategically designed to attack the government. On the one hand, the proposition of the interrogative implies that 'something went wrong'; on the other, the use of the temporal adverbial *THIS tIme* presupposes that this did not happen for the first time. In sum, the adverbials contextualise the reported speech in ways which provide coherence and emphasis, promoting the communicative goals of the local action.

The other way round, the non-production of circumstantial adverbials *de*contextualises the reported speech. This format is furthered by the valency of the verb SAY, which does not take obligatory adverbials and is so low in transitivity that it does not require an object. Note that decontextualised formats of reported speech are clearly preferred in the sample. This suggests that circumstantial information is methodically not provided (with the source representing the most relevant portion of the reporting clause) to the effect that the reported speech can be used for local communicative goals, which may have nothing to do with the original action. This is in line with Tannen's (2007) conceptualisation of reported speech as constructed dialogue. If speakers use quotations from contexts alien or maybe even contradictory to the communicative purposes of the present speaker in the here and now, giving too much circumstantial information may hinder the current communicative project.

2003–2013

On average, not even a third (99) of the 356 finite 2003–2013 reporting clauses contain circumstantial adverbials, a finding which roughly compares to the 1978–1988 sample.[12] This means that generally, reporting clauses in the 2003–2013 data set are formatted without circumstantial adverbials, that is, they constitute a format that underspecifies circumstantial information. Compared to the 1978–1988 data set, the reporting clauses from 2003 to 2013 feature a diversified set of adverbials, which includes adverbials of respect and manner as well as adverbials of time, space, and speech event (tables 5.15a, 5.15b, Appendix B).

The sample further shows a slight diversification in form, with a small amount of clausal forms in the group of temporal adverbials (Table 5.16).

Like in the 1978–1988 sample, adverbials of time are the most common semantic type. Typically, these are shaped as noun phrases in the 2003–1013 sample.[13] Here *LAST WEEK*, which is exemplified in Ex. (46), represents the

Table 5.16 *Syntactic and semantic distribution of circumstantial adverbials in finite clauses (2003–2013)*

Adverbials (n=110)	NP	PP	AdvP	Clause	Total
Time	27% (29)	20% (21)	20% (22)	5% (5)	72% (77)
Space	0% (0)	6% (6)	1% (1)	0% (0)	7% (7)
Speech event	0% (0)	18% (19)	0% (0)	0% (0)	18% (19)
Respect	0% (0)	5% (5)	0% (0)	0% (0)	5% (5)
Manner	0% (0)	1% (1)	1% (1)	0% (0)	2% (2)

[12] Some reporting clauses contain more than one of the total 110 adverbials presented in Table 5.16.
[13] This contrasts with the 1978–1988 data set, which does not contain any nominal adverbials and shows a tendency towards adverb phrases in temporal adverbials.

most common token of temporal adverbials across turn types and participant roles. The example shows how the formatting as an NP fosters dense information packaging. At the same time, the adverbial contributes to creating cohesion and emphasis.

(46)   PMQs 22 June 2005

MP: Dr Tony Wright (Lab); PM: Tony Blair (Lab); S: Michael Martin

```
1   S:          doctor WRIGHT-
2   MP:         (0.89) <<all>↑does the prime minister recall that> (0.35) LAST
                year;
3               (0.76) we had a celebration to mark (0.61) the cenTENary;
4               of the Entente cordiALE.
5               (0.67) [(2.79)]
6   MPs:               [1 1 1 ] [mur mur mur mur mur mur]
7   MP:   ->            [lAst (0.25) last ↑WEEK;]
8   MPs:        [mur mur]
9   MP:   ->    [(1.02) ] last WEEK the president of frAnce;
10  MPs:        [mur mur]
11  MP:         [0.73)  ] said that (.) my right honourable friend wAs (0.33)
                pathetic (0.58) and ↑TRAgic;
12  MPs:        [h l ch]
13  MP:         [(8.46)] ((resumes with speech))
```

The reporting clause begins with a noun phrase, which serves as a time adverbial. It is repaired in orientation to the audience responses (*lAst (0.25) last ↑WEEK;*, lines 6–7) until it is produced in the clear and integrated with the subsequent subject in a single intonation phrase (*last WEEK the president of frAnce;*, line 9). The noun phrase has a simple structure, with *last* functioning as the determiner and *WEEK* as the head. It contextualises the reported speech as topical and thus relevant to the ongoing debate. Note the dense information packaging of the intonation phrase in which it occurs – out of six words in total, it is built of four content words. At the same time, the temporal adverbial *last WEEK* sets up a relation of contrast with *LAST year* (line 2) in the previous speech, creating coherence and adding emphasis. Most frequently, the reporting clauses contain individual adverbials (as shown in Ex. 46) rather than clustered groups. The latter, infrequent case is exemplified in Ex. 47.

(47)   PMQs 30 March 2011
LO: Ed Miliband (Lab); PM: David Cameron (Con); S: John Bercow

```
1   PM:      °hh he Asked the quEstion about Arming the REBels.
2        ->  now I've said beFO:RE in this hOuse.
3            °h that we must do EVerything to comply with-
4            °h BOTH the security council resolutions;
5            °h and as i: ↑TOLD the house;=
6            =the ↑LEgal position is clear;=
7            that the ARMS embargo applies to the who:le (.) ↑TERritory of
             libya. ((turn continues))
```

The reporting clause is produced in line 2 (*now ↑I've said beFO:RE in this house*). Apart from the subject and verb ↑*I'VE said*, the intonation phrase in which the reporting clause is produced contains three more elements. The discourse marker *now*, which signals 'discontinuity' (Jucker 1986: 121), an adverb serving as an adverbial of time, *befo:re*, and an adverbial of place in the form of a prepositional phrase, *in this house*.

Turning to the second-most frequent type of adverbial, it is noticeable that space adverbials generally constitute figurative choices used to describe the speech event. Ex. (48) is an example.

(48)   PMQs 02 July 2008
PM: Gordon Brown (Lab); LO: David Cameron (Con); S: Michael Martin

```
1   LO:      the HEAD of the probAtion officers sAid, (.)
2        ->  ON the rAdio, (0.21)
3            well we BROUGHT it up last year
4            and as FAR as i can sEe,
5            they've dOne (.) NOTHing;
```

The prepositional phrase *ON the rAdio,* (line 2) labels the speech event where the quotation was taken in a metaphorical way. Here a speech event is conceptualised as space. The source domain (space) is mapped onto the target domain (i.e., a speech event; see Lakoff and Johnson 2003). The metaphorical space adverbial is produced in an 'incremental' (Schegloff 1996b) intonation phrase following the subject and verb of the reporting clause (*the HEAD of the probAtion officers sAid, (.),* line 1).

These findings suggest that like in the 1978–1988 sample, the circumstantial details of what was said are commonly left unstated in finite reporting clauses with SAY. The quotation construction is thus decontextualised, reduced to information about the source and the position stated, and streamlined and tailored to the in situ communicative goals of the participant doing the quoting.

Nevertheless, when these details are presented, the focus is on the timing and speech event. The most frequent choice of temporal adverbial, *LAST WEEK*, indicates a tendency to quote recent discourse, which frames the position claimed in the quotation as topical and thus relevant to the current argument. At the same time, it is formed as an NP, and is therefore a resource for dense information packaging, a finding which mirrors the patterns identified for the formatting of subjects of reporting clauses.

To come to a final point, as was shown in Ex. (48) above, adverbials can be produced in independent intonation phrases to the effect that the reporting clause is incrementally produced over time. Ex. (49), which constitutes an extended version of Ex. (24), shows an adverbial of place and an adverbial of time, which are produced in an intonation phrase prior to the intonation phrase that contains the subject and the verb.

(49)   PMQs 08 Dec. 2010
PM: David Cameron (Con); MP1: Richard Ottaway (Con) S: John Bercow

```
1  S:         rIchard OTtaway;
2             (0.31)
3  MP1: ->    IN: afghanistan on mOnday;=
4       ->    =the PRIME minister said;=
5             =BRITish troops;=
6             =could start coming home from afGHANista:n;
7             (0.33) as EArly as next YEAR;
8  MP2:       hear HEAR;
```

Note that the adverbials (*IN: afghanistan on mOnday;=*, line 3) are produced in an independent intonation phrase before the production of the core elements of the clause, the subject and verb (=*the PRIME minister said;=*, line 4). This kind of prosodic chunking of non-core elements into incomplete syntactic units seems to be a general feature of political speech in order to maintain audience attention, an observation that should be explored further in future research.

Nevertheless, note that the low percentage of indirect objects is afforded by the subcategorisation frame of SAY, where the naming of recipients is –

at least syntactically – optional. I argue that this low percentage is reflective and at the same time constitutive of turn-constructional and interactional formats at PMQs in that it allows participants to quote past speech from contexts where it was (possibly) aimed at other audiences and served different communicative goals, and to use it to address their own audiences for rhetorical purposes in a political setting (cf. Tannen 2007).

5.6 Entering Grammaticalisation? The Case of HE SAID

This section explores possible traces of grammatical change between 1978–1988 and 2003–2013. To that end, I examined both data sets to determine whether there are finite reporting clauses that consist of a pronominal subject and a verb with simple aspect, preceding a reported clause and not prefaced by the complementiser *that*. Past research (Thompson 2002; Thompson and Mulac 1991a) has shown that such formats in evidential, epistemic, and evaluative CTPs point to formulaicity, a springboard for grammaticalisation. Specifically, grammaticalisation in spoken discourse has been associated with loss of prime-categoriality, loss of syntactic constraints, a tendency to assume discourse functions, mobility in position, phonetic reduction, semantic bleaching, and subjectification (Dehé and Wichmann 2010; Bybee *et al.* 1994; Hopper 1991; Traugott 2010; Thompson and Mulac 1991a, 1991b).

1978–1988
The 1978–1988 data set has only one reporting clause with a pronominal subject which qualifies as a candidate for a formulaic construction. Tables 5.17 (Appendix B) and 5.18 show the relative frequency and absolute distribution of the candidate I SAID in the 1978–1988 data set.

Ex. (50) illustrates the use of I SAID in the 1978–1988 sample.
(50)   PMQs 06 Nov. 1986
Derek Conway (Con); PM Margaret Thatcher (Con); S: Bernard Weatherill

```
PM: -> i SAID at the moment we hAve no plans to chAnge it;
```

The reporting clause *i SAID* has a pronominal subject in first person singular and a verb in simple past. The subsequent reported clause *at the moment we hAve no plans to chAnge it;* is not marked by the complementiser *that*. Based on the assumption that formulaicity is coupled with frequency, I cannot make a case that this is a formulaic use of *i SAID*, since this is the only token of this kind in the sample. However, findings from American English conversational data suggest

Table 5.18 *Absolute distribution of I SAID in finite reporting clauses (1978–1988)*

Finite reporting clauses	I SAID	Other
1978–1988 (n=20)	5% (1)	95% (19)

that I SAID can be used as an evidential phrase (Kärkkäinen 2003: 38–45, 77–79).

2003–2013
In the 2003–2013 data set, the type and token frequency of candidates for formulaic constructions of the form [pronominal subject + SAY in simple aspect + bare reported clause] has skyrocketed.[14] Tables 5.19a, 5.19b (Appendix B) give an overview of the relative frequencies across turn types and speaker roles. They show a notable increase in type and token frequencies in the question–answer sequences between LO and PM, specifically regarding HE SAID. Recall that in the 1978–1988 sample, interactions between the LO and PM are shorter and thus not as prominent as in 2003–2013 (see Chapter 4). This suggests that the longer questioning has not only led to more multiple, lengthy question–answer sequences but also to an increase in the use of reporting clauses with SAY. This in turn might have created a fertile environment for grammaticalisation, which becomes specifically visible considering the heightened type and token frequency of the format [pronominal subject + SAY in simple aspect + bare reported clause]. Based on these observations, I argue that the data provide evidence for how – due to a politically calculated decision – a change in participant participation can prepare the ground for grammatical change.

Table 5.20 shows the general increase of formulaic candidates – those with this format – among finite reporting clauses. Compared to the 1978–1988 data set (5 per cent), their use has gone up to 24 per cent, although other formats still dominate the picture.

Ex. (51) represents a case of I SAID analogous to the findings from the 1978–1988 sample.

(51)   PMQs 10 June 2009

LO: David Cameron (Con); PM: Gordon Brown (Lab); S: John Bercow

```
1  PM: -> i SAID he'd moved on to pOlicy,
```

[14] I use the term 'bare reported clause' for reported clauses where *that* is omitted.

5.6 Entering Grammaticalisation? The Case of HE SAID

Table 5.20 *Absolute distribution of [pronominal subject + SAY in simple aspect + bare reported clause] and other formats*

Finite reporting clauses	[pronominal subject + SAY in simple aspect + bare reported clause]	Other
2003–2013 (n= 356)	23.9% (85)	76.1% (271)

Table 5.21 *Absolute distribution of candidates for 'formulaic' constructions in reporting clauses (2003–2013)*

	I SAID	WE SAY	WE SAID	HE SAYS	HE SAID	IT SAYS	IT SAID	THEY SAY	THEY SAID
2003–2013 (n=85)	4% (3)	2% (2)	5% (4)	32% (27)	39% (33)	4% (3)	2% (2)	4% (4)	8% (7)

As in the 1978–1988 excerpt, a first-person singular pronoun (*i*) functions as the subject, referring to the current speaker as the source of the quotation. The quotative verb has the primary accent (*SAID*), and the reporting clause is prosodically integrated with the quotation in an intonation phrase.[15] Table 5.21 shows the absolute distribution of pronominal subjects in the sample of formulaic candidates. (Since there are no second-person subjects (Table 5.6), they were not included in the table.)

Analogous to the 1978–1988 data set, the number of tokens of the reporting clause I SAID has remained at the same low token count. The most frequent type in the sample is the quotative clause HE SAID. Compared to the 1978–1988 sample, where there was only one type of the format [pronominal subject + SAY in simple aspect + bare reported clause] (I SAID), the number of types has diversified (I SAID, WE SAID, etc.) – but note there is no subject in third-person singular feminine (SHE) – and the number of tokens has generally increased.

These findings illustrate that compared with the 1978–1988 data set, the 2003–2013 sample indicates a 'generalization to greater type- as well as token frequency' (Traugott and Trousdale 2010: 12), which has been described as a correlate of grammaticalisation. Thompson and

---

[15] As in the 1978–1988 sample, all quotative clauses with a first-person singular pronominal subject were found in responsive turns.

Mulac (1991a) note two ways in which token frequency correlates with grammaticalisation. First, 'an increase in an item's text frequency is an important concomitant of its grammaticization' (Thompson and Mulac 1991a: 319). Second, 'out of a range of possible forms, only a small subset occurs with great frequency in the data, and these are the very forms that show up as grammaticized as EP's [sic!, epistemic phrases]' (Thompson and Mulac 1991b: 319). Both can be stated for the evidential phrases in my data set.

Following the assumption that frequency is linked to grammaticalisation, this is a finding worthy of further exploration. The data show a variety of HE SAID, which point to the reporting clause undergoing a process of grammaticalisation. Consider Ex. (52) for an illustration of the phenomenon. It is taken from an answer turn where the PM ridicules the LO for his PR (*pee Ar*, line 2).

(52)   PMQs 17 Oct. 2007

LO: David Cameron (Con); PM: Gordon Brown (Lab); S: Michael Martin

```
1   PM:        (xxx) mister spEaker-
2              he's [GOOD at pee Ar,]
3   MPs:            [sh sh sh sh sh ]
4   PM:        [(1.0) but didn't (0.33) didn't (.) ]
5   MPs:       [sh sh sh sh sh sh sh sh sh sh sh]
6              dIdn't he go too fAr last weekend when he went to caliFORnia;
               (0.59)
7       ->     and he SAID in an intervIew-
8              in the NEWSpaper-=
9       ->     =he SAID;
10             (0.31) LOOK at me he said. (.)
11      ->     <<all>he said> (.) LOOK at me he said. (0.22)
12      ->     <<all>he said> lOok at me (.) and thInk of Arnold
               SCHWARzenegger.
13  MPs:       [l sh l sh l sh l sh l sh l sh l sh l sh l sh l sh ]
14  PM:        [(1.07) <<ff> that's the LAST thing in anybody's mInd;>]
15  MPs:       [l sh ]
16             [(2.5)]
```

The excerpt has six tokens of HE SAID:

1. One is accented and integrated in a larger intonation phrase (*he SAID*, line 7).
2. One forms a separate, accented prosodic chunk (*he SAID;*, line 9).

5.6 Entering Grammaticalisation? The Case of HE SAID

3. Two are unaccented and positioned at the end of larger intonation phrases (*he said.*, lines 10, 11).
4. Two are anacrustic, that is, unaccented and produced in fast tempo, in initial position (<<*all*> *he said*>, lines 11, 12).

With reference to the prior discussion, HE SAID₁ represents a more schematic construction in that it is prosodically integrated with more lexical material, notably an adverbial in the form of a prepositional phrase (*in an intervIew-*, line 7). On the other hand, HE SAID₂₋₄ constitute a variety of fixed forms present in the 2003–2013 data set, which suggests that HE SAID has entered a cline of grammaticalisation. Based on these initial observations, I now systematically investigate the formal and functional variants of HE SAID. These can be summarised as follows:

- HE SAID₁ as a fixed formulaic 'projector construction' (Günthner 2011a, 2011b), with primary accent and full semantics;
- HE SAID₂ and HE SAID₃ reanalysed, that is, grammaticalised, as a parenthetical, without primary accent or non-accented and with bleached semantics, and used as a parenthetical;
- HE SAID₄ reanalysed as discourse marker (phonetically reduced, semantically bleached, redundant).

I begin with HE SAID₁, a fixed formula, which I consider the 'onset' of grammaticalisation in the sample. Consider Ex. (53).

(53) PMQs 11 May 2011
LO: Ed Miliband (Lab); PM: David Cameron (Con); S: John Bercow

```
1   LO:       °h now i ↑nOticed also he didn't mention,
2             °h his top down reorganis↑SA[tion;=
3   LO:       =[when he talked about his   HANdling; ]
4   MPs:      [h h h h h h h h h h h h h h h]
5   LO:       [(0.30) <<all>of the EN aitch es>; (0.33)]
6   MPs:      [h h h h h h h h h h h h h h h h h h]
7   LO:       ↑LET me remind him of what he sAId;
8             (0.39) JUST a mOnth agO;=
9             mister SPEAker;
10  ->        °h he SAID-
11            (.) ↑I've been involved in desIgning these changes-
12            °h WAY back;
13            (.) into oPposition;
14  LO:       (.) [with aNdrew (.) lAnsley; (1.44)]
15  MPs:          [h h h h h h h h h h h h h h h]
```

The LO produces a metapragmatic construction which pre-empts a quotation ((-)↑*LET me remind him of what he sAId;*, line 7). It is incrementally expanded through a tome adverbial ((-)↑*JUST a mOnth agO;=*, line 8). Next the LO appeals to the Speaker (*mister SPEAker;*, line 9), orienting to him as an addressee of his speech. This reorientation, from structuring and pre-empting turn-constructional space for a quotation to selecting an addressee, may explain why the LO next again pre-empts interactional space for the projected quotation, now using the reporting clause *he SAID-* (line 10). In terms of form, it is produced in an independent intonation phrase, with the verb bearing the primary accent. Functionally, it projects a shift in footing, providing an evidential framing for the subsequent portion of speech, a direct quotation (without an initial complementiser *that*): ((.)↑*I'VE been involved in desIgning these changes (…)*, lines 11–14). If *he SAID-* were left out, the deictic centre of the subsequent speech would not be clear. This is taken as evidence that *SAID* has retained its full semantics as a verb of communication in this situated position. The *he SAID-* clause functions as a fixed construction, contributing to the turn-internal progressivity and coherent organisation, pre-empting interactional space for the following quotation, and projecting a change in footing.

Ex. (54) is another case in point. Here HE SAID₁ represents the third event in a mini narrative, projecting and pre-empting turn constructional space for its climax.

(54)   PMQs 02 July 2008

LO: David Cameron (Con); PM: Gordon Brown (Lab); S: Michael Martin

```
1    LO:       a YEAR agO, (0.27)
               i Asked the prime minister WHY, (0.21)
2              under his nEw: Early release from PRIson scheme,
3              °h DANgerous criminals were being lEt out early;
4              a!GAINST! the express advice of probAtion officers.
5              °h the PRIME minister prOmised me,
6              that it would be looked iNto,
7              but it is STILL going on;
8       ->    °h ONE person <<all>released Early under the scheme>,
9       ->    reTURNED home and stabbed his girlfriend.
10      ->    °h he SAID;
11            (0.31) i CANnot belIeve,
12            they have LET me out;
13            °h i TOLD them,
14            i would DO it;
```

5.6 Entering Grammaticalisation? The Case of HE SAID 109

The narrative consists of three events: *ONE person <<all> released Early under the scheme>* (line 8) (1) *reTURNED home* (line 9), (2) *stabbed his girlfriend.* (line 9), and (3) *he SAID; i CANnot belIeve, they have LET me out; (...)* (lines 10–14). Again *he SAID;* (line 10) precedes the reported speech, is produced in a separate intonation phrase, and has the primary accent on the verb. Both members of the clause have retained their full semantics: the pronominal subject *he* makes anaphoric reference to *ONE person* (line 8); the verb *SAID* adds to the progressivity of the narrative, like the verbs *reTURNED* and *stabbed*. Finally, the clause *he SAID* projects a change in footing. Without the reporting clause, the deictic centre of the personal pronouns *I* and *me* (lines 11–14) in the quotation would be assigned to the current speaker. Ex. (55) is another example.

(55)   PMQs 03 Nov. 2010
MP: Heidi Alexander (Lab); PM: David Cameron (Con); LO: John Bercow

```
1   MP:      in MARCH of this year;
2            the prIme minister came to LEWisham college; (0.29)
3            and spOke to students about his PLANS; (0.34)
4       ->   he SAID, (0.22)
5       ->   and i QUOTE- (0.46)
6            we'll KEEP it; (0.57)
7            <<all>we've TAken a look at it,> (0.28)
8            <<all>we thInk it's a good iDEA.>
```

The reporting clause *he SAID* (line 4), produced in an independent intonation phrase with the primary accent on the verb, is functional in providing an evidential framing for the subsequent tripartite list (lines 6–8). The semantics of the personal pronoun *he* in subject position is evoked through anaphoric reference to the nominal subject, *the prIme minister* (line 2). Thus the semantics of the personal pronoun is also indexically constructed through discourse deixis. If the reporting clause were absent, the turn would be non-coherent but also – similar to Ex. (54) – the deictic centre of the personal pronoun *we* would be misaligned. This shows that the verb *SAID* has retained its full semantics, framing the list as reported speech. The excerpt further shows that while projecting and pre-empting interactional space for the quotation, *he SAID* and the subsequent speech do not enjoy a syntactic relation. The formula *and i QUOTE-* (line 5), which follows the reporting clause and precedes the quotation, provides evidence that *he SAID* has a formulaic quality and is not a matrix clause: produced in a separate intonation phrase, the *and*-prefacing coordinates the clause *i QUOTE-* with the reporting clause *he SAID*. While *he SAID* frames the list as past speech, *i QUOTE-* frames it as a verbatim quotation (see Chapter 6 on the function of (AND) I QUOTE). The two clauses can neither be arranged in reverse order, nor is it possible to put the construction in passive voice, a canonical test for objects.

This also suggests that HE SAID$_1$ does not serve as a matrix structure for the subsequent clause but is 'stored and retrieved' (Thompson 2002: 125) as a fixed formula which may combine in time and in a serially emerging gestalt with the formula (AND) I QUOTE. It pre-empts turn-constructional space and indexes a change in footing for subsequent (multi-unit) speech. Here is a summary of the features of HE SAID$_1$:

o primary accent
o precedes bare reported clause
o done in an independent intonation phrase
o retains full semantics
o has lost matrix clause status
o pre-empts turn-constructional space for a quotation
o indexes a change in footing for subsequent (multi-unit) speech
o fixed and formulaic

The data further contain two types of HE SAID which could be 'bridging' or 'switch' constructions (Heine 2002; cf. also Fischer 2007) in the continuum of constructions on the path of grammaticalisation. These two types are difficult to distinguish and have more in common than divides them. HE SAID$_2$ and HE SAID$_3$ both show prosodic reduction and integration to various degrees, as well as mobility in terms of their position within intonation phrases. This indicates that HE SAID$_2$ and HE SAID$_3$ are reanalysed as adverbs with bleached semantics and are used as parentheticals.[16] The finding that these variants exist is taken as evidence that the grammaticalisation is still in progress. Ex. (56) illustrates the use of HE SAID$_2$. This is the only token of this type in the sample.

---

[16] Parentheticals are units which are external to or 'at best loosely related to the syntactic structure of the host' (Dehé 2009: 571). This syntactic disintegration is contextualised through prosodic breaks surrounding parentheticals, as for instance, pauses (see Dehé 2009 for an extended literature review). It is typical for parentheticals to be inserted at a point before the unit under way is complete (Dehé and Kavalova 2007: 1; Dehé and Wichmann 2010: 1; Mazeland 2007: 1818–1819).

5.6 Entering Grammaticalisation? The Case of HE SAID

(56)   PMQs 17 Oct 2007
LO: David Cameron (Con); PM: Gordon Brown (Lab); S: Michael Martin

```
1   MPs:       [j j j j j j j j j j j j j j j j j j j j j j j j]
2   PM:        [but let me aLso quote (.) the new chief ꜜeXECuꜜtive, (0.43)]
3              of mAIdstone en aitch es ↑TRUST;
4   MPs:       [j j j j j j j j j j j j j j j j j j j j j j j ]
5   PM:  ->    [tArgets are there (.) he said (.) for a ↑REAson; (0.33)]
6              THAT should not stop us from [fOcusing-]
7   MPs:                                    [j j j j j]
8   PM:        [mAjorly on patient sAfety, (0.33)]
9   MPs:       [j j j j j j j j j j j j j ]
10  PM:        [thAt is the number one priORity;]
11  MPs:       [j j j j j j j j j j j j j j]
```

The preface in lines 2–3 (*but ↑LET me Also quote (…)*) projects and pre-empts interactional space for what is claimed to be a verbatim quotation. Next follows a copula structure (*tArgets are there (.) he said (.) for a ↑REAson;*, line 5) in an independent intonation phrase, which is followed by three more intonation phrases that comprise the quotation (*THAT should not stop us from fOcusing- mAjorly on patient safety, THAT is the number one priority;*, lines 6, 8, 10). The prepositional phrase *for a ↑REAson;* serves as an adverbial in the copula structure. In between two micro pauses, the speaker inserts *he said*, following the obligatory members of the copular clause (*tArgets are there*) and produced before the final constituent of the clause (*for a ↑REAson;*). In contrast to HE SAID$_1$, this is non-accentuated, that is, prosodically reduced, prosodically and syntactically dependent on the host (i.e., the reported clause) rather than separate from it. This suggests that *he said* is a parenthetical, which seems to have been reanalysed as an evidential adverb. This is further evidenced by the positioning of *he said* in 'end position', a slot after all obligatory members of the clause, where adverbials can occur in English sentences (Quirk *et al.* 1985: 498). It serves to reaffirm but not project or even index the shift of footing of the quotation. This is how HE SAID$_2$, is characterised:

o   prosodic reduction and weak disintegration
o   mobility: mediary position within intonation phrases
o   reanalysed/grammaticalised as an evidential phrase
o   used as a parenthetical

HE SAID₃ is similar but for its positioning in the final position of intonation phrases. Ex. (57), an extended version of Ex. (25), is a case in point.

(57)   PMQs 10 June 2009

MP: Gerald Kaufman (Lab); PM: Gordon Brown (Lab); S: Michael Martin

```
1   PM:     mi' mister SPEAker;
2           (0.25) speCIFically the shadow health secretary s'_sAid this
            morning;
3           (0.52) over THREE years after twO thousand eleven,
4           a !TEN! per cEnt reduction;
5           °h in the departmental [expenditure limits for other
6   MPs:                           [ch j ch j ch j ch j ch j
    PM:     dePARTments.]
    MPs:    ch j ch j ch ] [ch j ch j ch j ch j] [sh sh sh sh sh sh sh
7   PM: ->                 [(0.40) it is a vEry tough] [spending requirement
    MPs:    sh sh sh sh sh ]
    PM:     inDEED ↓he said;]
8   PM:     <<all>an' he said> the jOb of the shadow chancellor [is to be
9   MPs:                                                        [sh sh sh
    PM:     CLEAR ]
    MPs:    sh sh ]
10  PM:     about whEre [the spEnding re] strAint BITES;
11  MPs:                [sh sh sh sh sh ]
```

The evidential phrase is produced at the end of an intonation phrase (*(0.40) it is a VERy tough spending requirement indeed he said;*, line 7), which forms part of a multi-unit quotation (*over THREE years after twO thousand eleven (. . .)*, lines 3–5, 7–8, 10). The reported clause is initially introduced and pre-empted by a reporting clause (*speCIFically the shadow health secretary s' sAid this morning*, line 2), having a nominal subject (*shadow health secretary*) and adverbials (*speCIFically, this morning*). The unit in which the parenthetical is produced is built as another copular structure and is produced in an independent intonation phrase; in this sense it is syntactically and prosodically complete. The reporting clause *he said* follows the primary accent on *inDEED*, after the unit is prosodically possibly complete. It comes unaccented, on a stepdown in pitch and with a final plosive without audible release. Syntactically, it comes in a position typical for adverbials, that is, in end position after the obligatory clause elements. Although it is the final item in the local syntactic-prosodic unit, *he said* is produced at a point before the multi-unit quotation is finalised. Note that although the copular structure is semantically coherent with the

5.6 Entering Grammaticalisation? The Case of HE SAID

preceding talk, it is prosodically and syntactically disintegrated and its footing is not clear. This suggests that semantico-pragmatically, *he said* functions as an evidential parenthetical, indexing the footing of the unit in which it is integrated.

Ex. (58) shows a case similar to the previous example where HE SAID$_3$ is produced in final position in the intonation phrase and serves to index the footing of the prior speech in the unit. The excerpt is taken from an answer turn composed of a string of quotations. The LO is the co-present referent of the personal pronoun *he*.

(58) PMQs 01 Feb. 2006
LO: David Cameron (Con); PM: Tony Blair (Lab); S: Michael Martin

```
1   PM:    ↑THEN he was asked, (0.50)
2          whether (.)
3          ↑IF (.) schools wanted a return to selection by ability they
           could hAve that. (.)
4   ->     that's RIGHT ↓he said.
5   MPs:   [<<cresc>1 1>]
6   PM:    [(0.95)    ] then suddenly two weeks ago he SAYS- (0.33)
7          i guaranTEE; ((quotation continues))
```

Placed in final position, the reporting clause is prosodically integrated with a copular clause which it marks as a reported clause (*that's RIGHT he said.*, line 4). The quotation is constructed as the answer to an indirect question (↑*THEN he was asked, (0.50) whether (.)* ↑*IF (.) schools wanted (...)*, lines 1–3). Like in Ex. (57), *he said* follows the primary accent on a downstep in pitch and without an audible release of the final plosive in *said*. Syntactically, it comes in end position after the obligatory elements of the clause (i.e., subject, copula verb, and subject complement), a typical position for adverbials. Semantico-pragmatically, *he said* indexes the evidential grounding of the copula structure as a quotation, that is, it indexes a shift in footing. Without this evidential marker, *that's RIGHT* would be heard in the current speaker's voice. This shows that while it is syntactically optional as to its status as an adverbial, it is obligatory in terms of discourse coherence and turn structure. In sum, these are the features of HE SAID$_3$:

o prosodic reduction and integration in a larger intonation phrase: following the primary accent on a downstep in pitch and without an audible release of the final plosive in SAID
o mobility: final position in intonation phrase
o syntactic dependency: reanalysis as an evidential phrase

- evidential reframing of prior speech as quotation
- used as a parenthetical

The fourth type, HE SAID₄, is exemplified in Ex. (59), where the topic is VAT (Value Added Tax, transcribed as *vEe ay TEE*, line 4).

(59)   PMQs 01 Dec. 2010

LO: Ed Miliband (Lab); PM: David Cameron (Con); S: John Bercow

```
1   PM:     <<all, h, f> well first of all> let me deal with vee ay tEe
             preCISEly;>
2            because îthIs is what the FORmer chancellor,
3            °h <<all>the: m⁷ MEMber for edinburgh south west said>;
4       ->   °h <<all>he said> vEe ay TEE,
5            <<all>would have> alLOWED you;
6            to PAY off,
7            °h a sIzeable chUnk of the DEFicit;
8            [°h thAt is the pa⁷ POLicy,]
9   MPs:    [AH: : : : : : : : : : : ]
10  PM:     [(0.33) that the lAst chancellor supPORted;]
11  MPs:    [AH: : : : : : : : : : : : : : : : : ]
```

The object of interest, <<*all*> *he said*>, is produced in the initial position of the first intonation phrase, <<*all*> *he said*> *vEe ay TEE*, (line 4), of a multi-unit quotation (lines 4–7). The quotation is prepared for and pre-empted through prior metapragmatic constructions (*let me deal with vee ay tEe preCISEly; because* ↑*thIs is what the FORmer chancellor, (...) said*>;, lines 1–3).

This type of HE SAID is phonetically reduced in that it is produced in anacrusis before the first accented syllable of the intonation phrase. Semantically, it is bleached: the evidential framing it provides has been pre-empted by the metapragmatic construction and thus constitutes given information, and it is turn-constructionally redundant in that it does not contribute to the coherence and progressivity of the turn. This suggests that HE SAID₄ has been reanalysed as discourse marker. Ex. (60) shows another example of HE SAID₄.

(60)   PMQs 02 July 2008

MP: Bob Russell (LD); PM: Gordon Brown; S: Michael Martin

```
1   PM:     and AS for progress being made in afghAnistan,
2            i can Only rePORT;
3            (0.44) what sir jock STIRrup;
4            <<p,all> the chief of the defence staff has said> Only this
```

5.6 Entering Grammaticalisation? The Case of HE SAID   115

```
                  MORning;
5          ->     °hh <<all>he said> the PROgress we've made over the last few
                  months is remArkable.
6   (MP):         [((cough))]
7   PM:           [(0.44)     ] and he tAlked about bEing in helmand province;=
8                 =<<all>and said> the LAST time i was hEre-
9                 i WASn't able to come into the town at All,
10                °h it was a FULL scale bAttlefield.
11                °h NOW <<all>wE've jUst cOme twIce through the mAin street>.
```

The evidential particle is in line 5 (°hh <<all>he said> the PROgress we've made over the last few months is remArkable.). It prefaces a quotation projected by a metapragmatic construction (*and AS for progress being made in afghAnistan, i can Only rePORT; (0.44) what sir jock STIRrup; (...) has said> (...)*, lines 1–4). The metapragmatic construction provides an evidential framing of the subsequent talk. The information provided by <<*all*> *he said*> is thus given. Its anacrustic formatting goes along with semantic bleaching. Finally, the particle is turn-constructionally redundant. Ex. (61) provides further evidence that these constructions particles are indeed redundant.

(61)   PMQs 01 Nov. 2006
LO: David Cameron (Con); PM: Tony Blair (Lab); S Michael Martin

```
1   PM:       there ↑WAS of course the comprehensive report pUblished
              on the health service by the healthcare com↑mIssion;
2             °h just a few days a↑GO;
3       ->    and this is what it SAID;
4             °h there are ↑REAL improvements to applaud and celebrate?
5             °h ↑pAtients are seeing ↑REAL improvements to health care
              services in england and wales?
6             °h they're waiting ↑LESS time for treatments,
7             there are now more DOCtors,
8             more NURses,
9             and more health care pro↑FESsionals;
```

Line 3 contains a quotative construction (*and this is what it SAID;*) which pre-empts a slot for and projects the subsequent direct speech (lines 4–9). In contrast to Ex. (60) above, the direct speech is not prefaced by an evidential particle. This suggests that the quotative construction in line 3 is sufficient to index the subsequent speech as a direct quotation. This is how HE SAID$_4$ can be described:

- phonetically reduced: anacrustic
- fixed front position in first intonation phrase of quotation
- syntactically non-functional
- semantically bleached
- turn-constructionally redundant
- reanalysed as an evidential discourse marker

To sum up, I have explored the possibility of ongoing grammaticalisation, searching for the format [pronominal subject + SAY in simple aspect + bare reported clause] as a starting point in the 1978–1988 and 2003–2013 samples. The study revealed one single candidate, I SAID, in the former data set. In the latter, I identified a diversification in types instantiating the construction plus an enormous increase in type and token frequency. Here the type HE SAID was most widely used, and especially so in the question–answer turns in the sequences between the LO and PM. These findings correlate with an increased questioning activity by the LO during 2003–2013 compared to 1978–1988, and a particularly frequent use of reported speech with SAY in these question–answer sequences.

Based on the analysis presented, I propose that HE SAID has entered a path of grammaticalisation, involving the following continuum of constructions: HE SAID$_1$ as a fixed, formulaic clausal construction; HE SAID$_2$ and HE SAID$_3$ reanalysed as adverbs, used as parentheticals; and HE SAID$_4$ reanalysed as an evidential particle. This can be summarised as follows:

evidential clausal formula (HE SAID$_1$) > evidential parentheticals (HE SAID$_2$/HE SAID$_3$) > evidential discourse marker (HE SAID$_4$)

This suggests that HE SAID in the 2003–2013 data set is currently in a process of 'specialisation', one of the principles of grammaticisation – which I here call grammaticalisation – named by Hopper:

> Within a functional domain, at one stage a variety of forms with different semantic nuances may be possible; as grammaticization takes place, this variety of formal choices narrows and the smaller number of forms selected assume more general grammatical meanings. (Hopper 1991: 22)

Kärkkäinen (2003) and Imo (2009) study formulaic uses of pronoun + SAY and variants in American English and German contexts other than political discourse. Their findings suggest that the formulaicity (and potentially grammaticalisation) of HE SAID is a general phenomenon across speech communities. I show that the format [Temporal adverbial + THE PRIME MINISTER + SAY + quotation] examined in Section 5.7 constitutes a more local, genre-specific formation.

Despite the matching evidence from grammaticalisation research, a potential objection to the analysis presented above might be that the processes identified constitute pragmaticalisation rather than grammaticalisation in that the variants of *he said* are functional in the construction of discourse and the signalling of footing rather than being functional on the sentence-level. Diewald and others (see Diewald 2011 for a literature review) have argued that this depends on how grammar is conceptualised:

> If grammar (a grammatical sign) contains an indexical structure, it encodes 'pragmatic' information as part of its own inherent semantic structure. In other words; as grammar contains semanticized, schematized, and abstracted information about the localization of the utterance in the communicative situation, it is fundamentally rooted in pragmatics (cf. Givón 1979). To the extent that grammaticalization is the development of such an anchoring function in a linguistic item, it may be said that pragmaticalization is a subprocess of grammaticalization. (Diewald 2011: 458)

Diewald views pragmaticalisation as a 'subprocess of grammaticalisation'. I suggest going one step further and considering that if it is assumed that grammar stems from language use, a separation between pragmaticalisation and grammaticalisation may not be needed, since grammar and language use cannot be separated.

5.7 Entering Grammaticalisation? The Case of [Temporal adverbial + THE PRIME MINISTER + SAY + quotation]

This section is concerned with a second case study on how type and token frequency, that is, the repetition of linguistic structures and categories, occasions conventionalisation. In contrast to the case of HE SAID (Section 5.6), the structure examined here is specific to the activity of PMQs, representing a pre-patterned chunk, that is, a formula which makes the emerging turn type recognisable as a question turn under construction.

Recall that in the two data sets, THE PRIME MINISTER constitutes the most frequent nominal subject, with temporal adverbials being the most common choice in terms of adverbials in finite reporting clauses. I found that – at least in the 2003–2013 sample – there is a correlation in use between THE PRIME MINISTER and temporal adverbials in reporting clauses (Table 5.22): 51.4 per cent of the 2003–2013 finite reporting clauses with the NP THE PRIME MINISTER in subject position have a temporal adverbial. Even though the 1978–1988 sample is small, note that in both

Table 5.22 *Correlation between subject THE PRIME MINISTER and temporal adverbials in finite reporting clauses (1978–1988, 2003–2013)*

Reporting clauses with THE PRIME MINISTER as subject	+ Temporal Adverbial	– Temporal Adverbial
1978–1988 (n=2)	50 % (1)	50 % (1)
2003–2013 (n=37)	51.4 % (19)	48.6 % (18)

data sets, at least half of the uses of THE PRIME MINISTER in subject position co-occur with an adverbial of time.

I now explore the implications of these patterned co-occurrences to build reporting clauses.

1978–1988
Ex. (16′) illustrates the only case from the 1978–1988 sample where the use of THE PRIME MINISTER in subject position combines with adverbials of time in the reporting clause.

(16′)   PMQs 03 May 1988

MP1: Ernie Ross (Lab); PM: Margaret Thatcher (Con); S: Bernard Weatherill

```
1   MP:        [the prIme minister has said toDAY,]
2   MPs:       [mur mur mur mur mur mur mur mur mur      ]
3   MP:   ->   [(.) and last THURSday;]
4   MPs:       [mur mur mur mur mur mur]
5   MP:        [that she expects the SAME level of sErvice;]
6   MPs:       [mur mur mur mur mur mur mur mur mur mur mur]
7   MP:        delivered at the sAme STANDard of service-
8              ((click)) °h with uh: and (thus) resulting in the SAME community
               charge (xxx xxx xxx length and breadth xxx) the united kIngdom;
9   MP:        (.) does the prime minister not underSTAND; ((turn continues))
```

There are two adverbials of time in the reporting clause. The first, done in the form of an adverb phrase, is prosodically integrated with the subject and verb of the reporting clause (*the prIme minister has said toDAY,* line 1). After a pause, the second, shaped as a noun phrase, is incrementally produced in a new intonation phrase (*and last THURSday*, line 3), coordinated with the former unit through *and*. There follows indirect, *that*-prefaced speech (*that she expects the SAME level of sErvice; (. . .)*, lines 5, 7–8) in a new intonation phrase.

Note that the two adverbials of time are produced in positions subsequent to the verb. The analysis of the 2003–2013 sample reveals an

5.7 Entering Grammaticalisation? Quoting in question turns 119

emergent formulaic use with the temporal adverbials in initial position. This is investigated in what follows.

2003–2013

The 2003–2013 data set has cases similar to the single 1978–1988 example. Ex. (62) demonstrates a reporting clause with THE PRIME MINISTER as the subject, and an optional adverbial of time.

(62)   PMQs 13 Oct. 2004
LO: Michael Howard (Con); PM: Tony Blair (Lab); S: Michael Martin

```
1   MPs:        [mur mur mur mur mur mur mur mur mur mur mur ]
2   LO:    ->   [the=uh the prIme minister said on MONday,=]
3   MPs:        [mur mur mur mur]
4   LO:         [=that he wants] to see a conSENsus on pEnsions policy.
```

As in Ex. (16'), the subject, verb, and temporal adverbial are produced in a single intonation phrase, *the prIme minister said on MONday,* (line 2). The temporal adverbial (*on MONday*) follows the verb (*said*), and the *that*-prefaced indirect speech is produced in a new intonation unit (*that he wants to see a conSENsus on pEnsions policy,* line 4).

Nevertheless, note that in 42 per cent (eight) of the nineteen cases where the subject THE PRIME MINISTER occurs with a temporal adverbial in a finite reporting clause, the subject, verb, adverbial, and subsequent reported speech emerge in a recurrent serial pattern, which can be schematically described as a format with more abstract and fixed slots [Temporal adverbial + THE PRIME MINISTER + SAY + quotation]. This repeated, serial use of elements, which varies in prosodic chunking, points to the emergence of a formulaic construction in the 2003–2013 data set. Ex. (63) exemplifies such a case:

(63)   PMQs 24 May 2006
MP: Shailesh Vara (Con); PM: Tony Blair (Lab); S: Michael Martin

```
1   MP:   -> in nineteen ninety SEven;=
2         -> =the prIme minister says that things can only get BETter.
```

The MP first produces an adverbial of time (*in nineteen ninety SEven;=,* line 1) before the subject, verb, and quotation in the next intonation phrase (*=the prIme minister says that things can only get*

BETter, line 2). Ex. (64) illustrates another example, where the components are skilfully produced in three prosodic chunks.

(64)   PMQs 01 Nov. 2006

LO: David Cameron (Con); PM: Tony Blair (Lab); S: Michael Martin

```
1  MPs:       [j sh j sh j sh j ]
2  LO:    -> [back in JANuary,]
3  MPs:       [j sh j sh j sh j sh j sh ]
4  LO:    -> [the PRIME minister sAid;]
5  MPs:       [j sh j sh j sh sh j sh j sh j sh j sh sh j sh j sh j sh
6  LO: ->    [(0.30) i'm ABsolutely hAppy that gOrdon brown will be my
   MPs:      sh j sh j  ]
   LO:       succEssor;]
```

Here the adverbial of time (*back in JANuary,* line 2), the subject and verb (*the PRIME minister sAid;* line 4), and the quotation (*i'm ABsolutely hAppy that (...),* line 6) come in three separate intonation phrases. Recall also the observation in Section 5.5 about such an incremental production of core elements as a typical resource in political oratory to create suspense and maintain audience attention.

In sum, the findings point to an ongoing formulaicity of SAY reporting clauses with THE PRIME MINISTER as the subject. As was pointed out earlier, reported speech with THE PRIME MINISTER as source makes the turn under way typically recognisable as a question turn. This indicates that it is not only the case that reporting clauses citing the Prime Minister become fixed, but also that the design of question turns where such quotations are implemented as prefatory material is emergent as a formula in the 2003–2013 sample.

5.8 Summary and Conclusions

It has been demonstrated that – compared to the period of 1978–1988 – the more recent period of 2003–2013 shows a rise in the LO's questioning activity. This has led to PMQs as an activity format which culminates in the question–answer sequences between the LO and PM. The analysis presented in Chapter 5 has revealed a dramatic increase in the frequency of reporting clauses in the LOs' question turns and PMs' answer turns.

5.8 Summary and Conclusions

5.8.1 Reporting Clauses as Constructions

In both data sets, the subject and the verb SAY are always represented in the reporting clauses.[17] Based on these empirical findings, I conceptualise the reporting clause as a construction [Subject + SAY] with more and less 'central members' (Bybee 2013: 13; Bybee and Eddington 2006: 327), where 'exemplars with higher token frequency appear to function as central members' (Bybee and Eddington 2006: 326; see also Bybee 2013). Figures 5.1 and 5.2 illustrate the exemplar clouds of the 1978–1988 and 2003–2013 reporting clauses. In keeping with Bybee's conventions, the central members of these exemplar clouds are expressed in capital letters, and the non-central ones in lower case and parentheses.

The two figures show that in 1978–1988, I as well as HE and THE PRIME MINISTER, and SAID represent the central members of the exemplar cloud, in having the highest token frequency; in 2003–2013, it is HE and SAID.[18] What is crucial is that in the 1978–1988 sample, these subjects exclusively refer to/address government members. During 2003–2013 HE is used to refer to/address male sources on both sides of the House.

In terms of the non-central members shown, I included those with the highest token frequency, although the list for members to fill the subject and verb slots is much longer. Here as well it becomes visible that in the 1978–1988 subject slot, only government members (the present minister for the health service) are represented, which suggests a focus on the authority of the government (as a quoted source). This contrasts with the 2003–2013

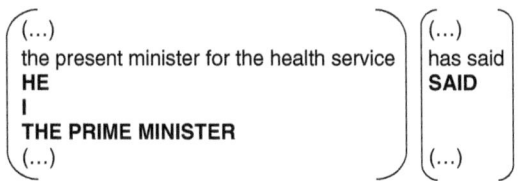

Figure 5.1 1978–1988 exemplar cloud of reporting clauses.

---

[17] This may not come as a surprise since subject and verb are treated as core elements in clauses with low-transitive predicates like *say*, but note that there are activities, such as narratives, where unexpressed subjects are common (see, e.g., Travis and Lindstrom 2016).
[18] Because of the small size of the 1978–1988 sample, the frequencies are so low that the differences between I/HE/THE PRIME MINISTER seem negligible. For this reason, I treat them all as central members.

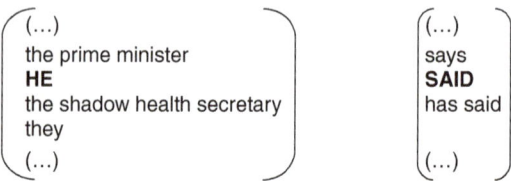

Figure 5.2 2003–2013 exemplar cloud of reporting clauses.

subject slots, which include members of the government (the prime minister) and of the opposition parties (the shadow health secretary, they) among its highly frequent members, indicative of an increasing focus on the confrontation between the PM and the LO as well as a general polarisation between the two sides of the House. In terms of the verb, HAS SAID is the second-most frequent token in 1978–1988, while in 2003–2013 it is SAYS.

Bybee argues that '[e]xtensions of the construction will be based on [the] central members' of a construction (Bybee 2013: 61). My analysis has shown in two case studies that type and token frequency of the subject and verb provided the basis for formulaic and even grammaticalised extensions:

1. During 2003–2013, the pronoun HE and the verbal form SAID represent the most frequent types of clause members, subject and verb. At the same time, HE and SAID are the most frequent tokens. In a study which included detailed phonetic-prosodic analysis, I argued that HE SAID has entered a path of grammaticalisation, which can be understood as an extension of the construction:

evidential clausal formula (HE SAID$_1$) > evidential parentheticals (HE SAID$_2$ /HE SAID$_3$) > evidential discourse marker (HE SAID$_4$)

2. I also found that reporting clauses can include indirect objects and adverbials, which do not differ in their frequency but vary between the two data sets: indirect object, adverbials of place and of time (1978–1988), versus indirect object, adverbials of place (also figurative), of time, of manner, and of respect (2003–2013). The case study on the sequence [Temporal adverbial + THE PRIME MINISTER + SAY + quotation] revealed that temporal adverbials in the reporting clause are also on the way to becoming part of a formulaic construction, losing their free compositionality. However, more research is needed to explore how adverbials are used as patterned extensions of this construction.

5.8　Summary and Conclusions

In sum, the findings suggest that the reporting clauses with SAY represent stripped-down constructions reduced to their core elements, the subject and verb, only. Such a syntactic form is enabled by the low transitivity of the verb SAY, which may account for the frequency of SAY as a quotative in the PMQs data. This form allows speakers to indicate quotations without needing to provide past recipients or other circumstantial details of the original situated context from which the quotation was taken. Furthered by the neutral semantics of SAY, speakers can choose to frame positions as context-free quotations, tailoring them as evidential building blocks for context-specific in situ actions and goals.

5.8.2　General Tendencies

The comparative analysis of the reporting clauses has revealed a general diversification of categories between the 1978–1988 and 2003–2013 samples. This may seem a natural outcome since the latter is much larger in size. However, a comparison reveals patterned differences which point to the following tendencies.

Agentival Authoritative Sources
What both data sets share is that reporting clauses are delivered with active verbs, framing the sources as agentival subjects. The sources themselves show in the majority a membership categorisation which constructs them as authoritative due to their office and function (in the state), which lends them elite, high status. This membership categorisation is reflective of and constructs the institutional context in which PMQs is performed.

Densification
In 1978–1988 and 2003–2013, subject NPs are heavy-headed if they do not occur as pronouns. This suggests dense information packaging, which can be explained by two related factors:

1. the time pressures under which turns at talk are delivered; and
2. a speaker orientation to name sources in a self-explanatory and disambiguating fashion, that is, to package them in a minimally but highly recognisable format.

The 2003–2013 sample additionally shows a frequent use of NPs in adverbials (along with PPs), for which I do not have evidence in the 1978–1988 data set. These are not necessarily heavy-headed but are still more tightly packaged than PPs. This suggests an increased tendency towards dense information packaging compared to the 1978–1988 data.

Polarisation

1978–1988 speakers almost exclusively recruit government sources, while in 2003–2013 they come from the government, the opposition, and (to a minor extent) from other groups. This trend towards polarisation is nicely reflected in the use of personal pronouns, with the stock of singular forms *I, he, she, it* (1978–1988) expanded to include the first- and third-person plural forms *we* and *they* in 2003–2013. The use of non-governmental sources can further be seen as a sign of democratisation, described as follows.

A More Interpersonal Style: Democratisation and Personalisation

As opposed to 1978–1988, there are 2003–2013 examples where speakers use continued pronominal third-person forms of address over turn boundaries in responsive moves. This indicates on the one hand that the organisation of sequences is more interactional and interpersonal, but on the other hand that speakers display less deference to the authority of office. It is also a sign of personalisation, which comes off as a more aggressive and confrontational style. Along the same lines, the 2003–2013 use of names (instead of professional titles) is more interpersonal, which can be interpreted as a trend towards personalisation and democratisation, described as the 'reduction of overt markers of power asymmetry' (Fairclough 1992: 98; as cited in Leech *et al.* 2009: 259; see also Leech *et al.*'s 2009 analysis of changing referring expressions to *the President of the United States* as a sign of democratisation).

Credibility Enhancement

The packaging of the 2003–2013 reporting clauses further suggests a growing orientation towards the credibility of speakers, which on the one hand becomes visible in an increased use of counter-interest sources to back up claims. On the other hand, while the proportion of circumstantial adverbials and the dominance of temporal adverbials in the reporting clauses has remained the same, it is noticeable that the second-most common adverbial in the 2003–2013 sample details the speech event where the quoted speech was produced. This figurative use of place adverbials along with those of respect and manner are completely absent from the 1978–1988 data. This indicates an orientation to greater detail in the delivery of past speech, which has been described as a strategy for credibility enhancement (van Dijk 2014: 269).

CHAPTER 6

Reported Clauses

In this chapter I analyse the (multi-)clausal units of what is framed as a quotation by the reporting clause, exploring patterned formal packages in the 1978–1988 and 2003–2013 data sets. From the perspective of the radio listeners, the packaging of quotations in the 1978–1988 data set is achieved through bundles of phonetic-prosodic, lexico-syntactic, and what I call audio-visual resources, that is, the visual manipulation of paper, which can sometimes be heard as crackling by the radio audience. Television audiences (and online users) perceive quotations as embodied performances, which involve visual-spatial embodied cues and sometimes the manipulation of documents.

I explore how these patterned packages of quotations compare between the 1978–1988 and 2003–2013 data sets, examining how these packages are distributed over turn types and speaker roles and whether new packages have come into use and/or some have been lost over time. To this end, I analysed the formal features of reported clauses in the real time of interaction and established categories based on the bundles of features found. I compared these categories between the two data sets and calculated the relative frequencies across participant roles and turn types.

This chapter shows that these formal packages can be generally categorised in grammatical terms: indirect speech, (types of) direct speech, and a third, more ambiguous format positioned 'in between' direct and indirect speech.[1] Considering a single 2003–2013 case in more detail, however, I suggest that these grammatical formats are not fixed, but that reporting clauses can be 'repackaged' in the emerging turn. In addition, independent of these grammatical formats, speakers in the 2003–2013 data set show a heightened speaker orientation towards building trust with their audience. They attempt to achieve credibility through demonstrating evidential access, which is claimed

---

[1] This metaphor is adopted from Günthner's (2000) study, entitled 'Zwischen direkter und indirekter Rede' (*In between direct and indirect speech*). The category also relates to Tannen's (2007) 'fadeout, fadein' dialogue.

through the staging of original documents and the use of the formula (AND) I QUOTE, which is also deployed as practice for framing a fourth type of quotation, that is, mixed quotations.

Based on these observations, the chapter is organised into the following sections: I begin with a review of past research on the contextualisation of reported speech in spoken data (6.1). Next indirect speech (6.2), quotations which are ambiguous with respect to their grammatical classification (6.3), and direct speech (6.4) are described and compared between the 1978–1988 and 2003–2013 data sets. I further discuss how quotations are repackaged contingent on the organisation of speech and turns in time (6.5) and how the formula (AND) I QUOTE is functional in framing entire or only smaller portions of quotations as verbatim (6.6). The chapter is completed with a summary and conclusions (6.7).

6.1 Past Research

To my knowledge, there is no substantial research on the phonetic-prosodic, lexico-syntactic, and visual contextualisation of quotations in political discourse, let alone parliamentary interaction (but see Atkinson 1984 on rhetorical structures in political speeches, outlined in Chapter 7). For this reason, the following review considers results generated from non-political spoken interaction.

To begin with vocal cues, systematic research on the prosodic contextualisation of reported speech in English is sparse. In her study of mundane interaction, Couper-Kuhlen (1999) points out that to make their talk coherent, participants need to index shifts in footing, which can be accomplished through animating the reported speech in a voice that is audibly different from the current speaker's own voice, that is, through prosodic and paralinguistic features. This finding is supported by Holt (1996), who shows how vocal resources are deployed for implicit stance-taking towards the reported talk (cf. also Niemelä 2005). Couper-Kuhlen further provides evidence that such 'vocal framing' (Couper-Kuhlen 1999: 23) is sufficient for indexing a shift in footing and constructing coherent talk when the reported speech is produced without a quotative.[2] Interestingly, she notes that 'non-projected quotation' (Klewitz and Couper-Kuhlen 1999: 468) of this kind is a common practice in her data, a finding which contrasts with the observations made for the

---

[2] Related to this, Mathis and Yule report on a 'paralinguistic modulation of voice quality' (Mathis and Yule 1994: 64), involving changes in pitch register, in what they call 'zero quotatives'.

PMQs data, where quotations are practically always lexically marked by quotative verbs. Klewitz and Couper-Kuhlen complement these findings by detailing the prosodic and phonetic features used to animate reported speech in English conversation. It is shown that the prosodic marking of reported speech can involve:

- 'a simple increase in overall pitch or volume' (Klewitz and Couper-Kuhlen 1999: 465) or
- 'global changes in speech rate' (Klewitz and Couper-Kuhlen 1999: 482) or
- 'a shift to perceptually isochronous timing' (Klewitz and Couper-Kuhlen 1999: 465) or
- a combination of some of these parameters:

> Clusters of prosodic shifts as marks of reported speech are actually more common than simple ones in our corpus, and they are often accompanied by changes in voice quality. The fact that multiple prosodic and paralinguistic shifts co-occur is indicative of the nature of the contextualization process involved [...]. The shifts contexualize the speech as reported, that is they serve as quasi-iconic signs of a shift in indexical ground [...]. (Klewitz and Couper-Kuhlen 1999: 468)

However, the authors concede that not all instances of reported speech in their data are marked by prosodic shifts nor do those shifts necessarily coincide with the boundaries of the speech reported. Rhythmic pausing is found as a unique resource for marking the left-hand boundary, that is, that between the quotative and the reported speech. This is corroborated by Jansen *et al.* (2001), who find a stronger likelihood of a prosodic break preceding direct speech than indirect speech (but the right-hand boundary does not have similar marking).

In sum, these studies show that prosodic cues are potentially functional in signalling a shift in footing to construct discourse coherence, in animating the voices of characters whose speech is claimed to be reported, and in marking the boundaries of quotations.

Günthner (2000) on German conversation reveals that the grammatical distinctions between direct and indirect speech do not lend themselves as descriptive categories for reported speech in spoken language. She proposes an alternative categorisation, drawing on prosodic and syntactic parameters (see also Günthner 1997).

In contrast to studies concerned with the prosodic and grammatical contextualisation of quotations in spoken interaction, quoting and embodiment has recently become a burgeoning research area. Perhaps the most radical finding is that bodily movements, such as dancing steps, can be treated as 'bodily quotations' (Keevalik 2010: 402). Here the teacher demonstrates students' dancing steps, simultaneously describing the movements for instruction. Based on Swedish, Estonian, and English data, Keevallik argues 'that verbal and bodily quoting are essentially the same kinds of activities. They serve to create coherence, make sense, provide proof, and give evidence' (Keevalik 2010: 402; see also Good 2015 on 'reported actions' and Sidnell 2006 on 'reenactments').

In a follow-up study, she shows how these bodily quotations are projected by specific, syntactically incomplete constructions, with the bodily movement filling in what has been left unsaid:

> The embodiments as a rule provide the new and focused information of the unit. The feature that binds all the patterns together is temporality: language first, embodiment later. The projective capacity of grammar is used to accomplish an interactional unit that includes a grammatically obligatory embodied component. (Keevallik 2013: 11)

Park (2009) finds a patterned correlation between the grammatical and embodied framing of quotations ascribed to self and co-present participants on the one hand and non-present third parties on the other in a study on Korean embodied interaction between friends and colleagues (cf. further Goodwin 2007 on reported speech in Aphasic embodied interaction). Stec *et al.* (2016) illustrate that – in addition to voicing – gaze, facial expression, body posture, and to a minor extent gesture are functional in signalling shifts in footing in narratives. Blackwell *et al.* (2015) reveal a correlation between the type of quotative and the type of reported speech (direct, indirect) with respect to bodily demonstrations. Here it was found that indirect speech introduced by *say* was performed with less vocal and bodily demonstration (see Clark and Gerrig 1990 for the distinction between direct and indirect speech as demonstrations and descriptions).

One dimension which combines the studies mentioned is how bodily and vocal resources are deployed to display the speaker's stance towards the quoted speech or bodily action. Importantly, Good (2015: 679) adds to these speaker-centred findings an audience perspective relevant to the present analysis: he observes that reported actions 'bring to life past events and make them accessible and assessable for a current audience'. It is shown that this can also be claimed for the reported speech at PMQs.

This literature review has shown that the prosodic and bodily contextualisation of reported speech serves to signal shifts in footing, perform demonstrations, and display speaker stance. Prosodic cues are especially designed to animate figures, create coherence, and index initial boundaries of reported speech. Bodily movements can themselves be quoted as bodily actions which can be performed in syntactically projected turn-constructional slots. In this way, these reported actions are made accessible and assessable for recipients. Here *say* seems to be a quotative which is least deployed in relation with such bodily or vocal demonstrations. I now turn to the analysis of reported clauses at PMQs.

6.2 Indirect Speech

In both data sets, quotations grammatically marked as indirect speech form the majority of quotations. The lexico-syntactic marking of indirect speech in English involves the potential production of the complementiser *that*, a possible backshift of the verb, and possible changes in pronominal expressions.

The complementiser *that* as an optional choice in complement clauses has received the most attention in past literature. For instance, Thompson and Mulac (1991b) argue that the production of the complementiser *that* can be predicted based on features of the CTP and the subject of the complement clause. Biber analyses the (non-)production of *that* as a normative feature of genres. Among the four genres (conversation, fiction, news, academic prose), conversation shows the highest percentage of *that* omission, as it is 'spoken and produced on-line', has 'involved and interpersonal purposes', and is 'casual and informal in tone' (Biber 1999: 145). Academic prose, on the other hand, which is characterised by 'careful production circumstances; an expository, informational purpose; and a formal tone' (Biber 1999: 145) has the lowest percentage of *that* omission.

I demonstrate that, as far as indirect speech is concerned, the main differentiating factors between the 1978–1988 and 2003–2013 samples include the production of the complementiser as well as the distribution of indirect quotations across turn types and speaker roles.

1978–1988
The 1978–1988 sample shows a tendency towards quotations which are grammatically formatted as indirect speech (seventeen out of twenty-four). The majority (sixteen) have explicit lexico-syntactic marking through the complementiser *that*. Table 6.1 summarises the relative frequencies of these variants across turn types and speaker roles.

In absolute terms, MPs' question turns are the home of indirect speech in the 1978–1988 sample. Moreover, the indirect speech is overwhelmingly built of past declarative utterances. To describe their prosodic formatting, the indirect speech can – but does not necessarily have to – be marked through

Table 6.1 *Relative frequencies of indirect speech across turn types and speaker roles (1978–1988)*

Turn types and speaker roles	IDS + *that*	IDS + *that* – omission	IDS wh-clause	Total
MPs Question turns (n=275)	4.0% (11)	0.4% (1)	0% (0)	4.4% (12)
Answer turns to MPs Question turns (n=275)	0% (0)	0% (0)	0% (0)	0% (0)
LO Question turns (n=44)	2.3% (1)	0% (0)	0% (0)	2.3% (1)
Answer turns to LO Question turns (n=44)	0% (0)	0% (0)	2.3% (1)	2.3% (1)
Leader of the Lib /SDP Question turns (n=12)	16.7% (2)	0% (0)	0% (0)	16.7% (2)
Answer turns to Lib/SDP Question turns (n=12)	8.3% (1)	0% (0)	0% (0)	8.3% (1)

single, global cues. While the left-hand boundary of the indirect speech is not consistently bounded in prosodic terms, for example, in that it begins in a new intonation phrase following the reporting clause, the sample shows a clear prosodic marking of the right-hand edge.

Before I illustrate the general case where *that* is produced, I begin with the one exception where *that* is omitted (Ex. 21′).[3] Here the pronominal change and the backshift of the verb function as grammatical cues of indirect speech. The reported speech, *who THREW at her one thousand jOb applications saying he hadn't got a JOB;*, is in lines 4–6.

(21′)   PMQs 03 May 1988
MP: Timothy Devlin (Con); PM: Margaret Thatcher (Con); S: Bernard Weatherill

```
1  MP:        dOes my right honourable frIend (.) recall mEeting mister eric
              FLETcher.
2             the thirty five year old mIddlesbrough man [during her tOur
3  MPs:                                                  [mur mur mur mur
   MP:        of TEEsside; (0.39)]
   MPs:       mur mur mur mur mur]
4  MP:   ->   [who THREW;]
5  MPs:       [sh sh sh   ]
```

---

[3] This example differs from the rest of the collection in many ways: the ascribed source constitutes an ordinary member of the public, a constituent of the questioning MP; the quotative comes in a nonfinite form of *say*; and the reported speech is produced as part of a mini-narrative scenario.

6.2   Indirect Speech

```
6    MP:    -> [(0.30) who THREW at her one thousand jOb applications saying
7    MPs:      [<<p>mur mur mur mur mur mur mur mur mur mur mur mur mur mur>
     MP:    -> he hAdn't got a JOB; (0.64)]
     MPs:      sh sh sh sh sh sh sh sh sh]
8    MP:       [and would (1.46) and (0.94) and (.) was (.) was she
9    MPs:      [sh sh sh sh sh sh sh sh sh sh sh sh sh sh sh sh sh
     MP:       ((turn continues))
```

The ascribed source of the quotation (*mister eric FLETcher. the thirty five year old MIDdlesbrough man;*) is named in lines 1–2. The reported clause *he hAdn't got a JOB* is indicated by the preceding quotative verb *saying* in the same intonation phrase (line 6).

The change of pronoun (*he*) and backshift of the verb (*hAdn't got*) in the quotation are indicative of indirect speech. The complementiser *that*, which is optional in indirect speech, is not produced. There is no change in voice quality and/or pitch range which would make it heard as an animated voice. Nevertheless, the indirect speech is produced in faster tempo and with dense accentuation: both the primary verb and object have accents, a prosodic contextualisation which sets the quotation off from the beginning of the intonation phrase, where the quotative verb is produced. The speaker continues his turn with speech characterised by self-repair *[(0.64) and ↑would] [(1.46) and] [(0.94) and (.) was (.) was she]* (line 8). The reset in pitch and the interrogative structure mark the end of the indirect speech in retrospect.

Nevertheless, the overwhelming majority of indirect quotations are produced with the complementiser *that*. Ex. (65) exemplifies an indirect quotation with the complementiser *that*. Like (Ex. 21'), it has a nonfinite quotative.

(65)   PMQs 05 May 1980
MP: Christopher Price (Lab); PM: Margaret Thatcher (Con); S: George Thomas

```
1    MPs:       [j j j j j j j j j j j j j j j j j  ]
2    MP:        [(3.29) ↑would the prime minister recon]SIDer her remarks;
3               (0.43)
4               just After (0.32) the brIxton (0.29) PROBlems;
5         ->    °h in SAYing;
6         ->    <<p>that unemployment;> (.)
7         ->    <<p> was nOt (.) a primary CAUSE;>
8         ->    <<p>(.) <<all>in in> those MATters;>
9               (0.57) ↑doesn't she think (.) in Any case. ((turn continues))
```

The reported clause (*that unemployment; (.) was nOt (.) a primary CAUSE; (.) <<all> in in> those MATters;*, lines 6–8) follows the nonfinite quotative verb (*SAYing;*, line 5). The implied subject, *the prime minister*, of the nonfinite in-clause, which refers to the ascribed source, is in line 2. Grammatically, the quotation is cued as indirect speech by the complementiser *that*, the backshift of the verb *was*, and the change of the demonstrative pronoun *those*. Prosodically, the quotation is set off from the prior talk in that it begins in a separate intonation phrase and is produced in a slightly softer voice than what was said before. Following a medium pause and a prosodic reset, there begins a new interrogative structure, *(0.57) ↑doesn't she think (.) in Any case.* (line 9), which marks the right-hand boundary of the indirect speech in retrospect. Ex. (66) exemplifies another case of prosodic emphasis. This time, the quotative comes in a finite form of the verb.

(66)   PMQs 03 Nov. 1983
MP: Norman Atkinson (Lab); PM: Margaret Thatcher (Con); S: Bernard Weatherill

```
1    MPs:      [mur mur mur mur mur mur mur mur ]
2    MP:       [0.80) dId she this morning REMons]trate with her secretary of
               state for emplOyment  (1.04)
3       ->     who SAID that unemplOyment had gone dOwn, (0.56)
4              when REALly he mEant; (0.68)
5              that the nUmber of people claiming unemployment BENefit had gone
               down,
```

The reporting clause and the reported clause are produced in one intonation phrase (*who SAID that unemplOyment had gone dOwn*, line 3). The complementiser (*that*) and backshift of the verb (*had gone dOwn*) mark the quotation grammatically as indirect speech. The slot of the ascribed source is filled by a relative pronoun, which refers to the antecedent in line 2 (*her secretary of state for emplOyment.*). The prosodic contextualisation of the reported clause makes it stand out from the surrounding talk through dense accentuation. With *go down* considered a two-word expression, the quotation has accents on every content word or expression (*unemplOyment, gone dOwn*). The quotative *SAID* is integrated into this emphatic structure with the primary accent in the intonation phrase. Note that the left-hand boundary of the quotation is only signalled lexically (through the quotative verb) but not prosodically. Next the speaker gives his interpretation of what the ascribed source meant (*when REALly he mEant;* line 4), at the same time contextualising the right-end boundary of the quotation in retrospect. Here any number of content words do not have accents (*that the nUmber of people claiming unemployment BENefit had gone down,* line 5), which supports the observation that dense accentuation is used to make the quotation stand out. This is, nevertheless, not always the case. In Ex. (67), which again has a finite quotative verb, the reporting clause rather than the quotation is prosodically marked.

(67)   PMQs 09 Nov. 1978
LLD: David Steel (Lib); PM: James Callaghan (Labour); S: George Thomas

```
1    PM:       °h uhm that let let me say to the right honourable g? right
               honourable gentleman-
2              °h i'm ↑stIll waiting to hear from FORD;
3              and i ↑cAnnot really beLIEVE;
4         ->   °h them when their SPOKESman sAys;
5         ->   that they don't know what efFECT;
6         ->   the impact of this wage settlement is going to have on the price
          ->   of their CARS next year.
7              °h it seems to me almost (.) VERy unlikely that a company of that
               sIze;
8              should take decIsions about PAY,
9              without KNOWing in advance,
10             how it's [going to feed THROUGH into their prices. ]
11   MPs:               [h h h h h h h h h h h h h h h h h h h h h][h h h ]
12                                                                 [(0.32)]
```

In line 4, the PM produces the ascribed source and the quotative, indexing what follows as reported speech (*(. . .) when their SPOKESman sAys;*). The dense accentuation on the subject and verb of the reporting clause adds emphasis to the talk. The subsequent quotation begins in a new intonation phrase but there is no audible shift in the prosodic setting. Grammatically, the complementiser *that* marks the reported speech as indirect (*that they don't know what efFECT; (. . .)*, lines 5–6; other grammatical markers are the change in pronouns *they* and *their*). Following an audible inbreath, the PM positions himself towards the quotation (*°h it seems to me almost (.) VERy unlikely that a company of that sIze; (. . .)*, lines 7–10), which closes off the quotation in retrospect.

The present analysis has shown that the grammatical features of indirect speech form consistent features of categorisation for quotations in the 1978–1988 data set. The grammatical cueing of indirect speech may be accompanied by global prosodic marking (but this need not necessarily be the case – instead the reporting clause may be prosodically marked), which adds extra emphasis. The indirect speech, however, is generally not heard as being uttered in an animated voice, to characterise the source quoted.

As regards the prosodic chunking of indirect speech, the data do not show a uniform trend as regards the left-hand boundary. Almost half of the instances (including the indirect speech in the LO's question turn) show a consistent pattern in that the indirect speech is produced in a new intonation phrase separate from the preceding reporting clause. The other cases are rather diverse, with both the source and the quotative or the quotative alone integrated into the same intonation phrase as (portions of) the indirect speech. Here the complementiser *that* can even be chunked together with the reporting clause before the quotation begins in the next intonation phrase. This finding suggests that the complementiser could also be conceptualised as part of the reporting clause, a possibility which should be explored on the basis of a larger collection.

Nevertheless, the left-hand boundary of the indirect speech is always made available through the reporting clause. The right-hand edge of the indirect speech in the 1978–1988 data set is consistently made recognisable in retrospect through prosodic and lexico-semantic cues which signal that the speaker has moved on to produce the next building block of the action turn.

2003–2013

Corresponding to the most common format in the 1978–1988 data set, most cases of indirect speech are marked by the complementiser *that*, although there is a 2003–2013 increase in bare indirect speech. Taken together, the interaction between the LO and PM is the locus where most indirect quotations are produced (Tables 6.2a, b).[4] Here bare indirect speech is even more often used than *that*-prefaced indirect speech, which suggests that this is due to a more interactional style. Taking these formal variants together and looking at individual turn types, indirect speech is most frequently used in the question turns by the Leader of the Liberal Democrats, while in the MPs' question turns it is the most infrequent compared to the other turn types and speaker roles.

To begin with prosodic contextualisation, the indirect speech can – but does not necessarily have to – be marked through single, global cues. While the left-hand boundary of the indirect speech is not always prosodically

---

[4] When comparing the relative frequencies of quotations and reporting clauses, the numbers do not match. This is because there may be more than one reporting clause preceding the quotation (e.g., in repair). On the other hand, one reporting clause may introduce more than one quotation.

6.2 Indirect Speech

Table 6.2a *Relative frequencies of indirect speech across turn types and speaker roles (MPs, LOs, and PMs, 2003–2013)*

Turn types and speaker roles (2003–2013)	IDS + *that*	IDS + *that*-omission	IDS wh-clause	Total
MP Question turns (n=828)	3.9% (32)	1.2% (10)	0% (0)	5.1% (42)
Answer turns to MP Question turns (n=828)	5.3% (44)	1.9% (16)	0% (0)	7.2% (60)
LO Question turns (n=257)	10.9% (28)	12.5% (32)	0% (0)	23.4% (60)
Answer turns to LO Question turns (n=257)	10.1% (26)	12.5% (32)	0% (0)	22.6% (58)

Table 6.2b *Relative frequencies of indirect speech in question–answer sequences between the Leader of the Liberal Democrats and the PM (2003–2010)*

Turn types and speaker roles (2003–2010)	IDS + *that*	IDS + *that*-omission	IDS wh-clause	Total
LLD Question turns (n=56)	17.9% (10)	3.6% (2)	0% (0)	21.5% (12)
Answer turns to LLD Question turns (n=56)	10.7% (6)	5.4% (3)	0% (0)	16.1% (9)

marked, the sample shows a clear prosodic marking of the right-hand edge in other- and third-party quotations, which represent the vast majority in the 2003–2013 data set (see the analysis of sources in Chapter 5). Consider Ex. (68), where the indirect speech is prefaced by a *that*-complementiser. It can be directly compared to the 1978–1988 examples shown, in being taken from an MP's turn.

(68)   PMQs 23 May 2007
MP1: Dr Tony Wright (Lab); PM: Tony Blair (PM); S: Michael Martin

```
1   S:      [dOctor tOny WRIGHT, ]
2   MPs:    [1 1 1 1 1 1 1 1 1 1] ((cough))
3           (0.80)
4   MP1:    <<all>thank you mister SPEAker>,
5           tha' (.) thas my honourable fr' my right honourable friend
            NOticed;
6     ->    (0.24) that (.) the FORmer head;
7     ->    (0.54) of his deLIVery unit,
```

```
8        -> sir michael BARber;
9        -> °h has been SAYing;=
10       -> =<<all>that the pOwer of a prIme minister> is too WEAK;
11       -> (0.53) uh? rather than too STRONG;
12       -> uh: that it needs to be STRENGthened,
13       -> (0.42) uh: <<all>and that there needs to be a prIme minister's>
         -> (0.30) de↑PARTment;
14 MP2:     [ha ha ha ha ha]
15 MP1:     [(0.63)         ] does (.) dOes my right honourable friend aGREE
            with this.= ((turn continues))
```

The reported speech, introduced by the reporting clause (the FORmer head; (0.54) of his deLIVery unit, sir michael BARber; °h has been SAYing;=, lines 6–9), is done in a tripartite list (=<<all> *that the power of a prime minister> is too WEAK; (...) that it needs to be STRENGthened, (...) <<all> and that there needs to be a prIme minister's> (0.30) de↑PARTment*, lines 10–13).[5] With each list item prefaced by the complementiser *that*, it is grammatically marked as indirect speech. Prosodically, the boundary between the reporting clause and the quotation is marked by a prosodic break, with the *that*-prefaced quotation beginning in a new intonation phrase. The first list item, =<<all> *that the pOwer of a prime mInister> is too WEAK; rather than too STRONG;* (lines 10–11), has accents on all content words. This dense accentuation frames the first list item as the most relevant portion of the quotation. The third list item is taken up with laughter by MP2 (line 14). Following this audience response, MP1 continues with an interrogative targeted at the PM in a new intonation phrase, *does (.) dOes my right honourable friend aGREE with this.* (line 15). This marks the right-hand edge of the quotation in retrospect.

The prosodic chunking of the reporting clause and the indirect speech with and without a complementiser would warrant an independent study in its own right, which must be left to future research. For reasons of space, I can only demonstrate for exemplary purposes that the chunking of reporting and reported clauses need not align with syntactic boundaries (Ex. 69; see also Barth-Weingarten 2016). At the same time, it exemplifies a rare case where the ends of the quotation are fuzzy. As I illustrate more below, this seems to be a particular problem of self-

---

[5] The list is combined with another rhetorical device, a relation of contrast between the stressed adjectives *WEAK* and *STRONG* in the first list item (=<<all> *that the power of a prime minister> is too WEAK; (0.53) uh? rather than too STRONG*, lines 10–11).

quotations where there is no shift in footing but the speaker continues to speak in his own voice.

(69)   PMQs 06 Feb. 2008

MP: Patrick Mercer (Con); PM: Gordon Brown (Lab); S: Michael Martin

```
1    PM:    the ↑stAtement that i made in (.) decEmber was wIdely WELcomed,=
2           when i SAID that our trOop nUmbers;
3           °h would be around sEven thousand Eight eight hUndred;
4           °h and we main↑TAIN them at around that lEvel for the foresEeable
             uh' FUture. (0.40)
5           as i rePEAT; ((turn continues))
```

The quotation (*that our trOop nUmbers; °h would be around sEven thousand Eight eight hUndred;*, lines 2–3) is marked as indirect by the complementiser *that* and the auxiliary *would* (instead of *will*). The reporting clause, the complementiser, and the subject are produced in one go, that is, integrated in one intonation phrase. There is no shift in voice quality or prosodic features which make the quotation heard in an animated voice. When the PM continues with his talk after an audible inbreath (*and we main↑TAIN them at around that lEvel; for the foresEeable uh' FUture*, line 4), there is no reset in pitch, duration, or loudness nor a shift in the deictic centre, which suggests that the speaker continues with the quotation. However, the present tense of the verb (*maintain* rather than *would maintain*) suggests that this is talk in the here and now and not reported speech.

In sum, the findings with respect to the prosody of 2003–2013 indirect speech largely match those of the 1978–1988 sample. Cues like dense accentuation can be used to emphasise (portions of) the indirect quotations. The beginning of the quotation is not always clearly marked through prosodic cues, for example through a start in a new intonation phrase, but is indicated through lexico-syntactic markers, for example, the complementiser and/or the quotative verb, which project a subsequent quotation. The ending of quotations tends to be marked in retrospect through the beginning of a new turn-constructional unit in the following intonation phrase.

To turn to visual contextualisation cues, speakers usually perform indirect speech without visual orientation to their notes. Ex. (70) shows a rare exception, where the Leader of the Liberal Democrats presents indirect speech, drawing on his notes in his question turn.

138 Reported Clauses

(70)   PMQs 08 June 2005
LLD: Charles Kennedy (LibDem); PM: Tony Blair (Lab); S: Michael Martin

```
1   LLD:    that with+↑OUT the american president# fUlly on board;
    cam     ≫ mid shot - - -≫
    lldH             +looks towards PM - - ->
    fig                                       #Fig. 6.1

2   LLD:    °h it's gonna be im↑POSsible (0.38) to a*chIeve a consensus on
    lldG                                       *takes notes into left
            these +mAtters.
    lldG    hand - - ->
    lldH         +looks down to notes - - ->

3   LLD:    #°h and so? *
    lldG            - - ->*
    fig     #Fig. 6.2

4   LLD: -> °h +↑whEn the prime minister said some TIME ago,
    lldH -> +

5   LLD: -> °h that ACtion on +clImate #change,
    lldH            - - -> +looks up  - - ->
    fig                                    #Fig. 6.3

6   LLD: -> +°h was gonna be one of the |two main# +PLANKS,
    lldH    +looks down to notes - - ->      - - ->+looks up towards PM->
    fig                                    #Fig. 6.4

7   LLD: -> °h on which ↑HIS presidency,

8   LLD: -> (0.31) of the gEe eight would be +JUDGED;
    lldH                      - - ->  +looks down to notes- - ->

9   LLD:    +°hh what# is he going to ↑SALvage;
    lldH:   +looks up towards PM - - -≫
    fig            #Fig. 6.5

10  LLD:    at glenEAgles,
11  LLD:    (0.23) if <<all>the american president will not sign UP,>
```

The quotation, *that ACtion on clImate change,* (...) (lines 5–8), is projected by a reporting clause, *°h ↑whEn the prime minister said some TIME ago,* (line 4), which ascribes the quotation to the PM. The reporting clause is marked by a step-up in pitch on the first accented syllable ↑*whEn*, which signals a 'new beginning' (Couper-Kuhlen 2004). However, there is no audible shift in the overall prosodic setting. The complementiser *that*, the backshift of the primary verb *was*, and the use of the auxiliary *would*, as well as the possessive pronoun ↑*HIS*, all frame the quotation as indirect speech. It is produced in a new intonation phrase, which prosodically cues a boundary between the reporting clause and the beginning of the quotation. Visually, the

6.2 Indirect Speech

Figure 6.1 The Leader of the Liberal Democrats displays visual orientation towards the PM.

Figure 6.2 The Leader of the Liberal Democrats orients down to his notes, tracing the point where he has written down the quotation with his left thumb.

performance of the quotation is prepared for by the speaker's kinetic and visual engagement with his notes. He first displays visual orientation towards the PM (Fig. 6.1) before he finally gazes down to his notes (line 2), eventually moving his left thumb to where he has put down the quotation (Fig. 6.2).

Next, he begins to produce the reporting clause (line 4). He largely sustains his visual orientation down to his notes before reorienting towards the PM

Figure 6.3 The Leader of the Liberal Democrats glances towards the PM.

Figure 6.4 The Leader of the Liberal Democrats sustains a downward gaze at his notes.

(Figs. 6.3–6.5). This display of visual engagement frames the quotation as what is presented as 'literalised' indirect speech (see Chapter 2 for discussion), with the speaker claiming to deliver a verbatim rendition of his sources.

Anticipated by shifts in visual orientation and a long filled pause, the production of the wh-interrogative verbally marks the right-hand boundary of the quotation in retrospect (*°hh what is he going to ↑SALvage;(...)*, lines 9–11).

Figure 6.5 The Leader of the Liberal Democrats displays visual orientation towards the PM.

'Literalised' indirect speech is rare in the 2003–2013 data, although it forms a common pattern for the most common type of direct speech (see Section 6.4). The vast majority of indirect speech is performed without visual orientation to prepared notes. Ex. (71) exemplifies this.

(71)   PMQs 30 March 2011
MP: Chris Leslie (Lab/Co-op); PM: David Cameron (Con); S: John Bercow

```
1  PM:    ->   ˙h <<all>‡we #SAID that <<p, l>en aitch es spending would increase
   cam           ≫ bird's eye view                                        - - ->
   pmH                    ‡sustained gaze towards opposition benches - - ->
   fig                           #Fig. 6.6
   PM:    ->   in|real terms# each yEar,≫
   cam         ->|medium close-up - - -≫
   fig                           #Fig. 6.7

2  PM:         (.) and it WILL. (.)‡
   pmH                           - - ->‡
```

The excerpt shows the full answer turn, which is unusually short. It begins with an indirect quotation by the PM, *'h <<all> we SAID that en aitch es spending would increase in real terms each yEar,>* (line 1). The indirect speech is marked by *that* and the use of the modal *would* (as a past form of *will*) in agreement with the simple past tense of the quotative. The reporting clause and the indirect speech are produced in one intonation phrase, with the

Figure 6.6 The Leader of the Liberal Democrats is midway into the production of the reporting clause without consulting his notes, orienting towards the opposition benches.

indirect speech produced at a slightly lower pitch and volume (beginning on the subject *en aitch es*) than the prior speech. The next portion of speech, *(.) and it WILL.* (line 2), is produced after a micro pause and is back at a normal pitch and volume in a new intonation phrase. The use of *will* frames the line as performed in the here and now. The prosodic and lexico-syntactic shifts demarcate the right edge of the quotation in retrospect. Visually, the speaker sustains a gaze towards the opposition benches at the beginning of the reporting clause (Fig. 6.6) and beyond the production of indirect speech (Fig. 6.7), not consulting his notes.

To summarise, there are two important differences between the 1978–1988 and 2003–2013 data sets which make visible how much the practices at PMQs have changed. First, there is a noticeable drop in the frequency of indirect speech in MPs' question turns, from most common to least common. This suggests that MPs do not, in 2003–2013 PMQs, primarily perform hostile actions. Second, there is a conspicuous rise in bare indirect speech, especially in the interaction between the LO and the PM, which points to a more conversational style in particular in these sequences.

6.3 'In Between' 143

Figure 6.7 The Leader of the Liberal Democrats sustains a gaze at the opposition benches towards the end of the quotation.

As regards the prosodic formatting, dense accentuation is deployed to put emphasis on (portions of) the quotation. The right boundaries tend to be signalled in retrospect through the beginning of a new intonation phrase, and through other prosodic and lexico-syntactic cues which indicate that a new turn-constructional move is under way. The left boundaries show varying degrees of integration, which warrants further study. In terms of the visual cues available during 2003–2013, indirect speech is generally delivered without the speakers' engagement with their notes, but there are exceptions where evidential access to their sources is visually displayed, which frames the quotation as 'literalised' indirect speech.

6.3 'In Between'

As has been described for German (Günthner 1997, 2000), speakers do not always deliver reported speech in ways which clearly match the features of direct or indirect speech. Although the speakers at PMQs show a strong orientation to mark the reported speech as direct or indirect, they

Table 6.3 *Relative frequencies of grammatically ambiguous speech across turn types and speaker roles (1978–1988)*

Turn types and speaker roles (1978–1988)	'In between'
MP Question turns (n=275)	0% (1)
Answer turns to MP Question turns (n=275)	0.7% (2)
LO Question turns (n=44)	0% (0)
Answer turns to LO Question turns (n=44)	0% (0)
Leader of the Lib/SDP Question turns (n=12)	0% (0)
Answer turns to Lib/SDP Question turns (n=12)	0% (0)

sometimes remain vague in their contextualisation. This section is concerned with such cases in the 1978–1988 and 2003–2013 data.

1978–1988

There are three cases in the 1978–1988 sample where – similar to indirect speech – there are global shifts in prosodic features, but the quotation is not prefaced by a complementiser, nor does it show a change of pronoun(s) and/or clear backshift. Table 6.3 shows that the relative frequencies of ambiguous markings of reported speech in the 1978–1988 sample are very low.

Ex. (72), a longer version of the same extract as in Ex. (50), illustrates the problem. The background murmuring of the MPs is not represented in the transcript.

(72)   PMQs 06 Nov. 1986

MP: Derek Conway (Con); PM Margaret Thatcher (Con); S: Bernard Weatherill

```
1    PM:        uh mister SPEAker;
2               (0.22) uh? I SAW that repOrt;
3               °h but AS our armed forces are based on the existence of a
                voluntary profEssional uh? armed forces,
4               <<all>we do not have any plans at the moment to> ↑CHANGE it;
5               °h there are a nUmber of youth trAining places which cAn be
                served ↑IN the armed forces,
6               °h uh? and thOse i think are EARnestly sought after;
7        ->     i SAID at the moment we hAve no plans to chAnge it;=
8               =it would be of course extrEmely expensive and alter the !WHOLE!
                nature °h <<all>o? of of> the: <<all>uh? uh?> the whole nature
                of our armed forces,
9               <<p>which i do not wish to DO.>
```

6.3 'In Between'

The reporting clause and quotation are produced in one single intonation phrase, *i SAID at the moment we hAve no plans to chAnge it;=* (line 7), which has a rhythmic structure (cf. Couper-Kuhlen 1993). This is illustrated in Ex. (72′).

(72′) Rhythmic structure of Ex. (72), line 7

```
1    PM:       i
2              /SAID at the /
3              /moment we   /
4              /hAve no     /
5              /plans to    /
6              /chAnge it;=
```

The rhythmic production makes the line stand out from the surrounding talk and frames it as the key message in the answer turn. Grammatically, the quotation could be either indirect or direct speech. Although there is no backshift of the verb, this is not a mandatory criterion for indirect speech if the statement framed as a quotation is still valid at the time of speaking. The problem of categorising it is also due to the first-person subjects in both the reporting clause and quotation, which means that there is no shift in the deictic centre which would involve a change in pronouns in direct speech. Ex. (73), a shorter version of the same extract as in Ex. (19), has a similarly ambiguous structure, yet it can be inferred from the prior talk that the quotation is indirect.

(73)   PMQs 12 Nov. 1981

MP: Christopher Price (Lab); PM: Margaret Thatcher (Con); S: George Thomas

```
1   MP:    ->   [where ↑SHE said; (0.43) ]
2   MPs:        [mur mur mur mur mur mur]
3   MP:    ->   [that there was ONE other indivIdual; (0.33)]
4   MPs:        [mur mur mur mur mur (h h h h h h h h h h) ]
5   MP:    ->   [to whom: inducements: had been GIven; (0.42)]
6   MPs:        [(h h h h h h h h h h h h h h h h h h h h h h)  ]
7   MP:    ->   and the at↑TORney said, (0.32)
8          ->   there were a ↑FEW other individuals.
```

There are two quotations in the excerpt. The first represents a clear case of indirect speech (*where ↑SHE said; (0.43) that there was ONE other individual; (0.33) to whom: inducements: had been GIven; (0.42)*, lines 1, 3, 5). Introduced by the reporting clause *SHE said;* with the quotative SAY in simple past, the quotation is indexed as indirect speech by the complementiser *that* and what could be a backshift of the verb *was*. Note that the second quotation (*and the at↑TORney said, (0.32) there were a FEW other individuals.*, lines 7–8) occurs in a parallel structure except for the complementiser. The ascribed source has been produced with the primary accent on a step-up in pitch; the reporting clause and the quotation each form two independent intonation phrases. The quotations contain the same existential copulative constructions. The primary accents are on the words which form contrasting concepts: *ONE* versus *FEW*. Because of the rhetorical set-up it can be argued that the second quotation can be heard in a parallel fashion as an indirect quotation even if its grammatical status as either indirect or direct speech remains ambiguous.

To sum up, 'in between' reported speech is not very common in the 1978–1988 sample, which suggests the speakers' tendency to use written norms in their speech. Reported speech where the grammatical formatting is ambiguous tends to be self-quotations or performed in environments where its status as indirect speech can be inferred from the prior context.

2003–2013

The 2003–2013 data set also contains quotations with ambiguous grammatical marking. Tables 6.4a and 6.4b show the relative frequencies of ambiguous markings of reported speech in the 2003–2013 sample.

'In between' cases are most widely deployed in answer turns to LOs' questions (and in LOs' questions turns) and are in total more frequent than in the 1978–1988 data. This suggests a more interactional, interpersonal style in the 2003–2013 data.

I first begin with an analysis of cases similar to what is found in the 1978–1988 sample. Ex. (74) corresponds to Ex. (72) in that the grammatical features of the reported clause do not mark it as either direct or indirect, and there are no cues from the prior context which would frame it either way.

Table 6.4a *Relative frequencies of grammatically ambiguous speech across turn types and speaker roles (MPs, LOs, PMs, 2003–2013)*

Turn types and speaker roles (2003–2013)	'In between'
MP Question turns (n=828)	0.4% (3)
Answer turns to MP Question turns (n=828)	1.5% (12)
LO Question turns (n=257)	3.5% (9)
Answer turns to LO Question turns (n=257)	5.5% (14)

6.3 'In Between'

Table 6.4b *Relative frequencies of grammatically ambiguous speech in question–answer sequences between the Leader of the Liberal Democrats and the PM (2003–2010)*

Turn types and speaker roles (2003–2010)	'In between'
LLD Question turns (n=56)	0% (0)
Answer turns to LLD Question turns (n=56)	1.8% (1)

(74) PMQs 14 Jan 2009
MP: Michael Spicer (Con); PM: Gordon Brown (Lab); S: Michael Martin

```
1    MPs:         [l l l l l l l l l l l l l   ]
2    PM:    ->    [(2.30) <<all>mister speaker] i've sAid there's no PLANS for
                  that>,=
3                 =<<all>and i> sAy aGAIN;
4                 <<l>there's no PLANS>.
```

The reporting clause *i've sAid* and the reported clause *there's no PLANS for that>,=* are produced in the same intonation phrase (line 1). There is no complementiser *that*, nor a shift in tense (the quotative verb and the verb of the reported clause are both in present tense), which would mark the quotation as clearly indirect. Moreover, the existential construction *there's* is built such that it remains the same, independent of a possible shift in the deictic centre. Thus, the status of the reported clause as direct or indirect is left ambiguous.[6]

Ex. (75) also shows a case of 'in between' reported speech in a copular construction. Similarly to Ex. (73), the reported speech comes in a string of quotations, which makes it heard as indirect.[7]

(75) PMQs 17 Oct. 2007
LO: David Cameron (Con); PM: Gordon Brown (Lab); S: Michael Martin

```
1    MPs:    [mur mur mur mur mur ]
2    PM:     [if he want? i? (0.44)]
3    MPs:    [mur mur mur mur mur mur mur mur mur  ]
4    PM:     [if he wAnts to trade QUOTES; (0.27)]
```

---

[6] Although lines 3–4 are formatted in similar ways, the simple present verb form of *sAy* (line 3) makes it heard as an affirmative metapragmatic construction rather than reported speech. Still, the example makes visible that the boundaries between quotative and more metapragmatic uses of SAY are fuzzy, an aspect which cannot explored here further for reasons of space.

[7] See Chapter 8 on the formula *if he wAnts to trade QUOTES*.

```
5     MPs:       [j j j j]
6     PM:        [let uh⁷] LET him listen to the chairman of his Own democracy
                 commission; [(0.96)]
7     MPs:                [ch l ch] [l l l l l l l] [mur mur mur mur mur
8     PM:    ->                                    [who sAys that] [the proposal for a
      MPs:       mur mur mur mur mur mur mur mur]
      PM:        referendum under the tory plans] is CRACKpot, (0.36)
9     MPs:       [l l l l l l l l l l l l l l   ]
10    PM:    ->  [(.) then he says it's DOTty,] (0.38)
11           ->  <<all>and then he says it's> frankly (.) abSURD;
```

The excerpt contains three instances of reported speech: (1) *[who sAys that] the proposal (...) is CRACKpot,* (line 8), (2) *then he says it's DOTty,* (line 10), and (3) *and then he says it's frankly absurd* (line 11). A comparison reveals that the reported clauses are constructed in parallel copular constructions but that the first is prefaced by the complementiser *that*, which marks it as indirect speech, and has a nominal subject (*the proposal*). The pronominal subjects (*it*) of the subsequent quotations are linked to the latter in an anaphoric chain but are not clearly formatted as direct or indirect speech. As the reporting clauses have the same ascribed source (again connected in an anaphoric chain), and due to the parallel production of the quotations, it can be inferred that the second and third also represent indirect quotations.

Recall that the 2003–2013 'in between' forms of reported speech are most frequent in the question–answer sequences between the LO and PM. Considering that these sequences are the most interactional in the 2003–2013 data set, this distribution is indicative of a more informal but also involved use. The latter becomes especially visible in Ex. (76). Here the reporting clause has a coordinated subject NP, which makes the quotation come off as 'choral dialogue' (Tannen 2007: 114–115).

(76)   PMQs 19 Jan 2011

LO: Ed Miliband (Lab); PM: David Cameron (Con); S: John Bercow

```
1     MPs:       [mur mur mur mur mur mur mur mur]
2     LO:        [dOctors and nurses +SAY, (0.22)]
      loH                           +gazes down to notes - - ->
3     MPs:       [mur mur mur mur    ]
4     LO:    ->  [his reFORMS,#(.)+]
      loH                         - - ->+
      fig                         #Fig. 6.8
```

```
5    MPs:         [mur mur mur mur mur mur mur  ]
6    LO:     ->   [are exTREMEly +risky, + (.)]
     loH                        +gazes down+
7    MPs:         [mur mur mur mur mur mur mur mur  ]
8    LO:     ->   [and +potentially+(.) diSAStrous.]
     loH                +gazes down+
```

The quotation (*his reFORMS (...)*, lines 4, 6, 8) is introduced by a reporting clause with the quotative verb in present tense (*dOctors and nurses SAY,* line 2). The reported clause is not prefaced by the complementiser *that.* The choice of the third-person personal pronoun (*his*) and present-tensed verb (*are*) make it grammatically ambiguous whether the quotation is direct or indirect, since they would remain the same if there were a shift in the deictic centre. The subject in the reporting clause is produced in a coordinated NP (*dOctors and nurses SAY,* line 2). This does not convey that doctors and nurses produced a joint utterance, but it is heard as 'choral dialogue', animating their position as a quotation as an 'involvement strategy' (Tannen 2007) aimed at the audience. Note, however, the speaker's repeated visual engagement with his notes, which displays a claim of direct evidential access to sources (Fig. 6.8; Ex. 76

Figure 6.8 The LO shows repeated visual engagement with his notes during the production of the quotation.

150 Reported Clauses

lines 2, 4, 6, 8). It is this combination of contextualisation cues which creates involvement as well as authenticity, making reported speech a particularly powerful rhetorical weapon.

The present analysis has shown that the frequency of reported speech with ambiguous formatting has increased in 2003–2013. It occurs especially often in the sequences between the LO and the PM, which are most dynamic because they span more than one single question–answer sequence. Although the environments which make the formatting of the quotation heard as 'in between' are similar in the 1978–1988 and 2003–2013 data sets, the study of the latter has revealed a rhetorical diversification, which draws on both the use of coordinated NPs and the presence of cameras, two more recent developments in the activity at PMQs.

6.4 Direct Speech

Direct speech constitutes the second largest category of reported speech in both samples but its distribution over turn types as well as the forms and functions have diversified in the 2003–2013 sample compared to the earlier footage.

1978–1988
There are only four direct quotations in the 1978–1988 sample, which are exclusively found in the PM's answer turns. Table 6.5 summarises the relative percentages of direct speech and their distribution across speaker roles and turn types.

Despite the small size of the sample, it is striking that the direct quotations are exclusively found in action turns by the PM. Recall that direct speech, in particular when it is 'literalised', signals direct evidential access to sources. This suggests that the direct quotations constitute a display of privileged access which lends the PM extra authority as head

Table 6.5 *Frequencies of direct speech relative to number of question and answer turns defined by speaker roles (1978–1988)*

Turn types and speaker roles (1978–1988)	Direct speech
MP Question turns (n=275)	0% (0)
Answer turns to MP Question turns (n=275)	1.1% (3)
LO Question turns (n=44)	0% (0)
Answer turns to LO Question turns (n=44)	2.3% (1)
Leader of the Lib/SDP Question turns (n=12)	0% (0)
Answer turns to Lib/SDP Question turns (n=12)	0% (0)

6.4 Direct Speech

of state. All examples of direct speech in the 1978–1988 sample were found in the answer turns of Margaret Thatcher. For this reason, it is open to conjecture whether the results are a description of her idiosyncratic style or an evidential resource reserved for PMs at PMQs during this period.[8] I show that these quotations represent 'literalised' direct speech, delivered in a 'voice of authority'.[9]

First, the prosodic analysis in all three cases reveals that the left-hand boundary is marked through a prosodic break between the reporting clause and the subsequent reported speech, that is, the quotation begins in a new intonation phrase. Ex. (77), which includes the same interaction seen in Ex. (14), illustrates this particularly well. The transcript does not contain the audience responses in full detail.

(77) PMQs 07 May 1985
LO: Neil Kinnock (Lab); PM: Margaret Thatcher (Con); S: Bernard Weatherill

```
1    PM:           mister SPEAker;
2                  $i'm GLAD the right honourable gentleman referr:ed$ to my rIght
     pmG       $   crackling noise of paper                         $
     PM:           honourable friend the secretary of state for energy's spEech;
3    PM:     ->    (0.51) i NOtice that he SAID,
4    PM:     ->    (0.56) that my RIGHT honourable friend the secretary of energy
             ->    sAid,
5            ->    (0.45) the lAbour party whilst ↑frequently interested in the
             ->    econOmic disconTENTment.
6            ->    (0.43) ap↑pEar $to be              $ ↑TOtally unwilling;
     pmG               $crackling noise of paper$
7    PM:     ->    to give the worker the higher STAtus and the higher [privilege
8    MPs:                                                              [h h h h h
     PM:     ->    he sEeks;]
     MPs:          h h h h h] [h h h h h]
9    PM:             [(1.28) he] wEnt ON,
10                 (0.29) they are aGAINST workers in cOuncil houses becoming
                   owner occupiers,
11                 they are aGAINST workers having frEedom of choice for their
                   chIldren in education;
12                 (0.48) to THEM it appEars;
13                 that workers are but fragments of a BLOCK vote at a lAbour party
                   conference-
```

---

[8] This is a general problem facing diachronic studies of spoken language which rely on media broadcasts (see Jucker and Landert 2015).
[9] See Raymond (2000) on the construction of a voice of authority – not related to reported speech – in live news broadcasts.

```
14          °h and nOt people whose responsibility and freedoms need to be
            in their ↑OWN hands,
15          (0.42) rAther than in the hands of a socialist politician or
            the BUReaucrat;
16          (0.58) <<f,h>thAnk you very MUCH mister speaker;>
17          i'm GRATEful to the right honourable gentleman;=
18          =for LETting me quote from my rIght honourable friend's speech.
```

Following an address to the Speaker (line 1), the PM displays a positive evaluative stance towards the questioner's prior mentioning of the secretary of state's speech (*i'm GLAD the right honourable gentleman referr:ed to my rIght honourable friend the secretary of state for energy's spEech*, line 2). The crackling noise of paper which accompanies the beginning of this move anticipates the upcoming quotation. It is also verbally projected by a reporting clause (*i NOtice that he SAID,* line 3), which subsequently undergoes repair (*that my RIGHT honourable friend the secretary of energy sAid,* line 4). After a medium pause, there follows what turns out to be the first portion of the quotation, produced in multiple intonation phrases (*(0.45) the LAbour party whilst ↑frequently interested in the econOmic discontentment. (0.43) ap|pEar to be ↑TOtally unwilling; to give the worker the higher STAtus and the higher privilege he sEeks;,* lines 5–7). This stretch of speech comes off as a 'literalised' direct quotation delivered in another voice. Compared to the previous speech, it is accompanied by more and higher pitch peaks and delivered with a greater pitch range. The lexico-syntactic choices are more formal: note the lexical choice of *whilst* and the syntactic position of the adverbial clause after the subject of the main clause. There is no backshift of the verbs *ap↑pEar* and *seeks*. This first portion of the direct speech is met with appreciation on the part of the government MPs (line 8). The PM orients towards the audience responses by pausing before signalling that she is resuming with the quotation (*he wEnt ON,* line 9). The audible crackling of paper and the fact that she claims to continue to retrieve and report on the secretary of state's past speech for her audience suggest that she is reading the verbatim quotation from a written source (lines 10–15).

The thank you formula <<*f,h>thAnk you very MUCH mister speaker;>* (line 16), which is explicitly addressed to the Speaker of the House of Commons, marks a shift in footing to the in situ interaction, cued by the terms of address *you* and *mister speaker*, and by a higher volume and higher pitch register. This return to the speaker's voice as PM indexes the right-hand boundary in

6.4 Direct Speech

retrospect. The PM next rewords her thanks, overtly labelling her prior action as quoting from the Secretary of State's speech ((...) *quote from my rIght honourable friend's speech*, lines 17–18).

Ex. (78) is another example of direct speech taken from the PM's answer turn. Again, it shows a shift in global prosodic marking, this time beginning in the reporting clause, and a shift to more formal lexico-syntactic choices. Other than the examples shown above, the right-hand edge of the quotation is fuzzy. The reporting clause is in line 14, the quotation in lines 15, 16, 18, 20, and 22.

(78)   PMQs 01 May 1984

Leader of SNP: Gordon Wilson (SNP); PM: Margaret Thatcher (Con);
S: Bernard Weatherill

```
1    PM:          NO mister speaker;=
2                 =i DID answer that question-=
3                 <<all>but perhaps> because of the NOISE,
4                 the: the hOnourable gentleman couldn't HEAR it;
5    MPs:         [chu chu chu chu chu chu chu chu chu chu chu chu chu chu chu]
6    PM:          [°h i dId indicate that i had already GIVen instructions;]
7    MPs:         [chu chu chu chu chu chu chu chu chu chu chu chu chu chu]
8    PM:          [for the cIrcumstances leading up to the events of the  ]
9    MPs:         [chu chu chu chu chu chu chu chu chu chu chu]
10   PM:          [seventeenth of april in saint james's SQUARE; ]
11   MPs:         [chu chu chu chu chu chu chu chu chu chu chu chu chu
12   PM:          [°h inꜛCLUding the intelligence and other information
     MPs:         chu chu chu chu chu chu chu chu chu ]
     PM:          available to be thOroughly reviewed;]
13   MPs:         [chu chu chu chu chu chu chu]
14   PM:    ->    [°h <<h>i went ON to sAy:;> ]
15          ->    °h <<h>if there are LESsons to be lEarnt;>
16          ->    <<h>in regard to the [arrangements for HANdling;>]
17   MPs:                               [chu chu chu chu chu chu chu ]
18   PM:    ->    [<<h>disseEminating and asꜛSESsing intelligence;>]
19   MPs:         [chu chu chu chu chu chu chu chu chu chu chu chu   ]
20   PM:    ->    [°h <<h>the nEcessary changes WILL be made,> ]
21   MPs:         [chu chu chu chu chu chu chu chu chu chu]
22   PM:    ->    [°h <<all, h>and i'm afraid it may well be ꜛINappropriate on
23   MPs:         [chu chu chu chu chu chu chu chu chu chu chu chu chu chu
```

```
PM:     ->   security grounds to make a pUblic announcement of any such
MPs:         chu chu chu chu chu chu chu chu chu chu chu chu chu chu chu
PM:     ->   changes.>]
MPs:         chu chu  ]
```

This extract is taken from the last question–answer sequence at this session of PMQs. The reporting clause °h i went ON to sAy:; (line 14), which projects the subsequent direct speech *if there are LESsons to be lEarnt; (...)* (lines 15, 16, 18, 20, 22), has an aspectual semantics due to the phrasal verb *went ON* that frames what follows as part of a past ongoing action where the PM continues to quote her own prior speech. It picks up on the previous lines (6, 8, 10, 12), where the PM delivered the wording of a prior answer turn, previously read out in response to a LO's question in indirect reported speech (°h i dId indicate that i had already GIVen instructions (...)).

There is a subtle shift to a higher pitch range on the production of the reporting clause, which is maintained during the subsequent direct quotation. The use of the passive voice (*to be lEarnt*, line 15; *WILL be made*, line 20) points to a written-language style.

In line 22, the PM speaks at a faster tempo but maintains the same pitch range as in the prior talk (<<*alb* and *i'm afraid it may well be* ↑*Inappropriate (...)*). The change in tempo and the contracted form of the verb *i'm* suggests that the line is not part of the quotation and thus marks the right-hand boundary in retrospect. However, since the deictic centre of the self-quotation, indexed by the first-person pronoun *I* in the reporting clause, and that of line 22 are the same, the boundaries are blurred.

The foregoing analysis has shown that the PM delivers direct speech with:

1. Global prosodic contextualisation cues which set it apart from the prior speech (this prosodic shift may begin in the reporting clause, a practice which has been called 'flagging'; Klewitz and Couper-Kuhlen 1999: 473).
2. Lexico-syntactic choices which make it come off as 'conceptually written', conveying 'communicative distance' (Koch and Oesterreicher 2007).
3. Sometimes it is accompanied by an audio-visual cue: an audible crackling of paper.
4. The beginning of the direct speech and the post-quotation talk are delivered in new intonation phrases.

These features make the reported speech heard as 'literalised' direct speech, performed in what I call the 'voice of authority' for the speaker's audience, to the end that the position conveyed is authenticated and authorised. The 2003–2013 sample also contains 'literalised' direct speech, which largely matches that in the 1978–1988 sample, but it has been demonstrated that its distribution and formatting has changed in ways which are indicative of more global factors affecting the activity at PMQs.

2003–2013
The direct quotations in the 2003–2013 data set fall into two types:

'Literalised' Direct Speech (Type 1)
This is characterised by:

- lexico-syntactic cues which mark it as direct speech and/or as what is heard as 'conceptionally written' (Koch and Oesterreicher 2007);
- an optional shift in voicing;
- a tendency to be produced in a new intonation phrase following the reporting clause; and
- visual cues that involve a visual engagement with the speakers' notes, a possible haptic manipulation of notes, and a possible shift in the orator's posture.

Summarising Direct Speech (Type 2)
This type resembles Tannen's notion of 'summarizing dialogue' (Tannen 2007: 114). In the data, what is summarised in direct speech can relate to what was just said in the prior in situ interaction or to a general position/policy by the party quoted. Crucially, what distinguishes Type 2 from Type 1 is that these performances are grammatically keyed as direct speech but characterised by an absence of the bodily conduct and involvement of written notes seen in Type 1. Moreover, the reporting clause and reported clause are not always produced in independent intonation phrases. Tables 6.6a and 6.6b show the relative frequencies over turn type and speaker roles.

Type 1 is clearly more common than Type 2 across all turn types and speaker roles. Corresponding to the 1978–1988 type of direct speech, it is also much more frequent than in the radio data. Type 1 is most common in

156   Reported Clauses

Table 6.6a *Relative frequencies of direct speech across turn types and speaker roles (MPs, LOs, PMs, 2003–2013)*

Turn types and speaker roles (2003–2013)	Type 1: 'Literalised' DS	Type 2: Summarising DS	Total
MP Question turns (n=828)	2.7% (22)	0.4% (3)	3.1% (25)
Answer turns to MP Question turns (n=828)	1.0% (8, incl. 1 reframing of IDS to DS)	0.5% (4)	1.5% (12)
LO Question turns (n=257)	12.5% (32)	2.0% (5)	14.5% (37)
Answer turns to LO Question turns (n=257)	6.2% (16, incl. 1 reframing of DS to IDS)	2.0% (5)	8.2% (21)

Table 6.6b *Relative frequencies of direct speech in question–answer sequences between the Leader of the Liberal Democrats and the PM (2003–2010)*

Turn types and speaker roles (2003–2010)	Type 1: 'Literalised' DS	Type 2: Summarising DS	Total
LLD Question turns (n=56)	1.8% (1)	0% (0)	1.8% (1)
Answer turns to Leader of the Lib Dems Question turns (n=56)	1.8% (1)	1.8% (1)	3.6% (2)

the question turns by the LO. Both types are most often used in the interaction between the LO and the PM.

'Literalised' Direct Speech (Type 1)

To begin with an illustration of Type 1, Ex. (79) exemplifies a 'literalised' direct quotation, delivered in lines 7–11.

(79)   PMQs 03 Dec. 2003

LO: Michael Howard (Con); PM: Tony Blair (Lab); S: Michael Martin

```
1    PM:      and ‡(.) if i can say we had an interesting     ‡$contriBUtion;#
     cam          ≫ medium close-up - - -≫
     pmH              ‡lets gaze drift downwards to folder - - ->‡looks to his
     pmG                                                       $opens page in
     fig                                                            #Fig.6.9
              (0.44)
     pmH      right down the aisle - - ->
     pmG      folder and holds page midway - - ->
```

6.4 Direct Speech

Figure 6.9 The PM is holding the page midway.

```
2   PM:         [to the big‡ conversa$tion this MORning,]    ‡  $#(0.44)
    pmH                    --->‡reorients down to folder  - - ->‡ looks up orienting
    pmG                              - - ->$ turns page completely $
    fig                                                              #Fig.6.10
3   MPs:        [chu chu chu chu chu chu chu chu chu chu  ]
4   PM:         from his Own (.) ↑SPOKESman; (0.21)
    pmH         towards opposition benches, Speaker's Chair and own benches - - ->
5   PM:         [on HIGHer educa‡tion; (0.57)]              ‡
    pmH                    --->‡gazes back down on notes‡
6   MPs:        [sh sh sh sh sh sh sh sh sh  ]
7   PM:    ->   [‡who SAID,]                      [‡ (0.29)]
    pmH         ‡orients towards opposition benches ‡ back down to notes - - ->
    MPs:        [sh sh sh sh]                     [chu chu]
8   PM:    ->   [when $ASKED,          $] (0.73)
    pmG                    $adjusts glasses$
    MPs:        [chu chu chu chu chu  ]
9   PM:    ->   i §↑DO accept;#
    pmP         §rests on dispatch box and leans forward - - ->
    fig                    #Fig.6.11
10  PM:    ->   there hAs been UNder fUnding;
```

Figure 6.10 The PM has turned the page completely.

```
11    PM:     ->    ˚h NOT jUst under the conservative gOvernment-
12    PM:     ->    but in the LAST seven years as ##wEll-
      pmH                                        ↑reorients towards opposition
      fig                                         #Fig.6.12
13    PM:     ->    §for uniVERsi[ties; (0.40)]
      pmH                benches - - -»
      pmP                §straightens up - - -»
14    MPs:                           [sh j sh j sh]
15    PM:                    [↑NOW;]
16    MPs:                   [sh j  ]
```

The quotation *i DO accept; there hAs been UNder fUnding; (...)* is performed in lines 9–13. It is prepared for and framed as relevant to the here and now in a preface (*and (.) if i can say we had an interesting an interesting contriBUtion (...)*, lines 1–2, 4–5). While producing the preface, the speaker orients his gaze down to his folder, opening a page midway, that is, 'freezing' (Streeck 1993: 293) the movement (Fig. 6.9) before opening the page completely (Fig. 6.10). The PM names the source of the subsequent quotation in the preface, (...) *his*

Figure 6.11 The PM rests on the dispatch box and leans forward.

Own (.) ↑SPOKESman; (0.21) on HIGHer education; (lines 4–5). The disaffiliative MPs' audience responses in orientation to head of the NP, ↑*SPOKESman*, display recognition and that a hostile move is projected. However, this also shows that the postmodifying PP *on HIGHer education* is produced in orientation to the mediated audience.

In what follows, the PM delivers the reporting clause *who SAID,* (line 7), accompanied by a gaze towards the opposition benches. The antecedent of the relative pronoun is the source which the PM has named in the preface.

The PM reorients his gaze down to his folder, accompanied by a pause and the subsequent production of an incremental adverbial of time (*when ASKED,* line 8). The subsequent quotation, which begins in a new intonation phrase and comprises five in total, is marked by a shift to a wider pitch range and by higher pitch peaks than the prior talk. The use of the pronoun *I* in first person singular as a reference to the third-person source indexes a shift in the deictic centre, framing it as direct quotation. While still gazing down to his notes, the PM rests on the dispatch box and leans forward, embodying his full focus on the notes (Fig. 6.11).

Figure 6.12 The PM looks up from his notes.

Towards the end of the second-to-last intonation phrase of the quotation, the PM shows disengagement with his notes, looking up towards the opposition benches (line 12, Fig. 6.12). This disengagement visually anticipates the completion of the quotation in the next line. Producing the discourse marker ↑*NOW;* (line 15) in a new intonation phrase and on a step-up in pitch, he marks his moving forward in the turn and the completion of the quotation in retrospect.

The foregoing analysis has demonstrated how the quotation is grammatically cued as direct speech, accompanied by prosodic features similar to the direct speech in the 1978–1988 sample. Compared to the noticeable lexico-syntactic 'literalisation' of direct speech during 1978–1988, however, there is more variation in the 2003–2013 data set. Not all Type 1 instances of direct speech are heard as formal, distancing talk, but its 'literalisation' is primarily achieved through visual cues. This might be due to the fact that not all direct quotations are based on conceptually written speech but may also refer to prior spoken speech. Moreover, there is a general '[tendency] for written norms to become more informal and move closer to speech' in present-day English, a development termed 'colloquialization' (Leech *et al.* 2009:

6.4 Direct Speech

20; Mair 2006: 183). This explains why the quotation in Ex. (79) certainly has a formal tone but does not sound as conceptually written as the direct speech in the 1978–1988 examples.

Ex. (80) is another example of direct speech where the LO's sources are visually recruited for the audience. It represents the uncommon case where the quotation is marked by a shift in voice quality.

(80)   PMQs 17 Oct. 2007
LO: David Cameron (Con); PM: Gordon Brown (Lab); S: Michael Martin

```
1    MPs:        [h h h h h h h h h h h h h h h h h h      ]
2    S:          [%(0.66)      %     |david CAMe°ron       °]-
     cam         ≫medium close-up |bird's-eye view - - ->
     pmW         %sitting down%
     loW                                          °standing up°
3    MPs:        [h h h h h h h h h h h h h h h h h h h h h h h h h h h ]
4    LO:         [*(2.0)*                    (1.28)* ↑THANK you;   *]
     loG         *puts notes on dispatch box and adjusts mic *fiddles with tie*
5    MPs:        [h h h h h h h h h h h h h]
6    LO:         [(.)↑THANK you mister spEAker;]
7                °h in the last four YEARS,
8                the ↑NUMber of people who've ↑dIEd;
9                from the ↑hOspital-acquired infection cee diffi↑CILE,
10               °h has TREBled,
11               °h NINEty patients died in one hospital trust alOne,
12   LO:   ->    +°h the *#↑HEALTH      *care commission *sAId    *last week,
     loH         + gazes down to notes - - ->
     loG              *chopping gesture*           *touches notes*
     fig              #Fig.6.13
13   LO:   ->    #where □trUsts□ are under se*↑VERE*  *prEs *sure to meet
     loG                                   *ch.g.*  *ch.g.*
     loP                 □rests on stretched left arm□
     fig         #Fig.6.14
     LO:   ->    *tAr * gets relating to *fI*nance and *Ac*cess,
     loG         *ch.g*          *ch.g.*       *ch.g.*
14   LO:   ->    *con*cern for in*↑FEC*tion control,+
     loH                                        - - ->+
     loG         *ch.g.*    *ch.g.*
15   LO:   ->    +may be under    +*MINED;*#
     loH         + gazes towards PM + gazes down --->
     loG                          *ch.g. *
     fig                          #Fig.6.15
```

```
16    LO:         °h                  □↑WILL□ the prime minister +↑nOw ac#cept;
      loH              to notes - - ->                            +gazes towards
      loP                        □straightens up slightly□
      fig                                                                  #Fig.6.16
17    LO:         that the ↑NUMber and extent;
18    LO:         °h of ↑HIS top-down +targets;           +
      loH                         - - -> +gazes down to notes+
19    LO:         +are con↑TRIButing to this [problem;] |+
      cam                                        - - ->|
      loH         +gazes towards PM          - - ->    +
20    MPs:                                     [chu chu ]
```

The sequence begins with a summons by the Speaker (line 2) which is appreciated by the MPs (lines 3, 5). The LO answers the appreciation and the summons (lines 4, 6) and begins his question turn with a question preface. Here he first quotes figures and statistics which show a rise in the number of people who have died from an infection they acquired in hospital (lines 7–11).

Next follows a reporting clause which projects a quotation by the healthcare commission, a public body (°h the ↑HEALTHcare commission sAId last week, line 12). This is marked by a step-up in pitch on the first accented syllable, ↑HEALTH, which signals a new beginning (Couper-Kuhlen 2004) and is produced in a wider pitch range. At the beginning of the clause, the PM orients his gaze down to his notes (Fig. 6.13). When he begins the quotation in the following intonation phrase, he maintains his sustained downward gaze, repositioning his posture (Fig. 6.14) before finally resting on his stretched out left arm.

This repositioning and manipulating of his notes displays a claim of full embodied engagement with them. Prosodically, the quotation is produced in a medium register and with a narrower pitch range than the prior reporting clause. Phonetically, it is performed in a slightly breathy voice. A change in voice quality in the delivery of quotations is uncommon in the data set. Grammatically, the passive voice of the bare infinitive in *may be underMINED* and the nominal style, that is, the high density of nouns, cue the quotation as conceptually written, which makes it heard as a direct quote read from the speaker's notes. The LO thus displays a direct evidential access to his sources, presenting himself as having evidential authority. This in turn constructs him as having credibility as a political leader and contender for the office of the Prime Minister.

Shortly before completing the quotation, he briefly looks up towards the PM before gazing down again (Fig. 6.15).

6.4 Direct Speech 163

Figure 6.13 The PM is positioned at the onset of the reporting clause.

Figure 6.14 The PM readjusts his posture at the initial boundary of the quotation.

Figure 6.15 The PM looks down at the final boundary of the quotation.

In a new intonation phrase, the PM implements his next turn-constructional move, an interrogative targeted at the Prime Minister, ↑*WILL the prime minister* ↑*nOw accept; (...)* (lines 16–19). Coordinated with the pitch accent on the first syllable, the LO readjusts his posture, straightening up before lifting his gaze from his notes and looking towards the PM (Fig. 6.16). This combination of prosodic, lexico-syntactic, and bodily signals mark the end of the quotation in retrospect.

Recall that the most frequent occurrence of direct speech is in question turns by the LO, whose interactional role and use of reported speech with SAY was – in comparison – marginal during 1978–1988, where direct speech was restricted to answer turns by the PM, and generally very limited in absolute and relative numbers. In 2003–2013, direct speech is also used in MPs' question turns, which only contained indirect speech in 1978–1988. An explanation for this overall rise in direct speech, and specifically in the LO's action turns, is that the presentation of the 'exact wording' in direct speech is a strategy to appear more impartial and unchallengeable. Research in political science suggests that trust in politics has diminished in the UK since the 1990s (Bromley *et al.* 2004). The rise in direct speech

Figure 6.16 The LO shifts his visual orientation towards the PM.

and orientation to the authentication of sources (see also Section 6.6) can be regarded as a strategy by politicians to boost their public image as a credible, trustworthy leader, which is in particular relevant to the self-presentation of LOs, the contenders for the premiership.[10]

To come to a final example of 'literalised' direct speech, recall that in the examples above, it was illustrated how the speaker achieves a clear marking of the boundaries of the direct quotation such that the speaker's voice and the voice quoted are audibly and visibly differentiated. Even though these represent the majority of cases, the contextualisation of footing is not always so clear. Ex. (81), an extended and multimodally transcribed version of Ex. (60), shows a case where a shift between a third-party direct quotation and the subsequent speech in the orator's own voice is only contextualised visually but is not distinctly marked through vocal or verbal cues. This deviant case gives us valuable insight into visual cues as well as the relation between vocal and verbal cues.

---

[10] I owe this point to Stephen Holden Bates, personal communication.

Reported Clauses

(81)   PMQs 02 July 2008

PM: Gordon Brown; MP: Bob Russell (LD); S: Michael Martin

```
1   PM:        $and AS for progress being made in afghAnistan,
    cam        ≫ medium close-up of PM - - ->
    pmH
    pmG        $left hand positioned beside notes on dispatch box- - ->
2   PM:        i can Only rePORT; $#
    pmG                - - ->$#
    fig                          #Fig.6.17
3   PM:        $(0.44)‡what sir jock# STIRrup;‡
    pmH              ‡downward gaze to notes‡
    pmG        $. . . . . . . . . .   - - - - - - -
    fig                          #Fig.6.18
4   PM:        <<p,all>‡the chief of $the defence staff has said>‡ Only this
    pmH                  ‡sideward gaze towards opposition benches‡ downward gaze
    pmG                   , , , , , , , , , , ,  $ left hand resting on notes - - ->
               MORning;$
    pmH        to notes   - - ->
    pmG           - - ->$
5   PM:    ->  $°hh <<all>he said> the PROgress we've made‡ over the last few $
    pmH                                     - - ->‡ sideward gaze tow.
    pmG        $. . . . . . . . .- - - - - - -x- - -x- - - -x- - -, , , , , , , , , , , , , , ,$
    fig                          #Fig.6.19
6          ->  $months         ‡is remArkable.
    pmH        opp. benches  ‡downward gaze to notes - - ->
    pmG        $ left hand positioned beside notes on dispatch box - - -≫
7   (MP):      [((cough))]
8   PM:        [(0.44)   ] and he  ‡tAlked about BEing in      ‡ helmand
    pmH                      - - ->‡sidew. gaze tow. opp. benches ‡ downward
               province;=
               gaze to notes - - ->
9   PM:    ->  =<<all>and said> the LAST time i was hEre-
10  PM:    ->  i WASn't able to come into the town ‡at All,
    pmH                                    --->‡ sidew. gaze tow. opp. b. --->
11  PM:    ->  °h it was‡ a FULL scale bAttlefield.
    pmH             --->‡ downward gaze to notes --->
12  PM:    ->  °h NOW <<all>wE've jUst# cOme ‡ twIce through the mAin
    pmH                             - - ->‡ gaze tow. opp. benches
    fig                          #Fig.6.20
           ->  street>.=
    pmH           -≫
13  PM:        =a SIGN-# (0.22)
    fig                 #Fig.6.21
```

```
14  PM:       that thIngs are imPROving <<all, p>as a result of the presence
              of british troops.>
15            °h I: ↑tOo agree with him,
16            °h that Every COUNtry,
17            (0.28) who has SIGNED up to the coalition fOrces,
18            should make (.) a CONtribution, ((turn continues))
```

The direct speech construction is prefaced by a metapragmatic unit which pre-empts turn-constructional space for the quotation to occur and in which the topic, the ascribed source, and the timing of the quotation are named (*and AS for progress being made in afghAnistan, i can Only rePORT; (...)*, lines 1–4). The production of the ascribed source (*sir jock STIRrup;*, line 3) marks a notable transition in the orator's bodily orientation in terms of gaze and manual manipulation (transcribed as 'gesture'). The orator reorients his gaze, which was directed towards his audience, towards his notes and moves his hand, which was placed beside his notes, to touch his notes (Fig. 6.17 and 6.18).

The touching of the notes is coordinated with the production of the proper name of the source, which visually cues the relevance of the naming of the source for the projected quotation (line 3, Fig. 6.18). When he begins the direct quotation, the orator traces his written notes with his fingers.

Figure 6.17 The PM looks towards the opposition benches before engaging with his notes.

Figure 6.18 The PM is touching the notes in synchrony with the proper name of the source, *jock STIRrup*.

The points where he actually touches his notes with his index finger are in coordination with the production of the syllables *PRO*, *we've*, and *made*, marked by 'x' in the transcript (line 5, Fig. 6.19).

Following this heightened manual and kinetic involvement with his notes, the orator moves his left hand back to its former position beside the notes (lines 5–6), displaying manual disengagement from the reading before it is fully completed. In doing so, he retrospectively contextualises *the PROgress we've made* (along with the naming of the source) as the key points of the quotation. This contrasts with the orator's orientation in gaze, which is – with temporary, brief suspensions – sustained towards his notes until the end of the TCU in line 12 (Fig. 6.20). When he begins with a new TCU in line 13, he maintains this visual reorientation towards the in-house audience (Fig. 6.21).

Semantically, the talk summarises the upshot of the quotation in a positive manner (=*a SIGN-(0.22) that thIngs are imPROving <<all, p> as a result of the presence of british troops>*, lines 13–14). I argue that the visual disengagement from the notes, which is maintained in the beginning

6.4 Direct Speech

Figure 6.19 The PM is tracing the direct quotation as written in the orator's notes.

Figure 6.20 The PM shows visual orientation to his notes.

Figure 6.21 The PM displays visual disengagement from his notes.

of the new unit, cues this evaluative summary as performed in his own voice rather than a continuation of the direct quotation. Note, however, that prosodically, this talk is framed as a continuation of the prior speech. This illustrates that visual and prosodic cues are independent from one another. Because of this mismatch between the visual and prosodic contextualisation as well as the lack of clear verbal cues in the wording of the ongoing speech, the footing of lines 13–14 remains ambiguous. It is only in line 15 (*°h I: ↑tOo agree with him*) that the use of the self-referential subject *I:* makes the PM's speaking in his own voice explicit. Here he positions himself towards the questioner in an affiliative fashion.

As in the 1978–1988 data set, there are only a few cases of ambiguous footing in the 2003–2013 sample. This shows that, on the one hand, speakers display a strong orientation to the clear footing of positions and building blocks of their speech. This also means that shifts in footing are signalled overtly. The analysis of the 1978–1988 audio data has evidenced that prosodic and lexico-syntactic cues suffice to this end. This suggests that the main function of visual displays and the manipulation of paper documents is to

6.4 Direct Speech

display evidential access and construct the authority and credibility of the speaker. The latter aspect is especially highlighted when putting what are claimed to be authentic documents on display (see Reber 2020b).

To continue this point, direct quotations are visually performed with orators displaying a (haptic and even kinetic) orientation to their notes, and/or making shifts in body posture and gaze. Notably, the visual orientation towards notes is prepared for before the production of the reporting clause. This suggests two things:

1. Quotations are built up and projected as major building blocks in turns far beforehand, which can be treated as a strategy to create suspense but also to attract the audience's attention.
2. These visual preparations are a window into the speaker's mind, showing the planning of quotations as turn constructional elements online.

Summarising Direct Speech

When orators do not show this visual orientation, the direct speech comes off as summarising dialogue of what was just said by the interlocutor in prior speech or a (general) position/policy. In these cases, the boundaries between the reporting clause and the reported clause tend to be integrated. In this sense summarising direct speech does not represent 'literalised' speech. This type of direct speech is illustrated in the remainder of the chapter.

Ex. (82), which represents a multimodal transcript of Ex. (36), is a case in point for a summary of in situ prior talk framed as reported speech. It is taken from a follow-up move of the LO responding to the PM's prior answer turn.

(82)   PMQs 01 Dec. 2010
LO: Ed Miliband (Lab); PM: David Cameron (Con); S: John Bercow

```
1   S:         Ed MILiband;
2   LO:        <<all>mister SPEAker>;=
3   LO:  ->    =<<all>#he says> #hOw do we get the #GROWTH of the economy up,
    fig              #Fig.6.22 #Fig.6.23      #Fig.6.24
4   LO:        (0.32) Absolutely RIGHT; ((turn continues))
```

In response to the Speaker's summons (*Ed MILiband;*, line 1), the LO answers with an address to the Speaker <<*all> mister SPEAker>;=*, (line 2). Next, he produces a direct quotation ascribed to the PM, grammatically formatted as a wh-interrogative (=<<*all> he says> hOw do we get the*

GROWTH of the economy up, line 3). Note that the reporting clause and the direct speech are done in one single intonation phrase.

The prior address of the Speaker both functions as an answer to the summons and appeals to the Speaker as the target of the subsequent talk, which is evidenced by the LO's visual orientation: he sustains a gaze towards the Speaker during the production of the reporting clause (Fig. 6.22) and the beginning of the direct speech (Fig. 6.23) until he turns to look towards the PM and the government benches (Fig. 6.24).

Thus displaying visible disengagement from his notes placed on the dispatch box, the LO frames the summarising direct speech as a follow up to the prior talk, seemingly performed off the cuff. To 'formulate' (Heritage 1985) the gist of the prior speech is a practice typical of interaction aimed at a split audience. Had the LO shown a visual orientation towards his notes and performed the quotation as being read from prepared notes, the quotation would not have been coherent with the prior interaction.

Ex. (83) exemplifies the second variant of summarising direct speech. Here a (general) position or policy is proposed. Again, the sentence type,

Figure 6.22 The LO looks at the Speaker during the reporting clause.

6.4 Direct Speech

Figure 6.23 The LO sustains his gaze, beginning the quotation.

Figure 6.24 The LO reorients his gaze towards the PM and government benches.

this time an imperative, cues the quotation as direct speech. The excerpt is taken from an answer turn to the LO's fifth question turn.

(83)   PMQs 10 June 2009

PM: Gordon Brown (Lab); LO: David Cameron (Con); S: Michael Martin

```
1   PM:         (there'll) be a chOice between a government that has actively
    cam         ≫ bird's eye view - - ->
2   PM:         intervened to |DEAL # with the recession?
    cam                        - - ->| medium close-up - - -≫
    fig                                      #Fig.6.25
3   PM:    ->  $‡°h and a ‡conSERvative# party that said;
    pmH          ‡g.t. opp.‡ gaze towards S- - ->
    pmG          $. . . . . . . . - - - - - - - - - - - - - - - - -
    fig                                      #Fig.6.26
4   PM:    ->  do #NOTHing.
    pmG          - - - - - - - - - -
    fig           #Fig.6.27
5   PM:         °h and there will be the‡$ #CHOICE nOw; ((turn continues))
    pmH                              - - ->‡
    pmG         ,,,,,,,,,,,,,,,,,,,,,,,,,,,.§
    fig                                      #Fig.6.28
```

The reporting clause in the form of a relative clause and the quotation *and a conSERvative party that said; do NOTHing* occur in lines 3–4. The position/policy framed as a quotation is constructed as marking a contrast to the government's policy depicted as an action (*a government that has actively intervened to DEAL with the recession?*, lines 1–2). What is conveyed here is that the government was active and acted, while the opposition was only talking.

Visually, the reporting clause, which pre-empts turn-constructional space for the (direct) quotation, and the quotation itself are contextualised as one single gestalt which is set off from the surrounding speech. Fig. 6.25 illustrates how the speaker's head position and left-handed gesture are oriented towards the Speaker and/or government benches in the unit preceding the reporting clause (line 2).

The orator shifts his orientation during the audible in-breath at the beginning of line 3, which is marked by a brief head turn towards the opposition benches and a move of his left hand. This becomes the preparation for a pointing gesture whose apex is reached in coordination with the accented premodifier of the NP, referencing the source (Fig. 6.26, line 3, *°h and a conSERvative party that said;*).

Figure 6.25 The PM orients his gesture and gaze towards the Speaker and the government benches.

Fig. 6.27 shows how the apex of the pointing gesture and the head positioning are maintained during the direct speech (*do NOTHing;*, line 4). Note that there are only slight changes in the appearance of the surrounding audience, which helps us to spot the difference between FIGURES 6.26 and 6.27. Finally, Fig. 6.28 shows how the orator has readopted his original posture of head position and gesture.

The retraction phase of the pointing gesture which accompanied the reporting clause and quotation constitutes the preparation for this next gesture. The PM's return to his original posture marks a visible shift in footing, signalling the end of the direct speech. This shift in posture thus functions as a boundary marker of the unit. The visual contextualisation of the right-hand boundary is coordinated with vocal signals which concordantly indicate a clear prosodic boundary between lines 3 and 4: a final prosodic movement falling to low at the end of what is heard as direct speech (line 3) and an audible in-breath at the beginning of what comes off as the orator's speech in his own voice.

Figure 6.26 The PM indexes the ascribed source gesturally and verbally while showing no orientation to his notes.

Figure 6.27 The PM maintains his bodily alignment during the quotation.

6.4 Direct Speech

Figure 6.28 The PM has readopted his original posture of head position and gesture.

Although summarising direct speech as illustrated in the two excerpts is relatively infrequent in the 2003–2013 sample, it represents a new development with respect to other- or third-party quotations in comparison to the 1978–1988 data set. As it represents a rhetorical involvement strategy which plays to the audience, it can be seen as indicating increased media skills on the part of the participants at PMQs. It is certainly not a coincidence that it is mainly the PM and – to a lesser degree – LOs who make use of the practice. They have the two participant roles in a position to perform responsive actions, where such (seemingly) spontaneous practices are best put to use, and they are the ones who arguably benefit from the best coaching in public speaking skills.

This analysis has shown how orators at PMQs use prosodic, lexicosyntactic, and visual cues to contextualise what is treated as two types of direct speech. While the 'literalised' direct speech (Type 1) constitutes an evolving continuation of the direct speech documented in the 1978–1988 sample, the summarising direct speech seems to be an expression of increased media skills, providing speakers with a resource for playing to a split audience.

6.5 Repackaging Quotations (2003–2013)

It has been suggested in the preceding sections that quotations are produced in fairly stable packages. Ex. (84) illustrates the point that the construction of a quotation as direct or indirect reported speech in the real time of speech is (displayed to be) contingent on the availability of notes. Here the PM recruits a written source to challenge the opposition party and the LO with a quotation. To fill a potential pause and save time, he produces the complementiser which contextualises it as indirect speech.

(84)   PMQs 03 Nov. 2010

PM: David Cameron (Con); MP1: Andrew Selous (Con); S: John Bercow

```
1    PM:         °h and ↑I think one of the bEst places to START; (0.32)
     cam         ≫ medium close-up - - ->
2    PM:         with HOUsing benefit,
3    PM:         °h ‡is the maniFESto;# (.)
     pmH            ‡gazes towards Speaker - - ->
     fig                         #Fig.6.29
4    PM;         PERsonally written, (.)
5    PM:         <<laughing> by the honourable GENtleman>=
6    PM:         ‡°h #sitting OPposite me-
     pmH         ‡gazes down to his folder - - ->
     fig            #Fig.6.30
7    PM:         $(.) <<all>because because> # THIS is what °h it sAId; (.)
     pmG         $ engages with notes and browses through folder - - ->
     fig                         #Fig.6.31
8    PM:    ->   it said VERy vEry clEarly,
9    PM:    ->   °h [that hOUsing BEN$ efit;]
     pmG                - - ->$
10   MPs:        [ j sh j sh j sh j sh j           ]
11   PM:    ->   [(0.25) HERE we ‡are,# $ (0.4sh j sh j2)$]
     pmH                   - - ->‡
     pmG    ->                      $ rips out paper noisily$
     fig                         #Fig.6.32
12   MPs:        [j sh j sh j sh j sh j sh j sh j ]
13   PM:    ->   [housing ben?=§]
     pmP                  §rests on right elbow, holding paper- - ->
14   MPs         [j sh j sh j sh ]
15   PM:         |=[<<all, f>thIs was the LAbour manifesto;>]
     cam         |medium close-up of LO--->
16   MPs:         [Ooh:::::::::::::::::::      ]
17   MPs:         [Ooh:::::::::: ]
```

6.5 Repackaging Quotations (2003–2013)

```
18  PM:         [(1.45) <<laughing>well>;]
19  PM:         [°h they All |STOOD on it, (.)]
    cam:                    - - ->|medium close-up of PM--->
20  MPs:        [chu chu chu chu chu chu chu]
21  PM:         [they should be re‡MINDed of #it;]
    pmH                             ‡gazes to notes - - ->
    fig                                      #Fig.6.33
22  MPs:        [chu chu chu chu chu chu chu]
23  PM:    ->   [(0.50) housing BENe‡fit; (0.25)‡]
    pmH                - - ->  ‡looks up  ‡
24  MPs:        [chu chu chu chu chu chu chu]
25  PM:    ->   [‡will be reFORMED; # (0.32)]
    pmH         ‡gazes to notes - - ->
    fig                            #Fig.6.34
26  MPs:        [chu chu chu chu chu chu]
27  PM:    ->   [to ensUre we dO not SUBsidise people,    ]
28  MPs:        [chu chu chu chu chu chu chu chu]
29  PM:    ->   [°h to live in the ↑PRIvate sector, (0.30)]
30  MPs:        [chu chu chu chu chu chu chu chu]
31  PM:    ->   [on RENTS;]
32  MPs:        [chu chuc]
33  PM:    ->   [that Other ordinary working $families‡] [could not
    pmG                      - - ->$ puts notes down
    pmH                                        ->‡
34  MPs:        [chu chu chu chu chu chu chu chu][j j j j
    PM:    ->   af#fOrd; (1.0)          $| (1.67)]
    cam                                 - - ->|medium close-up of LO
    pmG         to dispatch box         - - ->$|
    fig         #Fig.6.35
    MPs:        j j j j j j j j j j j j j j j]
35  PM:         (<<laughing> i say>) (0.36|0.36)]
    cam                              - - ->|bird's eye view - - ->
36  MPs:        j j j j j j j j j 1 j 1 j 1 j j ]
37  PM:         [<<laughing>the level> (0.52)]
38  MPs:        [j 1 j 1 j 1 j 1 j 1 j 1 j 1]
39  PM:         [the LEvel of opportunism is] |sO great;
    cam                                 - - ->|medium close-up of PM--->>
40  MPs:        [j 1 j 1 j 1 j 1 j 1 j 1 j]
41  PM:         that Even when we introduce their ↑OWN policies they oppose
                [them;]§
    pmP          - - ->§
42  MPs:        [ch ch] ch ch ch
```

Figure 6.29 The PM marks the source, while gazing towards the Speaker and gesturally referring to the author of the source, the LO sitting on the opposite bench.

The ascribed source of the quotation is introduced in an *and*-prefaced unit (*and I think one of the bEst places to START (...)*, lines 1–6). The source marking, *the manifEsto PERsonally written, <<laughing> by the honourable gEntleman>; °h sitting OPposite me-*, is accompanied by the speaker's shift in visual orientation from gazing towards the Speaker (Fig. 6.29) down to his notes (Fig. 6.30). At the same time, the verbal reference to the LO, who authored the source, is anticipated and framed by repeated hand gesturing.

When the speaker next projects the quotation in a quotative construction (*((.) <<all> because because> THIS is what °h it sAId*, line 7), he begins to display a heightened kinetic and manual involvement with his notes (Fig. 6.31), searching for the quotation. This process explains the multiple self-repair in this and the subsequent line, where a new reporting clause is produced (*it said VERy vEry clEArly*, line 8).

While still searching his notes, the speaker begins with the quotation *°h that hOUsing BENefit* (line 9) in an independent intonation phrase. The complementiser *that* frames it as indirect speech. In overlap with the beginning of the quotation, the MPs respond with jeering and shouting.

6.5 *Repackaging Quotations (2003–2013)*

Figure 6.30 The PM gesturally references the author of the source.

Figure 6.31 The PM shows kinetic, manual engagement with notes, searching for the quotation in his folder.

Figure 6.32 The PM rips out the page from his folder.

The speaker next abandons the quotation and announces that he has found it, ripping out the page (line 11, Fig. 6.32).

He begins to perform the quotation (line 13) but cuts it off, attending to the disaffiliative audience responses in a side sequence (lines 15, 18–19, 21). His full visual engagement with his notes (Fig. 6.33) marks his re-orientation to the suspended quoting, which he resumes in a restart (*housing BENefit (...)*, lines 23, 25, 27, 29, 31, 33), sustains a gaze at his notes (Fig. 6.34). Bringing the quotation to completion, he gradually disengages from his notes, putting the paper back down on the open folder (Fig. 6.35). This is accompanied by audience responses in overlap.

Note that on both occasions when the speaker resumes the quotation, the *that* complementiser does not get produced, which contrasts with the first initiation of the quotation. Moreover, the grammatical choices with respect to the auxiliary and personal pronoun (*will, we*) in the multi-unit quotation mark it as direct speech with the LO as the principle and author of the manifesto, animated by the PM.

6.5 Repackaging Quotations (2003–2013)

Figure 6.33 The PM displays full engagement with his notes before resuming with a restart of the quotation.

Figure 6.34 The PM performs a 'literalised' quotation.

Figure 6.35 On completion of the quotation, the PM puts the paper back down on the dispatch box.

In sum, what was initiated as indirect speech while searching for notes is reframed as direct speech when the written source becomes available. This shows two things:

1. The complementiser is not functional as a marker of syntactic subordination but signals that the speaker is merely paraphrasing the position quoted. When the notes are available, he repackages the quotation as direct speech, displaying a claim of more direct evidential access to the source. So the availability of notes is used for claims of direct access to sources (which does not mean that this always goes together with direct speech; see Section 6.2).
2. More generally, the grammatical formatting of quotations can be redone in ongoing speech, and this may be explained through the availability of sources. While it can be assumed that notes are used for similar claims of direct access in the 1978–1988 data set, there is no example where this is verbalised, nor does the older sample contain a comparable grammatical repackaging.

6.6 The Formula (AND) I QUOTE (2003–2013)

The analysis of Ex. (84) has further shown that the complementiser *that* may be produced as a filler when speakers are searching their scripts for a quote, something which may be subsequently repaired. This implies that the distinction between direct and indirect speech is not a rhetorical choice as such but may reflect the availability of evidential access to sources. I continue the discussion about how evidential access is contextualised at PMQs in Section 6.6.

6.6 The Formula (AND) I QUOTE (2003–2013)

I have argued that the changed visual media conditions of the television broadcast PMQs, allowed for an interactional differentiation between direct quotations performed in orientation to the speaker's written documents and those done without that visible orientation. The speaker's visible orientation towards his documents was analysed as a claim of authenticity and authority, which, as Reber (2020b) shows, can be increased when displaying what is claimed to be an original copy of the document for credibility enhancement. In this section I propose that a verbal way to maximise claims of authenticity and authority through evidential access is to label the quotation explicitly as a literal, verbatim quotation. The collection contains examples in which participants display an orientation towards quoting the 'exact words'. This is illustrated in Ex. (85).

(85)   PMQs 19 Jan 2011
MP: Grahame M. Morris (Lab); PM: David Cameron (Con); S: John Bercow

```
1    PM:           he should have a look at his OWN pArty's mani[fEsto:; (.)]
2    MPs:                                                       [j sh j sh j sh]
3    PM:           [that SAID,]
4    MPs:          [j sh j sh j ]
5    PM:    ->     [and i QUOTE it almost dirEctly-]
6    MPs:          [j sh j sh j sh j sh j sh j sh j]
7    PM:    ->     [(0.24) the ↑prIvate sector should be alLOWED; (0.27)]
8    MPs:          [j sh j sh j sh j sh j sh j sh j sh j sh j sh j sh]
9    PM:    ->     [INto the en aitch Es:-]
10   MPs:          [j sh j sh j sh j sh j]
11   PM:    ->     [aLONGside the en aitch es:.]
12   MPs:          [j sh j sh j sh j sh j sh j]
```

```
13    PM:    ->   [(0.21) thOse are WORDS:,]
14    MPs:        [j sh j sh j sh j sh j sh ]
15    PM:    ->   [(0.30) from the LAbour manfEsto,]
16    MPs:        [j sh j sh j sh j sh j sh j sh j sh j ]
17    PM:    ->   [(0.27) ↑↑WRITten (.) by his rIght honourable friend. ]
18    MPs:        [j sh j sh j sh j sh j sh j sh j sh j sh j sh ]
```

The speaker produces a reporting clause (*that SAID*, line 3), which projects a quotation in what follows. During the entire extract, the speaker does not consult his notes (not shown here). In an *and*-prefaced clause, *and i QUOTE it almost directly-* (line 5), he frames the quotation that is forthcoming in lines 7, 9, and 11 (*the ↑prIvate sector should be alLOWED; (...)*) as being almost direct. Following the quotation, he upgrades its authenticity as actual wording recorded in writing (*thOse are WORDS:, (0.30) from the LAbour manifEsto, (0.27) ↑↑WRITten (.) by his rIght honourable friend*, lines 13, 15, 17). This shows that while SAY merely projects a shift in footing, QUOTE frames what follows as a direct or verbatim quotation.

It was noted in Section 5.6 that quotations are sometimes introduced not only by a reporting clause but also by the formula (AND) I QUOTE. This practice is only found in the 2003–2013 sample. Although related in meaning, note the difference in semantics between the two verbs:

quote *verb* [...] [I or T] to repeat the words that someone else has said or written[11]

say *verb* [...] [T] to pronounce words or sounds, to express a thought, opinion, or suggestion, or to state a fact or instruction[12]

In this section, I show that the data provide evidence that – in line with these semantic distinctions – there is a division of labour between the two verbs: using the verb QUOTE, speakers claim that the subsequent chunk of speech constitutes a verbatim quotation, authenticating the quoted material performed. The quotative SAY, on the other hand, merely provides an evidential framing for the following speech. This point was made with respect to Ex. (55), which is reproduced as Ex. (55') for convenience.

---

[11] https://dictionary.cambridge.org/dictionary/english/quote
[12] https://dictionary.cambridge.org/dictionary/english/say

6.6 The Formula (AND) I QUOTE (2003–2013)

(55′)   PMQs 03 Nov. 2010
MP: Heidi Alexander (Lab); PM: David Cameron (Con); LO: John Bercow

```
1    MP:            in MARCH of this year;
2                   the prIme minister came to LEWISham college; (0.29)
3                   and spOke to students about his PLANS; (0.34)
4           ->      he SAID, (0.22)
5           ->      and i QUOTE- (0.46)
6                   we'll KEEP it; (0.57)
7                   <<all>we've TAken a look at it,> (0.28)
8                   <<all>we thInk it's a good iDEA.>
```

The speaker first projects the quotation, using the formula *he SAID*, (line 4). She next produces the chunk *and i QUOTE-* (line 5), which is followed by the direct speech (lines 6–8).

Because of the semantics of QUOTE, I suggest that the additional use of (AND) I QUOTE in combination with a reporting clause makes the direct quote 'literalised' and thus more authentic. Ex. (86) is another example of a direct quotation, where the speaker visually frames his performance as consulting his notes (see Chapter 8 for a visual analysis).

(86)   PMQs 11 May 2011
LO: Ed Miliband (Lab); PM: David Cameron (Con); S: John Bercow

```
1    PM:            °h [now i'm GLAD; (0.54)]
2    MPs:              [j j j j j j j j j j]
3    PM:            i'm ↑GLAD that he mentioned °h wAiting times,
4                   because it was it was ↑TWO weeks ago,
5           ->      °h that ↑AT that dispatch box,
6           ->      HE said;
7           ->      and i QUOTE,
8                   °h ↑WAIting times have risen,
9                   °h MONTH on month,
10                  °h <<all>under this GOvernment>;
11   PM:            ↑THAT [is nOt trUE;]
12   MPs:                 [sh sh sh sh ]
```

Like in Ex. (55′), the speaker produces a reporting clause, which precedes the formula (AND) I QUOTE (*that ↑AT that dispatch box, HE said; and i QUOTE*, lines 5–7). These provide an evidential and literal framing for what follows. The quotation in lines 8–10 (*WAIting times have risen, (. . .)*) is formatted as direct speech.

However, (AND) I QUOTE can also be used to introduce indirect speech. Ex. (87) exemplifies this.

(87)   PMQs 07 Dec. 2005

LO: David Cameron (Con); PM: Tony Blair (LO); S: Michael Martin

```
1    LO:    wE support the GOAL;
2           of a new kyOto STYLE:;
3           treaty that will tAckle CARbon emIssions.
4           ↑EARlier this yEar;
5           the prime MINister said <<all>and i quOte>;
6           he has been (.) chAnging his thInking on this ISsue.
7           can he set out his NEW thinking, ((turn continues))
```

After a claim of his party's position (*wE support the GOAL; of a new kyOto STYLE:; treaty (...)*, lines 1–3), the speaker produces a reporting clause which consists of two intonation phrases (↑*EARlier this yEar; the prime MINister said*) with the formula (AND I QUOTE being integrated in the second intonation phrase (<<*all> and i quOte>*, lines 4–5). Displaying visual engagement with his notes (not shown here), the speaker next delivers a quotation, *he has been (.) chAnging his thInking on this Issue* (line 6). The use of the personal pronoun *he* and the possessive pronoun *his* index an indirect quotation.

The example shows that indirect quotations can be framed as literal quotations through the use of the formula (AND) I QUOTE. This implies that speakers can claim a difference between verbatim indirect quotations and non-verbatim ones and that they show an orientation to this at PMQs.

The routine (AND) I QUOTE can further be used to mark mixed quotations.[13] In the spoken interaction at PMQs, (AND) I QUOTE functions similarly to quotation marks, contextualising what follows as direct or even verbatim quotation. Consider Ex. (88).

(88)   PMQs 24 May 2006

PM: Tony Blair(Lab); LO: David Cameron (Con); S: Michael Martin

```
1    PM:    the ↑new home SECretary,
2           has said that the IMmigration (.) and nAtionality directorate,
3           (0.24) after nIne yEArs: of a labour GOVernment,
4           °h is inAdequate? (0.45)
5           dysFUNCtional, (0.36)
6           and nOt fIt for PURpose;
7    ->     °hh more than two YEARS ago:,
```

---

[13] There are multiple examples of this practice in Hansard. Interestingly, what is marked as mixed quotation with quotation marks in the written record does not mirror what was really said in the recordings. In other words, what is marked as mixed quotation in Hansard is not necessarily framed as such in the spoken performance by the speaker.

6.6 The Formula (AND) I QUOTE (2003–2013)

```
8            ->    in fEbruary two thousand and FOUR,
9            ->    °h the prime ↑MInister said, (.)
10           ->    that the immigration and nationality diRECtorate,
11           ->    IS <<all>and i quOte>,
12   PM:     ->    °h A transFORMED (.) pArt [of the hOme office;]
13   MPs:                                   [1 1 1 1 1 1 1 1 1]=
14   MPs:          =[1 1 1 1 1 1 1 1 1 1]
15   LO:           [(2.59) does he (0.79)] ((turn continues))
```

The excerpt contains two quotations. Both are *that*-prefaced, which introduces them grammatically as indirect speech. The first is in lines 2–6 (*that the IMmigration (...)*). The second is in lines 10–12 (*that the immigration (...)*). Here the speaker produces the formula <<*all> and i quOte*>, (line 11) after the copula verb, framing the subject complement as verbatim, *°h A transFORMED (.) pArt of the hOme office;* (line 12). This shows that (AND) I QUOTE represents a formulaic construction which serves to 'literalise' subsequent clausal and phrasal structures. That speakers use the formula to frame short chunks of longer quoted material as verbatim evidences their heightened orientation towards 'literalisation', authentication, and, ultimately, credibility enhancement.

Tables 6.7a and 6.7b show the percentage of quotations framed by (AND) I QUOTE across speaker roles and turn types. Technically, the tokens of direct and indirect speech which occur together with (AND) I QUOTE represent variants of the respective types (described in Sections 6.2 and 6.4), while the mixed quotations are treated as an additional type.

In total, the formula is more widely used in question rather than answer turns, with the LO using it most often. (AND) I QUOTE is deployed to

Table 6.7a *Relative frequencies of (AND) I QUOTE across turn types and speaker roles (MPs, LOs, PMs, 2003–2013)*

Turn types and speaker roles (2003–2013)	DS	IDS	Mixed quotation	Total
MP Question turns (n=828)	0.7% (6)[14]	0% (0)	0.5% (4)[15]	1.2% (10)
Answer turns to MPs (n=828)	0% (0)	0% (0)	0.1% (1)	0.1% (1)
LO Question turns (n=257)	2.0% (5)	0.8% (2)	1.6% (4)	4.4% (11)
Answer turns to LOs (n=257)	0.4% (1)	0% (0)	0.8% (2)	1.2% (3)

[14] Includes the variant THEN I QUOTE (PMQs 16 July 2003).
[15] Includes the variant AND I QUOTE FROM HIS ADVISOR (PMQs 9 January 2013) where the source is named.

Table 6.7b *Relative frequencies of (AND) I QUOTE in question–answer sequences between the Leader of the Liberal Democrats and the PM (2003–2010)*

Turn types and speaker roles (2003–2010)	DS	IDS	Mixed quotation	Total
LLD Question turns (n=56)	0% (0)	0% (0)	1.8% (1)	1.8% (1)
Answer turns (n=56)	0% (0)	0% (0)	0% (0)	0% (0)

frame the subsequent quoted material as verbatim, which can comprise the entirety or only portions of the quotation. If claims of evidential access and authority are regarded as practices to construct credibility, this may explain why the formula is highest in LO question turns, where the LO presents himself as a contender for the office of the prime minister. Seen the other way round, the finding that there is no example of a comparable usage in the 1978–1988 data set suggests that the authentication of sources and building trust with the (mediated) audiences was not as pressing at the same time. Moreover, the older data set does not have mixed quotations of a comparable format, if at all. Methodologically, the analysis shows that a low percentage does not mean an item should be neglected. It rather sheds new light on the findings, in this case that the grammatical formatting of reported speech is only one layer of performing evidentiality in English.

6.7 Summary and Conclusions

In this chapter, I have examined the packaging of reported clauses in 1978–1988 and 2003–2013, especially considering how they are heard and seen by the mediated audiences. What contribute to the contextualisation of reported clauses from the perspective of a radio audience are prosodic, lexico-syntactic, and audio-visual cues. The television and online audience, who have the visual channel available, receive quotations as embodied performances, involving phonetic-prosodic, lexico-syntactic, bodily, and material resources. The analysis has yielded the following categories based on the grammatical features: in the 1978–1988 sample, indirect, 'literalised' direct speech, and 'in between' quotations with ambiguous formatting were identified. With respect to 2003–2013, I have shown that 'literalisation' pertains to all types of reported speech in the 2003–2013 data set. The major types of quotations I have identified include: indirect, 'literalised' (Type 1), and summarising (Type 2) direct speech, as well as 'in between', and mixed quotations.

6.7 Summary and Conclusions

6.7.1 Contextualisations of Reported Clauses in Public Speaking in Parliament over Time

The 2003–2013 reported clauses are contextualised through a variety of resources which is summarised here. Moreover, I discuss what general conclusions can be drawn from these patterns of use.

Indirect Speech
Indirect speech in both data sets is dominated by formats with the complementiser *that*, with an increase in the use of bare forms during 2003–2013. In both data sets, *that*-prefaced clauses tend to be nonintegrated with the prior talk, while bare quotations tend to be integrated. Some (portions of) indirect speech can be marked through rhythmic structures or dense accentuation. While the beginning of the indirect speech is not always prosodically bounded, its final boundaries are generally recognisable in retrospect: the subsequent speech is produced in a new intonation phrase.

'In between'
Both 1978–1988 and 2003–2013 contain grammatically ambiguous forms of reported speech. Their use increases in the more recent sample, which seems to be due to a more interpersonal and dynamic style in the sequences between the LO and the PM, where it is used most often.

'Literalised' Direct Speech
In both data sets, there are corresponding forms of 'literalised' direct speech. In 1978–1988, it has the following features, which authenticate and authorise the quotation in what is heard as a voice of authority:

1. beginning in a new intonation phrase, and ending in an intonation phrase separate from the post-quotation talk;
2. global prosodic shift, which may begin in the reporting clause;
3. conceptually written lexico-syntactic choices, sometimes accompanied by
4. audio-visual cues that suggest the manipulation of paper notes.

Features 1 and 2 are similarly observable in the 2003–2013 formats. As regards 3, while there can be conceptually written framing, it is generally heard as less distancing talk than in 1978–1988. With respect to 4, the visual cues involve a visible engagement with the speakers' notes, a possible haptic manipulation, and a possible shift in bodily posture.

In contrast to the 1978–1988 data set, the 2003–2013 sample shows how speakers can recategorise quotations when visibly engaging with their notes, changing from indirect to direct framing of quotations and vice versa. This suggests that – apart from a more informal style – the grammatical framing of quotations may depend on the availability of sources.

Summarising Direct Speech
Only observable in 2003–2013, this category describes 'non-literalised' direct speech where speakers do not display visual orientation to their notes, and the reporting and reported clause can be prosodically integrated. It can summarise the position just expressed in situ by interlocutors or a (general) position/policy ascribed to a third-party source or the interlocutor.

Mixed Quotations
Marked through the formula (AND) I QUOTE, these are only found in the 2003–2013 sample. Using the formula, speakers can explicitly frame portions of the reported speech as verbatim, which are otherwise non-literal (and marked as indirect speech).

Reported Speech as Building Blocks in Public Speaking in Parliament
Both data sets show a strong preference for clearly marked boundaries of reported speech across types of quotations, displaying a strong orientation towards indicating shifts in footing unequivocally. Other than in everyday conversation, where recipient difficulty over the deictic centre of current speech can be repaired (Couper-Kuhlen 1999), this is not possible for the (mediated) audiences for which the interaction at PMQs is performed.[16] This preference for clear boundaries suggests that the formatting of quotations is recipient designed for a split audience – in line with a general orientation to index overtly what speakers are doing in and through their talk. It is noticeable that despite very different media conditions, this is achieved in equal measure in both periods. The observation that verbal and vocal cues suffice suggests that they constitute different signalling systems compared to bodily and material resources.

With regard to 'literalised' direct speech, the analysis has shown that the manipulation and orientation towards written notes can begin well before the source and/or subject of the reporting clause is named. The reported

---

[16] The data do not contain any instance where a co-present participant makes such trouble in understanding relevant.

speech is also projected and prepared for through a variety of linguistic constructions, pre-empting turn-constructional space for the quotation. This projection suggests that reported speech constructions are well planned and substantial building blocks of turn construction and argumentative interaction.

6.7.2 General Tendencies

In comparison, speakers from both periods are strikingly conservative in the contextualisation of the quotations, with indirect and 'literalised' direct speech representing the two dominant practices. However, the range of the 2003–2013 formats is more diversified, which is indicative of general processes as to how the practices of reported speech at PMQs have evolved. This is discussed in what follows.

Credibility Enhancement
Reported speech has been analysed as an evidential resource which displays speakers' claims about their access to sources. In this way it is a rhetorical resource for constructing a speaker's credibility. The 2003–2013 sample shows an orientation to claims of direct evidential access to an extent which is not visible in the 1978–1988 data set:

- 'Literalised' direct speech, where quotations are staged as verbatim is a particularly powerful format since it displays maximum access to the source. In the 1978–1988 sample, this practice is rare and seems to be reserved for the PM. In contrast, the 2003–2013 sample not only shows a rise in the practice but also demonstrates that it is now distributed across turn types and speaker roles. Here the claimed literal wording of prior discourse is enacted as a visual performance of written sources. (Given that the crackling of paper can be heard in some of the older recordings, it is open to conjecture whether direct speech was staged in a similar fashion.)
- However, claims of direct access are not only displayed with 'literalised' direct speech but also when indirect speech is performed in engagement with paper notes.
- The use of the formula (AND) I QUOTE is only observed with reported speech in the 2003–2013 sample. It is deployed in addition to visual practices to claim direct evidential access overtly, framing what follows as a verbatim quotation. The practice of marking portions of

reported speech as direct quotations has led to the emergence of a new spoken category, mixed quotations, in the 2003–2013 sample.

This heightened orientation to 'literalised' direct speech and claims of direct evidential can be explained by two potential factors. First, a drop in public 'trust in government' since the 'early 1990s' (Bromley *et al.* 2004: 5), which politicians seem to counter with strategies for regaining credibility; second, better access to archives of speech and texts due to recent technological developments, which allows for wider direct, verbatim quoting and furthers claims of direct evidential access; and third, a tendency to play to a mediated viewing audience.

A More Interpersonal Style
A more interpersonal style has been developing in two respects. First, although indirect speech with *that*-prefacing dominates in both data sets, there is a noticeable rise of bare indirect speech in 2003–2013. This points to a more interactional and 'spontaneous' – rather than prepared – production of speech, which comes off as a more interpersonal and involved style (see Biber 1999: 145; Koch and Oesterreicher 2007). Second, the emergence of more varied summarising reported speech: there is already evidence for summarising dialogue in the 1978–1988 sample, but the 2003–2013 sample shows a new tendency in the production of summarising dialogue ascribed to others and third parties (rather than oneself). This represents a general tendency towards a more involved style, which also involves a personalisation and – especially in other-quotations – a polarisation of positions.

CHAPTER 7

Reported Speech and Rhetorical Structures

As was illustrated in Chapter 6, reported speech represents a rhetorical resource in political oratory deployed for the authentication and authorisation of positions as well as for creating audience involvement. Further rhetorical structures typical of political speeches involve lists, contrasts, combined structures such as list and contrast, and puzzle–solution (also known as riddle–solution). I show in this chapter how reported speech can be densely packaged in these structures to lend extra emphasis to the position of speakers and to convey their message in an especially pointed way, and how this packaging has changed between the 1978–1988 and 2003–2013 samples.

The chapter begins with a review of past literature (7.1), before presenting the analytic results concerning lists (7.2) and contrast (7.3) found in 1978–1988 and 2003–2013, as well as combined structures (7.4) from 2003 to 2013, illustrating a more recent development. The chapter is wrapped up with a summary and conclusions (7.5).

7.1 Past Research

In his seminal book on political speeches in the UK, Atkinson identifies two rhetorical devices that are designed to solicit applause, which he calls 'claptraps': lists of three and contrast, or the use of the two combined (Atkinson 1984: 57). He states that 'the secret of successful claptrap production lies in the simultaneous and co-ordinated use of relatively few verbal and non-verbal techniques which signal to audiences *that* they should start clapping and *when* they should' (Atkinson 1984: 83; italics in the original). At the same time lists and contrasts have a high quotability: 'The fact that they feature in some of the best-known quotations of all time suggests that they are peculiarly susceptible to being noticed, reported, and remembered' (Atkinson 1984: 131). In other words, if speech is organised in lists and/or contrasts, these portions are likely to be quoted in other discourse contexts. However, this only explains in part why the quotations at PMQs might come in these rhetorical structures. Before turning to the data analysis, in what follows I present a review of past research concerned with the relevant rhetorical structures.

The typical format of list structures in English political oratory as well everyday interaction is three-part (Atkinson 1984; Heritage and Greatbatch 1986; Jefferson 1990; but see Couper-Kuhlen 1986; Selting 2007 on longer list formats). The list items in examples from the literature vary with respect to their syntactic forms: they may be composed of clausal or subclausal structures. Although there is a preference for similarity between list members, which can be achieved on various levels, the examples in the literature suggest that, in general, formal similarity is not necessarily a requirement for chunks of talk to be treated as items in a list.

However, lists in political speeches 'normally take the form of triples of noun phrases [...] or of qualifying adjectives' (Heritage and Greatbatch 1986: 126) which can further be integrated through, for example, 'alliteration and the use of rhyme and repetition' (Heritage and Greatbatch 1986: Fn 18). Prosodically, lists can be characterised as complete or incomplete with respect to the pattern of pitch accents formed by the list items (Couper-Kuhlen 1986: 150, with reference to Schubiger 1958: 72–3).

Ex. (89), taken from a speech by Margaret Thatcher at a Conservative Party Conference, illustrates a recurrent list intonation in political speeches:

(89)   Conservative Party Conference, 1980 (adapted from Atkinson 1984: 63)

```
Thatcher:     Soviet Marxism is
         1-> ideol↑ogically
         2-> pol↑itically
         3-> and mor↓ally bank↓ru[pt|------(9.0------|
                              [xxXXXXXXXXXxx-x
```

Here the first two items (*ideol↑ogically*, *pol↑itically*) are realised with rising final pitch movement, 'and the third with a fall on the last beat' (*and mor↓ally bank↓ru[pt*; Atkinson 1984: 63, see also Erickson 1992 on lists in English conversation). As is indicated by the multiple x's in the last line, the list is taken up in overlap with applause by the audience. Rhetorically, lists are deployed for emphasis (Heritage and Greatbatch 1986: 126), which means that lists in reported speech at PMQs should represent an especially pointed means of claiming a position.

7.1 Past Research

The second type of structure, contrast, serves as a rhetorical device to categorise positions as similar to or different from that of the speaker. Connal states:

> Rhetoricians made use of the topic of difference in order to develop arguments that would confirm or refute their positions. Comparisons of similarities and differences (contrasts) can also be used to restate a position in order to highlight the weakness of an opposing position in an argument or to develop a refutation of opposing arguments. (Connal 1996: 145)

For political speeches, this means that orators usually construct contrasts between 'us' and 'them', conveying positive assessments of 'us' and negative ones of 'them' (Atkinson 1984: 37–46, 73–85; see also Chilton 2007).

To describe how contrast and opposition is organised on the text level, Rhetorical Structure Theory (RST; Mann and Thompson 1988) offers a framework to analyse relations between two portions of a text (generally, but not exclusively, clausal units), 'whether or not they are grammatically or lexically signalled' (Mann and Thompson 1988: 244). A contrast relation holds between two text portions which are:

(a) comprehended as the same in many respects,
(b) comprehended as differing in a few respects and
(c) compared with respect to one or more of these differences

(Mann and Thompson 1988: 253)

Drawing on RST, Ford (2000) notes that contrast is a rhetorical move which comes in larger discourse patterns: '[A]cross contexts, contrasts are treated as needing resolution in subsequent talk; that is, they are regular building blocks for larger actions involving explanations or solutions for problematic states of affairs' (Ford 2000: 285). As regards the formal packaging of contrasts in political speeches, Atkinson (1984) stresses 'the importance of producing two contrasting pairs which resemble each other in length and content' (Atkinson 1984: 77) in order to be rhetorically effective, that is, to solicit applause. Similar to lists, the intonation contour of the first contrastive part projects 'more to come' (Atkinson 1984: 74), while the second has a final pitch movement signalling completion. In coordination with lexico-semantic and syntactic properties, this intonation provides strong cues for timely audience responses.

Barth-Weingarten (2006, 2009) on English everyday conversation describes in detail how contrasts are built of similar pairs, a format labelled parallel-opposition structure. She identifies two construction patterns: AXBY, where two subjects (A, B) and their properties (X, Y) are contrasted; and ZXY, where the two properties (X, Y) of one single subject (Z) are contrasted. Based on these patterns, a third variant is categorised: ZAXZ'BY, where the subject remains the same (Z, Z') and two contrastive properties in non-subject position are compared (A, B and X, Y; Barth-Weingarten 2006: 156). In her everyday data, parallel-opposition constructions are generally realised as AXBY and ZAXZ'BY: here the contrastive parts relate to the same topic, come in declarative sentence types, have a fixed order, and are typically produced by the same speaker in one single turn. Prosodically, the first part commonly bears a contrastive accent and projects a continuation of the turn (and structure; Barth-Weingarten 2006: 160–4).

Puzzle–solution structures, to my knowledge – unlike lists and contrasts – have only been described with respect to political discourse, for example, parliamentary interaction (Antaki and Leudar 2001) and political speeches in UK and US contexts (Atkinson 1984; Heritage and Greatbatch 1986; Sato 2014). The puzzle–solution is described as a device to emphasise a point the speaker wishes to make:

> In this comparatively straightforward device, the speaker begins by establishing some kind of puzzle or problem in the minds of the listeners and then, shortly afterward, offers as the solution to the problem a statement that stands as the core to the message that he or she wishes to get across. The adumbrated message is emphasised by the puzzle, which invites the audience to anticipate or guess at its solution and, by the same token, to listen carefully to the speaker's own solution when it is delivered. (Heritage and Greatbatch 1986: 127)

Antaki and Leudar point out that in parliamentary debates, puzzles do not constitute a real source of confusion but are only rhetorically staged as such: 'Of course, given the public nature of this genre and its transparency to its hearers, the revelation that the person quoted is the speaker's opponent is something of an open secret: yet the trick retains its power, just as any properly executed stagecraft does' (Antaki and Leudar 2001: 481).

While the prosodic and lexico-syntactic formatting of lists and contrasts is relatively well researched across discourse contexts, the foregoing literature review has revealed a gap in the research with respect to the linguistic analysis of puzzle–solution structures.

All relevant rhetorical structures (lists, contrasts, and puzzle–solutions) are functional in emphasising the speaker's point or message in such a way that it invites applause, that is, an affiliative audience response. This means

7.2 Lists

that they serve as an involvement strategy, engaging either present or mediated, non-present audiences in emotional ways. As regards contrast, the construction of opposition and contrast between 'us' and 'them' may be particularly functional in processes of polarisation between the government and the opposition, which is also made visible in the ecology of space in the House of Commons.

7.2 Lists

Both data sets, 1978–1988 as well as 2003–2013, contain examples of list constructions. The focus of the analysis is three-part lists.

1978–1988
The 1978–1988 data set contains five quotations with lists, which are all tripartite and contextualised as complete lists but are syntactically and prosodically diverse. Ex. (90), which includes the interaction shown in Ex. (18), exemplifies such a case.

(90)   PMQs 07 May 1985
MP: David Alton (LD); PM: Margaret Thatcher; S: Bernard Weatherill

```
1    PM:           [i notice also that he refers to the speech of my]
2    MPs:          [sh sh sh sh sh sh sh sh sh sh sh sh sh sh sh ]

     PM:           [rIght honourable friend the secretary of state for ENergy-
     MPs:          [chu chu chu chu chu chu chu chu chu chu chu chu chu chu

     PM:           (0.27)]
3    MPs:          h h h ]

4    PM:      ->   [with regArd to unemployment i notice that my right honourable
5    MPs:          [chu chu chu chu chu chu chu chu chu chu chu chu chu chu chu

     PM:      ->   friend SAID;]
     MPs:          chu chu chu ]

6    PM:      ->   [(0.39) to obtAin GROWTH;]
7    MPs:          [chu chu chu chu chu chu ]

8    PM:      ->   [(0.35) we must obtAin the right relationship between PAY and
9    MPs:          [chu chu chu chu chu chu chu chu chu chu chu chu chu chu

     PM:      ->   invEstment and productIvity.]
     MPs:          chu chu chu chu chu chu  ]

10   PM:           [(0.37) an inflationary wage round linked with] produc'
11   MPs:          [chu chu chu chu chu chu chu chu chu chu ]

12   PM:           ↑UNlinked with productIvity-
13   PM:           °h would do imMENSE dA[mage to britain's economic
```

```
14   MPs:                                    [chu chu chu chu chu chu chu
     PM:       opportunity;]
     MPs:      chu chu chu ]
15   PM:       [i WHOlly] [agrEE. (.) ]
16   MPs:      [chu chu ] [chu chu ch ]
17   MP:              [h h h h h ]
```

The reporting clause, *(-) with reGARD to unemployment i nOtice that my right honourable friend sAid;* (line 5), projects the quotation *(-)to obTAIN grOwth;(-) we must obtAin the right relationship between PAY and invEstment and productIvity; (...)* (lines 6, 8, 10, 12–13). A portion of the quotation is delivered in a three-part list composed of three accented items: *PAY, invEstment,* and *productIvity* (line 8). Each of these accented syllables has a high-rising pitch, a pitch movement which is anticipated in the prior intonation phrase on the syllable with primary accent, *GROWTH* (line 6). The list items are integrated in one single intonation contour with a final low-falling pitch movement, which is produced on the last list item (see Ex. (90′)).

(90′)   List structure of Ex. (90), lines 6 and 8.

```
1        (0.39) to obtAin GRÓWTH;
2     ->1 (-) we must obtAin the right relationship between PÁY
3     ->2 and invÉstment
4     ->3 and productÍvity.
```

The list in the example is characterised by syntactically parallel list items, each composed of an NP, which are prosodically contextualised as a complete list and produced in a single intonation phrase. Finally, the PM herself displays an affiliative stance towards the position claimed in the list (*i WHOlly agrEE,* line 15), which is shared by a soft affiliative uptake (line 17).

To sum up, the list structures found in the 1978–1988 data match those illustrated in previous studies on political discourse. All instances in the sample represent prosodically complete lists, showing syntactically diverse formats. However, despite being formally recognisable as lists, these lists do not (necessarily) serve as claptraps. Note that affiliative audience responses are only forthcoming following the PM's claim of agreement in Ex. (90).

2003–2013
Probably due to the rather small collection of lists, the 1978–1988 sample is too diverse to be compared with the sample from the 2003–2013 data set.

Nevertheless, what can be noted is that the three-part lists in the 2003–2013 sample are also syntactically diverse and prosodically complete. What is different, however, is that each of the list items tends to be listed in an independent intonation phrase and the list often constitutes the entire quotation (rather than being presented as a part of a longer quotation). This is exemplified in Ex. (91).

(91)   PMQs 02 July 2008
LLD: Nick Clegg (LD); PM: Gordon Brown (Lab); S: Michael Martin

```
1   LLD:         [there is a MENtal health crisis; (0.20)]
2   MPs:         [chu chu chu chu chu chu chu chu chu]

3   LLD:         [in this cOuntry toDAY;=]
4   MPs:         [chu chu chu chu chu]

5   MP1:         [=<<all>hear hear HEAR;>= ]
6   MPs:         [chu chu chu chu chu chu  ]

7   LLD:  ->     [=Ev[en the new          ] president of the royal
8   MP1:            [<<all>hear HEAR;>]
9   MPs:         [chu chu chu chu chu chu chu chu chu chu chu chu chu

    LLD:  ->     college of psychiatrists psyCHIatrists;]
    MPs:         chu  chu  chu                          ]

10  LLD:  ->     [(0.30) himself] said this week-
11  MPs:         [chu chu chu chu]

12  LLD:  ->     that our mEntal health wArds (0.25) ARE i quOte;
13        ->     (0.39) unacCEPtable,(.)
14        ->     uninHABitable,
15        ->     and †DANgerous.
16               [(0.20) there's no exCUSE for the prime minister's complAcency.]
17  MPs:         [chu chu chu chu chu chu chu chu chu chu chu chu chu chu chu  ]
```

The list *unacCEPtable,(.) uninHABitable, and DANgerous.* (lines 13–15) is composed of three parallel adjective phrases, with the first two characterised by alliteration. The last list item is taken up with disaffiliative audience responses on the part of MPs (line 17). In contrast to the list in Ex. (90), which also consists of three syntactic phrases, the three list items in the present example are done in three separate intonation phrases, which lends them more prominence. Prosodically, the list is contextualised as a complete list: the intonation phrases of list items 1–2 end on a mid-rising final pitch movement, while the final contour on list item 3 falls to low (Ex. 91′). The pitch movements on the accented syllables are falling (items 1–2) and rising (3): *unacCÈPtable,(.) uninHÀBitable, and ↑DÁNgerous.* The last list item is taken up with disaffiliative audience responses on the part of MPs (Ex. 91, line 17).

(91')   List structure of Ex. (91), lines 13–15.
```
1    ->1    (0.39) unacCÈPtable,(.)
2    ->2    uninHÀBitable,
3    ->3    and ↑DÁNgerous.
```

Even though more research is necessary, this first comparison with the 1978–1988 list structures suggests that the performance of listed quotations seems to be done more skilfully in the 2003–2013 data set. Generally presented without any further quoted material following the list, they tend to present the point of the quoted position in a short and sweet fashion. Moreover, the presentation of the list items in independent intonation phrases makes them more prominent and adds more emphasis to each item, inviting audience responses on the part of the parliamentary MPs.

7.3   Contrast

Contrast can be enacted in various ways at PMQs. In this section, I focus on contrast relations constructed between two quotations indexed by SAY.[1] In the argumentative interaction at PMQs, such contrastive constructions are deployed to claim contradictions in the argument/positions of the political opponent or to claim disagreement with the political opponent, which creates an opposition between 'us' and 'them'.

1978–1988
When quotations feature contrasts, the most common format in the 1978–1988 data set is a parallel opposition type of construction, which tends to be used in question turns. Consider Ex. (92), which includes the interaction represented in Ex. (19). Here two quotations indexed by SAY are put into opposition.

---

[1] The data sample suggests a wider variety of contrastive structures which operate on a broader level. For instance, constructions of contrast between what is/was said and what is/was done (see Ex. 83) seem to be a patterned component of specific turn-internal structures of action formation, an observation which should be explored in future research.

7.3 *Contrast* 203

(92) PMQs 12 Nov. 1981
MP1: Christopher Price (Lab); PM: Margaret Thatcher (Con); S: George Thomas

```
 1  S:        christopher PRICE;
 2  MP1:      [((clears throat)) could (.) ↑could the prime minister (0.42)
 3  MPs:      [mur mur mur mur mur mur mur mur mur mur mur mur mur mur mur
    MP1:      clear up (0.51) one: disCREPancy.]
    MPs:      mur mur mur mur mur mur mur mur ]
 4  MP1:      [(0.48) which (.) stands between HER statement (0.26) about
 5  MPs:      [mur mur mur mur mur mur mur mur mur mur mur mur mur mur mur
    MP1:      mister leo lOng's espionage actIvities,]
    MPs:      mur mur mur mur mur mur mur mur mur mur ]
 6  MP1:      [˙h and that of the attorney GENeral. (0.48)]
 7  MPs      [mur mur mur mur mur mur mur mur mur mur mur]
 8  MP1: ->  [where ↑SHE said; (0.43)]
 9  MPs:      [mur mur mur mur mur mur]
10  MP1: ->  [that there was ONE other indivIdual; (0.33)]
11  MPs:      [mur mur mur mur mur (h h h h h h h h h h) ]
12  MP1: ->  [to whom: inducements: had been GIven; (0.42)]
13  MPs:      [(h h h h h h h h h h h h h h h h h h h h)]
14  MP1: ->  the at↑TORney said,    (0.32)
15       ->  there were a ↑FEW other individuals.
16  MPs:      [mur mur mur mur mur mur mur mur mur mur mur mur mur mur mur
17  MP1:      [(0.53) could the? (0.23) could the prIme minister TELL the
    MPs:      mur mur]
    MP1:      house;]
18  MPs:      [mur mur mur mur mur mur mur mur mur ]
19  MP1:      [what the fActs ARE in these mAtters,]
20  MPs:      [mur mur mur mur mur mur mur mur mur mur mur mur mur mur
21  MP1:      and how mAny uh is the NUMber that the attOrney was referring
    MPs:      mur]
    MP1:      to;]
22  MPs:      [mur mur mur mur mur mur mur mur mur mur mur mur mur mur   ]
23  MP1:      [in a FEW individuals (.) being offered inducements to confEss;]
24  MP2:      and how [many      ] uhm=
25  MP3:              [HEAR hear;]
26  PM:       =((begins with answer turn))
```

The contrastive structure occurs in lines 8, 10, 12, and 14–15, reproduced below for convenience (Ex. 92′).

(92′)   Contrastive structure in Ex. (92), lines 8, 10, 12, and 14–15.

```
1   ->A    where ↑SHE said; (0.43)
2   ->X    that there was ONE other indivIdual; (0.33)
3          to whom: inducements: had been GIven; (0.42)
4   ->B    and the at↑TORney said, (0.32)
5   ->Y    there were a FEW other individuals.
```

Here a position framed as a quotation ascribed to the PM (Ex. (92′), lines 1–3) is opposed to a quoted position by the attorney (lines 4–5) on the same topic. The PM (↑*SHE*) and *the at↑TORney* share their function as ascribed source, being produced in a syntactically parallel fashion in subject position. *ONE* and *FEW* are syntactically parallel elements of the quotations. Note that these contrasted items between the clauses each have primary accents and are heard as contrastive accents: in this way, they form a parallel-opposition structure of the form AXBY: A (↑*SHE*) X (*ONE*) B (*the at↑TORney*) Y (*FEW*). The structure emphasises a contradiction in the position of the government in an encapsulated fashion. Ex. (92) (lines 10–13) suggests that the X-part is taken up with affiliative audience responses but not the final Y-part, where it is unclear from the recording how it is treated. In any case, the contrast does not solicit strong audience responses, which is in line with the observations made for lists in the 1978–1988 sample.

2003–2013

Ex. (93) is taken from the 2003–2013 data set and corresponds to the 1978–1988 example in Ex. (92) in terms of structure.

(93)   PMQs 14 Jan. 2009
MP: Gregory Campbell (DUP); PM: Gordon Brown (Lab); S: Michael Martin

```
1   S:     gregory CAMPbell-
2   MP:    <<all>THANK you mister speaker;>]
3   MPs:   [chu chu chu chu chu chu chu chu]
4   MP:    [next wEek=uh: the new PRESident of the united states of
5   MPs:   [chu chu chu chu chu chu chu chu chu chu chu chu chu chu
    MP:    America takes up office;]
    MPs:   chu chu chu chu chu chu]
6   MP:    [((click)) ˙h ↑whAt other differences are there betWEEN them;]
7   MPs:   [chu chu chu chu chu chu chu chu chu chu chu chu chu chu]
```

```
8   MP:   -> [˙h apart from the prIme MINister; (0.30)]
9   MPs:     [chu chu chu chu chu chu chu chu chu chu]
10  MP:   -> [inadvErtently saying that he's alREAdy saved the world,]
11  MPs:     [chu chu chu chu chu chu chu chu chu chu chu chu chu]
12  MP:   -> [˙h and the prEsident's saying that he NEEDS to;]
13  MPs:     [chu chu chu chu chu chu chu chu chu chu chu]
14  MPs:     chu l l l l
```

The contrast is organised in an AXBY structure, coordinated by *and* (lines 8, 10, 12). This is illustrated in Ex. (93′).

(93′) AXBY structure in Ex. (93), lines 8, 10, and 12

```
1   ->A   ˙h apart from the prIme MINister; (0.30)
2         inadvErtently saying
    ->X   that he's alREAdy saved the world,
3   ->B   ˙h and the prEsident's saying
    ->Y   that he NEEDS to;
```

Note that the parallel, opposing items are again stressed (with the Prime Minister, at whom the question turn is targeted, even bearing two accents): A (*prIme MINister*) vs. B (*prEsident's*), X (*alREAdy*) vs. Y (*NEEDS*). They are both about the same topic, that is, saving the world. Here a contradiction is created which serves to ridicule the PM, evidenced by the responsive collective laughter (Ex. 93, line 14). Ex. 94 shows another parallel-opposition structure from an MP's question turn, which has a more complex format (AXZBYZ′).

(94) PMQs 08 Dec. 2010
MP: Jack Dromey (Lab); PM: David Cameron (Con); S: John Bercow

```
1   S:       jack DROmey;
2   MP:      (0.51) uhm [(0.45) is the: prime minister aWARE;]
3   MPs:                [chu chu chu chu chu chu chu chu   ]
4   MP:      [(0.37) mister speaker that PARliament;]
5   MPs:     [chu chu chu chu chu chu chu chu chu chu]
6   MP:      [(0.69) ]may have been infiltrated by (.) an imPOSter;
7   MPs:     [shh shh]
8   MPs:     [(.) ((scattered, quiet laughter))]
9   MP:   -> [(0.86) uh?                       ] [the DEPuty prime
10  MPs:                                         [1 mur 1 mur 1 mur 1 mur
    MP:   -> minister; (1.64)]
    MPs:     1 mur 1 mur 1 mur ]
```

```
11  MP:   -> [the dep? (1.40)]   [the deputy (0.81) the deputy prime MINister;]
12              [l chu l chu l  ]  [l sh l sh l sh l sh l sh l sh l sh l sh l ]
13  MP:   -> [(3.89) the deputy prime MINister;]
14  MPs:      [l sh l sh l sh l sh l sh l sh l sh]
15  MP:   -> [(1.38) the deputy prIme minister has SAID;]
16  MPs:      [chu sh chu sh chu sh chu sh chu sh chu sh ]
17  MP:   -> that he will VOTE (.) to trEble tuItion fees-
18  MPs:      and aBOLish the education mAintenance allowance.
19  MP:   -> (0.58) befOre the general election the [leader of the liberal
20  MPs:                                             [l chu l chu l chu l
    MP:   -> ↑DEMocrats, (0.90)]]
    MPs:      chu l chu l chu l   ]
21  MP:   -> [sAid (.) that he would vOte to a↑BOLish tuition fees, ]
22  MPs:      [chu sh chu sh chu sh chu sh chu sh chu sh chu sh chu]
23  MP:   -> [and ↑KEEP the educational mAintenance allowance.]
24  MPs:      [chu sh chu sh chu sh chu sh chu sh chu sh chu sh ]
25  MP:      [(0.87) mister SPEAker;]
26  MPs:     [chu sh chu sh chu sh  ]
27  MP:     [(0.34) can the prime MINister; (1.41)]
28  MPs:    [chu sh chu sh chu sh chu sh chu sh    ]
29  S:     the ↑HONourable gentleman will have a chance to fInish his
           Question;=
30         =without CHUNtering and shOuting from a sedentary position;
31         (0.68) the LAST sentence. (0.33)
32  MP:    mister SPEAker; (0.50)
33         cAn the prime minister TELL the house;
34         (0.48) are there TWO;
35         (0.20) nick CLEGGS.
36  MPs:   [ch sh ch sh ch sh ch sh ch ]
37  PM:    [(1.30) ((begins with turn))]
```

The parallel opposition structure is produced in lines 9, 11, 13, 15, 17, 19, 21, and 23. It is asyndetic. The structure is formatted as AXZBYZ′, as illustrated in Ex. (94′).

(94′) AXZBYZ′ structure in Ex. (94), lines 9, 11, 13, 15, 17, 19, 21, and 23

```
1  ->A  (1.38) the deputy prIme minister has SAID;
2  ->X  that he will VOTE (.) to trEble tuItion fees-
3  ->Z  and aBOLish the education mAintenance allowance.
4  ->B  (0.58) befOre the general election the leader of the liberal
        ↑DEMocrats, (0.90)]
```

```
5         sAid (.)
6    ->Y  that he would vOte to a↑BOLish tuition fees,
7    ->Z' and ↑KEEP the educational mAintenance allowance.
```

The parallel sets of key items each are accented, which is heard as contrastive stress. A (*deputy prIme minister*) vs. B (*leader of the liberal ↑DEMocrats*), X (*trEble*) vs. Y (*a↑BOLlish*), and Z (*abolish*) vs. Z' (*↑KEEP*). Note the accents on the second, contrasting items (B, Y, and Z') are all produced with a step-up in pitch, which adds extra emphasis. The relation of opposition is constructed through different labels for one and the same referent (*deputy prIme minister, leader of the liberal ↑DEMocrats*), which serves to emphasise contradictions between the past positions of the deputy PM. This attacks the credibility of the government. The additional rhetorical device to refer to the deputy PM in various ways creates extra involvement (see also the first label, *imPOSter*, set up as a puzzle; Ex. 94, line 6).

The foregoing analysis has shown that speakers use parallel-opposition structures of varying complexity to construct relations of opposition in the two data sets, attacking the government on various levels. Similar to mundane interaction, they are performed within the same turn, and relate to the same topic. What is different is the contrastive accents on all parallel items, which adds extra emphasis but also transparency to facilitate understanding in the context of mediated, public speaking. While the 1978–1988 example has a contrastive construction that expresses a conflict in a non-figurative way, the 2003–2013 examples stage oppositional positions, adding extra rhetorical layers.

7.4 Combined Structures (2003–2013)

Marking a stark contrast between the two data sets is the fact that 2003–2013 speakers use combined rhetorical devices to present quotations. This is not to say that there are no combined structures in the 1978–1988 set. However, they do not include quotations with SAY. I illustrate the practice in the 2003–2013 sample, beginning with combined list, contrast, and puzzle–solution structures before turning to the analysis of single puzzle–solution formats.

7.4.1 Combined List, Contrast, and Puzzle–Solution

Ex. (95) exemplifies how quotations are presented in a list, in combination with a contrast structure and puzzle–solution. Note that it is not the quoted list which is appreciated by the audience but the moment when it is put in contrast. The excerpt is taken from an answer turn in response to the Leader of the Liberal Democrats, the second biggest opposition party at the time. The pronominal address *(hE,* line 12) makes deictic reference to the questioner. The Conservative party named in line 4 was the largest opposition party at the time of the recording. In the excerpt, P stands for puzzle, and S for solution.

(95)   PMQs 24 May 2006
LLD: Sir Menzies Campbell (LD); PM: Tony Blair (Lab); S: Michael Martin

```
1   MPs:            [chu chu chu chu chu chu chu chu chu ]
2   PM:             [now i was ↑sAying a moment or two aGO.]
3   MPs:            [chu chu chu chu chu chu chu chu chu chu chu chu chu chu chu
4   PM:     ->A     [(0.57) that the consErvative party (.) had vOted agAinst
    MPs:            chu chu chu chu chu chu chu chu chu chu chu chu ]
    PM:     ->X     mAny of the mEasures nEcessary to STRENGthen the lAw,]
5   MPs:            [chu chu chu chu chu chu]
6   PM:     ->1     [(0.24) ON immigration,]
7   MPs:            [chu chu chu]
8   PM:     ->2     [on aSYlum,]
9   MPs:            [chu chu chu chu chu ]
10  PM:     ->3     [an_on ↑CRIME. (0.70)]
11  MPs:            [chu chu chu chu chu chu chu chu chu chu chu chu]
12  PM:     ->P     [hE at least has been THORoughly consistent. (0.24)]
13  MPs:            [chu chu chu chu chu chu chu chu]
14          ->S:BY  [he's voted against (.) !EVE!ry meas] [ure nEcessary. (1.17)]
15  MPs:                                                  [l ch l ch l ch l ch l ]
16  MPs:            [chu chu chu chu chu chu chu chu chu chu chu chu]
17  PM:     ->1     [to strEngthen the law against ilLEgal immigrAtion,]
18  MPs:            [chu chu chu chu chu chu chu chu]
19  PM:     ->2     [against UNfounded asylum seekers-  ]
20  MPs:            [chu chu chu chu chu hu ]
21  PM:     ->3     [an=in respect of CRIME.]
```

The *now*-prefaced reporting clause, *i was ↑sAying a moment or two aGO.* (line 2), projects the subsequent indirect quotation, *that the consErvative party (. . .)* (lines 4, 6, 8, 10). The last portion of the quotation is made up of the prepositional phrases *ON immigration,* (line 6), *on aSYlum,* (line 8), *an_on ↑CRIME.* (line 10), which build a three-part list with parallel members. Prosodically, it is framed as a complete list: the first two items

7.4 *Combined Structures (2003–2013)* 209

are done in intonation phrases with mid-rising final contours, while the last is falling to low. In what follows, the speaker sets up a puzzle (*hE at least has been THORoughly consistent*, line 12), which leaves the audience guessing what is meant by him being consistent. Next the solution is presented (*he's voted against (.) !EVE!ry measure nEcessary*, line 14). This marks a contrast to line 4 in an AXBY structure: A (*the consErvative party*), X (*mAny*), B (*he*), Y (*!EVE!ry*). This is appreciated by laughter and cheering by the government MPs (line 15). The subsequent list (*to strEngthen the law against (. . .)*, lines 17, 19, 21) recycles the list items from the first. Ex. (96) illustrates another combined list and contrast structure, set up as a puzzle–solution but organised in a slightly different way.

(96) PMQs 08 Dec. 2010
LO: Edward Miliband (Lab); PM: David Cameron (Con); S: John Bercow

```
1   MPs:        [chu chu chu ch chu ]
2   PM:         [the ↑FACT is; (0.48)]
3   MPs:        [chu chu chu chu chu chu chu chu chu]
4   PM:         [they WENT into the lAst election;     ]
5   MPs:        [chu chu chu chu chu chu chu chu    ]
6   PM:         [(0.54) he WENT into the last election,]
7   MPs:        [chu chu chu chu chu chu chu chu chu chu chu chu chu chu
8   PM:         (0.31) with a twEnty five percent cut planned in the bUsiness
    MPs:        chu chu chu chu chu]
    PM:         de↑PARTment; (0.34)]
9   MPs:        [chu chu chu chu chu chu chu chu chu chu]
10  PM:         [and he's got !AB!solutely no wAY, (0.21)]
11  MPs:        [chu chu chu chu chu chu chu chu ]
12  PM:         [of mAking the numbers add ↑UP; (0.79)]
13  MPs:        [chu chu chu chu chu chu chu chu  ]
14  PM:    ->   [what ↑Everybody KNOWS mister spEAker;]
15  MPs:        [chu chu chu chu chu chu chu chu chu chu chu chu chu]
16  PM:    ->   [(0.30) they ↑SAID they wouldn't introduce tuItion fees,]
17  MPs:        [chu chu chu chu chu    ]
18  PM:    ->   [(.) thEY introDUCED them,]
19  MPs:        [chu chu chu chu chu chu chu chu chu chu chu chu  ]
20         ->   [(0.31) they ↑SAID they wouldn't introduce topup fEEs;  ]
21  MPs:        [chu chu chu  ]
22  PM:    ->   [(.) they intro][DUCED them; (0.50)
23  MPs:                        [ch ah ch ah ch ah ]
```

```
24  MPs:        [chu chu chu chu chu chu chu chu chu chu]
25  PM:    ->   [they sAid they supPORted the brOwne revIEw,]
26  MPs:        [chu chu chu chu chu chu chu chu    ]
27  PM:    ->   [(0.30) he !WROTE! it into their manifEsto.]
28  MPs:        [chu chu chu chu chu chu chu chu chu chu chu chu
29  PM:    ->   [(0.30) WHY are they breaking (.) their plEdge about the
    PM:         brOwne review; (1.7)]
30  MPs:        j sh fp sh fp j sh fp]
31  MPs:        [j sh fp j sh]
32  PM:    ->   [↑WHY; (6.37)]
33  MPs:        [j sh fp j sh fp j sh fp j sh fp j sh   ]
34  PM:         [<<laughing>he> (1.47) he SAW; (0.77)]
35  MPs:        [j sh fp j sh fp j sh]
36  PM:         [the FACT is; (1.25)  ]
37  MPs:        [j sh fp j sh fp j  ]
38  S:          [<<f>!UH!;> (1.60)]
39              ↑ALL this finger pointing is vEry unsEEmly;
40  MPs:        h h [h h h h h
```

The extract contains a combined list and contrast structure with reported speech which is set up as a solution to the puzzle, namely *what ↑Everybody KNOWS mister spEAker;* (line 14). The three list items are: *they ↑SAID they wouldn't introduce tuItion fees* (line 16), *they ↑SAID they wouldn't introduce topup fEes;* (line 20), and *they sAid they supPORted the brOwne revIEw,* (line 25). Each list member is produced in an independent intonation phrase. In particular, the first two have a parallel format in terms of syntax, prosody, and to a lesser extent, lexis.

The first two are put in contrast with lines 18 (*thEY introDUCED them*) and 22 (*they introDUCED them*). By running counter to the expectation that item 3 is also contrasted in the following line, line 27 (*he !WROTE! it into their manifesto*) surprises the audience. This element of surprise is resolved in line 29 (*WHY are they breaking; (...)*), which again conforms to the normative expectations that the speaker emphasises the contradictions and misconduct of the other side of the House. This is taken up by shouting and finger pointing on the part of the opposition party, displaying disaffiliation with the PM's attack. These adversarial audience responses are even further pursued by the PM's recycling of ↑*WHY;* (line 32). Heritage and

Greatbatch comment on the practice: 'The tactic of pursuing, in that it involves reiterating or otherwise drawing attention to a point that has just been made, inevitably serves to reemphasize the point. In so doing, pursuits also provide audiences with a further opportunity to respond to the point' (Heritage and Greatbatch 1986: 135).

The foregoing analysis has shown how combined list and contrast structures are designed to achieve opposition and even polarisation between the two sides of the House, audibly evidenced by the affiliative and disaffiliative audience responses on both sides, and potentially also involving the mediated public audience. Moreover, Ex. (96) has illustrated that the speakers' rhetoric not only serves to rally their own benches behind them but also to provoke the opposite benches.

7.4.2 Puzzle–Solution

In this section I examine the puzzle–solution format as a single device (not combined with other structures as illustrated above). In this format, puzzle–solution structures constitute a rather rare phenomenon in the 2003–2013 data set. In total, they comprise seven instances (tables 7.1a and 7.1b).

Table 7.1a *Absolute distribution of puzzle–solution structures in the question–answer sequences between the LO or MPs and the PM (2003–2013)*

n=6	Quotation as puzzle		Source as puzzle	
	Question turns	Answer turns	Question turns	Answer turns
LO–PM	66.7% (4)	0% (0)	0% (0)	16.65% (1)
MP–PM	0% (0)	0% (0)	0% (0)	16.65% (1)

Table 7.1b *Absolute distribution of puzzle–solution structures in the question–answer sequences between the LLD and the PM (2003–2010)*

n=1	Quotation as puzzle		Source as puzzle	
	Question turns	Answer turns	Question turns	Answer turns
LLD–PM	100% (1)	0% (0)	0% (0)	0% (0)

Despite the small sample, the distribution shows a striking consistency. The puzzle–solution schema is used in two ways: either the contents of the quotation or the identity of the source is presented in a puzzle. The former choice is found in question turns only, while the latter is exclusive to answer turns. All quotations are in direct speech.

I begin with the instances of the quotation as the puzzle, which constitutes the most frequent choice. Consider Ex. (97), taken from the beginning of the second question turn by the LO, where he follows up on a prior answer in which the PM has claimed his support for identity cards, quoting two opposition sources.

(97)   PMQs 09 Jan. 2008
LO: David Cameron (Con); PM: Gordon Brown (Lab); S: Michael Martin

```
1    LO:           [(2.5)] [<<f>whAt we've LEARNED over the last few] mOnths;>
2                  <<f>is it's complEtely unsAfe to trust the government
     LO:           with any more of our [identity inforMAtion;> (1.27)]
3    MPs:                               [h h h h h h h h h h h h h h h]
4    MPs:          [h h h h h h h h]
5    LO:           [if he wAnts to trade] QUOTES;
6    LO:    ->P    <<all>what about THIS one from the chAncellor of the
                   exchEquer;> [(0.38)]
7    MP:                          [AH::::] [::::::::::]
8    LO:    ->S                            [who SAID,]
9           ->S    idEntity cards are unNECessary; [(0.29)]
10   MPs:                                          [chu chu]
11   MPs:          [chu chu chu chu chu chu chu chu chu chu chu]
12   LO:    ->S    [i do not want my WHOLE life to be redUced;]
13   MPs:          [chu chu chu chu chu chu chu chu chu chu]
14   LO:    ->S    [°h to a magnEtic strIp on a plAstic CARD;  ]
15   MPs:          [1 1 1 1 1 1 1 1 1 ]
16   LO:           [(1.1) i have to SAY;]
17   MPs:          [1 chu 1 chu 1 chu 1 chu 1 chu 1 chu 1 chu 1 chu 1 chu]
18   LO:           [(0.49) compared with being chancellor in his GOvernment;>]=
19   MPs:          [1 chu 1 chu 1 chu 1 chu 1 chu 1 chu 1 ]
20   LO:           =[<<all>BEing a magnetic strip on a] plastic cArd,>
21                 <<all>is probably a welcome relLIEF;>
22   MPs:          1 1 1 1 1 1
```

The LO picks up on the PM's prior quotes, saying *if he wAnts to trade QUOTES;* (line 5; see also Chapter 8), before setting up a puzzle,

<<all>what about THIS one from the chAncellor of the exchEquer;> (line 6). The puzzle labels the ascribed source, a member of government, but not what quotation will be performed. Marked by the reporting clause *who SAID,* (line 8), the quotation is produced as direct speech in what follows (*idEntity cards are unNECessary; (...)*, lines 9, 12, 14). It constitutes the solution to the puzzle, celebrated by laughter on the part of the opposition MPs (line 15). Emphasised by the metapragmatic preface *i have to SAY;* (line 16) in overlap, the LO next picks up on the point just made ((...) =<<all>BEing a magnetic strip on a] plastic cArd,> (...)*, lines 18, 20–21) in an attempt to further ridicule the government. The example shows how the quotation is set up as the punchline, which is appreciated with audience responses, in this case laughter, to ridicule the political opponent.

Ex. (98) exemplifies the case where the ascribed source of the quotation rather than the quotation itself is presented as the puzzle. It is produced in the answer turn in response to the first question turn in a sequence between the LO and PM.

(98)   PMQs 01 Nov. 2006
LO: David Cameron (Con); PM: Tony Blair (Lab); S: Michael Martin

```
1   PM:        and ↑If he wants the best evidence of im↑PROVEment in the
               national health service,
2       ->P    °h ↑SOMEone said this mOrning,
3              °h ↑IF you were to say to mE,
4              Is the en aitch es bEtter NOW,=
5              than it was in nineteen ninety SEven?
6              °h <<:-)>i think there've been im↑PROVEments;>
7       ->P    °h ↑WHO was that-
8       ->S    °h the ↑SHAdow hEalth spokesman;=
9   MPs:       =ch ch ch ch ch ch ch ch
```

In talk not shown here the PM first rebuts the accusation made by the LO about the National Health Service, citing figures and statistics, which is appreciated by the government MPs. He next delivers reported speech framed by a puzzle–solution structure. First, he sets up a puzzle in an *if-then* construction, *and ↑If he wants the best (...)* (lines 1–2), which contains a reporting clause in which the ascribed source (*↑SOMEone*) is not specified. This is followed by direct reported speech (*°h ↑IF you were to say to mE (...)*, lines 3–6). The solution is again set up by a puzzle: *↑WHO was that- the ↑SHAadow* *hEAlth spokesman* (lines 7–8). Note that the solution completing the structure solicits loud cheering on the part of the government MPs (line 9).

Ex. (99) represents an exceptional case, and one worth considering. Here the PM exploits the puzzle–solution structure but leaves the solution unstated. With the solution being shared knowledge among the audience (see Ex. 96 for an excerpt of some of the previous interaction in the same parliamentary session), the speaker creates a rhetorical effect by not producing the solution.

(99)   PMQs 08 Dec. 2010
MP1: Nigel Dodds (DUP); PM: David Cameron; S: John Bercow

```
1   S:      nigel DODDS;=
2   MP1:    =uhm (0.30) in lIght of his experience of the world CUP bid;
3           in zUrich uh: last WEEK;=
4   MPs:    [chu chu ch chu chu chu chu chu chu    ]
5   MP1:    [=uh: cAn the prime minister TELL us;]
6   MP1:    °h what his view NOW is;=
7           =of an organisation that engages in the most CONvoluted and
            bizarre vOtIng arrangements-=
8   PM:     =ha ha ha ha ha [ha
9   MP1:                    [which says uh ONE thing and then votes exactly
10  MPs:                    [chu 1 chu 1 chu 1 chu 1 chu 1 chu 1 chu 1 chu
    MP1:    the Opposite] [way; (2.17)    ]
    MPs: 1 chu chu 1][1 1 1 1 1 1 1 1  ]
11  MP2:                  [(1.89) VERy good;]=
12  MPs:    [1 1 1 1 1][1 1 1 1]
13  MP1:    [and who has] [uh (.)   ]
14  MP2:                  [<<p>VERy][ good;>
15  MP1:                            [who has a LEAder that seems] more
16  MPs:                                        [1 1 1 1 1 1 1 1 1 1 1 1 1]
    MP1:    interested in power and prestige than accountability;=
17  MPs:    =[h h h h h h h h h h]
18  MP1:     [(1.19) And_uh (0.58)]
19  MP1:    <<all>after he is finished with the lib DEMS;>=
20          =<<all>can he tell us what he thinks of FIfa;>
21  MPs:    [h h h h h 1 1 1 1 1 h h h h 1 1 1 1 1 1 1 1]
22  PM:     [(1.88) <<:-)>i:> (1.12) i_um (2.34) i certainly (0.26)]
23  MPs:    [1 1 1 1 1 1 1 1 1 1 1 1 1 1 1 1 1]
24  PM:     [i cErtainly learned ONE thing; (0.49)]
```

```
25  PM:   <<all>i cErtainly learned one thing when it comes to breaking
          PROMises;>=
26        =POLiticians have got nothing on <<laughing>football>
          management;
27  PM:   <<laughing>uhm> °h [there's no doubt about THAT;]
28  MPs:                   [chu chu chu chu chu chu chu]
29  MPs:  [chu sh chu sh chu sh chu sh ch sh ch sh ch]
30  PM:   [(0.52) uhm (0.61) but i_uh (0.87) ha? (0.80)]
31  MPs:  [chu chu chu chu chu chu chu chu    ]
32  PM:   [be↑FORE they all start pOInting;]
33  MPs:  [chu chu chu chu chu chu]
34  PM:   [we COULD just remember;]
35  PM:   °h WHO was it who said;
36  MPs:  [chu chu]
37  PM:   [(0.22) ] we will nEver introduce tuITion [fees;]
38  MPs:                                            [h h h ]
    MPs:  [h h h h h h h h]
39  PM:   [(1.10) WHO sAId;]
40  MPs:  [h h h h h h h h h h h h h h  ]
41  PM:   [we will never introduce (.)] [TOP up fe[es;]
42  MPs:                                          [ch ] ch
    MPs:  [ch ch ch ]
43  PM:   [WHO said-]
44  PM:   thAt we will back the BROWNE review;
45  MPs:  [ch ch ]
46  PM:   [(1.28)] whO is now an ORganised hypocrisy;
47  MPs:  ch ch ch ch ch l ch l
```

The question challenges the PM with respect to FIFA, implicitly accusing him of lacking credibility when collaborating with FIFA, framed as an organisation of low morale (lines 2–20). It is taken up by the opposition MPs with laughter (line 21). The PM begins his turn in overlap with the laughter, with the multiple self-repair at the beginning indicating a dispreferred turn-format and trouble (lines 22–24). In lines 25–26, the PM asserts that *POLiticians have got nothing on <<laughing>football> management*. This assertion is framed as being based on his own experiential perception (*learned*, line 25). He next upgrades his claim (*there's no doubt about THAT*, line 27), which is taken up by disaffiliative responses from the opposition MPs (lines 28–29). The PM restarts with repair markers (line 30) before orienting to the chuntering and gesturing of the opposition party (*be↑FORE they all* *start pOInting;*, line 32). At PMQs, 'finger-pointing' constitutes an embodied action of blaming and is subject to sanctioning by the Speaker. He next appeals to the collective memory of his audience: *we COULD just remember;* (line 34). This appeal serves as a preface to a multi-unit puzzle organised as a list. In the first three list items, the PM asks for the source of the direct speech enacted (*WHO was it who said; (...), WHO sAId; (...),* and *WHO said- (...),* lines 35, 37, 39, 41, 43–44). The solution to the puzzle remains consistent – the opposition Labour party – but never gets produced. Instead, it is treated as shared knowledge, the mentioning of which would be redundant. This is evidenced by the audience responses: each of the puzzles solicits strong agreement on the part of the government MPs (lines 38, 42, 45). In doing so, the PM draws on the prior discourse where the same quotations were produced and explicitly ascribed to a source, the Labour party. Finally, the PM produces a parallel fourth list item, *whO is now an ORganised hypocrisy;* (line 46), which again is constructed as puzzle, and on that has the same solution. With respect to its content, the solution presents the punchline. Again, it is not produced, but the slot is filled by cheers and laughter (line 47), which celebrates the implied accusation that the opposition party (Labour) is hypocritical and to blame themselves. By challenging the opposition's moral and political authority and restoring his own, this display of rhetoric rebuts MP1's question and the opposition audience's responses. This shows that puzzle–solution structures can be conceived of as schematic constructions with slots to be filled; and if these slots are not filled, as in the example, the blanks are filled inby the recipients based on their prior knowledge, which creates a rhetorical effect.

To conclude, it has been shown how sources presented in puzzle–solution structures can be a powerful rhetorical device to rebut accusatory actions by the political opponent, orchestrating audible audience responses on the part of the speaker's party backbenchers. In general, the distribution of formats over turn types illustrates that the contents of quotations are the part treated as most relevant in question turns, while the choice of sources is crucial in answer turns. In this way, the choice of source is treated as vital in the dynamics of argumentative interaction, in asserting and defending one's own position (see also Chapter 8).

7.5 Summary and Conclusions

In this chapter I have been concerned with the ways in which reported speech is packaged in terms of further rhetorical structures in political speeches. The 1978–1988 and 2003–2013 data sets both yielded lists and contrasts, while only the latter showed combined structures, that is, a list, contrast, and puzzle–solution used in combination.

7.5.1 Rhetorical Structures as a Resource for Public, Mediated Speaking in Parliament

The organisation of reported speech in more simple and complex rhetorical structures shows an orientation to the contingencies of public, mediated speaking in parliament.

Denser Packaging of Incisive Messages
Both samples (1978–1988 and 2003–2013) exhibit reported speech organised in lists and contrasts. The lists show diversity in the syntactic formatting of list items and are prosodically complete in both samples. The 2003–2013 lists, however, display a more skilful delivery. They tend to comprise the entire quotation (rather than only portions of it), with each list item delivered in a separate intonation phrase. With quotations thus being shorter, this means that messages are presented in a denser and more incisive fashion.

The study of uncombined contrast structures centred on contrast between two instances of reported speech with SAY in the same turn. Contrast relations in both samples are delivered in parallel opposition structures, which differ from those in mundane interaction in that they generally have contrastive accents on the parallel items. Unlike the 1978–1988 data set, 2003–2013 contrastive structures can be enriched by additional rhetorical effects, for example, when the same referent is named through multiple labels. This again constitutes a practice to convey a message in the most dense and incisive fashion possible (but also in an engaging way; see below).

Forming Hostile Actions in an Engaging Way
Combined list, contrast, and puzzle–solution structures have only been found in the 2003–2013 sample. This combination of devices achieves an intensification of the rhetorical effect, creating a densely packaged, incisive message which, in the context of adversarial parliamentary interaction, means that hostile actions are formatted in a way that engages and mobilises the audience to rally behind or to oppose the speaker that polarises the House.

7.5.2   General Tendencies

Audience Involvement

The more engaging style of how reported speech is presented comes off as more interpersonal, creating more involvement with the audiences. This can be treated as more lively and entertaining (see also Chapter 8) and interpreted as a 'shift towards more accessible, oral styles', generally observed across genres, called 'popularization' (Biber 2003: 169).

Polarisation

As mentioned above, the mobilisation of audiences in the House in favour of or against the current speaker, which can be assumed to translate to mediated audiences, contributes to an increased polarisation of the two sides of the House.

CHAPTER 8

Reported Speech in Recurrent Courses of Action

It has been illustrated in Chapters 5 and 6 that reported speech with SAY is most frequent in the 2003–2013 LO–PM question–answer sequences, and deployed in more interactional ways than in the 1978–1988 data set. Some of the implications of this repeated use named in these previous chapters were the grammaticalisation of reporting clauses and a heightened orientation to the 'literalisation' of reported speech. This chapter addresses another implication, namely that reported speech with SAY is pervasive in 2003–2013 action formation and constitutes a building block for recurrent courses of action between the LO and PM (but not in the 1978–1988 data set).

As was also demonstrated in Chapter 4, the steep increase in the relative frequency of reported speech in LO–PM encounters correlates with the increasingly dominant institutional role of the LO at PMQs (which in turn has led to an overall decline in total questions asked per question time and a weakening of backbenchers' roles.): in the 1978–1988 data set, LOs asked an average of four questions per week (i.e., two per session), while in the 2003–2013 data set they averaged a total amount of six questions per week and session.

The aim of the present chapter is to explore how this historical development plays out in terms of action formation, and, specifically, in the construction of courses of action involving reported speech with SAY. I found that a higher frequency of reported speech with SAY correlates with patterned courses of action where quoting is constitutive of action formation (2003–2013). Seen the other way round, a low frequency of reported speech with SAY meant that it was not possible to identify patterned results for 1978–1988.

There are a variety of ways in which the LO and the PM can engage in adversarial (but also friendly) courses of action at PMQs. I show that what is crucial to the trajectory of the activity is that the LO can solicit a new question–answer sequence of sequences with a 'simple' or 'prefaced' question (Clayman and Heritage 2002b), with the subsequent trajectories of actions having very diverse dynamics. Based on these findings, this chapter identifies two recurrent 2003–2013 courses of action, one initiated by a simple question, which is called 'Enticing sequence', and the other by a prefaced question, 'Trading-quotes sequence'. The chapter shows how reported speech with SAY is functional for action formation and the progressivity of the sequence. As to trading-quotes sequences, I argue that the 1978–1988 sample provides evidence that the practice of trading quotes is deployed in similar ways. This suggests that this practice was known and used in ways which seem to be a precursor to what is later moulded into more conventionalised courses of action. This bears the theoretical implication that not only linguistic structures but also courses of action may become conventionalised and formulaic/ritualised.

The chapter is organised as follows: first a review of relevant past research is presented (8.1); next the enticing sequence, a 2003–2013 phenomenon, is described (8.2); and the 2003–2013 emergence of trading quotes as a ritualised course of action is analysed and traced to the 1978–1988 data set (8.3). Section 8.4 summarises and concludes the discussion.

8.1 Past Research

There is very little research on how political interaction is organised in sequences of sequences, and how these sequences 'embody' courses of action (Levinson 2013: 121). For instance, it is poorly understood how participants can engage in question–answer sequences to pursue different courses of action in news interview shows, civil protests in the street, or parliamentary sessions. Notable exceptions are Reynolds (2011a, 2011b, 2013, 2015) and Roth (2005), whose work presents recurrent courses of action which are constructed to achieve political goals. For this reason, their findings are summarised in more detail as follows. What they have in common is that both authors stress the relevance of epistemic access and authority (see also Streeck 2008; Vincze et al. 2016).

Reynolds describes a 'practice in which participants would ask uncontroversial, "enticing" questions which do not transparently oppose the addressed speaker, manipulating epistemic displays and epistemic rights in order to establish a basis for a later, oppositional, action' (Reynolds 2011a: 2, drawing on Gruber 2001). This practice is typically found in the public sphere. Here the questioners strategically solicit an anticipated, known answer in order to use it as a basis for their subsequent challenge. This is illustrated in Ex. (100). C is the challenger, T the target.

8.1 Past Research

(100) GIC:EJR:2009:11:C1 'Argument with Anti-birth Control'
(modified from Reynolds 2015: 301; see also Reynolds 2011a: 2)[1]

```
92.   C:    what's poisonous for one plant- for one creature,
93.         may not be foo:d for another.=
94.         [you ca:n't destroy all the food.       ]
95.   T:    [>but we're talking about< <human beings.>]
96.         we're not talking about destro:ying anything.
97.         you're ju:mping to conclu[sions.    ]
98.   C:                              [>let me a]sk you
99.         something.=do you eat eggs.<
100.        (2.0)
101.  T:    <yes.>
102.  C:    that's a foe:tus. couldn't it be¿
103.        if there's a blood thi:ng
104.        [it's->it's a foetus.<]
105.  T:    [<we are talking >] about <the pi:ll ki:lling
106.        wo:men.>you're going off topic.>we're talking
107.        about the< PI::LL being harmful to women.=
```

This is Reynolds' analysis: the target produces an 'arguable' (*we're not talking about destro:ying anything*, line 96), which occasions the enticing sequence. The challenger first produces a pre-pre (*let me ask you something*, lines 98–99) before he asks an enticing, uncontroversial question (*do you eat eggs*, line 99).[2] The latter is conducive of a positive answer, which constitutes the enticed response. This is forthcoming in line 101 (*yes.*). There follows a challenging upshot (*that's a foe:tus. (...)*, lines 102–104), followed by a so-called reaction (*we are talking about the pi:ll ki:lling wo:men. (...)*, lines 105–107; Reynolds 2015: 300–302). The organisation of the enticing sequence is summarised in Table 8.1.

Reynolds' analysis demonstrates how recipients are set up such that they are enticed to provide a response which is challenged and used against them by the questioner to make a political argument. Section 8.2 examines similar courses of action in the 2003–2013 data set, with quoting having a specific position and function in a sequential slot which I call 'accusation', that is, Reynolds' 'challenge.'

Roth (2005) identifies an activity in news interviews with US presidential candidates which he calls journalistic 'pop quiz questioning'. He shows how the questioning through which the factual knowledge of the

---

[1] The video from which this excerpt is taken can be retrieved from www.youtube.com/watch?v=tC6GxktGdww [05:19–05:37].
[2] Pre-pres (Schegloff 2007) open up interactional space for a subsequent speaker action.

Table 8.1 *The sequence of enticing a challengeable**

Phase	Action
Preface	Pre-pre
	Pre-question
Pre-challenge	Enticing interrogative
	Enticed response
Challenge	Challenging upshot
Reaction	Various

* Adapted from Reynolds (2013: 60–61).

candidates is tested may 'transform the news interview into a kind of a 'degradation ceremony' (Garfinkel 1956)' (Roth 2005: 40), in which political candidates are potentially discredited.

The work by Reynolds and Roth shows that questioners may use the question–answer format to pursue specific agendas, which may be hidden from their recipients and audiences. In their work on news interviews, Clayman and Heritage (2002b) point out that agenda-setting of this kind is typical of adversarial talk. Here question design plays a crucial part, as it makes specific responses on the part of the recipient relevant. For this reason, their work is summarised in more detail in what follows.

Clayman and Heritage convincingly conceptualise news interviews as a distinctive type of 'genre' (Clayman and Heritage 2002b: 7–8) that has 'fuzzy boundaries' with related formats such as, for example, talk shows or panel discussions, without, however, identifying distinct courses of action. Their focus lies on action formation in interviews, arguing that the turn-constructional design of interviewers' question turns is relevant for agenda-setting in terms of:

1. Topic: as first pair parts, they '[identify] a specific topical domain as the appropriate or relevant domain of response' (Clayman and Heritage 2002b: 196) and a non-response on this topic will be heard as noticeably absent.
2. Action: they 'also identify *actions* that the interviewee should perform in relation the topical domain' (Clayman and Heritage 2002b: 197), for example, agreeing or disagreeing with yes/no questions.

Table 8.2 *Dimensions of questioning**

Interviewer questions	Interviewee responses
Set agendas:	Engage/Decline to engage:
(i) Topical agendas	(i) Topical agendas
(ii) Action agendas	(ii) Action agendas
Embody presuppositions	Confirm/Disconfirm presuppositions
Incorporate preferences	Align/Disalign with preferences

* Reproduced from Clayman and Heritage (2002b: 192).

Questions further embody certain presuppositions and set up certain preference frames. Interviewees, on the other hand, can engage with or decline the topical and action agendas, (dis)confirm presuppositions, and align or disalign with preferences (see Table 8.2).

So how are the dimensions of question and answer design modelled on news interviews relevant to parliamentary question–answer sequences? My analysis shows that agenda-setting is pervasive to parliamentary questioning. In contrast to interviewers who display an orientation towards neutralism, questioning at PMQs is not a neutral or personal enterprise: the questioner speaks in their capacity as member of a political party or holder of an office and represents their interests and policies. Moreover, presuppositions have been described as a resource for political propaganda (Holly 1989: 124). These can be expected to be challenged by political opponents in the courses of action at PMQs.

The turn design of questions is crucial for agenda-setting in that it can set 'narrower' or 'broader' agendas. For instance, yes/no questions, which make a yes- or no-answer relevant, are designed to set a narrower agenda (Clayman and Heritage 2002b: 198–200), which contrasts with wh-questions, in particular *what*, *how*, and *why* questions, which solicit a more open-ended agenda (Clayman and Heritage 2002b: 200–201). Although this terminology has often been criticised for being misleading (Jucker 1986: 110), I use it here because it is widely shared in the relevant past research.

It is not only the interrogative form of the question component itself but also the design of the overall question turn that contributes to shaping the interviewer's agenda: Clayman and Heritage distinguish between what they call 'simple questions' and 'prefaced questions'. In simple question designs, 'a single question makes up the entire interviewer turn with no other turn component of any kind' (Clayman and Heritage 2002b: 104).³ In prefaced questions, on the other hand, as exemplified in Ex. (101), 'a "prefatory" sentence (arrow 1) supplies background information for the news audience, presenting it as a simple fact known to the parties, and establishes a context for the subsequent question (arrow 2)' (Clayman and Heritage 2002b: 201–203).

(101)   UK BBC Radio World at One: 25 Jan 1979: Letters
(Clayman and Heritage 2002b: 105)

```
1    IR: 1    ->    .hhh The (.) price being asked for these letters
2                   is (.) three thousand pou::nds.
3    IR: 2    ->    Are you going to be able to raise it,
4                   (0.5)
5    IE:             At the moment it ... (continues)
```

Note that question prefaces constitute a turn component designed 'to make the agenda of a question more complex, constraining or problematic' (Clayman and Heritage 2002b: 201). In this way, they represent a questioner's resource to 'tighten the agenda' so as to make the interaction more adversarial (Clayman and Heritage 2002b: 201–203).

Based on these distinctions, I differentiate between the question component, which in my data is usually made up of a yes/no-, a wh-interrogative, or an alternative question, the potential preface, and the overall question turn performed in the LO's allocated slot. Following Clayman and Heritage, I adopt the terms 'prefaced' question for interrogatives introduced with prefatory material, and 'simple' for unprefaced questions. But note that there may be talk before simple interrogatives directed at the PM, which does not technically function as its preface but sets the tone with which the interrogative question is produced.

I now turn to the analytic description of a recurrent course of action at PMQs where reported speech plays a constitutive role, beginning with what is called enticing sequences (see also Reber 2019, 2021), solicited by a simple question on the part of the LO, before turning to trading-quotes sequences.

---

³ The authors note that questions can come in various formats defined by syntax, prosody, epistemic access, and/or footing.

8.2 The Enticing Sequence (2003–2013)

Enticing sequences at PMQs are characterised by an initial, simple question that serves to entice a pre-figured answer on the part of the PM. This answer is taken as a basis for an accusation, which is implemented in the LO's second question turn slot. Here quotations are relevant for action formation: they are deployed as systematic building blocks for accusations, positioned as prefatory material in prefaced question turns. Although instantiated throughout the 2003–2013 sample, there is no evidence for enticing sequences in the 1978–1988 data set, which suggests that they are a more recent formation (at least not pre-1988). This recurrent course of action in the 2003–2013 data is organised as follows:

LO: enticing question
PM: pre-figured answer
LO: accusation (including quotations)
PM: account, counter-accusation, or a combination of the two
LO: accusation (on-topic or topic-shift)

The activity is initiated with an uncontroversial, enticing question, which invites a pre-figured answer. The LO next uses what the PM has just made publicly available in situ as a basis for his accusation.[4] Such accusations are built as question turns with quotations in the preface. In his answer turn, the PM may perform an account, a counter-accusation, or a combination of the two. Following more accusations and counter-accusations, varying in number, the activity is terminated.

Note that the LO does not pursue agreement or compromise with the PM in this course of action but constructs disagreement as required by their institutional roles (see Blum-Kulka *et al.* 2002). To this end, the LO dictates a hidden agenda whose goal is to attack and damage the PM's credibility and authority as head of government and in which an asymmetric relationship is constructed. The 2003–2013 data set yielded twelve instances of this course of action (Table 8.3).

Typically, the first, simple questions are formatted as (indirect) wh-interrogatives (58 per cent, 7). Other forms include (indirect) yes/no-interrogatives (25 per cent, 3) or alternative interrogatives (17 per cent, 2; Table 8.4). The quotations in the second question turns show great variation in form, although SAY dominates as a verb of communication with quotative function (63 per cent). Most such quotations introduced by

---

[4] The collection included only male LOs.

Table 8.3 *Collection of enticing sequences (2003–2013)*

PMQs		Prime Minister	Leader of the Opposition
1	16 July 2003	Tony Blair (Lab)	Iain Duncan Smith (Con)
2	14 Jan. 2004	Tony Blair (Lab)	Michael Howard (Con)
3	14 July 2004	Tony Blair (Lab)	Michael Howard (Con)
4	16 Nov. 2005	Tony Blair (Lab)	Michael Howard (Con)
5	06 Feb. 2008	Gordon Brown (Lab)	David Cameron (Con)
6	02 July 2008	Gordon Brown (Lab)	David Cameron (Con)
7	08 Dec. 2010	David Cameron (Con)	Ed Miliband (Lab)
8	19 Jan. 2011	David Cameron (Con)	Ed Miliband (Lab)
9	27 April 2011	David Cameron (Con)	Ed Miliband (Lab)
10	11 May 2011	David Cameron (Con)	Ed Miliband (Lab)
11	18 April 2012	David Cameron (Con)	Ed Miliband (Lab)
12	09 Jan. 2013	David Cameron (Con)	Ed Miliband (Lab)

Table 8.4 *Absolute distribution of initial, simple questions*

Syntactic form of initial, simple question (n=12)	
Wh-interrogative	58.3% (7)
Yes/no interrogative	25.0% (3)
Alternative interrogatives	16.7% (2)

Table 8.5 *Distribution of verbs of communication with quotative function in prefaces of second question turns*

Quotatives in second question turn (n=19)	SAY +visual	SAY -visual	Other
	47.4% (9)	15.8% (3)	36.8% (7)

SAY are enacted by LOs showing direct evidential access to their sources, by displaying visual engagement with their notes (Table 8.5). Thus, what characterises the practice of quoting in the second question turn is not a pervasive linguistic construction but the visual performance of 'literalised' evidential access, which serves to construct the LO's evidential authority.

The following exemplary analysis of an extract illustrates the single, contingent actions which build the course of action summarised above. The extract has been selected because it contains 'literalised' direct speech with SAY as a quotative marker, where the speaker shows visual engagement with his notes, in the second question turn. It further exemplifies a frequent

8.2 The Enticing Sequence (2003–2013)

case where the enticing question is designed as a wh-interrogative and the LO claims a K- status (Heritage and Raymond 2012). The analysis illustrates the forms and functions of reported speech as well as common patterns of action formation identified across all instances of the activity found.

1. *The Enticing Question*

The initiating action of the sequence always has a simple question design, that is, it is not prepared for by prefatory material.[5] It can come in various interrogative forms (wh-, yes/no, or alternative questions), with wh-interrogatives representing the most frequent grammatical choice in the collection. The question turn functions as an uncontroversial but enticing question. This means that while questions in this slot clearly challenge the PM, they are not treated as openly hostile, a point which is also evidenced by the fact that they are generally not produced with 'more-than-normal involvement' (Selting 1994) and are often responded to by type-conforming answers:[6]

Ex. (102) exemplifies an enticing question (lines 4–7), which constitutes the first question turn in the question–answer sequence with the PM. The LO marks the boundary between the prior action component, condolences (line 3; not shown here), and the first question turn, by addressing the Speaker (line 3). Addressing the Speaker constitutes a resource for turn-structuring in signalling a transition point from one action component to the next. NHS (*EN aitch es*, line 7) stands for the National Health Service, the British healthcare system.

(102) PMQs 11 May 2011
LO: Ed Miliband (Lab); PM: David Cameron (Con); S: John Bercow

```
1    S:          ed ↑MILiband;
2    MPs:        h h h h h h
3    LO:         ((condolences, 34 sec omitted))
4                °h <<all>mister SPEAker;>
5          ->    (.) a YEA:R into his gOvernment.
6          ->    °h hOw would the prime minister rate his HANDling;
7          ->    (0.20) of the EN aitch es.
```

---

[5] The finding that the sequence does not have or need a preface phase contrary to Reynolds' (2013, 2015) results may be explained by the fact that PMQs represents a restricted speech setting (see Atkinson and Drew 1979).

[6] The concept of type conformity was introduced by Raymond (2003) in his work on yes/no interrogatives but can also be applied to wh-interrogatives (Schegloff 2007: 78). Preferred second pair parts come unmitigated, unelaborated, by default, and on time (Schegloff 2007: 63–73).

The LO begins the first question–answer sequence with an open question, a wh-interrogative, *hOw would the prime minister rate his HANDling; of the EN aitch es.* (lines 6–7). It is preceded by an adverbial of time *a YEA:R into his gOvernment* (line 5), which qualifies the temporal scope of the question.[7] Prosodically, lines 5–7 are not produced with unusual loudness, duration, or pitch. The wh-interrogative is designed to elicit a self-assessment of the PM, which in the context of parliamentary power talk and political rhetoric in general, can be expected to be positive. Because of the predictable dynamics, the interrogative functions as an 'enticing question' for the PM, enabling him to praise the achievements of his premiership. In terms of sequence organisation, it constitutes a pre- to the second question.[8]

2. The Pre-figured Answer

In response to enticing questions shaped as wh-interrogatives, PMs typically comply with the constraints set up by the question format, treating it as uncontroversial. The response can be anticipated in the sense that it is predictable due to the dynamics of political rhetoric, where PMs (or politicians in general) tend to make positive attributions to and assessments of their own party and present themselves as having credibility and authority, while making negative attributions to and assessments of the opposition.[9] In line with these dynamics, answer turns in response to enticing questions are commonly performed in a preferred turn format, that is, undelayed and to the point. Vocally, this preference orientation is contextualised in the timing of the response. The turn begins without repair, pausing, and/or hedges. All in all, this turn slot provides PMs with an opportunity to promote the government's success and/or claim credibility and authority. In a deviant case in the collection (not shown here), where this pre-figured answer is not forthcoming, the LO provides the answer himself in a follow-up to the PM's response. This indicates that the response in the first answer turn slot is both anticipated by the LO in the build-up of his agenda and, if it is not forthcoming, is relevantly absent in the trajectory of actions.

---

[7] Since in this position in the turn and sequence, the adverbial does not represent a statement or assertion in its own right, it is not regarded as a question preface.

[8] A pre- or pre-sequence represents an adjacency pair which is produced 'preliminary' to a base adjacency pair (Schegloff 2007: 28).

[9] Exceptions to the rule in the data are questions on national security where national interests are foregrounded or speeches where tributes are paid and unity across party lines is displayed.

8.2 The Enticing Sequence (2003–2013)

Consider Ex. (103), which begins where Ex. (102) left off. Here the PM praises the achievements under his government in his answer turn.

(103)   PMQs 11 May 2011
PM: David Cameron (Con); LO: Ed Miliband (Lab); S: John Bercow

```
8                        (2.23)
9    PM:    ->   <<all>i ↑thInk the most> im↑PORTant thing we've done,=
10   PM:    ->   =[<<len>is incrEAse ↑SPEN]ding> on the en aitch [Es; (0.73)
11   MPs:   ->    [l l l l l l l l l l l l l ]              [h h h h h]
12   MPs:   ->   [h h h h h h h h h h h h h]
13   PM:         [<<len>which is ↑SOMEthing;]
14   PM:         that has ↑ONly happened,
15               because of the com↑MITment; (.)
16          ->   ↑WE made at the last election;=
17               =so an ↑EXtra;
18               °h elEven point six °h ↑BILlion pounds;
19               will be ↑GOing into the en aitch Es;
20          ->   ((click) °h beCAUSE of the decision we've tAken.
21               °h in ad↑DItion to that,
22               °h there's a ↑twO hundred million cancer DRUGS ↑fund?
23               °h <<all>so people get the DRUGS they need;>
24               °h and for the ↑FIRST time in a lOng time;
25               °h the number of ↑dOctors is growing very ↑QUICKly;
26               °h <<all>and the number of ↑bUreaucrats is actually [FALling.>]
27   MPs:                                                             [h h h h h]
                 [h h h h h h h h h h h]
```

In his answer, the PM delivers the pre-figured self-praise of the government's achievements (lines 9–10, 13–26), which are loudly appreciated by the government MPs (line 27). The turn beginning is delivered to the point, without turn-initial hedging, self-repair, or pausing. The pause transcribed in line 8 is due to the time the PM needs to stand up to speak. In fact, he begins his talk before fully positioning himself at the dispatch box. The turn begins with an evaluation, *i ↑thInk the most im↑PORTant thing we've done is incrEAse ↑SPENding on the en aitch Es;* (lines 9–10). The first portion, *i ↑thInk the most im↑PORTant thing we've done*, is met with laughter by opposition MPs (line 11), who ridicule the evaluation, claiming an evidential stance that they have done nothing important. Note that the turn-initial production of *i ↑thInk* frames the subsequent positive evaluation as 'subjectively qualified information' (Fetzer 2014d: 73), which '[makes] explicit [...] inferred information by the speaker from cognitive context, viz. both episodic and long-term memory' (Fetzer 2014d: 73–74). Using the first-person singular pronoun *I* for self-reference, the PM marks the evaluation as type-conforming to the question to rate his handling of the NHS, a move that is celebrated by the government MPs (lines 11–12). Nevertheless, he deploys the first-person plural pronoun *we* (lines 9, 16, 20) for self-reference in what follows. The choice of the plural pronoun is more indeterminate and has the potential to defer responsibility (from 'me' to 'us'), as it can refer to, for example, the government, the Conservative Party, or the coalition with the Liberal Democrats, at the same time highlighting a 'binary' opposition between 'us', that is, the group in power, and 'them', that is, the opposition (see Chilton 2007: 203 for binary representations as a typical feature of political discourse).

In lines 13–16, the PM reframes the policy of increased spending on the NHS as a kept election promise, claiming credibility. The subsequent *so* marks what follows as the upshot of his speech (lines 17–26), which frames it as a formulation targeted at a public audience. The upshot is rhetorically structured as a list: it presents policies and achievements claimed for his premiership, presented as three points based on figures and numbers. The last point, organised in a contrastive structure, *°h the number of ↑dOctors is growing very ↑QUICKly; °h <<all>and the number of ↑bUreaucrats is actually FALling.>* (lines 25–26) initiates appreciation by the government MPs (line 27).

3. *The Accusation*

The accusation comes in the form of a prefaced question, which typically contains one or more quotations presented as prefatory material. These question turns challenge the PM not only by presenting prepared, compromising evidence in the form of quotations but also in the context of the pre-figured answer, which was just publicly performed by the PM and is now used against him.

The LO's bodily orientation in the performance of question turn 2 makes this visible. Consider Ex. (104), which is an extended version of Ex. (53). Question turn 2 is produced in the context of the PM's prior positive claims about his government's achievements with respect to the NHS. Performing the direct quotation, the LO draws on his written

8.2   *The Enticing Sequence (2003–2013)*   231

sources, to present his evidence against the government and to create involvement with his (mediated) audience, visibly mobilising his backbenchers and rallying them behind him.

(104)   PMQs 11 May 2011
PM: David Cameron (Con); LO: Ed Miliband (Lab); S: John Bercow

1	S:	[(0.78) <<ff>ed ↑MILliba:nd>;]
	cam	>> bird's eye view --->
2	MPs:	[mur mur mur mur mur mur mur mur mur mur]
3	LO:	[(0.40) +mis (.) <<all>mister speaker->]
	loH	+ gazes towards S--->
4	LO:	in ↑CASE the prime minister didn't realIse;|
	cam	-->|
5	LO:	|it takes +seven YEARS to train a #doc[tor;]
	cam	| medium close-up of LO --->
	loH	--->+orients towards PM
	fig	#Fig.8.1
6	MPs:	[1 1]
7	MPs:	[1 1 1 1 1 1 1 1 1 1 1 1 1 1 1 1 1 1 1 1 1 1 1 1 1 1
8	LO:	[°h so i would like to ↑THANK him for his congratulations# on
	fig	#Fig.8.2
	MPs:	1 1 [h 1 h 1 h 1 h 1 h 1 h 1 h 1 h 1 h]
	LO:	our [record (-) on the +en aitch es; (1.1)]
	loH	--->+
9	MPs:	[1 h 1 h 1 h 1] [1 sh 1 sh 1 sh 1 sh 1 sh 1 sh 1]
10	LO:	[<<all>now now] [(0.60) and i have to SAY to him;]|
	cam	-->|
11	MPs:	[1 sh 1 sh 1 sh 1] [mur mur mur mur mur mur mur mur]
12	LO:	|[(0.70) uh' (2.1)] [<<all>i? i> have to |SAY to him;]
	cam	|medium close-up of PM ->| medium close-up
13	MPs:	[mur mur mur mur mur mur mur mur mur mur mur mur]
14	LO:	[(0.38) if it's all (.) if it's ↑ALL going so wEll,]
	cam	of LO --->
15		↑WHY do we see the nUmber of pEOple,
16		°h WAIting for diagnosis,
17		rising a↑GAIN this morning-
18		°h over ↑TEN thOUsand pEOple,
19		(.) wAIting to get their ↑TEST;
20		that's thrEE ↑TIMES the number it wAs,
21		°h a YEAR ago;
22		°h now i ↑NOticed also he didn't mention,

```
23              °h his top down reorganis↑SA[tion;=
24     LO:      =[when he talked about his |HANdling;]
       cam                              -->|camera from right angle
25     MPs:     [h h h h h h h h h h h h h h h]
26     LO:      [(0.30) <<all>of the EN aitch es>;(0.33)]
27     MPs:     [h h h h h h h h h h h h h h h]
28     LO:      ↑LET me remind him of what he sAId; |
       cam                                        ->|
29     LO:      |(0.39) JUST a mOnth a+gO;=
       cam      | medium close-up of LO --->
       loH                      +gazes down onto notes --->
30     LO:      #mister SPEAker;
       fig      #Fig.8.3
31     LO:  ->  °h he SAID-
32     LO:  ->  (.)↑I've been *□in#volved in de+sIgning + these changes-
       loH                                --->+looks up+reorients to notes
       loG              *rests both hand on dispatch box --->
       loP                     □fairly relaxed and upright posture ->
       fig                     #Fig.8.4
33     LO:  ->  +*°h WAY + back; *
       loH      +looks up+ reorients to notes--->
       loG       *lifts briefly left hand*
34     LO:  ->  *(.)+ into OPposition;
       loH      -->+looks towards speaker--->
       loG      *rests both hand on dispatch box ->
35     LO:  ->  (.) +[with ANdrew (.) lAnsley;(0.30)+ #(1.14) +*]
36     MPs:        [h h h h h h h h h h h h h h h h]
       loH      -->+ reorients to notes           +looks up+
       loG                                                --->*
       fig                     #Fig.8.5
37     MPs:     [sh sh sh sh sh sh sh sh sh sh sh sh sh]
38     LO:      [*↑cAn he th?  *cAn he therefore conFIRM,]
       loG       *lifts both hands*
39     LO:      (0.33) that the ↑FAIling en aitch es plans,
40     LO:      (0.33) □ are ↑NOT the hEAlth secretary's fAUlt,
       loP             -->□
41     LO:      (.) they're HIS; (.)
42     MPs:     [h h h|][h h h]
       cam           -->|bird's eye view --->>
43              [(0.15)][(2.00)]
```

8.2 The Enticing Sequence (2003–2013)

In response to the Speaker's summons (line 1), the LO begins his turn, addressing the Speaker (line 3). The LO next produces two follow-up responses to the PM's answer (lines 4–5, 8, 10, 12, 14–21). The first follow-up, *in ↑CASE the prime minister didn't reallse it takes seven YEARS to train a doctor*, constitutes a challenge to the PM's competence and knowledge (epistemic access) of the NHS: in stating that it takes seven years to train a doctor, the LO implies that the groundwork for the current success of the NHS was laid under the previous Labour government. In doing so, he claims to expose the PM's ignorance of the health system and at the same time points out the achievement of his own party. Note that he does not look at his notes but gazes towards the PM here (Fig. 8.1): this contextualises his assertion as general knowledge, which he knows by heart and need not retrieve from his notes. At the same time, he addresses the PM.

This is met by the MPs' extended laughter (lines 7, 9–11), which treats it as ridicule of the PM. Displayed claims of epistemic access at the cost of the political opponent are a common practice of enacting

Figure 8.1 The LO displays visual disengagement from his notes and orientation towards the PM.

Figure 8.2 The LO thanks the Prime Minister, accompanied by the opposition MPs' audible laughter.

asymmetries of power and authority and even degradation in political interaction. In overlap, the LO thanks the PM for his congratulations on his party's achievements in terms of the NHS (°h so i would like to ↑THANK him for his congratulations (...), line 8, Fig. 8.2). In follow-ups to the PM's answers, claims of gratefulness routinely project challenging moves.

The following occurs in the subsequent talk. In a second follow-up the LO contrasts the PM's claims about the improvement of the NHS with figures about waiting times, which he claims provide evidence for the opposite, attacking the credibility as well as the epistemic and evidential authority of the PM, ((...) if it's all (.) if it's ↑ALL going so wEll, ↑WHY do we see the nUmber of pEOple, °h WAIting for diagnosis, rising a↑GAIN this morning- (...), (lines 14–21). With his next move, the LO prepares for the question preface. He claims that the PM did not mention the top-down reorganisation of the NHS (now i ↑NOticed also he didn't mention, °h his top down reorgani↑SA[tion, lines 22–23), although this was at least implied in the PM's answer. This may

8.2 The Enticing Sequence (2003–2013) 235

Figure 8.3 The LO displays an orientation to his notes to read out the quotation.

explain why this only gets a soft uptake on the part of the opposition MPs. The LO continues with an increment, an adverbial of time, *when he talked about his HANdling of the EN aitch es;* (lines 24, 26). Its wording is identical to portions of his first question. This suggests that the increment, at least in part, constitutes rehearsed, prepared speech.

The subsequent preface *LET me remind him of what he sAId (. . .)* (lines 28–29) projects a quotation to come. On completion of the construction, the LO orients his gaze down to his notes (Fig. 8.3), which also visually projects the production of the quotation.

Following an appeal to the Speaker (*mister SPEAker,* line 30), and maintaining a gaze to his notes, the LO produces the reporting clause *he SAID-* (line 31). This is produced in an independent intonation phrase and followed by a clause not introduced by *that* (↑*I've been involved in desIgning these changes- (. . .)*, lines 32–35). It was shown in Chapter 5 that *he SAID-* of this shape constitutes a formulaic construction, functional in indicating a shift in footing and projecting reported speech. The third-person singular pronoun *he* makes anaphoric reference to a nominal labelling of the

Figure 8.4 The LO sustains a gaze onto his notes.

source, *the prime minister*, at the same time deictically pointing to the (co-referential) interlocutor as the ascribed source of the quotation. The quotation is grammatically formatted as direct speech, having no change in pronouns (*I*), determiner (*these*), nor backshift of the present-tensed verb. The quotation positions the Prime Minister as having designed the top-down organisation together with his current Secretary of Health, Andrew Lansley, which provides evidence that he is not solely responsible for the health policy. This contradicts the self-presentation of the PM in the previous answer, where he claimed the success of his health policy as head of government. Fig. 8.4 shows the LO's visual engagement with the notes and his posture, which he maintains, even when occasionally looking up.

When this is appreciated in overlap by the opposition MPs (line 36), the LO looks up (Fig. 8.5) before lifting both hands in overlap with the unit-initial repair of the interrogative question component, which he produces next, *(. . .) ↑CAN he thErefore confirm, that the ↑FAIling en aitch es plans, are ↑NOT the hEAlth secretary's fAUlt, they're HIS;* (lines 38–41).

His visual and gestural disengagement thus constitute local boundary signals, embodying the LO's move to the next-positioned question

8.2 The Enticing Sequence (2003–2013) 237

Figure 8.5 The LO looks up towards the government benches post-completion of the quotation.

component. In light of the quotation ascribed to the PM, which seems to contradict his prior answer, the LO asks the PM to confirm that the failing NHS plans are his responsibility alone. According to Jucker (1986: 103), such questions concern' the truth conditional status of the proposition' expressed in the *that*-clause. Being framed as a question to test the truthfulness of the PM, the interrogative implicitly accuses the PM of not having told the truth in his prior answer.

4. *The Account, Counter-accusation, or a Combination of the Two*
The data show different kinds of responses towards the LO's accusations. PMs may perform accounts, counter-accusations, or a combination of the two. Note that counter-accusations often imply claims of hypocrisy. Ex. (105), which includes the interaction shown in Ex. (86), exemplifies how a counter-accusation is performed, drawing on quotations. This illustrates further that quotations can also be implemented in other positions than the second question turns. The counter-accusation begins where Ex. (104) left off.

(105)   PMQs 11 May 2011
LO: Ed Miliband (Lab); PM: David Cameron (Con); S: John Bercow

```
1    PM:     ->    the ↑LEAder of the opposition‡§ himsElf has said;
     cam           >>
     pmH                                           ‡gaze towards S --->
     pmP                                              §rests himself on right arm -->

2    PM:     ->    that NO |chAnge,#
     cam           -->|medium close-up of PM --->
     fig                         #Fig.8.6

3    PM:     ->    °h is not an ‡↑OPtion;
     pmH                  --> ‡

4    MPs    :     [ch ch ch ch ch ch ch ch ch AH::::::]
5    PM:          [°h so what we're seeing is the ↑Usual,]

6    PM:          (.) empty |oppo↑SITion;
     cam           -->| medium close-up of LO --->

7    PM:          °h [now i'm GLAD; (0.54)]
8    MPs:             [j j j j j j j j j]

9    PM:          °h wAiting times, i'm ↑GLAD |that he mentioned
     cam                                     -->| medium close-up of PM --->

10   PM:     ->   because it was it was |↑TWO weeks a↑go,
     pmH                                      ‡gazes down onto notes --->

11   PM:     ->   °h that ↑AT that dis‡patch #box,
     pmH                         ‡gazes down onto notes --->
     fig                         #Fig.8.7

12   PM:     ->   HE said;
13   PM:     ->   and i QUOTE,
14   PM:     ->   °h ↑WAIting times have risen,‡
     pmH                                   --->‡

15   PM:     ->   ‡°h MONTH on month, ‡
     pmH          ‡gazes towards S -->‡

16   PM:     ->   ‡°h <<all>under this GOvern‡ment>;           ‡
     pmH          ‡ gazes down onto notes -->‡looks up towards LO‡

17   PM:          ↑THAT [is nOt trUE;]
18   MPs:               [sh sh sh sh]

19   MPs:          [AH:::::::::::::::::::::::::]
20   PM:           [(0.54) those (.) the ↑FIgures,]

21   MPs:          [sh sh sh sh sh sh sh sh sh sh]
22   PM:           [which he ↑HAD at the tIme, (0.54)]

23   PM:          the lo? the ↑fIgures SHOW,
24                that for ↑IN patient waiting times,
```

8.2 The Enticing Sequence (2003–2013) 239

```
25            °h they ↑FELL from nine point one to nine weeks,
26            °h and for ↑OUT patients,
27            ↑they went DOWN,
28            °h from ↑FOUR point eight weeks,
29    PM:     °h [to three point ↑FIVE weeks; (0.30)]|
30    MPs:       [chu chu chu chu chu chu chu chu]
      cam                                    -->|
31    PM:     |[↑that is the lOwest (.) for a YEAR; (0.51)]
      cam     | bird's eye view --->
32    MPs:    [j j j j j j j j j j j j j j j j j]
33    PM:     [now it is im↑PORtant;=]
34    MPs:    [chu chu chu chu chu chu]
35    PM:     [=when we ↑COME to |this house,]
      cam                        -->| medium close-up of PM --->>
36    MPs:    [chu chu chu chu chu chu chu chu]
37    PM:     [and we MAKE statements,]
38    MPs:    [mur sh mur sh mur sh]
39    PM:     [(.) that are in↑Accurate;]
40    MPs:    [mur sh mur sh mur sh mur]
41    PM:     we corrEct the REcord,
42    PM:     at the first [available oppor↑TUnity; (1.60)]
43    MPs:                 [h h h h h h h h h h h h h]
44    MPs:    [h h h h h h h]
45    PM:     [hold ON; (0.64)] [(4.37)]
46    MPs:                      [l l l]
47    PM:     so wOuld he (.)
48            would he like to ↑TAKE this opportunity,
49            °h to correct that spe↑CIfic mistake.=
50    MPs:    =[h h h h h h h h h]
```

In his response, the PM does not comply with the constraints set up by the yes/no interrogative but begins his turn with a quotation ascribed to the LO *the ↑LEAder of the opposition himsElf has said; that NO chAnge, °h is not an ↑OPtion;* (lines 1–3). The quotative verb SAY is in present perfect form. The reported clause is introduced by the complementiser *that*, marking it as indirect. Visually, the PM displays no orientation to his notes during the projecting reporting clause and quotation (Fig. 8.6) but claims to present a summary of the LO's position retrieved from memory.

Figure 8.6 The PM looks towards the S, showing disengagement from his notes.

The quoted utterance ascribes a position to the LO, which depicts him as in favour of change himself, a move which rebuts the LO's prior attack and frames him as being hypocritical. Formatted as reported speech, it serves as a rhetorical move, providing what seems to be independent evidence and creating involvement. This is evidenced by responsive cheering by the government MPs. Note that the PM tacitly accepts the presupposition made by the LO that he alone is responsible for the government's policies but does not pick up on the quotation delivered by the LO in his prior speech. Directed at the public audience, the PM next makes the upshot of this quotation explicit in a *so*-prefaced formulation, *so what we're seeing is the ↑Usual, (.) empty oppo↑SITion;* (lines 5–6), again attacking the opposition. He next refers to the issue of waiting times, displaying a positive evaluative stance (*i'm ↑GLAD that he mentioned °h waiting TIMES,* line 9). In what is framed as an account for the positive evaluation, he produces an it-focus construction which projects another quotation ascribed to the LO (*because it was it was ↑TWO weeks ago, °h that*

↑*AT that dispatch box, HE said*, lines 10–12). Chunks of this type were described as formulaic constructions in Chapter 5, projecting a shift in footing. The pronoun *HE* makes both anaphoric reference to the PM's prior nominal reference to the leader of the opposition, and at the same time evokes deictic reference, addressing the questioner. Next the PM produces the formula AND I QUOTE (see Section 6.6), framing what follows as a verbatim quotation. In the reported speech, the LO's position claimed in the prior question turn is repeated (°*h* ↑*WAIting times have risen,* °*h MONTH on month,* °*h <<all>under this GOvernment>*, lines 14–16). Shortly before the production of the reporting clause, the PM reorients towards his notes, showing visual engagement until the end of the reported clause (Fig. 8.7). This visual recruiting of his notes serves to authenticate and authorise the evidence provided.

But why is this position reproduced by the PM in the form of a verbatim quotation presented as visual evidence, when he could just as well have summarised the LO's prior in situ talk? Consider what

Figure 8.7 The PM displays visual engagement with his notes.

happens next: back in his own voice, the PM positions himself (Du Bois 2007) with respect to the quotation, assessing it as not true (line 17). This is appreciated by the government MPs (line 19). In what follows, he substantiates his assessment, by seemingly correcting the presentation of the figures, ((...) *the ↑Figures, which he ↑HAD at the tIme, the lo? the ↑fIgures SHOW (...)*, (lines 20, 22–29, 31). This attack on the moral but also evidential authority of the LO constitutes an attack on the general credibility of the PM's contention for premiership. This is met by jeering on the part of the opposition MPs (line 32). To refute an argument based on figures with more figures is a common rhetorical device at PMQs. In this context, this means that to restore his own authority and credibility, the PM quotes an old accusation by the LO based on figures from that time in the past, claiming that it was a lie, in order to rebut the current figures that form the basis of the LO's accusation in the here and now. This argumentative strategy culminates in the remainder of the turn, where the PM attacks the LO, *(...) to correct that spe↑CIfic mistake* (lines 47–49), which again frames the LO as lacking credibility. Note that this challenge mirrors the LO's prior wording in his question for the PM to confirm his *fAUlt,* framing it as a direct rebuttal of this move.

5. *The Accusation (On-topic or Topic-shift)*
At this point in the interaction, the LO can solicit an extended course of action, performing another on-topic accusation or move to a closing of the local activity, by implementing a topic shift and initiating a new action trajectory. In Ex. (106), the LO objects to the PM's claims about waiting times and makes a general attack on his authority and leadership before eventually shifting to other issues of the PM's health policy in his next question. The continuous audience responses, which are present almost throughout his speech, illustrate the confrontational nature of the interaction.

(106)   PMQs 11 May 2011
LO: Ed Miliband (Lab); PM: David Cameron (Con); S: John Bercow

```
1    S:      [(0.60) <<f>ed ↑MILliband>;  ]
2    MPs:    [j j j j j j j j j j j j]
3    LO:     [(0.54)↑NO mister speaker-=]
4    MPs:    [j j j j j j j j j j j j j j j j j j j j j j
5    LO:     [waiting (.) waiting times (0.45) waiting times are
     MPs:    j j j j]
     LO:     ↑RIsing;]
```

8.2 The Enticing Sequence (2003–2013)

```
 6   MPs:   [sh sh sh sh sh sh sh sh]
 7   LO:    [(0.21) and i ↑NOtice;]
 8   MPs:   [sh sh sh sh sh sh sh sh sh sh sh sh sh sh sh sh sh sh]
 9   LO:    [(0.38) i ↑notice he ↑DIDn't even take the opportunity;]
10   MPs:   [sh sh sh sh sh sh sh sh sh sh sh sh    ]
11   LO:    [°h to take responsi↑BIlity for the health poli] [cy.(0.73)]
12   MPs:                                                    [h h h h h]
13   LO:    [whe? where ↑IS the health secretary after] [All; (0.28)]
14   MPs:   [sh sh sh sh sh sh sh sh sh sh sh sh sh][h h h h h ]
15   MPs:   [h h h h h h h h h h h h h h h h h h h]
16   LO:    [where (.) where ↑IS the health sEcretary;]
17   MPs:   [sh sh sh sh sh sh sh sh sh sh sh sh sh sh]
18   LO:    [(0.65) and (0.24) and i have to SAY to him; (.)]
19   MPs:   [sh sh sh sh sh sh sh sh sh]
20   LO:    [i have to SAY to him; (0.31)]
21   MPs:   [sh sh sh sh sh sh sh sh sh sh sh sh]
22   LO:    [it's becoming (.) it's becoming a ↑PAT]tern with this
             prime minister mister spEaker;
23   LO:    °h because this MORning in the pApers,
24          °h we see the univERsities minIster?
25          (.) being DUMPED on;
26   LO:    °h [for his tuItion fees pOlicy,]
27   MPs:      [h h h h h h h h h h h h h]
28   LO:    °h we see the? ↑SCHOOL secretary?
29   LO:    °h being DUMPED on for his [free schools pOlicy, (0.63)]
30   MPs:                              [h h h h h h h h h h h h h]
31   MPs:   [h h h h h h h h]
32   LO:    [and the ↑POOR depu]ty prime mInister;
33   LO:    °h hE just gets dumped on Every day of the [WEEK; (1.81)]
34   MPs:                                              [h h h h h h]
35   MPs:   [h h h h h h h h h h h sh sh sh]
36   LO:    [now? (0.26) <<all>now now> (0.52)]
37   MPs:   [sh sh sh sh sh sh sh sh sh sh sh sh sh sh sh sh sh]
38   LO:    [now (.) now he mUst he mUst believe that ↑SOMEthing has]
             gone wrong with his health policy,
39   LO:    °h mister SPEAker-
40   MPs:          [chu chu chu chu chu chu chu chu chu chu chu chu chu
41   LO:    (0.25) [because he'S LAUNCHED his sO called (.) lIstening
     MPs:   chu chu chu chu ]
     LO:    exercise; (0.56)]
```

```
42            NOW; (0.40)
43            ↑CAN he reassure, (0.23)
44            DOCtors: (.) nUrses and patients, (0.29)
45            that it's a ↑GENuine exercise;
46    MPs:    [h h h]
47            [1.69)]
```

The LO begins his turn with a follow-up on the PM's response, repeating his position on waiting times ((...) *waiting times are* ↑*RIsing;*, line 5) without, however, presenting more back-up evidence. This is accompanied by jeering from the government MPs.

He next attacks the PM for not taking responsibility, a challenge of his authority as head of government, (...) *he* ↑*DIDn't even take the opportunity; to take responsi*↑*BIlity for the health policy.* (lines 7, 9, 11). This is appreciated by the opposition MPs. The LO expands his follow-up in attacking the PM for the general condition of the government. Producing a three-part list as part of this move, he rallies his MPs, who take up each item with affiliative responses behind him (lines 23–35). Introducing it with the discourse marker *now*, the LO finally shifts to a new turn component, which serves as the preface to the next interrogative question (lines 36, 38, 41). Following another use of *NOW* (line 42), he produces the question component of the turn (↑*CAN he reassure (...)*, lines 43–45).

By way of discussion, the foregoing analysis has shown how reported speech is deployed for adversarial action formation in enticing sequences; it represents a regular building block for the LO to construct the accusation in the second question turn slot. Here it provides independent evidence for the accusation and solicits audible affiliative responses on the part of the opposition backbenchers (involvement), which further serve to mobilise the public (mediated) audience. The observation that most reported speech is recruited from written sources in this turn slot not only shows how quotations are presented as a visual rhetorical device for the cameras but also how prepared and rehearsed these moves are in a rhetorical enterprise which seeks to undermine the credibility and authority of the government and ultimately to win the votes of the mediated audience.

In the specific excerpt shown, the PM further deploys reported speech in his turn to rebut the LO's accusations in an argument about truth(fulness). On both sides, reported speech is exploited for the self-presentation of evidential (and even moral) authority and credibility, and for attacks on political opponents in claims that they are lacking these very qualities.

Although truth(fulness), authority, and credibility are also negotiated in the 1978–1988 data between the two sides of the House, there is no example of a similar sequence which would point to a similar practice of enticing as evidenced for 2003–2013. In the next section I am concerned with the practice of trading quotes, already observable during 1978–1988, which came to be performed as a recurrent course of action solicited by prefaced questions in 2003–2013.

8.3 Trading-Quotes Sequences

Generally, 'trading quotes' is a member's label to describe a particularly adversarial practice in which the two speakers enact their relation of opposition by quoting sources to support their respective – and often tacitly claimed – positions. I begin the discussion with an illustration of the practice, illustrating how it constitutes a general, conventionalised practice at PMQs before examining more data from the 1978–1988 and 2003–2013 sets. It is argued that the practice has become constitutive of recurrent courses of action.

Ex. (107), a longer version of the same extract as in Ex. (97), illustrates how the general conventionalisation becomes visible in the use of the formula *if he wAnts to trade QUOTES;* (line 10) as a label for the practice.

(107)   PMQs 09 Jan 2008
PM: Gordon Brown (Labour); LO: David Cameron (Con); S: Michael Martin

```
1    PM:              if i mAY SAY sO;
2             ->      hIs poLICE adviser sIr jOhn stEvens,
3             ->      <<all>lAdy neville jones is his secUrity spokesman in the
              ->      house of LORDS>,
4             ->      <<all>bOth of them support <<f>i[DENtity cArds>>;]
5    MPs:                                       [h h h h h hh h]=
6                     =[hhh][h h h h h h h h h h h h h h h h h h]
7    LO:              [(2.5)][<<f>whAt we've LEARNED over the last few] mOnths>;
8                     <<f>is it's complEtely unsAfe to trust the government
                      with any more of our [identity inforMAtion>; (1.27)]
9    MPs:                                 [h h h h h h h h h h h h h h h]
10   MPs:             [h h h h h h h h]
11   LO:       ->     [if he wAnts to trade] QUOTES;
```

```
12    LO:          <<all>what about THIS one from the chAncellor of the
                   exchEquer>; [(0.38)]
13    MP:                          [AH::::][::::::::::]
14    LO:                                  [ who SAID, ]
15                 idEntity cards are unNECessary; [(0.29)]
16    MPs:                                                   [chu chu]
17    MPs:         [chu chu chu chu chu chu chu chu chu chu]
18    LO:          [i do not want my WHOLE life to be redUced;]
19    MPs:         [chu chu chu chu chu chu chu chu chu]
20    LO:          [°h to a magnEtic strIp on a plAstic CARD;]
21    MPs:         llllllll
```

In the question turn (not shown), the LO challenges the PM over his policy on identity cards. In response, the PM accounts for it (not shown here) before he launches a counter-attack: wrapping up his turn, the PM quotes two close aides of the LO as supporting identity cards (lines 2–4), a move which accuses the LO' political camp of disunity. This finally leads to a loud cheering on the part of the government MPs (lines 5–6), restoring the PM's authority in the Chamber.

In overlap, the LO begins his question turn with a follow-up in which he attacks the government on their credibility regarding identity information, *<<f>whAt we've LEARNED over the last few] mOnths>; (...)* (lines 7–8). Locally, the LO attacks the claims the PM has just made about the government's measures for identity protection. On a broader level, this seems to be a reference to a scandal which came to light in late autumn of 2007, where two CDs with confidential child benefit data sent by HM Revenue and Customs (HMRC) were lost in the post.[10] This is loudly celebrated by the opposition MPs (lines 9–10). The LO next explicitly follows up on the PM's prior quote, projecting a quotation to come in a conditional construction, *if he wAnts to trade QUOTES;* (line 11). This is followed by a puzzle–solution structure where the quote is the solution. The puzzle contains the ascribed source, a member of government (line 12), *<<all>what about THIS one from the chAncellor of the exchEquer>;)*. The solution is formatted in terms of direct reported speech, introduced by the quotative SAY (*who SAID, idEntity cards are unNECessary; (...)*, lines 14–15, 18, 20). The quotation presents a

---

[10] See, for example the BBC News report 'Data lost by Revenue and Customs', 21 November 2007, http://news.bbc.co.uk/2/hi/uk_news/7103911.stm

position which contradicts the official line of the government just claimed by the PM. Moreover, the LO directly rebuts the attack performed through the quotation presented by the PM, accusing the government of the same lack of unity within their ranks as was done by the PM with regard to the opposition party. The rebuttal is taken up by chuntering on the part of the government MPs in overlap (lines 16–17, 19) and post-completion laughter on the part of the opposition MPs (line 21).

The excerpt suggests that the practice of rebutting an adversarial quotation through another quotation constitutes such a well-tried, conventionalised routine that it has been given its own label, that is, trading quotes. Note that I find evidence in the 1978–1988 sample that participants already knew and performed this routine, which contrasts with the findings for enticing sequences. The 2003–2013 sample provides further evidence that trading quotes has become conventionalised as a recurrent practice for building courses of action. To illustrate this, I begin the analysis with a 1978–1988 excerpt before turning to 2003–2013 instantiations of trading quotes.

1978–1988
Although the analysis of the interaction between the LO and PM in the 1978–1988 sample did not yield recurrent trading-quotes sequences, the study of the MPs' question–answer sequences revealed what seems to be a precursor of what becomes a constitutive practice for recurrent courses of action in the 2003–2013 data set.

Ex. (108), which represents an extended version of Ex. (22), shows how an opposition MP and the PM trade quotes in a question–answer sequence. In the excerpt, Greenham Common refers to the Women's Peace Camp located next to the RAF Greenham Common Airbase, Berkshire, set up to demonstrate against the deployment of ninety-six Cruise nuclear missiles by the US Air Force there.[11] Michael Heseltine is the 1983–1986 Secretary of State for Defence. X refers to an unidentified participant, that is, an MP or the Speaker.

(108) PMQs 03 Nov. 1983
MP1: Syd Bidwell (Lab); PM: Margaret Thatcher (Con); S: Bernard Weatherill

```
1    S:        bidWELL?
2              (0.38)
```

[11] See www.greenhamwpc.org.uk

```
3    MP1:         (has the) right honourable lady had a CHANCE to- (0.66)
4           ->    <<all>look at the> wIdespread COMment:,
5           ->    on television=n PRESS- (0.60)
6           ->    on the pOssibility (0.33) of pEace demonstrators getting SHOT-
7           ->    [(0.30) at grEenham common and elseWHERE, (0.47)]
8    MPs:         [j j j j j j j j j j j j j j  j j j j j j]
9    MP1:         [does she parTICularly, (0.48)]
10   MPs:         [j j j j j j j j j j j j j]
11   MP1:   ->    [look at an interview with One woman demonstrator] [who SAID
12   MPs:         [j j j j j j j j j j j j j j j j j j j j j j j ] [chu chu
     MP1:   ->    that;]
     MPs:         chu  ]
14   MP1:   ->    [british sOldiers would not FIRE, (0.37)]
     MPs:         [chu chu chu chu chu chu chu chu chu chu]
15   MP1:   ->    [but MAYbe; (0.28)]
16   MPs:         [chu chu chu chu  ]
17   MP1:   ->    [american defEnce forces might FIRE, (.)]
18   MPs:         [chu chu chu chu chu chu chu chu chu]
19   MP1:         [and In those circumstances will she °h disOWN;] (0.23)
20   MPs:         [chu chu chu chu chu chu chu chu chu chu chu]
21   MP1:         the clUmsy remarks of the defence sEcre[tary      ]
22   MP2:                                                [hear HEAR;]
     MP1:         [two or three days aGO; (0.51)]
23   MPs:         [h h h h h h h h h h h h h ]
24   MP1:         [and (.) at? (0.31) does] she reallse that there will be a
25   MPs:         [h h h h h h h h h h h]
     MP1:         demonsTRAtion, (0.19)
26   MP1:         the biggest we've ever seen in our HIStory; (0.20)
27   MP1:         [if such eVENTS took] [plAce.]
28   MPs:         [mur mur mur mur mur] [h h h h] [h h h]
29                                     [1.66)] (1.33)
30   PM:          mister SPEAker;
31                the arrAngement for the protEction of NUclear installAtions in
                  this country;
32                are precIsely the sAme as they have ALways [been; (0.74)]
33   MPs:                                                    [h h h h h h ] [h ]
34   PM:                                                                    [NO]
                  difference at All; (0.25)
35                and we did ĭnot sUddenly get this aLAR:M and these questions on
                  previous occasions;
```

8.3 Trading-Quotes Sequences

```
36         ->   ˚h <<all>if $the right        $ if the honourable $gentle$man>
     pmG                      $crackling paper$            $crackling paper$
     PM:   ->   re$[fers$ to what the PRESS have said abOut it-]
37   MPs:       [chu chu chu chu chu chu chu chu chu chu chu]
     pmG                   $crackling paper$
38   PM:   ->   [˚h may i refEr him to] <<all>to to> what the [guardian] has
39   MPs:       [chu chu chu chu chu]                       [chu  chu ]
40   PM:   ->   said about it toDAY, [(0.54) ]
41   MPs:                            [chu chu] [chu chu chu chu chu chu chu
42   PM:   ->                                  [uh: (0.25) the prime mInister and
     MPs:       chu chu chu chu chu    ] [chu chu ] [chu chu chu    ]
     PM:   ->   mister heseltine will] [go to inor] [dinate LENGTHS-]
43   (X):                                            [shh::::::]
44   MPs:       [chu chu chu chu chu chu chu chu chu chu chu chu chu
45   PM:   ->   [to prevent the business of crUise deployment leading to
     MPs:       chu chu chu]
     PM:   ->   BLOODshed;]
46   MPs:       [chu chu chu chu chu chu ]
47   PM:   ->   [˚h the Army and the police] in their thousands are NOT there for
           ->   fun;
48         ->   (.) they are there precIsely to aVERT (.) such incidents;
49         ->   ˚h but cAn one lOgically envIsage a crowd of dEmonstrators
           ->   bouncing all over cruise wArheads whilst the parachute regiment
           ->   stands silently BY; [(0.26) ]
50   MPs:                           [chu chu] [chu chu  ]
51   PM:                                      [<<:-) >NO;>]
52   MPs:       [chu chu chu chu chu chu  ]
53   PM:   ->   [˚h <<:-) >and SHE,> (0.55)]
54   PM:   ->   ˚h <<:-) >is RIGH[T,> (0.62)]
55   MP1:                        [he he he ]
56   PM:   ->   [<<:-) >to SAY,> (0.50)]
57   MPs:       [l l l l l l l l l l]
58   PM:   ->   [<<:-) >that one couldn't expect a CHURchill,> (0.20)]
59   MPs:       [l l l l ch l ch l ch l ch l ch l ch l ch l ch]
60   PM:   ->   <<:-) >or an ATTlee,> (.)
61         ->   <<:-) >or a CALlaghan government,>
62         ->   <<:-) >or a prospective ↑KINnock one,>
63         ->   to reach Any Other con[CLUsion.]
64   MPs:                             [h h h h] [h h h h ]
65                                              [(4.17)]
```

Following the summons by the speaker (*bidWELL?,* line 1), the opposition MP begins with two quotations: in the first construction, a 'noun of communication' *the> wIdespread COMment:,* (line 4) is deployed to index a subsequent shift in footing. Like verbs of communication, nouns can serve as quotatives and provide an evidential framing (Fetzer and Reber 2015: 112–113). What follows is presented as a summary of the positions claimed by the ascribed sources *on television=n PRESS-* (line 5). The quoted position, *the pOssibility (0.33) of pEace demonstrators getting SHOT- at grEenham common and elseWHERE,* (lines 6–7), is taken up in overlap by audible jeering after the first possible completion point. This signals disagreement with what is treated as a controversial position. The second quotation, which is ascribed to a single source, is projected by a reporting clause with SAY: *an interview with One woman demonstrator who SAID that; british sOldiers would not FIRE, but MAYbe; american defEnce forces might FIRE,* (lines 11–17). The quotation, framed as indirect speech by *that,* claims a position similar to the first made by the MP, namely that peace demonstrators may be shot by soldiers on British soil. The production of the second quotation is accompanied by chuntering on the part of the audience, which is a sign of dissent.

Both quotations, which are prefaced by two interrogative structures (*((has the)right honourable lady had a CHANCE to- (0.66) <<all>look at,* lines 3–4; *does she particularly, look at,* lines 9–11) serve to stage a dramatic scenario relevant to the here and now and to prepare for the two subsequent questions, which constitute an attack and a threat. In an *and*-prefaced construction, the questioning MP first asks the PM to *disOWN; the clUmsy remarks of the defense sEcretary two or three days aGO;* (lines 19–21). The demonstrative determiner *those* in the adverbial *In those circumstances* (line 19) makes deictic reference to the possible scenario evidenced by the quotations. The question does not merely implement a request for action but also attacks the PM for the awkward handling of what is claimed to be a dangerous scenario by her government. This move is appreciated by opposition MPs in overlap at a possible point of completion (lines 22–23). MP1 continues with his turn, producing another *and*-prefaced question component, *and (.) at? (0.31) does she reallse that there will be a demonsTRAtion, the biggest that we've ever seen in our HIStory; if such eVENTS took plAce.* (lines 24, 26–27). The expression *the biggest that we've ever seen in our HIStory* represents an extreme case formulation (Edwards 2000;

8.3 Trading-Quotes Sequences 251

Pomerantz 1986). Such formulations state – as the term suggests – the extreme case of a scenario or state-of-affairs. In this way they are '[o]ne practice used in legitimizing claims' (Pomerantz 1986: 219). Again, the interrogative does not serve as a request for information *(does she reaIIse that)* but performs a threat that the anti-government protests will escalate. This is again met by affiliative audience responses on the part of the opposition MPs.

The PM begins her responsive turn by addressing the Speaker (line 30) in an appeal to his authority, before claiming that the government's handling of nuclear weapons has not changed (*the arrAngement for the protEction of NUclear installAtions in this country; are precIsely the sAme as they have ALways been;(. . .)*, lines 31–32). The expressions *precisely the sAMe* and *ALways* mark it as an extreme case formulation, which is met by displays of agreement by the government MPs (line 33). In overlap, this is upgraded with another extreme case formulation (*NO difference at All*, line 34). The PM continues to claim that it is the responses to the government policy which are different (*and we did ↑not sUddenly get this aLAR:M and these questions on previous occasions;*, line 35). In doing so, she defers the responsibility for the conflict to the demonstrators and political opponents, constructing a contrast between 'us' and 'them', and dismisses the MP's suggestion that she is responsible.

She next produces a conditional if-clause, picking up on the MP's quotation of the press (*if the right if the honourable gentleman> refers to what the PRESS have said abOut it-* (line 36). Its form resembles the expression *if he wAnts to trade QUOTES;* (Ex. 107) in that it constitutes another instantiation of the format [IF + 3rd person reference to a co-present party + V]. This suggests that speakers of the 1978–1988 period were already using a format still in use during 2003–2013. The move is accompanied by an audible crackling of paper, which suggests that the PM is recruiting her documents. The interrogative *then*-part contains a reporting clause in the form of what has been called an indefinite relative clause or nominal relative clause (Quirk at al. 1985: 1056–1061, *may i refEr him to what the guardian has said about it today*, lines 38, 40). The subject of the nominal relative clause makes reference to the source, *the guardian*, a hyponym of the source quoted in the question turn, the press. It contains two adverbials: the adverbial of respect (*about it*) makes vague anaphoric reference to prior topical talk; the adverbial of time (*today*) makes relative reference to the timing of the quoted speech, framing it as topical and newsworthy. After a medium pause, the PM begins with the quotation (lines 42, 45, 47–49, 51, 53–54, 56, 58, 60–63), which has no change in nominal or pronominal reference (e. g., *the prime mInister, SHE* to *I*) or backshift of the verb (e.g., *will go, are*), which marks it as direct speech; it is produced with faster tempo and higher register. This shift in the prosodic setting, coupled with the grammatical markers of direct speech, indexes it as performance of a verbatim quotation. The position cited supports the government's policy, rebutting the assessments and positions quoted in the question turn (*the prime mInister and mister heseltine will go to inordinate LENGTHS to prevent the business of crUise deployment leading to BLOODshed*, lines 42, 45). Again, it is formatted with an extreme case formulation (*inordinate LENGTHS*).

This shows that the format [IF + 3rd person reference to a co-present party + V] serves to project reported speech, presenting a counter-position to what was quoted in the prior turn. (As illustrated in Chapter 7, using opposition and contrasts is a common rhetorical device to rebut the opponent's position.) In this way, it matches the *if*-prefaced construction in the 2003–2013 example with regard to its lexico-syntactic form as well as its interactional implications.

In her own voice, the PM next signals affiliation with what she has just quoted (*NO*, line 51) in a smile voice. Moving back into the voice of The Guardian, she continues with the quotation in this smile voice until it is almost completed. This second portion of the reported speech further supports the governmental position (*and SHE is RIGHT to SAY that one couldn't expect a CHURchill or a CALlaghan government or a prospective ↑KINnock one to reach Any Other conCLUsion*, lines 53–54, 56, 58, 60–63). This rebuts the quoted position ascribed to the press in the question turn and at the same time attacks the credibility and evidential authority of the opposition MP and his party. In this context, the smile voice can be interpreted as a display of ridicule, which is aligned with and shared by the government MPs through initial laughter and eventual cheering (lines 55, 57, 59). The quotation and the rebuttal it accomplishes are celebrated by the government MPs on completion (line 64).

The foregoing analysis has provided evidence that participants in the 1978–1988 data set deploy the practice of trading quotes in similar ways as between 2003–2013. The 1978–1988 speaker makes her understanding of the practice explicit, using a metapragmatic move to project the quotation which matches the lexico-syntactic form used in the 2003–2013 example, [IF + 3rd person reference to a co-present party + V].

Although the 1978–1988 example is a single case, it illustrates that trading quotes represents a practice that participants in this community of practice have known and deployed for at least one or two generations. The use of the [IF + 3rd person reference to a co-present party + V] construction further suggests that speakers' procedural knowledge of how to counter first quotations through second quotations may have triggered a conventionalised form for labelling the practice which had already been deployed in the 1978–1988 data set.

I take this discussion further in what follows, showing that trading quotes emerges as a practice in recurrent courses of action in the 2003–2013 sample.

2003–2013
The course of action in which participants recurrently engage in 'trading quotes' has the following structural features: the LO opens the sequence with a prefaced question, which sets an adversarial agenda openly and right away. Characteristically, the question preface contains reported speech presenting a position designed to attack the PM in the context of the larger action format. In the second turn slot in the sequence, the LO implements a question turn with the same design. I found twenty-six instances of this pattern.

In response to the first question turn, PMs do not always respond with actions which contain reported speech in their turn. But when they do, this co-constructs a trajectory of actions in which the LO and PM engage in 'trading quotes'. In the following analysis, I focus on such instantiations. These amount to 35 per cent in the sample (nine out of the twenty-six cases mentioned above). The sequence is typically closed after the third question turn, which does not necessarily have a quotation, but may also be expanded further. The sequential organisation of trading quotes is depicted as follows.

LO: Challenging Question turn 1
              Preface incl. quotation
              interrogative question
PM: Answer turn 1 incl. quotation
LO: Challenging Follow-up Question turn 2
              Preface incl. quotation
              interrogative question
PM: Answer turn 2
LO: Follow-up Question turn 3
PM: Answer turn 3

Table 8.6 *Trading-quotes sequences in the 2003–2013 sample*

	PMQs	Prime Minister	Leader of the Opposition
1	16 July 2003	Tony Blair (Lab)	Iain Duncan Smith (Con)
2	22 June 2005	Tony Blair (Lab)	Michael Howard (Con)
3	11 Oct. 2006	Tony Blair (Lab)	David Cameron (Con)
4	01 Nov. 2006	Tony Blair (Lab)	David Cameron (Con)
5	23 May 2007	Tony Blair (Lab)	David Cameron (Con)
6	17 Oct. 2007	Gordon Brown (Lab)	David Cameron (Con)
7	09 Jan. 2008	Gordon Brown (Lab)	David Cameron (Con)
8	14 Jan. 2009	Gordon Brown (Lab)	David Cameron (Con)
9	30 March 2011	David Cameron (Con)	Ed Miliband (Lab)

Table 8.7 *Absolute distribution of interrogatives in first, simple question turns in trading-quotes sequences*

Syntactic form of question component	Wh-interrogative	Yes/no interrogative	Alternative interrogatives
First question turn (n=9)	0% (0)	100% (9)	0% (0)
Second question turn (n=9)	44.4% (4)	44.4% (4)	11.2% (1)

All LOs in the 2003–2013 data set – the Conservatives Iain Duncan Smith, Michael Howard, and David Cameron, as well as Ed Miliband (Labour) and the (acting) Labour LO – use this agenda (Table 8.6).

Table 8.7 shows that trading-quotes sequences are opened exclusively through question turns with question components in the form of yes/no-interrogatives, which have been described by Clayman and Heritage (2002b) as setting a narrower agenda than, for example, the wh-question formats most frequently used in the first action slot of enticing sequences.

The choices in the second question slot are diverse; however, I demonstrate that it cannot necessarily be inferred from these choices that they correlate with different action trajectories, as the interrogatives often only serve as dummies and are not treated as the actionable part of the multi-unit turn.

As shown in Table 8.8, SAY is the quotative marker most widely used across the second and third turns in the sequence. There were only two other quotative markers each occurring more than once, that is, *tell*, *attack* (two tokens each).

8.3 Trading-Quotes Sequences

Table 8.8 *Distribution of SAY and other quotative markers in the first three turns of the trading-quotes sequence*

Turn types and sequential positions	Quotative markers	
	SAY	all others
First question turn (preface, n=12)[12]	41.7% (5)	58.3 % (7)
First answer turn (n=12)[13]	75.0% (9)	25.0% (3)
Second question turn (preface, n=11)[14]	72.7% (8)	27.3% (3)

In the following sections, I present analyses of how the practice of trading quotes is deployed in such sequences, showing how reported speech with SAY is constitutive of building adversarial courses of action in this sequential context. I demonstrate that:

i. the source of the quotation is as relevant to the argument as the position quoted, and that
ii. quotations implement accusations.

Finally, I:

iii. discuss whether self-quotations are functional in providing evidence for a position in the same way as other- or third-party quotations.

I begin with an illustration of points i. and ii.

i The source of the quotation is as relevant to the argument as the position quoted

ii Quotations implement accusations

One of the key findings of Chapter 5 was that the low transitivity of SAY allows for a structural make-up of the reporting clause where the essential information is condensed in the subject NP. In Chapter 7, it was argued that the source constitutes a part of the quotation that is (almost) as important as the reported clause itself. In this section I provide further evidence for these observations from a functional perspective, examining how the relevance of the source and quoted position is interactionally constructed and addressed by speakers, and showing how this interrelates with the formation of adversarial actions.

---

[12] There were multiple quotative markers or verbs of communication in two of the question prefaces.
[13] One answer turn contained four instances of SAY as a quotative marker.
[14] Two question turns came with two SAY-quotatives, each in the preface.

Consider Ex. (109), which illustrates this particularly well. It represents the first question turn of the trading-quotes sequence, which is performed in the first turn slot allocated to the LO during this day's PMQs. It contains 'literalised' direct speech in the question preface (lines 12–15; see Ex. (80), for a detailed multimodal analysis). *C. difficile* (*cee diffi↑CILE*) is an abbreviation for *Clostridium difficile*,[15] a bacterium which can cause serious infections.

(109)   PMQs 17 Oct. 2007
LO: Mr David Cameron (Con); PM: Gordon Brown (Lab); S: Michael Martin

```
1     MPs:           [h h h h h h h h h]
2     S:             [(0.66) david CAMeron] -
3     MPs:           [h h h h h]
4     LO:            [↑THANK you;]
5     MPs:           [h h h h h h h h h h h h h h]
6     LO:            [(.)↑THANK you mister spEAker;]
7     LO:            °h in the last four YEARS,
8                    the ↑NUMber of people who've ↑dIEd;
9                    from the ↑hOspital-acquired infection cee diffi↑CILE,
10                   °h has TREBled,
11                   °h NINEty patients died in one hospital trust alone,
12              ->   °h the ↑HEALTHcare commission sAId last week,
13              ->   where trUsts are under se↑VERE prEssure to meet
                ->   tArgets relating to fInance and Access,
14              ->   concern for in↑FECtion control,
15              ->   may be underMINED;
16                   °h ↑WILL the prime minister ↑nOw accept;
17                   that the ↑NUMber and extent;
18                   °h of ↑HIS top-down targets;
19                   are con↑TRIButing to this [problem;]
20    MPs:                                     [mur  mur ] [ch] [ch ch ch]=
```

The summons by the Speaker, which comes in overlap with ongoing audience responses to the prior answer turn (lines 1–2), is appreciated by the opposition MPs (lines 3, 5). In overlap, the LO responds to the appreciation and the summons (↑*THANK you mister spEAker*, lines 4, 6) and begins his speech by presenting figures which are designed to provide evidence for a dramatic rise in the number of people who died from a hospital-acquired infection (°*h in the last four YEARS, the* ↑*NUMber of people who've* ↑*dIEd;* (. . .) *has TREBled,* (. . .),

---

[15] Since 2016, *Clostridium difficile* has been reclassified as *Clostridioides difficile* (see, e.g., Lawson et al. 2016).

lines 7–11).[16] He next quotes what is embodied as direct, verbatim speech by a governmental elite source,[17] introduced by the reporting clause with SAY (*the ↑HEALTHcare commission sAId last week, where trUsts are under se↑VERE pressure to meet tArgets (…), lines 12–15*). Using a government body as epistemic authority, the LO uses the quotation as evidence that the government's targets constitute a threat to infection control in hospitals. Positioned directly next to one another, the increase of infections contracted in hospital and the effect of the government's targets on infection control are implicitly related to one another, in a move which attacks the PM's authority and credibility. In terms of turn-internal organisation, the figures and reported speech serve as the preface to the subsequent yes/no-interrogative (*↑WILL the prime minister ↑nOw accept (…), lines 16–19*). With the proposition (*that the ↑NUMber and extent; of ↑HIS top-down targets; are con↑TRIButing to this problem;*) summarising and reaffirming the gist of the scenario staged in the preface, the LO repeats the attack on the PM in his own voice. This action is celebrated by the opposition MPs (line 20).

In sum, it has been shown that reported speech with SAY in question prefaces serves – along with figures, which are another type of evidence often used at PMQs – to construct accusations that attack the PM in terms of his credibility as head of government. Specifically, this is achieved through a quoted position ascribed to a government source which criticises the PM's policy on the topic. Pointing out disunity is a common strategy for attacking the political opponent.

Ex. (110) continues where Ex. (109) left off. It shows the PM's answer turn in response to the accusation. Here reported speech is used to rebut the attack. MRSA (*EM ar es ay*, line 4) is a hospital-acquired infection caused by an antibiotic-resistant bacterium.

(110)   PMQs 17 Oct. 2007
LO: Mr David Cameron (Con); PM: Gordon Brown (Lab); S: Michael Martin

```
1    PM:                              [(0.91)] [it (0.43)]
     cam                                      >>
2    MPs:       =[chu chu chu chu chu chu chu chu chu chu chu  ]
3    3 PM:     [<<all>it it it> it is beCAUSE uh mister speaker;]=
4    PM:       =we are |concerned about EM ar es ay,=
     cam                ---> | medium close-up
```

---

[16] Figures constitute a special form of quotation, in that only the base – but almost never the source – is indicated at PMQs.
[17] www.gov.uk/government/organisations/healthcare-commission

258   Reported Speech in Recurrent Courses of Action

```
 5  PM:         =and CE difficIle,
 6              °h that in the ↑LAST few weeks
 7              we have taken ↑VERy special measures;
 8  MPs:        [chu chu chu chu chu chu chu chu ]
 9  PM:         [(0.37) in (.) isolation (0.77)]|
    cam                                     --->|

10  MPs:         [chu chu chu chu chu chu ]
11  PM:         |[↑ISolation wArds, (0.63)]
    cam         |bird's eye view--->

12  MPs:        [chu chu chu chu chu chu chu chu chu chu chu chu chu chu chu chu
13  PM:         [we? we have apoin? we are a↑BOUT to appoint three thousand more

    MPs:        chu  chu  ]
    PM:         matrons,]

14  MPs:        [chu  chu  chu  chu  chu  chu  chu  chu  chu  chu  chu  chu  chu chu]
15  PM:         [°h we are ↑ALso about |to do a dEEp clean of hOspitals,]
    cam                          --->  |medium close-up

16  MPs:        [chu chu chu chu chu chu chu chu chu chu chu chu ]
17  PM:         [$‡ °h and ↑WHEN he comes #to the issue of §targets,]
    pmG           $ takes pile of notes --->
    pmP                                                      §rests himself on
    pmH           ‡gaze towards LO --->
    fig                                    #Fig.8.8

18  MPs:        [chu chu chu chu chu chu chu chu chu]
19  PM:         [and ↑QUOTES the health care commIssion,]‡
    pmP         dispatch box --->
    pmH                                                 --->‡

20  MPs:        [chu chu chu   ]
21  PM:         [‡↑LET me# che?]
    pmH          ‡gazes down on notes --->
    fig                    #Fig.8.9

22  MPs:        [chu chu chu chu chu chu chu chu chu chu chu chu
23  PM:    ->   [↑lEt me quote him the ‡CHAIRman #of the health care
    pmH                                 --->‡ gazes towards PM --->
    fig                                          #Fig.8.10

    MPs:       chu chu chu  ]
    PM:    ->  commission,‡]
    pmH                 --->‡

24  MPs:        [chu chu chu chu chu chu ]
25  PM:    ->   [‡ (0.20) sir ian KENnedy,]
    pmH          ‡ gazes down on notes --->

26  MPs:        [chu chu chu chu ]
27  PM:    ->   [(0.44) he SAYS-]
```

8.3 Trading-Quotes Sequences   259

```
28   PM:    ->   TARgets;
29          ->   or their eQUIvalent,
30          ->   are an in↑Evitable feature‡
     pmH                                ---> ‡
31   PM:    ->   ‡(.) of a ‡↑MOdern twenty first century  ‡[healthcare sYstem,‡
     pmH         ‡towards LO‡gazes towards own benches  ‡gazes down on notes‡
32   MPs                                                  [h h h h h h h h h h
     PM:    ->   ‡(0.91)     ‡]
     pmH         ‡towards LO‡
     MPs         h h h h h h h ]
33   PM:    ->   ‡he SAYS, (.)]
     pmH         ‡gazes down on notes
34   MPs:        h h h h h h ]
35   PM:    ->   [the ‡↑Obligation‡ to mEEt ‡targets,‡] (0.40)
     pmH              ‡towards S‡        ‡towards LO‡
36   MPs:        [sh sh sh sh sh sh sh sh ((sporadic))    ]
37   PM:    ->   ↑CANnot be used as an ex↑cUse;
38   PM:    ->   for ↑FAIling to meet Other mana[gerial ‡objectives,‡ (1.20)§]
     pmH                                       ‡down onto notes ‡
     pmP                                                         --->§
39   MPs:                                      [h h h h h h h h h h h h h h h   ]
40   PM:    ->   %‡he ↑ALso says; ‡
     pmP         % straightens himself --->
     pmH         ‡gazes towards LO‡
41   PM:        ‡uh² §and i ↑HOPE the oppositional leader will ↑tAke this into
     pmP    ->       § rests himself on dispatch box --->
     pmH        ‡gazes onto folder --->
     PM:        account-
42   PM:    ->  targets are |↑NOT to blame for the trust leaders taking their
     cam                --->| medium close-up of LO, looking sternly --->
     PM:    ->  [Eye Off the] [bAll; (0.93)] |
     cam                                --->|
43   MPs:       [chu chu chu] [h h h hhh ] |
44   MPs:       [chu chu chu chu chu chu chu chu chu  ]
45   PM:    ->  [|‡and he says‡ that ↑MANagers; (0.77)]
     cam         |medium close-up of PM --->
     pmH          ‡gazes towards PM‡ down onto notes --->
46   PM:    ->  ALways have to deal with [conflicting priorities,]
47   MPs:                                [chu chu chu chu chu chu]
48   MPs:       [chu sh chu sh chu sh chu sh chu sh chu sh chu sh chu sh chu sh  ]
49   PM:    ->  [‡$%and plenty% of ‡organisations do it successfully;(0.37)$]
```

```
           pmH         ǂlooks up towards Sǂ gazes towards opposition benches
           pmG         $puts notes back down onto dispatch box, turns back page $
           loP         %straightens himself%
    50   MPs:          [chu chu chu chu chu chu   ]
    51   PM:           [ǂin ↑OTHer words; (0.36)]
           pmH         ǂ gazes towards S   --->
    52   MPs:          [chu chu chu chu chu chu ]
    53   PM:           [it is not (.) $TAR $gets] #that are to blame? (0.43)
           pmG                         $taps on folder with open hand$
           fig                                   #Fig.8.11
    54   MPs:          [chu chu chu chu chu chu chu chu chu chu chu chu chu    ]=
    55   PM:           [<<f>we have gOt to in$↑VEST$ in the hEAlth service>,]
           pmG                                   $taps on folder with open hand$
    56   MPs:        =[chu chu chu chu chu chu chu chu chu chu chu chu chu chu ]=
    57   PM:           [(0.30) <<ff>now will $↑HE$ invest in the health service>,]
    58   MPs:        =[chu chu chu chu chu chu chu]
    59   PM:           [(0.34)<<ff>as ↑WE$ will>;|ǂ]
           cam                                   --->|
           pmH                                   --->ǂ
           pmG                         $takes notes--->
    60   MPs:          |[h h h h h h h h h h h]
    61                 |[%° (3.00)$ %°*(0.29)*]
           cam         |bird's eye view --->>
           pmG              -->$
           pmW              %sitting down%
           loW              °standing up°
           loG                        *puts notes onto dispatch box*
```

In his answer turn, the PM does not comply with the constraints of the prior yes/no question, that is, to agree or disagree. Both are impossible choices, since both options would do damage to his credibility and authority as head of government. In this sense, the question represents an 'unanswerable question' (Bates et al. 2014: 263). Instead, the PM rebuts the accusations made in the question preface, first responding to the incriminating figures.

The PM's self-repair in overlap delays the turn beginning of his answer turn, contextualising it as dispreferred. This shows an orientation to not complying with the terms of the yes/no question. He begins with an it-focus construction (*it it it> it is beCAUSE uh mister speaker; we are concerned about EM ar es ay, and CE difficIle,* lines 3–5), which explicitly picks up on the infection named in the figures and claims concern, setting up an evaluative/affective frame of governmental past and future measures next presented in three points ((...) *we have taken ↑VERy special measures (...)*, lines 6–7, 9, 11; *we are a↑BOUT to appoint three thousand more matrons,* line 13; and *we are ↑ALso about to do a dEEp clean of hOspitals,* line 15). Presenting the government as taking action and acting in a responsible way, he rebuts the positions presented in the preface, restoring his authority and credibility. According to Sealey and Bates (2016: 29), it is typical of prime-ministerial answers at PMQs 'to project not only authority and command within and beyond the Chamber but also empathy and representativeness', a finding which is interpreted as a reflection of the PM's 'identification with presumed societal norms' (Sealey and Bates 2016: 29). While this generally holds here as well, the PM's claim of concern, together with his listing of measures to tackle the problem, also locally reframes the LO's figures as 'old news', that is, as knowledge the government has long had access to and has already acted upon.

Next the PM picks up his pile of notes from the dispatch box and gazes towards the LO (Fig. 8.8), which is later followed by a bodily repositioning. This is accompanied by a verbal move in which he picks up on the LO's prior quotation, referring to its topic and source (*and ↑WHEN he comes to the issue of targets, and ↑QUOTES the health care commIssion,* lines 17, 19). I have suggested that speakers use the construction [IF + 3rd person reference to a co-present party + V] to mark the practice of trading quotes. The expression deployed here, [WHEN + term of address + V], seems to belong to this family of constructions, in that it serves similar functions. What is interesting here is that the PM's bodily moves project a quotation to come, while his words are backward-looking, pointing to talk and constructing coherence with the prior talk.

In a preface (*↑lEt me quote him the CHAIRman of the health care commission, sir ian KENnedy,* lines 21, 23, 25), the PM also makes verbally explicit what was only projected through bodily cues. His preface labels the subsequent move, that is, quoting, and gives the source in an appositive construction. This is accompanied by the PM's visual reorientation to his notes (Fig. 8.9). Now the verbal and visual cues are aligned.

Note that in recruiting *the chAIrman of the health care commission,* and making explicit reference to the chairman's title and name, *sir ian KENnedy,* the PM trumps the LO – who only recruited the general *↑HEALTHcare commission* (Ex. 109) as a source for his quotation – in

262 Reported Speech in Recurrent Courses of Action

Figure 8.8 The PM takes his notes, preparing for a visual presentation of his sources.

Figure 8.9 The PM reorients his gaze towards his notes.

8.3   *Trading-Quotes Sequences*   263

Figure 8.10 The PM disengages from his notes to look towards the opposition benches.

terms of the evidential authority displayed. This stance also seems to be contextualised through the PM's short gaze towards the opposition benches (Fig. 8.10).

The PM next produces four 'counter-quotes', which present positions in favour of the criticised government targets. In terms of form, the first three reporting clauses have a parallel syntactic and prosodic structure. They consist of the third-person pronoun *he* and a present-tensed quotative SAY: *he SAYS* (lines 27, 33; a form which I described as a candidate for a formulaic fragment in Chapter 5), and *he ALso says* (line 40). All reporting clauses are produced in independent intonation phrases and introduce 'literalised' direct speech: *TARgets; or their eQUIvalent, (. . .)* lines 28–31), *the ↑Obligation to mEEt targets (. . .)* (lines 35, 37–38), and *targets are ↑NOT to blame for (. . .)* (line 42).

The fourth quote breaks this pattern in that it is produced as an indirect quote: in line 45, which is linked to the previous talk by *and*, the reporting clause is produced in a prosodic unit together with the complementiser and subject of the quoted speech (*and he says that ↑MANagers;(. . .)*, lines 45–46,

49). The video analysis shows why: as line 45 is being delivered, the PM looks up before again orienting his gaze to his notes towards the end of the line. I argue that because of the PM's visual – and possibly also cognitive – disengagement from his notes, the PM produces the complementiser as a kind of filler, indicating that he is not producing verbatim past speech. In the medium pause that follows, he scans his notes for the right line until it is read out in what comes off as a 'literalised' quote.

Functionally, the quotations serve to provide evidence and account for the legitimacy of the government policy (targets are required in a modern healthcare system) and to defer the responsibility for failures to others (the managers), as well as to create involvement with a split audience. The first three quotations are celebrated by the government MPs (lines 32, 39, 43), who display affiliation with and support of their PM. Thus, in producing the quotations and showing evidential access to his sources, the PM rebuts the LO's accusations but, more importantly, is able to rally the government MPs behind him and have their visible support in front of a split audience. Exploiting the functions of reported speech to display evidential access and authority as well as creating involvement, he defends his authority and credibility, currently under attack in the House.

His answer turn culminates in a final summary that presents the upshot of the positions claimed in the quotations (*in ↑OTHer words it is not TARgets (...)* lines 51, 53, 55). The haptic gesture of touching his notes which the PM enacts reinforces the persuasive value of visual aids (Fig. 8.11). The summary is followed by a counter-challenge to the LO (*now will ↑HE invest in the health service (...)*, lines 57, 59), which is once more celebrated by loud cheering (line 60).

This analysis has shown that trading quotes is a recipient's practice to rebut position(s) quoted in prior talk, used to attack the government. In performing quotations that counter these positions, the PM claims evidential access and authority in addition to creating involvement with his audience, thus reconstructing his authority and credibility as head of government. The PM claims evidential access and authority not only by presenting positions likely to refute the LO's evidence, but also sources which are treated as superior and more authoritative. This shows that not only the position but also the source quoted is interactionally relevant to the construction of the speaker's argument and standing in the Chamber.

In terms of action formation, the example has illustrated how the preface including the reported speech, and not the question component, is treated as the actionable part by the recipient. This suggests that in such questions

Figure 8.11 The PM taps on his notes with his open hand.

turns, the interrogative only serves as a dummy to fulfil the requirements of the institution to ask a question of the PM.

Ex. (111) continues where Ex. (110) ended. Here the LO challenges the answer, specifically the quotations presented, performing more quotations attacking the PM. Like the PM, he does not comply with the constraints set up by the question asked by his interlocutor.

(111)   PMQs 17 Oct. 2007

LO: Mr David Cameron (Con); PM: Gordon Brown (Lab); S: Michael Martin

```
1    MPs:      [h sh h sh h sh h sh h sh h sh h sh h]
2    LO:       [|□it's ↑QUITE clear +mister speaker,+]
     cam       |>> bird's eye view --->
     loH                          +gazes towards S +
     loP       □rests himself onto dispatch box -->
3    MPs:      [h sh h sh h sh h]           [h sh h sh h sh h sh h]
4    LO:       [|+he hAsn't rEAd] the +hEAlthcare [commIssion re↑PORT;+]
     cam       |medium close-up --->
     loH          +gazes down onto notes+gazes towards PM         +
```

```
 5   MPs:          [chu  h  chu  h  chu  h ]
 6   LO:           [+(0.42) the re↑PORT; +]
     loH           +gazes down onto notes+

 7   MPs:          [chu sh chu sh chu sh chu ]
 8   LO:           [(.) ↑COULD not be clearer;]

     MPs:          [chu sh chu sh chu sh chu sh chu sh chu sh chu sh  ]
 9   LO:     ->    [(0.33) on the +↑MAIDstone hospital it sAYs,# (0.22)]
     loH                       + gazes down onto notes --->
     fig                                                       #Fig.8.12
10   LO:     ->    °h ↑SEnior managers were reLUCtant to ↑Implement major
             ->    infection control measures, +
     loH                                      --->+

11   LO:     ->    +becAUse of the nEEd to +meet ↑TARgets; +
     loH           +gazes towards PM      + down onto notes+

12   MPs:          [chu sh h chu sh h chu sh h chu sh h chu sh h chu]
13   LO:     ->    [+(0.60) and it WASn't just that ↑One +hospital, ]
     loH           +gazes towards own benches, headshake+ towards LO--->

14   MPs:          [chu sh chu sh chu sh chu sh chu sh chu sh chu]
15   LO:     ->    [(-) the re↑pOrt +into stoke ↑MANdeville said,#]
     loH           --->            +gaze down onto notes --->
     fig                                                       #Fig.8.13

16   MPs:          [chu chu chu chu chu chu chu chu chu chu chu chu]
17   LO:     ->    [°h the aCHIEVEment of the government's tArgets;+]
     loH                                                       --->+

18   MPs:          [chu sh chu sh chu sh chu sh chu sh chu]
19   LO:     ->    [+(.)was seen as + MORE important,= +]
     loH           + gazes towards PM+ down onto notes+

20   MPs:          [chu chu chu chu chu chu]
21   LO:     ->    [+=than the MANagement,]
     loH           +gazes towards S--->

22   MPs:          [chu chu chu chu chu chu chu chu chu chu chu
23   LO:     ->    [°h of the clInical risk inhErent (.) +in cee
     loH                                        --->+gazes down onto notes --->

     MPs:          chu chu chu chu chu  ]
     LO:        -> diffi↑CILE; (0.40) +]
     loH                              --->+

24   MPs:          [chu chu chu chu chu chu chu chu chu]
25   LO:     ->    [+thIs was a significant +FAIling; +]
     loH           +gazes towards PM       +gazes down onto notes+

26   MPs:          [chu chu chu chu chu chu chu chu chu chu]
27   LO:           [+°h ↑Almost one in two +↑HOSpitals agree,]
     loH           +gazes towards PM      + gazes down onto notes --->
```

8.3 Trading-Quotes Sequences

```
28   MPs:   [chu chu chu chu chu chu chu chu chu chu chu chu chu chu
29   LO:    [°h + that ↑TARgets are getting in the wAy of +infection
     loH    --->+ gazes towards S                        + down onto notes
     MPs:   chu]
     LO:    con] [trol;+]
     loH         --->+
30   MPs:   [h h h h ] [h h h h h h h h h h chu]
31   LO:    [+(0.60)] [the nAtional ↑AUdit of ]fice:;
     loH          + gazes towards PM --->
32   LO:    the pu? publIc [accOUnts committee + (.) both aGREE;+]
     loH                                       --> +down onto notes+
33   MPs:                  [chu chu chu chu chu chu chu chu chu]
34   MPs:   [chu chu chu chu chu chu chu chu chu ]
35   LO:    [+(-)<<all>WHAT makes him think>;(.) ]
     loH    + gazes towards PM               --->
36   MPs:   [chu chu chu chu chu chu chu]
37   LO:    [<<all,f>!HE! is right>;(.)]
38   MPs:   [chu chu chu chu chu chu chu chu ]
39   LO:    [<<all,f>and !THEY! are wrong>.=|]
     cam                                 --->|
40   MPs:   [|=h h h h h h h] [h h h]
     cam    |bird's-eye view --->
```

The LO begins his turn in overlap with the cheering of the government MPs. In a move that follows up on what the PM has quoted, the LO questions the credibility and evidential authority of the PM, calling into question the PM's knowledge of what he has presented as relevant sources (*it's ↑QUITE clear mister speaker, he ↑hAsn't rEAd the hEAlthcare commIssion re↑PORT*, lines 2, 4). His visual reorientation to his notes indexes an orientation to prepared speech. The subsequent assessment, in which the report is evaluated as easy to understand (*the re↑PORT; ↑COULD not be clearer;*, lines 6, 8), serves as a preface to the subsequent two direct quotations: both quotations are produced in direct speech projected by reporting clauses with forms of SAY. Again, these quotations are presented as visual evidence, authenticating and authorising the quoted positions. During the production of the adverbial of respect with which the reporting clause is initiated (*on the ↑MAIDstone hospital it sAYs*, line 9), the LO looks down to his notes (Fig. 8.12), a posture which he sustains until a moment during the first chunk of what comes off as a direct quote *(↑SEnior managers were reLUCtant to ↑Implement major infection control measures,* line 10). He looks up when delivering a *because*-clause in an increment

Figure 8.12 The LO displays visual engagement with his notes.

(*becAUse of the nEEd to meet ↑TARgets;* line 11), which suggests a shift in footing.[18]

Next the LO projects more to come, setting up a puzzle (*and it WASn't just that ↑One hospital,* line 13). The reporting clause which follows provides the solution, projecting another quotation (*the re↑pOrt into stoke ↑MANdeville said,* line 15). Re-engaging with his sources (Fig. 8.13), the PM produces another piece of 'literalised' direct speech (*the aCHIEVEment of the government's tArgets; (. . .),* lines 17, 19, 21, 23, 25). It makes the same point, namely that the government's targets were prioritised above the patients' safety.

---

[18] A look at the Hansard reveals that the production of the first quotation shows a clear orientation to a split audience. What comes off as a direct quote in lines 10–11 seems to be so only in parts, with the Hansard treating only line 10 as a direct quote (*On the Maidstone hospital, it says: 'senior managers were . . . reluctant to implement major infection control measures' because of the need to meet targets.* Hansard, HC, vol. 464, col. 817, 17 October 2007). This gives an insight into the LO's assumptions about the epistemic access of his audience: he adds the causal clause to provide extra information needed for audiences not familiar with the report to understand the state of affairs presented in the quote and to make the quotation coherent with his line of argument.

8.3 Trading-Quotes Sequences

Figure 8.13 The LO again displays visual engagement with his notes.

Neither of the quotations gets audible support by the opposition backbenchers but there is continuous chuntering on the government benches. It is only when the LO next cites figures which back up the points made in the quotations (lines 27, 29) that he achieves loud cheering on by the MPs (line 30). The LO next expands on this point (lines 31–32), which can be treated as a pursuit of further affiliative responses. These, however, are not forthcoming.

In what follows, the LO completes the question turn with a question component in the form of a wh-interrogative (*WHAT makes him think; (.) !HE! is right; (.) and !THEY! are wrong*, lines 35, 37, 39). Produced with parallel extra strong accents on the subjects, and with the two final lines organised in a contrastive construction accompanied by increased loudness, this comes off as the climax of the turn, in which the opposition between the prime-ministerial position and that of the LO's quoted sources culminate. This is celebrated by the government MPs in response (line 40).

In Ex. (112), in which the sequence continues, the PM again does not comply with the constraints set up by the interrogative. Similar to the first answer turn, he treats the reported speech presented by the

LO as the actionable part. Moreover, he mirrors the LO's strategy in accusing him of a lack of evidential access. This shows how access to (the relevant) sources is normatively constructed as a sign of authority and power (see also Sealey and Bates 2016; van Dijk 2014: 269–270).

(112)   PMQs 17 Oct. 2007

LO: Mr David Cameron (Con); PM: Gordon Brown (Lab); S: Michael Martin

```
1    PM:      [(1.7)] [<<well> MISter speaker;>]
2             he has NOT (.) dOne his resEArch.=
3    MPs:     =[j  h  j ][h  j  h  j  h  j  h  j]
4    PM:      [(1.50)] [mister SPEAker;]
5    MPs:     [j  chu  j  chu  j  chu  j  chu]
6    PM:      [(1.01) tar? (.) TARgets;]
7    MPs:     [sh   sh   sh   ((sporadic))       ]
8    PM:      [(0.53) TARgets are responsible,]
9    PM:      (0.28) for ↑wAIting lists which were a ↑QUARter of a million;
10            °h being almost ↑ZEro for thOse people-(0.26)
11   PM:      [at ↑SIX months; (0.90)]
12   MPs:     [h h h h h h h h h h ][h h h h h h]
13   PM:                           [↑tArgets are] responsible for a
              sEventeen per cent fall in HEART disease;     (.) [(0.48)]
14   MPs:                                                      [h h h h] [h h h
15   PM:                                                                 [tArgets
     MPs:     h h] [h h h h h h h h h h h]
     PM:      are] [responsible for a FORty] per cent fall, (0.21)
16   PM:      in [↑CORonary disease; $ (0.55)]
     pmG                             $ takes notes --->
17   MPs:     [h h h h h h h h h h h     ][h h h h h h h]
18   PM:                                  [and let (0.71)]
19   PM:      §and he (.) ↑WANTS to quote the healthcare
     pmP      §rests himself onto dispatch box--->
     PM:      (.) ‡commIssion, (0.36) ‡
     pmH          ‡gazes towards LO   ‡
20   PM:      ‡i have ↑QUOted sir ian ‡kEnnedy,
     pmH      ‡gazes towards S        ‡ gazes down onto notes
21   PM:      $who is the ↑CHAIRman of the healthcare commission, ‡
     pmH                                                      --->‡
     pmG      $lifts sheet of paper --->
```

8.3   Trading-Quotes Sequences   271

```
22   PM:          ‡°h saying tArgets are nOt to$ ‡↑BLAME; [(0.40)]  $
     pmH          ‡gazes towards LO              ‡gazes down onto notes--->
     pmG                                         --->$ puts sheet down again$
23   MPs:                                                       [j j j j]
24   MPs:         [sh sh sh sh sh sh ((sporadic))                        ]
25   PM:     ->   [but let me ALso quote (.) the new chief ‡eXECu‡tive, (0.43)]
     pmH                                               --->‡gazes towards LO‡down
26   PM:     ->   of mAIdstone en aitch es ↑TRUST; ‡
     pmH          onto notes              --->‡
27   PM:     ->   $‡tArgets ‡are there‡ (.) he said (.) for a ↑REAson; (0.33)
     pmH                    ‡looks up  ‡
     pmG     ->   $puts index finger on paper and traces text --->
     fig          #Fig.8.14
28   PM:     ->   THAT should not stop us from fOcusing-
29   PM:     ->   MAjorly on patient sAfety, (0.33)
30   PM:     ->   #thAt$ is the number one priORity; ‡
     pmH          ‡gazes towards the Speaker    ---> ‡
     loG          --->$
31   PM:          § (0.23) now the? (.) LEAder of the Opposition should rEcognise;
     pmP          § slightly straightens himself and assumes upright position --->
32   PM:          °h that the |↑REAson we can invest more in tackling ↑Em ar es
     cam                       --->|medium close-up of LO ->
     PM:          ay; (0.22)
33   PM:          and |↑CE difficile;
     cam          --->| medium close-up of PM
34   PM:          °h is that we are SPENding more money on the hEAlth service,
35   PM:          (0.32) <<all,f> hE voted aGAINST that [spending.>] §|
36   MPs:                                               [h h h h] =
     cam                                                        --->|
     pmP                                                        -->§
37   MPs:         = [h h h h] =
                  [(3.34) ]
```

The *well*-prefacing of the answer turn and address of the Speaker as authority (*well MISter speaker;* line 1) displays that what follows will be dispreferred (Heritage 2015; see also Jucker 1986). This becomes evident when the PM calls the LO's evidential access and authority into question (*he has NOT (.) dOne his research*, line 2), a move which is similar to what the LO did in his prior speech. The backbenchers respond with loud jeering and cheering (line 3). The PM's addressing the Speaker marks a boundary (line 4). In what follows, the PM first cites figures in a three-part list *((. . .) TARgets are responsible for*

↑*wAiting lists which were a* ↑*QUARter of a million being almost* ↑*Zero (...)*, lines 6, 8–11, 13, 15–16). Through citing these, the PM constructs evidence in favour of the government's position. Each of the list items is celebrated by the government backbenchers (lines 12, 14, 17). After the completion of the third list item, there follows a medium pause, where the PM takes his notes. He resumes his speech (*and let (0.71)*, line 18) but cuts it off and after more pausing, begins a new unit in repair. Marked by a concurrent repositioning in posture, this unit is the first of several to summarise what is treated as the gist of the prior argument (*and he (.)*↑*WANTS to quote the healthcare commIssion, i have* ↑*QUOted sir ian kEnnedy, (...)*, lines 19–22). At the same time, this summary repeats and reaffirms a quoted position in support of the government policy that targets are not to blame.

Introducing it with *but*, the PM next produces a preface to project a new quotation (*but* ↑*LET me Also quote the new chief executive, (-) of mAIdstone en aitch es TRUST*, lines 25–26). The preface contains the reference to a source which relates to the source just quoted by the LO. As in his first answer turn, the PM responds to the LO's prior quotation, by quoting a seemingly more senior, personalised source. In what follows, he begins with a direct quotation (see Chapter 5 for a phonetic-prosodic and grammatical analysis), displaying partly visual and haptic engagement with his notes during his speech (Fig. 8.14). The position quoted reconfirms the governmental position maintained throughout the sequence (*((-) tArgets are there he said for a* ↑*REAson; (...)*, lines 27–30). When coming to the end of the quotation, the PM looks up towards the LO and repositions himself post-completion. There is a noticeable absence of audience response. More systematic research on audience responses at PMQs is needed but an explanation for this absence might be that the quoted position is treated as 'no news', since it only repeats the line of argument pursued in the first answer turn.

After a medium pause, the PM closes his turn with an attack on the LO in which the opposition between the government and opposition policies are claimed (*now the? (.) LEAder of the Opposition should rEcognise; (-) that the* ↑*REAson we can invest more in tackling* ↑*Em ar es ay; (...)*, lines 31–35). In overlap, the government MPs respond with extra loud and long cheering (lines 36–37), which continues when the LO takes his turn (not shown here).

The analysis has shown that, again, the PM does not answer the interrogative but treats the LO's quotations as an accusation which has to be rebutted. Specifically, the analysis suggests that not only the contents

Figure 8.14 The PM shows haptic and visual engagement with his notes.

of the quoted position but also the ascribed sources are used for attacks and rebuttals. The recruiting of (what seem to be) more senior sources (the healthcare commission vs. the chairman of the healthcare commission; the healthcare commission report vs. the new chief executive of Maidstone NHS Trust) are exploited to display better evidential access and more evidential authority. Moreover, evidential access is equated with epistemic access and authority and normatively constructed as a sign of authority, credibility, and power.

Notably, all instances of reported speech deployed to this end represent prepared speech: the speakers are analysed as displaying visible engagement with their notes, presenting their quotations as visible evidence. The reported speech is projected through verbal and visual resources, securing the attention of the audience.

In data not shown here, the LO continues to attack the PM in his third question turn on the NHS, again evidencing his position with quotations. This is rebutted by the PM in his answer turn. After a follow-up, the sequence is closed when the LO moves to another topic in his fourth question turn.

iii. Self-quotations: Weaker Evidence?

The excerpts shown above in this section have illustrated the vital role of sources in reported speech ascribed to members of the opposite party or a third party. They are deployed to oppose the positions quoted in the prior turn and to rebut the accusations made. Ex. (113) exemplifies a case where the PM is not in a position to recruit other or third-party sources but presents himself or non-independent government bodies as his sources. The excerpt further illustrates particularly nicely how the LO presents his notes as physical evidence.

As to the background of this excerpt, this question–answer sequence deals with a political affair at the time surrounding the second war in Iraq. Notoriously, Blair justified the participation of British troops in the war by claiming that Saddam Hussein possessed chemical weapons. However, events prior to the recording of the excerpt suggested that information was leaked to the BBC that these claims were not true. One day before this session of PMQs, the alleged BBC source, a civil servant at the Ministry of Defence, Dr David Kelly, was questioned by the Foreign Affairs Select Committee. The question turn transcribed in Ex. (113) constitutes the first one allocated to the LO during this session of PMQs.

(113)   PMQs 16 July 2003
PM: Tony Blair (Lab); LO: Iain Duncan Smith (Con); S: Michael Martin

```
1    S:              Iain dUncan SM |°[ITH-]
2    MPs:                           |°[h h h]*[h h°]        [h h h h h h]*
     cam:        >> medium close-up of PM|extreme long shot --->
     loW:                            °walks towards dispatch box°
     loG:                                   *places notes onto dispatch box*

3    LO:    ->                      [(1.54)][(1.15)]□+[the #↑FOR+eign
     loP:                           □rests on dispatch box->
     loH:                                   +gaze down onto notes
     fig                                    #Fig.8.15
     MPs:          h h h h h h h h h h h h]

     LO:    ->    affairs select committee chairman|*has #sAId;]+=
     cam                                  -->| medium close-up
     loH                                     -->+
     loG                                     *holds notes in right hand -->
     fig                                     #Fig.8.16

4    LO:    ->    +=<<p>then i QUOTE;>+=
     loH          +gaze towards PM      +
```

8.3 *Trading-Quotes Sequences*   275

```
5    LO:      ->    =<<rall>+it's MOST unlIkely>,=
     loH                  +gaze down onto notes --->
6    LO:      ->    =that dOctor kelly was the prIme source for the story +about
     loH                                                              -->+ gaze

     LO:      ->    the government's + manipu[lation of inTELLigence;]+
7    MPs:                             [<<pp> mur mur mur mur    ]=
     loH                 towards PM    + down onto notes                    +

8    LO:      ->    +°h [↑AND that he has been + pOorly treated by the
9    MPs:               [<<pp> mur mur mur mur mur mur mur mur mur mur mur

     loH            +gaze towards PM       + down onto notes
     LO:            gOvernment;]+
     MPs:           mur mur mur>]=
     loH                  -->+

10   LO:            +[°h will the# ↑PRIME minister□*now apOlogise;] □*|
11   MPs:           =[<<pp> mur mur mur mur mur mur mur mur mur>  ]=
     cam                                                          --> |
     loP                                -->□straightens himself□
     loH            +gaze towards PM --->>
     loG                                        *picks up notes   *
     fig                       #Fig.8.17

                    |□§‡ (0.21) [(0.46)] [(1.17)] □§
12   MPs:                    [mur mur] [1 1 1] [j j j j]
     cam:           |long shot --->>
     loP            □sitting down            □
     pmP                §standing up              §
     pmH                ‡ downward gaze -->>
```

The Speaker's summons of the LO (*Iain dUncan SMITH*, line 1) is taken up by loud displays of agreement on the part of the opposition MPs (line 2). When he takes his turn, the LO immediately begins with a quotation taken from the questioning of the alleged BBC source, Dr Kelly, by the Foreign Affairs Select Committee the previous day. It is introduced by a reporting clause, a declarative main clause in an independent intonation phrase, which projects the production of the quotation. It consists of a subject, which makes reference to the source, and the verb SAY in present perfect (*the ↑FOReign affairs select committee chairman has sAId,* line 3). The source, the Committee chairman, is a government MP. The present perfect of the verbum dicendi SAY places the quotation at an indefinite time in the past. The LO next produces the formula =*then i QUOTE;=* (line 4), a variant of the form (*AND) I QUOTE,* framing what follows as a verbatim quotation. Using the formula, he authenticates the quotation and substantiates the objectivity of the source while at the same time explicitly distancing himself from the contents of the quotation. The quotation is delivered in two parts. The first begins on the subsequent intonation phrase (*it's MOST unlIkely, that dOctor kelly was the prIme source (...)*, lines 5–6). The use of the impersonal pronoun *it* as the dummy subject in the it-extraposition does not indicate whether there is a shift in deictic centre. Grammatically, the reported speech could thus be direct or indirect. The quotation is taken up by the MPs' displays of dissent. In overlap, the LO produces an *and*-prefaced second portion (↑*AND that he has been pOorly treated by the gOvernment*, line 8), with indirect speech prefaced by the complementiser *that*. Visually, the LO displays embodied engagement with his notes, holding the paper in his hand and maintaining a gaze to his notes. This is only sometimes suspended when looking towards the PM, until he finally reorients his gaze towards the PM during the production of the question component (Fig. 8.15–8.17).

The quoted material contains two statements that implicitly challenge the credibility of the government and accuse its members of misconduct: Dr Kelly was not the primary source who leaked confidential information about the government's actions to the BBC, and the government treated its civil servant poorly. These quotations by a government MP provide for the political relevance and justify the LO's next action component, a

Figure 8.15 The LO rests on the dispatch box.

Figure 8.16 The LO displays haptic and visual engagement with his notes.

Figure 8.17 The LO disengages his visual orientation from his notes.

request to apologise, *will the ↑PRIME minister now apOlogise* (line 10). The use of the modal *will* and the temporal adverb *now* make the question component particularly pressing and challenging. The grammatical form of this yes/no-interrogative is conducive to a positive answer. Following a short pause, this is responded to by laughter on the part of the opposition MPs (line 12).

278   Reported Speech in Recurrent Courses of Action

Ex. (114), which shows a longer, multimodal version of the transcript presented in Ex. (34), shows the answer turn of the PM. It begins where Ex. (113) left off.

(114)   PMQs 16 July 2003

PM: Tony Blair (Lab); LO: Iain Duncan Smith (Con); S: Michael Martin

```
1    PM:                    §$ [mi? mister SPEAker;] §$‡
     cam        >>long shot --->
     pmP                    §positions himself at dispatch box§
     pmH        >>                            ---->‡
     pmG                    $places open folder onto dispatch box$
2    PM:        $°h $‡<<all>the FOReign affairs select commi²s::elect committee
     pmG        $adjusts glasses$ places left forearm on folder, right hand
                grasping folder --->
     pmH        --->‡ gaze towards opposition -->
     PM:        have given their |opinion as to the sOurce,>
     cam:                   --->| medium close-up --->
3    PM:  ->    °h ‡ <<all>WE have‡ said #to the ministry of de↑fEnce
     pmH        -->‡ downward gaze‡ gaze towards opposition -->
                           #Fig.8.18
                that we don't #know who the source Is?>
     fig                    #Fig.8.19
4    PM:  ->    °h bUt the [bee bee ↑CEE,]
5    MPs:                  [j  j j  j  j j]
6    PM:  ->    [°h are in the position (.) ↑TO know who the source is;]
7    MPs:      [j j j j j j j j j j j j j j j j j j j j j j j]
8    PM:       [((click)) and they can say SUREly,]
9    MPs:      [j j j j j j j j j j j j j j j ]
10   PM:       [(0.34) whether this mAn $is that source or ‡↑NOT;]‡$|
11   MPs:      [j j j j j j j j j j j j j j j j j j j j j j ]
     cam:                                                 -->|
     pmH                                          -->‡ quick downward gaze‡
     pmG                     $moves left hand to grasp folder$
12   MPs:      [j h j h ]
13              |‡%+°[(0.50)]+
     cam       |long shot --->>
     pmH        ‡gaze towards LO --->>
     pmW           %sitting down with open folder in both hands --->>
     loH           +gaze towards Speaker+
     loW            °standing up ->>
```

Addressing the Speaker (line 1) in overlap with the opposition's laughter, the PM does not accept the constraints of the yes/no-interrogative (a request to apologise) imposed by the question. Instead, he dismisses the first accusation that Dr Kelly was not the primary source by downplaying the import of the quote delivered in the LO's question turn, treating it not as evidence but as a mere opinion (*the FOReign affairs select commi? s::elect committee have given their opinion as to the sOurce*, line 2). He next produces a self-quote, in which it is claimed that they are ignorant of who the source is (*WE have said to the ministry of de↑fEnce that we don't know who the source Is*, line 3). Note that the sources of the two positions being negotiated, that is, whether Dr Kelly was the prime source or not, each bear a primary accent, prosodically contextualising a relation of contrast (*FOReign affairs select committee, WE*).

The reporting clause and quotation, framed by the *that*-complementiser as indirect speech, are produced in one intonation phrase. Using the personal pronoun *WE* as the subject of the quotative verb SAY, the PM makes reference to himself and an underspecified collective, deferring the full responsibility of the subsequent quotation. Note that the self-quotation does not function as counter-interest, unchallengeable evidence but as a reaffirmation of a previously stated position, the truthfulness of which has not been confirmed.

In the prepositional object, the receiver of the message, the Ministry of Defence, is made explicit. This detailing constitutes a resource to enhance the credibility of what is framed as a past utterance. However, Figures 8.18 and 8.19 show that the PM shows a visual orientation towards the opposition benches. The quotation is one not backed by physical evidence, that is, written notes, which would authenticate and authorise it as an official position. The fact that the PM does not avert his gaze from the opposition benches can be interpreted as a sign of non-submission (see Holland *et al.* 2017; Reber 2019).

Next, the PM's use of *but* constructs a syndetic, contrastive link to what follows, a claim about the epistemic state and access of the BBC (*bUt the bee bee ↑CEE are in the position ↑TO know who the source is; (...)*, lines 4, 6, 8, 10). These claims of ignorance and deferring of the accountability to a third party (the BBC) position him as not being accountable for the state-of-affairs and actions he is being accused of in addition to allowing him to resist the constraints made relevant by the yes/no-interrogative and the question preface. The opposition MPs respond to the production of the

Figure 8.18 The PM sustains a gaze towards the opposition benches.

Figure 8.19 The PM sustains a gaze oriented towards the opposition benches.

contrastive marker with jeering, which is continued until after the turn is completed (lines 5, 7, 9, 11–12).

I have shown that, like in the excerpts above, the PM treats the quotation in the question turn as the actionable part of the LO's turn, using a quotation himself to rebut the accusation made. The self-quotation, however, constitutes weaker evidence for a state-of-affairs because it does not come from another or third-party source objectivising the position claimed. It merely reaffirms a position previously claimed by the PM, which does not constitute impartial evidence. This (lack of) function is also visually contextualised in that it is not read out from the speaker's notes: when given the right to the floor, the PM stands up with his open folder in both hands, placing it onto the dispatch box while addressing the Speaker.[19] During the production of his answer, the PM maintains a general visual orientation towards the opposite benches and does not gaze down to recruit the notes in his folder placed open before him. These visual cues construct the quotation as speech for which the speaker has no authoritative basis.

Ex. (115), which includes the interaction shown in Ex. (31), shows how the sequence continues. It begins where Ex. (114) left off. Here the LO calls the PM's answer into doubt, performing another quotation ascribed to government sources and staging his papers as physical evidence against the PM's claimed position. Alastair Campbell was the PM's Director of Communications and Strategy at the time.

(115)   PMQs 16 July 2003
PM: Tony Blair (Lab); LO: Iain Duncan Smith (Con); S: Michael Martin

```
1    S:         [(iain duncan SMITH;)]=°
2    MPs:       [j j j j j j j j j]
     cam        >> long shot --->
     loW        >> long shot          --->°
3    LO:        =[+*□#WELL; ⁑%°] [(0.58)]*
4    MPs:       [j j j j j j j][j j j]
     loH           +orients towards handling of papers --->
     loG           *places papers onto dispatch box*
     loP           □ positions himself at dispatch box --->
     pmH        >> gaze towards LO ǂ
     pmW        >> sitting down with open folder in both hands%
     fig           #Fig. 8.20
5    LO:        [*mister SPEAker;]°=
```

---

[19] According to William Hague, the former leader of the Conservative party, Tony Blair had answers on any topic and in alphabetical order in his folder. See www.totalpolitics.com/articles/news/william-hague-reveals-tactics-beating-tony-blair-pmqs

```
6   MPs:        [j  j   j   j    j j j j]
    loW         >> standing up and positioning himself at dispatch box°
    loG         *picks up paper sitting to the left of dispatch box -->

7   LO:         =[<<all>he's #↑rApidly] becoming a #stranger* to the ↑TRUTH>;=+
8   MPs:        [j  j j j j j j j j  ]
    loH                                                              -->+
    loG                                              -->*paper in both hands--->
    fig                  #Fig.8.21            #Fig.8.22

9   LO:     ->  +=the □ #↑TIMES |on the [tEnth of ju↑lY;]+
10  MPs:                        [l l l l  h h ]
    cam                 --->| medium close-up --->
    loH         +gazes onto notes                    +
    loP                 □ rests on left forearm on dispatch box --->
    fig                 #Fig.8.23

11  MPs:        [j j j j j j j j j j j j j j j j j j j j j
12  LO:     ->  [+ (0.50)       +  (0.48)<<f>on the ↑tEnth of july+ the
    loH         +gazes towards S+ onto notes              --->+towards S -->
    MPs:        j j j j]
    LO:     ->  ↑TIMES>];+
    loH         --->+

13          ->  +[(0.59)          + <<f>has a ↑QUOTE from number tEn>,]+
14  MPs:        [j j j j j j j j j j j j j j j j j j j j j  ]
    loH         +gazes onto notes + gazes towards PM          --->+

15  LO:     ->  +[(0.43) <<f>saying that they were] ↑nInety-nine per cent*□
16  MPs:        [j j j j j j j j j j j j j j j]
    loH         +gazes onto notes   --->
    loG                                                              -->*
    loP                                                              -->□

    LO:     ->  con+*↑↑VIN+#CED!>; *
    loH         -->+gazes towards PM+gazes onto notes--->
    loG                 *points at paper*
    fig                 #Fig.8.24

17  LO:     ->  +*that the GILligan source-+
    loH                          -->+
    loG         *holds paper in both hands --->

18  LO:     ->  +°h was *□DAvid kelly;
    loH         +gazes towards PM --->
    loG             --->*puts paper down left to dispatch box --->
    loP                 □ straightens himself --->

19  LO:         °h [so they ↑DI]D belIeve (.) [it* was david +kelly;] □
```

8.3 Trading-Quotes Sequences   283

```
20   MPs            [AH::::::::::]          [ah: yes            ]
     loH                                    --->+downward gaze onto notes-->
     loG                                 -->*
     loP                                                        -->☐
21   LO:    ->    ☐ °h and+ his ↑OWN labour mEmber of the commIttee Actually +
     loH                  + gazes towards PM                              +
     loP           ☐ rests himself on dispatch box --->
     LO:    ->    +says,
     loH           + gazes onto notes --->
22   LO:    ->    °h +that the ↑cIvil servant has been used as a F:ALL guy by
     loH           --> + gazes towards PM --->
     LO:    ->    the govern+ment.☐ [(.)]
23   MPs:                                   [h h] [h h h h h h h h h h h h h h h h]
     loH           --> + gazes onto notes --->
     loP                    --->☐
24   LO:                                    [°h +↑THIS has all the fingerprint]s of
     loH                        --->+
     LO:           Alastair campbell;
25   LO:           [°h who is using the ma↑CHInery of government;]
26   MPs:          [h h h h h h h h h h h h h h h h h h h h h   ]
27   LO:           [(0.55) as a venDETta;]=
28   MPs:          [h h h h h h h h h h]
29   LO:           [=a PERsonal vendEtta; (0.99)]
30   MPs:          [h h h h h h h h h h h h h]
31   LO:           ↑HOW long's the prime minister gonna let this continue;=
32                 =or ↑IS it correct as [alastair ↑cAmpbell] says;
33   MPs:                                  [j j j j j j j j j]
34   LO:    ->    +°h when ↑HE said;
     loH           + gazes towards PM --->>
35   LO:    ->    °h TOny couldn't cOpe withOUt #me-(.) |
     cam                                            --->|
     fig                                       #Fig.8.25
36   MPs:          |°%[l l l l ]=
     LO:              [(1.53)]
     cam:          | bird's-eye view --->>
     loW:              °sitting down --->>
     pmW:                 %standing up with open folder in his hands --->
```

The LO's subsequent turn builds on, as well as attacks, the PM's response, challenging it with regard to his displayed epistemic access and evidential authority. It shows that he neither acknowledges nor accepts the PM's response.

Figure 8.20 The LO places his notes on the dispatch box.

With the opposition MPs still softly jeering, the Speaker summons the LO by his name (line 1). While standing up, the LO puts his notes onto the dispatch box with his right hand and at the same time produces a *well*-preface in an independent intonation phrase (line 3, Fig. 8.20), foreshadowing a dispreferred move.

He next looks down to the left of the dispatch box. As if pulling a rabbit out of a hat, he picks up a second batch of notes from the table on which the dispatch box is placed. Note the displayed disengagement from the LO's actions on the part of the PM, who shows visual involvement with the notes in his folder (Figures 8.21, 8.22). At the same time, this disengagement nicely illustrates how the interaction during PMQs constitutes a performance for the cameras, targeted at a public audience, rather than the interlocutors.

In a concurrent verbal move, the LO appeals to the authority in the House, the Speaker, and accuses the PM of lying (*mister SPEAker he's ↑rApidly becoming a stranger to the ↑TRUTH*, lines 5, 7). In this way, he assesses the PM's prior speech in a follow-up, in particular with respect to the displayed epistemic stance in the self-quotation, calling the PM's credibility and authority explicitly into doubt. Rhetorically, the accusation sets up a riddle. The solution is presented in the form of two quotations: settling into a reading posture (Fig. 8.23), the LO makes reference to the source of the first quotation (*the ↑TIMES on the tEnth of ju↑lY*, line 9). In overlap,

8.3 *Trading-Quotes Sequences*   285

Figure 8.21 The LO produces more written evidence while the PM consults his notes.

Figure 8.22 The LO prepares to quote.

there is derisive laughter and audible agreement by the opposition MPs (line 10). On post-completion, the government MPs respond with jeering, which is oriented to by delay and repair on the LO's speech (lines 11–12). After more delay, he resumes with his speech, bringing the reported speech construction

286   Reported Speech in Recurrent Courses of Action

Figure 8.23 The LO delivers 'literalised' indirect speech.

to completion (*has a ↑QUOTE from number tEn saying that they were ↑nInety-nine per cent con↑!VINCED! (...),* lines 13, 15, 17–18). Note that this is a rare case in the data where the quotation of a quotation, as it were, is presented and the evidential authority is not constructed through the authority of a named, elite source but through the reference to an absolute date (*tenth of July*) and media outlet (*The Times*) from which this quotation was sourced. The source quoted by the newspaper comes from the heart of the government – number 10 represents the residence and office of the Prime Minister himself. The quotation is grammatically formatted as indirect speech through the complementiser *that*, a change of pronouns *we > they*, and backshift of the verb *are > were*. While performing the quotation, the LO generally maintains a sustained orientation to his notes (Fig. 8.23). Again, this represents an uncommon case in the data in that indirect speech is presented as a visual performance, drawing on written evidence.

In the quotation, the position is claimed that the PM's office was convinced that David Kelly was the source, which directly contradicts the PM's claimed position in the prior answer. What was treated as a key word in the quote, *con↑!VINCED!,* is accompanied by a pointing gesture with the LO's righthand index finger (Fig. 8.24). In this way, the paper embodies physical evidence against the claims the PM just made. The gesture is at a later stage accompanied by the LO quickly looking towards the PM,

Figure 8.24 The LO points at his evidence in coordination with the key word in the quotation.

contextualising the chunk as addressed to and relevant to the PM. The quotation is taken up by affiliative responses on the part of the opposition MPs, which can be treated as (orchestrated and staged) displays of surprise (*AH:::*, line 20).

In a new intonation phrase, the position is next recycled in a *so*-prefaced formulation addressed to the television audience: *so they ↑DID belIeve it was david kelly* (line 19). This is accompanied by the LO repositioning his posture, which also visually frames the completion of the quotation in retrospect.

The LO next again repositions himself, displaying visual engagement with his notes, producing the second instance of reported speech (*and his ↑OWN labour mEmber of the commIttee Actually says that the ↑cIvil servant has been used as a F:ALL guy by the government (. . .)*, lines 21–22). The indirect quotation is again ascribed to the PM's own political camp, repeating the accusation of misconduct from the first question turn. The construction is introduced by an *and*-preface which presents the quotation as providing a concordant position. The verbum dicendi SAY appears in simple present, which presents the reported speech in the here and now.

In his own voice, the LO now attributes the responsibility for the state of affairs claimed in the quotations to the PM's Director of

288 Reported Speech in Recurrent Courses of Action

Figure 8.25 The LO produces direct speech in the question component without visually recruiting his sources.

Communications and Strategy (↑ *THIS has all the fingerprints of Alastair campbell (...)*, lines 24–25, 27, 29). This move implicitly constructs the PM as powerless and as not having authority over his own government and is taken up with audible agreement by the opposition MPs (lines 26, 28, 30). The following question component is built on this assertion: ↑*HOW long's the prime minister gonna let this continue;* (line 31). Note that the alternative interrogative itself contains reported speech designed to back up the attack on the PM's authority and power (*or* ↑*IS it correct as alastair* ↑*cAmpbell] says when* ↑*HE said;°h TOny couldn't cOpe withOUt me-* (lines 32, 34–35, Fig. 8.25).

This presents a major challenge to the PM's competence, credibility, and authority as head of government. It is taken up with extensive (derisive) laughter by the opposition MPs (line 36), which continues when the PM takes his turn in overlap (Ex. (116), lines 1–2). In what follows, I show how the PM maintains his line of argument, claiming ignorance and deferring responsibility to third parties.

(116)   PMQs 16 July 2003

PM: Tony Blair (Lab); LO: Iain Duncan Smith (Con); S: Michael Martin

```
1     MPs:     =[1 1 1 1 1 1 1 1 1 1 1]
```

8.3 Trading-Quotes Sequences

```
2    PM:    [$uh? $% ↑FIRST of all,] $
     cam    >> bird's-eye view --->
     pmG    $places open folder onto dispatch box $ adjusts glasses$
     pmW       >>%

3    MPs:   [l sh ch sh ch sh ch sh ch sh ch sh ch sh]
4    PM:    [‡§ (0.78) the uh: (0.65) the |↑MINistry;]
     cam                              -->|medium close-up -->
     pmH    ‡gaze towards opposition --->
     pmP    §rests himself on dispatch box --->

5    MPs:   [<<f>ch ch ch ch l sh sh sh sh sh sh sh sh ]
6    PM:    [(1.37) ((smack)) (0.99) the ↑MINistry of defen]ce #(.) made it
     fig                                                      #Fig.8.26
     PM:    clear,=

7    PM:    =that of ↑COURSE;=
8    PM:    =they #don't KNOW who the source is,=
     fig         #Fig.8.27

9    PM:    =there's only one body that DOES?=
10   PM:    =and ‡that's <<p>the bee bee ↑CEE;> ‡
     pmH    -->  ‡ gaze towards own benches        ‡

11   MPs:   [j j j j j j j j j j j j j j j j j j ]
12   PM:    [‡ (0.36) and ↑IF there's some doubt about It?]
     pmH    ‡ gaze towards opposition --->

13   MPs:   [j j j j j j j j j j j j j j j j j j j]
14   PM:    [(.) it's very sImple for them to clear that ↑UP;]

15   MPs:   [j j j j j j j j j j j j j j j j j j j j j j]
16   PM:    [(0.81) but I: would have thought it is perfectly obvIous?]

17   MPs:   [j j j j j j j j j j j j j]
18   PM:    [(0.28) that ALL they need to dO,]§
     pmP                                  --->§

19   MPs:   [j j j j j j j j j]
20   PM:    [§is SIMply to say,]
     pmP    §straightens himself --->

21   MPs:   [j j j j j]
22   PM:    [yEs or $NO,] |
     pmH              --->|
     pmG             $grasps folder --->

23   MPs:   [j j j j j j j j j j j j j j j]
24   PM:    [|is he|   the source or NOT? §]
     pmH    |gaze towards own benches| towards opposition --->
     pmP                                ---->§

25   MPs:   [j j j j j j j j j j j j j j j]
26   PM:    [§they can dO it why ↑DON'T they; §]
     pmP    §leans forward                   §
```

```
27    MPs:    [|%☐j]
28            [(1.1)]
      cam     |bird's-eye view --->>
      pmW     %sitting down --->>
      loW     ☐standing up --->>
```

The PM's cut-offs and repair on turn beginning show an orientation to the MPs' continuing laughter. As in his previous response, the PM does not comply with the constraints set up by the interrogative but treats only the first quotation in the preface as the actionable part of the question turn. In doing so, he reiterates the same position as in his previous answer, this time citing the Ministry of Defence (rather than himself as part of an underspecified collective) to claim ignorance, (. . .) *the ↑MINistry of defence made it clear that of↑COURSE they don't KNOW who the source is* (lines 4, 6–8). The pausing and repair display an orientation to the MPs' cheering and shouting on both sides of the House.

The quotation is introduced by the expression *made it CLEAR* and produced with indirect speech, indicated by the complementiser *that* and a shift in pronoun (*we> they*). The fact that there is no backshift of the verb frames the quoted assertion as still valid at the time of speaking.

The PM shows no visual engagement with his notes when producing the quotation, framing it as a summarising dialogue retrieved from memory of what the ministry's claimed position is, rather than as an authorised quotation recruited from his sources (Figures 8.26–8.27). There is a shift in principalship during the use *of ↑COURSE*. This phrase displays his own stance towards the summarised position, which treats the position presented by the LO as 'morally problematic' (Stivers 2011: 104). There follows no audible display of agreement on the part of the government MPs in response to the quotation. This shows that while seeking to respond to and rebut the accusation made in the question turn, this move does not solicit support on the part of his backbenchers. This may be because the position of claimed ignorance displayed is only reiterated from the previous answer turn.

The PM next repeats the self-evident claim that the BBC knows the source (*there's only one body that DOES and that's the bee bee ↑CEE*, lines 9–10). This is responded to by soft jeering, a display of dissent, on the part of the opposition MPs (line 11). Amidst this continued soft jeering, the PM again defers the responsibility of the unclear situation to the BBC (*and ↑IF there's some doubt about It? (. . .)*, lines 12–27). There is a noticeable absence of audible support for the PM's speech among the government MPs, which

8.3 Trading-Quotes Sequences

Figure 8.26 The PM produces the quotation, showing multiple orientations towards the opposition benches.

Figure 8.27 The PM continues to produce the quotation, showing multiple orientations towards the opposition benches.

displays a lack of support, challenging the authority of the PM. This shows that not only the evidence delivered for his position, claiming ignorance, but also the general line of argument fails to rally the government MPs behind the PM.

In material not shown here, the sequence culminates in the LO performing an overall attack on the credibility and truthfulness of the PM and his government without providing further evidence. This is rebutted by the PM in a response where he accuses the LO of opportunism when claiming that they were misled over Iraq. Following this third answer turn, the sequence is closed and an MP is allocated the next turn.

In sum, I have demonstrated that although they are used in similar turn slots, self-quotations are not successful in claiming impartial, unchallengeable, and counter-interest evidence in the same way as other- or third-party quotations in responsive action formats. Rather, they serve to reaffirm positions previously made by speakers. In the example shown, this further becomes visible through the speaker's conduct, which does not display visual engagement with his notes. In this way, self-quotations are not suited in the same way to (re)construct the speaker's credibility and authority in interactional environments when a speaker is under attack.

8.4 Summary and Conclusions

This chapter has been concerned with the forms and functions of reported speech in the question–answer sequences between the LO and the PM. Based on the observation that the use of reported speech with SAY has increased most sharply in these encounters between the periods of 1978–1988 and 2003–2013, I examined how this relative frequency becomes visible in a sequential analysis. As a first result, the small number of 1978–1988 examples did not allow me to identify patterns of use. The study of the 2003–2013 sample, on the other hand, revealed two recurrent adversarial courses of action where reported speech is deployed in patterned ways: enticing sequences and trading-quotes sequences. In terms of the latter, I discussed how the procedural knowledge of trading quotes, which is evident in the 1978–1988 sample, has been constructionalised.

8.4.1 *Building Sequences with Quotations: Enticing and Trading-quotes Sequences*

Enticing sequences come in a number of variants across communities of practice.[20] The enticing sequences described in the PMQs data seem to

---

[20] Reynolds (pers. comm.) has commented that when comparing the enticing sequences as observed on the street in his data with these in parliament, the question is who has copied whom. In other words, have professional politicians adopted the practice of asking enticing questions from people on the street, or vice versa?

8.4 Summary and Conclusions

constitute a more recent phenomenon in that no comparable sequences were found between 1978–1988. Initiated by an uncontroversial simple question, reported speech is routinely used by LOs in the second question turn. In terms of form, the data show a clear tendency towards SAY as the quotative verb (63 per cent) in a variety of constructions. Almost half of the quotations (47 per cent) are performed as 'literalised' speech, with speakers showing visual engagement with their notes. This manipulation of objects displays evidential access, authenticating and authorising the positions presented. The practice of quoting in second action slots contributes to building accusatory actions which attack the credibility of the prime-ministerial answer that has just been made publicly available.

Trading quotes constitutes a practice in which speakers rebut attacks implemented through quotations with quotations in their own turn. In my data, it can be traced back to a single case in the 1978–1988 sample where it is deployed by the PM in an answer turn to an opposition backbencher. This indicates that the practice represents procedural knowledge which has been shared in this community of practice for at least one or two generations. It has been found that participants in both data sets can use expressions such as *if he wants to trade quotes, if the honourable gentleman refers to what the press has said about it* to project reported speech designed to counter the first quotations. This shows that the practice is so conventionalised that participants have found routine ways to talk about their procedural knowledge, which has, in turn, become frozen in a construction [IF + 3rd person reference to a co-present party + V], and that it has become constitutive for building adversarial courses of action between the LO and the PM. In contrast to enticing sequences, trading-quotes sequences are initiated with prefaced questions in which quotations serve to present controversial positions. These attack the PM and make the interaction hostile right from the start. Here SAY is the verb of communication most frequently used. The data analysis revealed three characteristic dimensions:

Quotations as the actionable part of turns
The study of quotations in larger courses of actions revealed that quotations are treated as the actionable part of turns. The analysis of trading-quotes sequences exemplifies this particularly well: I showed that reported speech presented in the preface of question turns implements the accusation, with the subsequent interrogative question component only serving as a dummy to perform what is required as the LO's action by the institution. In response, PMs engage in 'trading quotes', that is, they

rebut the reported speech in the question preface with reported speech ascribed to third parties (or others, i.e., the interlocutor) which squarely counters the position claimed. In not responding to the constraints set up by the interrogative but to the accusations made in the preface, PMs treat the preface as the actionable part. In the second question slot, LOs produce another prefaced question with reported speech as prefatory material designed to attack the PM's prior answer.

Ascribed sources and quoted material as key features of evidence
The analysis demonstrated that the attributed source of the quoted material may be presented as the key feature in a piece of evidence, which again confirms the point made in previous chapters that not only the position claimed in the quoted speech (what was said) but also the ascribed source (who said it) are crucial in the design of reported speech as a rhetorical device for constructing evidential authority and credibility on both sides at PMQs. Moreover, speakers were shown to present 'literalised' reported speech as authentic evidence through displays of visual and haptic engagement with their notes.

Self-quotations as reaffirmations but not evidence
Prime-ministerial self-quotations do not work in the same way to rebut hostile question designs in trading-quotes sequences. They are not treated as impartial, unchallengeable, counter-interest evidence for a counter-position, nor are they necessarily backed by physical evidence, that is, written notes, which would authenticate and authorise the counter-position as an official position. This is further evidenced by the observation that self-quotations are not used to construct controversial question designs at PMQs.

8.4.2   General Tendencies

Personalisation
The increased concentration on the polarising interaction between the LO and PM, staged as the climax of PMQs, has contributed to a personalisation of the opposition between the two sides of the House, embodied through the party leaders of the two biggest parties. The merging of the two fifteen-minute sessions into one thirty-minute one and the decision of LOs to make use of the full set of six allotted turn slots has granted LOs the space to solicit agendas stretching over several question–answer turns. The enticing and trading-quotes

8.4 Summary and Conclusions

sequences, which can comprise sequences of three to four question–answer sequences, represent one product of this development. Here other- and third-party quotations represent an especially powerful resource for attacking the credibility and authority of the PM, and on the other hand, for promoting the self-presentation of the LO, the contender for the office of the PM, as impartial, counter-interest, and morally superior. The construction [IF + 3rd person reference to a co-present party + V] is symptomatic of a personalised exchanging of quotations, which was already known to participants in the 1978–1988 sample but has arguably evolved into a ritualised course of action in the 2003–2013 sample.

Visualised 'literalisation' of reported speech

As demonstrated in the analysis, enticing and trading-quotes sequences are environments where a preference for 'literalised' reported speech is displayed, because it is functional in constructing impartial, counter-interest, and unchallengeable evidence to build hostile actions. I have shown in the comparative analysis of direct speech (Chapter 6) that direct speech can be heard as 'literalised' in both audio (1978–1988) and video recordings (2003–2013). The phenomenon is thus not new from the perspective of the mediated audience. However, the video broadcasts also allow speakers to make use of visual aids, performing visualised verbatim speech which plays to the audience. In this sense, it can be assumed that the interaction between the LO and the PM has also been mediatised, in the sense that participants engage in courses of action in a way that is conditioned by the visual media.

Audience involvement

As shown in the sequential analysis, speakers in enticing and trading-quotes sequences show an orientation towards engaging their audiences, that is, soliciting audience responses, thereby polarising the two sides of the House. It can be assumed that this conduct, which comes off as much more entertaining and lively, also involves the mediated audience to a greater extent

CHAPTER 9

Summary and Conclusions

This study has been concerned with the evolution of reported speech as an evidential practice at PMQs. Analysing two collections of reported speech culled from authentic recordings of 1978–1988 (audio) and 2003–2013 (video), I conducted a study which stands for a new research programme, Diachronic Interactional (Socio-) Linguistics. The focus was on reported speech with the quotative verb SAY, which was found to be the most frequent type of quotative verb in the 2003–2013 data set. The study yielded results concerning reporting clauses and reported clauses, the packaging of reported speech in rhetorical structures and its uses in recurrent courses of action. These findings are summarised in Section 9.1.

On a broader level, the study was designed to contribute to our theoretical understanding of evidentiality in English, to further our understanding of constructions, interaction, and change, and to offer insight into the workings and development of PMQs as a community of practice. It also serves as a proposal for how Interactional Linguistics can approach the short-term diachronic study of spoken data. The conclusions drawn from these considerations are outlined in Section 9.2.

9.1 Summary of Findings

The comparative study of the 1978–1988 and 2003–2013 data sets has shown that reported speech with SAY is an evidential practice which has changed from both quantitative and qualitative perspectives. I summarise the analytic findings from Chapters 5–8 in what follows.

Chapter 5 has analysed the emergence of reporting clauses in the 1978–1988 and 2003–2013 samples. Based on the finding that they are always realised with the subject and the verb (but only sometimes include other elements), reporting clauses are conceptualised as constructions of the format [Subject + SAY]; however, they have different 'exemplar clouds' which are reflective of changing social factors (see below). Reporting clauses

9.1 Summary of Findings

can thus be thought of as being similar to 'dense constructions' (e.g., Günthner 2011c) such that reporting clauses tend to convey only the most basic information, showing a preference for leaving out circumstantial detail from the original situated context where the past utterance was produced. Also due to the grammatical and semantic features of SAY, speakers can frame political positions as context-free quotations, tailoring them as evidential building blocks for context-specific in situ actions and goals.

I have argued that the data suggest two emergent extensions of the evidential construction: 1) the ongoing grammaticalisation of HE SAID, described as a continuum involving the path *evidential clausal formula* (HE SAID$_1$) > *evidential parentheticals* (HE SAID$_2$/HE SAID$_3$) > *evidential discourse marker* (HE SAID$_4$); and 2) a partially filled formulaic construction [Temporal adverbial + THE PRIME MINISTER + SAY + quotation]. Corroborated by evidence from other English contexts, the grammaticalisation of HE SAID indicates, in particular, that evidential meaning is entering the emergent grammar of English (see Section 9.2.1).

In both data sets, sources are constructed as agentival and authoritative, and are usually named in a self-explanatory and disambiguating fashion. However, the comparison between 1978–1988 and 2003–2013 shows the following general changes with respect to how reporting clauses are built: densification, polarisation, a more interpersonal style, and credibility enhancement.

Chapter 6 has been concerned with the contextualisation of reported clauses from the perspectives of listeners (1978–1988 audio) and viewers (2003–2013 video). It is found that from these perspectives, reported clauses are constructed through prosodic, lexico-syntactic, and audio-visual cues in 1978–1988, while in the 2003–2013 sample they constitute visual performances, constructed through bundles of prosodic, lexico-syntactic, and embodied cues, where speakers may be seen to recruit their sources through the haptic manipulation of notes and documents. I suggested that the quotations are formatted as building blocks due to the contingencies of public speaking: both data sets show a strong preference for clearly marked boundaries of the reported speech across types of quotations, displaying a strong orientation towards unequivocally indicating shifts in footing. Crucially, this proved to be equally effective for both the listening and viewing audiences, which shows that prosodic and lexico-syntactic resources suffice to serve this function. I proposed a grammatical continuum for the forms of reported speech, from indirect speech, to 'in between', to direct speech. Note, however, that the distribution across speaker roles and turn types differs in both data sets, with the PM having exclusive direct access to sources in 1978–1988, claimed through 'literalised' direct speech. The 2003–2013 sample on the other hand displays a strong orientation to the 'literalisation' of sources, a resource for authentication and authorisation, which is achieved across types of reported speech through the visual manipulation of (original) documents, and through the use of the verbal formula (AND) I QUOTE, which is also deployed to 'literalise' segments of reported speech. The use of the verbal formula (AND) I QUOTE points to an emergent practice of using of mixed quotations, which is not observed in 1978–1988. The repackaging of indirect to direct speech depending on the availability of written sources in 2003–2013 further points to the relevance of 'literalised' quotations. Syntactically, this finding suggests that the complementiser *that* does not serve as a subordinator but as an explicit lexical marker for indirect speech. This means that the complementiser is deployed as a lexical contextualisation cue to emphasise that the speaker does not have direct access to a source rather than marking syntactic relations.

Generally, the comparison between 1978–1988 and 2003–2013 points to a greater credibility enhancement and a more interpersonal style when quoting.

Chapter 7 has offered an analysis of the organisation of reported speech in rhetorical structures that are characteristic of political oratory. Lists and contrast relations are both found during 1978–1988 and 2003–2013 in the delivery of reported speech, while combined structures (list and contrast as well as puzzle–solution) are only performed during 2003–2013 in this context. The use of these rhetorical structures constitutes a resource for speakers to accomplish a denser packaging of incisive messages delivered through reported speech, and the findings show that this rhetorical effect has even been increased through a tighter chunking of 2003–2013 reported speech in list constructions, and in the overall use of combined structures. Crucially, these rhetorical devices serve to form hostile actions in an engaging way, which in the 2003–2013 data set rallies the audience behind speakers, leading to an audible (and visible) opposition and polarisation in the House which communicates in a more accessible, that is, popularised, style to mediated audiences.

Chapter 8 has investigated the question of how the heightened prominence of the interaction between the LO and the PM – which is evidenced by the 50 per cent increase of question–answer pairs between 1978–1988 and 2003–2013, from a weekly average of four (distributed over two sessions) to six question–answer pairs (concentrated in one session) – and the sharp increase in the use of reported speech in the same periods become visible in the performance of courses of action. The small sample of reported speech in the 1978–1988 LO–PM interaction does not allow generalisation. In the

2003–2013 sample, however, two recurrent adversarial courses of action with a patterned use of reported speech were identified: enticing sequences and trading-quotes sequences. In contrast to enticing sequences, evidence from an MP–PM question–answer sequence shows that trading quotes, where speakers rebut hostile moves accomplished through other- or third-party quotations with quotations in their own turn, constitutes a practice in the 1978–1988 data. Like in 2003–2013, this procedural knowledge can be explicitly addressed in a construction of the format [IF + 3rd-person reference to a co-present party + V], as in for example, *if he wAnts to trade QUOTES;*. This suggests that there are early precursors of this practice, which in the 2003–2103 sample has emerged as a patterned building block for recurrent adversarial courses of action.

9.2 Conclusions

At the beginning of this study, I asked how we could explain why it sounds so distant to us when we hear participants at PMQs engage in reported speech in recordings from the late 1970s and 1980s. The answer is that not only have the practices of how to do reported speech changed during the thirty-six years that the study examined, but so have the prominence of individual participant roles, the ways of implementing turns and activities at PMQs, and the broadcast media.[1] This has implications for our understanding of: evidentiality in English (9.2.1), constructions, interactions, and change (9.2.2), the House of Commons as a community of practice in change (and PMQs as an activity in change, 9.2.3), and the potential for a new research strand, Diachronic Interactional (Socio-)Linguistics (9.2.4). I discuss these points in what follows.

9.2.1 Evidentiality in English

Based on the findings of the study, I suggest the following theoretical conclusions on evidentiality in English:

Evidential practices are not optional in the adversarial interaction at PMQs
In providing an evidential grounding for the subsequent reported speech, reporting clauses index the voice in which what follows is said, contributing

---

[1] Of course, it can be assumed that there has been sound change in the participants' speech as well (see, e.g., Harrington 2006, 2007, and Harrington *et al.* 2000a, 2000b, 2005 for phonetic change in the Queen's televised speech) but this aspect must be left to future research.

to the internal coherence of turns at talk. If a shift of footing implemented through reported speech were not indicated through a reporting clause in the argumentative interaction at PMQs, the speaker's speech would be incoherent. In this sense, the evidential marking of quotations through reporting clauses is obligatory for meaning-making.

When reported speech is presented in the preface of question turns, it can be treated as the actionable part of a hostile action to which recipients respond and rebut in their talk. In this way, reported speech is constitutive of action formation.

The dichotomy between languages with and without evidentiality as a linguistic category cannot be maintained
I have demonstrated how reporting clauses with SAY are constructions which can undergo grammaticalisation. While the emergence of the formula [Temporal adverbial + THE PRIME MINISTER + SAY + quotation] is specific to question turns and more genre-specific than the case of HE SAID, which is evidenced across turn types in the study but has also been described across other varieties of English, this nevertheless shows that linguistic forms that express evidential meaning are entering the grammar of English.

Based on this evidence, I propose that the dichotomous conceptualisation of evidential and non-evidential languages needs to be modified in favour of a view where evidential and non-evidential languages form two extremes on a continuum. Here English would be positioned in between. This is because evidentiality is not (yet?) a verbal category expressed in the morphosyntax (like tense or aspect) but, as shown here, evidential expressions with SAY are grammaticalising into discourse markers, which represent typical forms of new grammatical evidentials across languages (see Aikhenvald 2004: 140–141; Deutscher 2011; Keevallik 2008).

Evidentiality, modality, and evaluation are separate dimensions
The results largely corroborate the findings for the use of the perception verb *see* as an evidential practice at PMQs (Reber 2014a): these suggest that evidentiality, evaluation, and (epistemic) modality should be conceptualised as separate dimensions (see further Couper-Kuhlen and Thompson 2006). Other than through the use of *see*, however, SAY verb phrases tend not to be qualified through epistemic markers. If they are, SAY tends not to be used in contexts where it functions as a quotative.[2]

---

[2] At least in the examples taken from PMQs. See Janney (1999) for different observations in a courtroom trial.

Evidential practices are indexical of their (changing) contexts
The choice and membership categorisation of sources at PMQs represent a strategic resource which have undergone diversification and change between the two data sets. In terms of form, the sources are realised as NPs. Roughly half of them constitute pronouns; the majority of the nominal representations are heavy-headed, which indicates dense information packaging. Dense information packaging is indexical of discourse environments with heavy time and space constraints, for example, news reports or technical texts. At the same time, the differentiating and self-explanatory design of the source labels secures quick identification and recognition, which is required in speech for a large audience (and) in mass media communication, where recipients cannot implement understanding checks.

The diversification of sources from largely government-only (1978–1988) to government, opposition, and other sources (2003–2013) suggests a 'democratisation' and a decline of the discursive authority of the government.

As to the types of reported speech across the two data sets, the general classification of direct, indirect, and 'in between' speech has been shown to be quite stable. However, the rise of direct speech, which is visually performed, and the additional use of (AND) I QUOTE in 2003–2013 suggests the speakers' orientation towards displays of claimed direct access to sources, authenticating the quoted material, and lending them authority and credibility. On the one hand, this was interpreted as another sign of 'democratisation', because this goes hand in hand with a diversification of speaker roles. In the 1978–1988 sample, direct speech was constructed as a privileged resource of the PM; in 2003–2013 it was found across all speaker roles. On the other hand, this development can be analysed as a response to the decline in trust of the British people in politics.

Finally, the finding that visual resources can be deployed to deliver reported speech at PMQs shows that evidentiality is not only a linguistic category but also an interactional practice, contextualised through embodied resources.

SAY as an ideal quotative verb at PMQs
In line with the previous point, SAY constitutes an ideal resource to index reported speech at PMQs. SAY has been described as an old, high-frequency, 'neutral' (both in terms of semantics and syntax) quotative verb across contexts, which conveys its high status. I expanded these findings, by showing that the low transitivity of the verb allows for reporting clauses which only have the subject (i.e., the source) and the verb (naming the action and projecting the

reported speech). The low relative frequency of optional elements (indirect objects and circumstantial adverbials) in both data sets suggests that Subject–Verb constructions with SAY are indeed treated as sufficient information in reporting clauses by participants at PMQs. In other words, I have argued that this low percentage is reflexive and at the same time constitutive of turn-constructional and interactional formats at PMQs. Here it is a resource for participants to quote past speech from contexts where it was (possibly) aimed at other audiences and served different communicative goals, and to use it to address their own audiences for rhetorical purposes in a political setting (see Tannen 2007). Moreover, the 'neutral' semantics of SAY frames the act of quoting as a potentially impartial, unbiased act of presenting what independent authorities have said with respect to the topic agenda.

9.2.2 *Constructions, Interaction, and Change*

Drawing on exemplar theory, I proposed an interactional, usage-based diachronic perspective on the study of constructions and change.

However, work informed by usage-based grammar theory based on the inductive investigation of English spoken data which takes phonetic and prosodic detail into account is still rare (see Reber 2020a for discussion), and the diachronic analysis of constructions still represents a young research programme (see, e.g., Fried 2013; Traugott and Trousdale 2013: 39–43 for literature reviews). In terms of the latter, Bergs and Diewald make two fundamental observations, which squarely match my findings made with respect to changes in the reporting clause:

> When we look at it closely, two ideas seem to underlie most constructional approaches to linguistic change: (a) linguistic change often does not affect only single linguistic items, like words, morphemes, or phonemes, but also syntagmatic structures up to the sentential and utterance levels (i.e. the relevant *co-text* comprises all levels of explicitly expressed linguistic material) and (b) linguistic change can be very *con-text* sensitive, i.e. motivated, triggered or influenced by pragmatic extra-linguistic factors. (Bergs and Diewald 2008: 3–4, italics in the original)

These observations confirm the results of the present study as follows: the analysis has evidenced changes on the clausal level, that is, in the reporting clauses, in terms of form and meaning/function. I have suggested linking these changes to what the authors call pragmatic extra-linguistic factors, that is, the correlation between the increased frequency of reporting clauses and the rise of question turns on the part of the LO to gain a heightened political profile.

In this vein, I wish to suggest that the changes observed in reporting clauses can be theorised in terms of Traugott and Trousdale's (2013) notions of constructionalisation and constructional changes. This is how these concepts are described by the authors:

> Minimally, constructionalization involves neoanalysis of morphosyntactic form and semantic/pragmatic meaning; discourse and phonological changes may also be implicated at various stages. Formal changes alone, and meaning changes alone cannot constitute constructionalization. We characterize such changes as constructional changes. [. . .] Gradual constructionalization requires prior constructional changes to have occurred (the 'succession' of small-step neoanalyses). The new pairing of both meaning and form is a new unit or sign. It is therefore a change to the system, i.e. a type/node change. (Traugott and Trousdale 2013: 22)

My analysis showed that in terms of token frequency, there was a change in the representations of exemplar clouds in the data: there was a shift from HE SAID, I SAID, and THE PRIME MINISTER SAID as dominating forms of reporting clauses in the 1978–1988 sample towards HE SAID as the single most frequent form. I have argued that this increased frequency of a single token fostered an environment for grammaticalisation processes, involving both formal and functional change in the 2003–2013 data. Drawing on Traugott and Trousdale (2013), I suggest that the ongoing grammaticalisation processes involving HE SAID can be understood as indicative of ongoing constructional change and constructionalisation: the forms of what I call *evidential clausal formulas* (HE SAID$_1$), which are used together with accented forms of HE SAID integrated in a larger intonation phrase, suggest a first phase of constructional change where there is a change in form but with the full evidential semantics and function of a quotative retained. At the other end of the continuum, the evidence provided for *evidential discourse markers* (HE SAID$_4$) in the data, which show changes in form *and* function, point to effects of constructionalisation in Traugott and Trousdale's sense.

9.2.3 The House of Commons as a Community of Practice in Change – PMQs as an Activity in Change

The study of reported speech in two time spans, 1978–1988 and 2003–2013, has revealed that not only is reported speech an emergent structure, but

PMQs is also emergent on more global levels. Further research is surely needed, but my findings suggest that PMQs as a political community of practice is changing quickly, which has an influence on the practices deployed by participants to engage in courses of action. This means that it is not only the composition and the PM that have changed, but also 'the ways of doing things' during the thirty-six years studied (and they are still changing at the time of writing; see also Hall-Lew *et al.* 2017: 346 for this challenge in the study of political data).

A Transformation of Mediated Access to PMQs
Perhaps most evidently, the public access to PMQs as it is mediated through the mass media has changed between the 1978–1988 and 2003–2013 data sets in that the media through which the data from these two periods are available are audio and audio-visual. The observation that direct speech could be contextualised through audio-visual cues (i.e., the crackling of paper in the audio recordings) illustrates, however, that these distinctions are not as clear-cut as it might seem. The type of direct speech in the video recordings, which corresponds to that in the audio recordings, is characterised by a visual performance of sources which plays to the (mediated) audience (see also Reber 2020b). Since we do not have video recordings of the audio broadcasts available, it is open to conjecture whether and how these visual aids were rhetorically deployed during the 1978–1988 period. Nevertheless, the analysis of camera work in 2003–2013 reveals a carefully staged choreography of camera angles that visualise the interaction for the mediated mass audience. This suggests that not only the medium but also the conduct of the participants has changed.

A General Change in Action Formation
While there is a general sharp increase of reported speech in terms of relative frequency across turn types and speaker roles in the 2003–2013 data, it is particularly noticeable in the question–answer sequences between the LO and PM. This correlates with the more prominent role of the LO at PMQs, which becomes visible in a conspicuous increase in question turns per week (an observation corroborated by Bates *et al.* 2014) compared to the 1978–1988 sample. From the state of the art today, it may not be surprising that reported speech is particularly widely used in action turns which are intended to be hostile, because of the LO's position as contender for the office of the PM. As mentioned above, Antaki and Leudar (2001: 477), drawing on Hansard from the 1990s, describe hostile actions as the home of literal quotations in British parliamentary debates. My findings

show that participants between 1978–1988 did not use reported speech as frequently for action formation, and verbatim quotations seemed to be only used in the PM's speech. If reported speech is primarily deployed in adversarial rather than friendly action formats, this suggests that participants used to build adversarial action formats in different ways (or that the interactions were not as hostile). More research is surely needed but this points to a general change in practices for action formation between the two data sets.

Emergent Courses of Action
In the 2003–2013 data set, the higher relative frequency compared to the earlier data set of reported speech with SAY, especially in the question–answer sequences between the PM and LO, co-occurs with recurrent courses of action where reported speech is systematically deployed in specific positions: enticing sequences and trading-quotes sequences. Reported speech with SAY had an extremely low relative frequency in the 1978–1988 interaction between the PM and the LO, and the earlier data set had a lower average length of question–answer sequences, so no such patterns could be identified. The practice of trading quotes, which lends the sequence its name, was used in the 1978–1988 set, while enticing sequences were not. This suggests that the trading-quotes practice has been known for longer but only came to emerge as a building block for recurrent courses of action after 1988.

9.2.4 Diachronic Interactional (Socio-)Linguistics

This study has proposed a Diachronic Interactional (Socio-) Linguistics method that can be used for the diachronic comparison of corresponding data sets from the same community of practice during different time spans. A comparison between data sets over time allows us to describe the changing and varying conventions and categorisations reflexive and constitutive of social structures, which constitute a desideratum in the study of social interaction. Such an analysis is now possible due to the recent availability of archives of audio and video recordings dating from the early twentieth century to today. The diachronic comparison of data taken from a relatively small community of practice provides valuable insights into the evolving contextualised forms and functions of language used and shared by entire linguistic communities.

The analytic interest of this study, reported speech as an evidential practice, was explored by a comparison of two periods of time on the following different levels: its composite linguistic and visuo-material elements, rhetorical structures, action formation, courses of action, and whether as a linguistic structure exclusively heard (by the listening radio audience) or both heard and watched (as an embodied performance by TV and internet audiences). Any of these levels or (mediated) settings (whether everyday or institutional) would lend themselves as diachronic objects of analysis in their own right in future research.

While drawing on Interactional Linguistics/Conversation Analysis, the research programme of Diachronic Interactional (Socio-) Linguistics necessarily expands these existing methodologies. I propose that studies of recent change in English from a diachronic interactional (socio-)linguistic perspective should be designed in line with the following considerations:

- The analysis should be grounded in authentic recordings of naturally occurring interaction. The compilation of the corpus should involve two or more comparable data sets and a structured data selection from the outset.
- The phonetic-prosodic and lexico-syntactic structures (as well as bodily movements and the manipulation of objects) should be described in the real time of interaction from a participant's perspective. In mediatised discourse, this can also mean from the perspective of the mediated audience.
- Depending on the communty of practice, the data sets should be compiled such that they span at least half a generation (Labov 1981). Other recent work has demonstrated the richness of findings gained from corpora which comprise longer periods (Jucker and Landert 2015).
- The approach should employ a combination of qualitative and quantitative methods. As a first step, categories should be established on the basis of qualitative analysis. Next, the tokens instantiating these categories (types) should be counted to determine change and variation between the data sets included. The implications of these findings should again be explored through qualitative study.

It will be exciting to see how the new possibilities opening up by the recent availability of historical spoken corpora will further foster the development of new methodologies in the future. To my mind, for example, the use of software tools represents a research desideratum that will add a new dimension to the interface of Interactional Linguistics and Digital Humanities, which is still underresearched today.

APPENDIX A

GAT 2 Transcription Conventions

Adapted from Couper-Kuhlen and Barth-Weingarten 2011.

Sequential structure

[ ] overlap and simultaneous talk
[ ]

In- and outbreaths

°h / h°	in- / outbreaths of appr. 0.2–0.5 sec. duration
°hh / hh°	in- / outbreaths of appr. 0.5–0.8 sec. duration
°hhh / hhh°	in- / outbreaths of appr. 0.8–1.0 sec. duration

Pauses

(.)	micro pause, estimated, up to 0.2 sec. duration appr.
(-)	short estimated pause of appr. 0.2–0.5 sec. duration
(--)	intermediary estimated pause of appr. 0.5–0.8 sec. duration
(---)	longer estimated pause of appr. 0.8–1.0 sec. duration
(0.5)/(2.0)	measured pause of appr. 0.5 / 2.0 sec. duration (to tenth of a second)

Other segmental conventions

and_uh	cliticisations within units
uh, uhm, etc.	hesitation markers, so-called 'filled pauses'

Laughter

`haha hehe hihi`	syllabic laughter
`((laughs))`	description of laughter
`<<laughing>>`	laughter particles accompanying speech with indication of scope
`<<:-)> so>`	smile voice

Other conventions

`((coughs))`	non-verbal vocal actions and events
`<<coughing>>`	... with indication of scope
`( )`	unintelligible passage
`(xxx), (xxx xxx)`	one or two unintelligible syllables
`(may i)`	assumed wording
`(may i say/let us say)`	possible alternatives
`((unintelligible, appr. 3 sec))`	unintelligible passage with indication of duration
`((...))`	omission in transcript
→	refers to a line of transcript relevant in the argument

Sequential structure

`=`	fast, immediate continuation with a new turn or segment (latching)

Other segmental conventions

`:`	lengthening, by about 0.2–0.5 sec.
`::`	lengthening, by about 0.5–0.8 sec.
`:::`	lengthening, by about 0.8–1.0 sec.
`?`	cut-off by glottal closure

Accentuation

`SYLlable`	focus accent
`!SYL!lable`	extra strong accent

Final pitch movements of intonation phrases

?	rising to high
,	rising to mid
-	level
;	falling to mid
.	falling to low

Other conventions

<<surprised> >	interpretive comment with indication of scope

Accentuation

SYLlable	focus accent
sYllable	secondary accent
!SYL!lable	extra strong accent

Pitch jumps

↑	smaller pitch upstep
↓	smaller pitch downstep
↑↑	larger pitch upstep
↓↓	larger pitch downstep

Changes in pitch register

<<l> >	lower pitch register
<<h> >	higher pitch register

Intralinear notation of accent pitch movements

ˋso	falling
ˊso	rising

Loudness und tempo changes, with scope

<<f> >	forte, loud
<<ff> >	fortissimo, very loud
<<p> >	piano, soft
<<pp> >	pianissimo, very soft
<<all> >	allegro, fast
<<len> >	lento, slow
<<cresc> >	crescendo, increasingly louder
<<dim> >	diminuendo, increasingly softer
<<acc> >	accelerando, increasingly faster
<<rall> >	rallentando, increasingly slower

Changes in voice quality and articulation, with scope

<<creaky> >	glottalised
<<whispery> >	change in voice quality as stated

Rhythm

Each line represents a foot, that is an interval which consists of an accented syllable perceived as a rhythmic beat and subsequent unaccented syllables, ending on, but not including the following accented syllable. Left-hand slashes indicate the beginnings, right-hand slashes the ends of such intervals (Couper-Kuhlen 1993: 74). Slashes lined up under one another indicate that the next beat, that is, the beginning of the next foot, is perceived rhythmically on time. This is exemplified as follows (Couper-Kuhlen and Barth-Weingarten 2011: 33):

```
71 JEFF: /thEy:       /
         /brOught it up /
         /On them      /
         /↑`SELVES.
```

If the next beat is produced earlier or later than expected, the rhythmic structure breaks off.

Appendix A

Conventions for Multimodal Transcription*

* *	Gestures and descriptions of embodied actions are delimited between two identical symbols and are synchronised with correspondent stretches of talk.
| |	The same goes for descriptions of camera angles (cam).
*--->	The action/ camera angle described continues across subsequent lines
---->*	until the same symbol is reached.
≫	The action/camera angle described begins before the excerpt's beginning.
-≫	The action/camera angle described continues after the excerpt's end.
.....	Action's preparation.
----	Action's apex is reached and maintained.
,,,,,	Action's retraction.
fig	The exact moment at which a screen shot has been taken
#	is indicated with a specific sign showing its position within turn at talk.

Speaker roles	Head movement and gaze	Hand movements and gesture	Posture	Body movement / Walk
LO (questioning)	loH +	loG *	loP ☐	loW °
MP (questioning)	mpH +	mpG *	mpP ☐	mpW °
LLD (questioning)	lldH +	lldG *	lldP ☐	lldW °
PM (answering)	pmH ǂ	pmG $	pmP §	pmW %

* Adapted from Mondada (2019a, 2019b).

Audience Responses

ch	cheering
chu	chuntering
fp	finger pointing
h	hear! hear!
j	jeering
l	laughter
mur	murmuring
sh	shouting
shh	shushing

APPENDIX B

Table 5.1 Relative frequencies of heavy and light noun phrases over turn types and speaker roles in subjects of finite reporting clauses (1978–1989)

(n=20)	Light NPs			Heavy NPs				Total
	Pronoun	Simple Noun	Name	Compound	Single modification	Multiple modification	Other	
MPs Question turns (n=275)	1.8 % (5)	0.4% (1)	0% (0)	0.7% (2)	0% (0)	0.7% (2)	0% (0)	3.6% (10)
Answer turns to MPs Question turns (n=275)	1.1% (3)	0.4% (1)	0% (0)	0% (0)	0% (0)	0.4% (1)	0% (0)	1.9% (5)
LO Question turns (n=44)	0% (0)	0% (0)	0% (0)	2.3% (1)	0% (0)	0% (0)	0% (0)	2.3% (1)
Answer turns to LO Question turns (n=44)	0% (0)	0% (0)	0% (0)	0% (0)	0% (0)	2.3% (1)	0% (0)	2.3% (1)
Leader of the Lib/SDP Question turns (n=12)	16.7 % (2)	0% (0)	0% (0)	0% (0)	0% (0)	0% (0)	0% (0)	16.7 % (2)
Answer turns to Lib/SDP Question turns (n=12)	0% (0)	0% (0)	0% (0)	8.3% (1)	0% (0)	0% (0)	0% (0)	8.3% (1)

Table 5.3a *Relative frequencies of noun phrases in subject position of finite reporting clauses across question turns (MPs, LOs) and answer turns (PMs, 2003–2013)*

n=335	Light NPs				Heavy NPs			Total
	Pronoun	Simple Noun	Names	Compound	Single modification	Multiple modification	Other[1]	
MPs Question turns (n=828)	2.4% (20)	0.5% (4)	0.6% (5)	2.2% (18, incl. 15 *the Prime Minister*)	1.1% (9)	0.1% (1)	0.2% (2)	7.1% (59)
Answer turns to MPs Question turns (n=828)	5.9% (49)	0.6% (5)	0.1% (1)	0.6% (5, incl. 1 *the Prime Minister*)	0.7% (6)	0.2% (2)	0.6% (5)	8.7% (73)
LO Question turns (n=275)	17.8% (49)	1.5% (4)	0.4% (1)	8.7% (24, incl. 18 *the Prime Minister*)	7.3% (20)	1.8% (5)	1.8% (5)	39.3% (108)
Answer turns to LO Question turns (n=275)	30.2% (83)	0.4% (1)	0.4% (1)	1.1% (3)	2.2% (6)	0% (0)	0.4% (1)	34.7% (95)

1 Coordinated subjects, abbreviations, and appositions are subsumed under Other.

Table 5.3b *Relative frequencies of noun phrases in subject position of finite reporting clauses in question–answer sequences between the Leader of the Liberal Democrats and the PM (2003–2010)*

n=21	Light NPs				Heavy NPs			
	Pronoun	Simple Noun	Names	Compound	Single modification	Multiple modification	Other	Total
LLD Question turns (n=56)	3.6% (2)	0% (0)	0% (0)	10.7% (6, incl. 3 *the Prime Minister*)	3.6% (2)	1.8% (1)	0% (0)	19.7% (11)
Answer turns (n=56)	16.1% (9)	0% (0)	1.8% (1)	0% (0)	0% (0)	0% (0)	0% (0)	17.9% (10)

Table 5.9 *Relative frequency of verb forms across turns types and speaker roles (1978–1988)*

n=24	Finite clauses					Nonfinite clauses				Total
	Present simple	Present progressive	Present perfect	Past simple	modal/ aspectual	to-infinitive	bare infinitive	ing-form		
MPs Question turns (n=275)	0.4% (1)	0% (0)	0.4% (1)	2.9% (8)	0% (0)	0% (0)	0.4% (1)	0.7% (2)		4.8% (13)
Answer turns to MPs Question turns (n=275)	0% (0)	0% (0)	0.4% (1)	1.1% (3)	0.4% (1)	0% (0)	0% (0)	0% (0)		1.9% (5)
LO Question turns (n=44)	0% (0)	0% (0)	0% (0)	2.3% (1)	0% (0)	0% (0)	0% (0)	0% (0)		2.3% (1)
Answer turns to LO Question turns (n=44)	0% (0)	0% (0)	0% (0)	2.3% (1)	0% (0)	0% (0)	0% (0)	2.3% (1)		4.6% (2)
Leader of the LibParty/ SDP Question turns (n=12)	0% (0)	0% (0)	0% (0)	8.3% (1)	8.3% (1)	0% (0)	0% (0)	0% (0)		16.6% (2)
Answer turns to Lib/SDP Question turns (n=12)	8.3% (1)	0% (0)	0% (0)	0% (0)	0% (0)	0% (0)	0% (0)	0% (0)		8.3% (1)

Table 5.10a *Relative frequencies of verb forms across turns types and speaker roles (LOs, MPs and PMs, 2003–2013)*

Verb phrases in reporting clauses	Finite verb phrases (n=335)							Nonfinite verb phrases (n=53)		Total
	Present simple	Present progressive	Present perfect progressive	Present perfect	Past simple	Past progressive	to-infinitive	ing-form		
MPs Question turns (n=828)	1.1% (8)	0.1% (1 passive)	0.1% (1)	0.6% (4active +1 passive)	5.3% (44)	0% (0)	0.2% (2)	1.3% (11)		8.7% (72)
Answer turns to MPs Question turns (n=828)	1.8% (15)	0.1% (1 passive)	0.1% (1)	1% (9)	5.4% (45)	0.2% (2)	1.0% (8)	1.4% (12)		11.2% (93)
LO Question turns (n=275)	17.5% (48)	0% (0)	0% (0)	1.5% (4)	20.4% (56)	0% (0)	0.4% (1)	1.8% (5)		41.5% (114)
Answer turns to LO Question turns (n=275)	14.2% (39)	1.1% (3)	0% (0)	4.0% (11)	15.3% (42)	0% (0)	0.7% (2)	2.9% (8)		38.2% (105)

Table 5.10b *Relative frequencies of verb forms in the sequences between the Leader of the Liberal Democrats and the PM (2003–2010)*

Verb phrases in reporting clauses (2003–2013)	Finite verb phrases (n=21)						Nonfinite verb phrases (n=4)		Total
	Present simple	Present progressive	Present perfect progressive	Present perfect	Past simple	Past progressive	to-infinitive	ing-form	
LLD Question turns (n=56)	0% (0)	0% (0)	0% (0)	1.8% (1)	17.9% (10)	0% (0)	1.8% (1)	1.8% (1)	23.2% (13)
Answer turns to LLD Question turns (n=56)	7.1% (4)	0% (0)	0% (0)	5.4% (3)	3.6% (2)	1.8% (1)	0% (0)	3.6% (2)	21.4% (12)

Appendix B

Table 5.11 *Relative frequency of indirect objects across turns types and speaker roles (1978–1988)*

Turn types and speaker roles (1978–1988)	Indirect objects
MPs Question turns (n=275)	0% (0)
Answer turns to MPs Question turns (n=275)	0% (0)
LO Question turns (n=44)	0% (0)
Answer turns to LO Question turns (n=44)	0% (0)
Leader of the Lib/SDP Question turns (n=12)	8% (1)
Answer turns to Lib/SDP Question turns (n=12)	0% (0)

Table 5.12a *Relative frequency of indirect objects across turns types and speaker roles (LOs, MPs and PMs, 2003–2013)*

Turn types and speaker roles (2003–2013)	Indirect object
MPs Question turns (n=828)	0% (1)
Answer turns to MPs Question turns (n=828)	1% (6)
LO Question turns (n=275)	0% (1)
Answer turns to LO Question turns (n=275)	0% (1)

Table 5.12b *Relative frequency of indirect objects in question–answer sequences between the Leader of the Liberal Democrats and the PM (2003–2010)*

Turn types and speaker roles (2003–2010)	Indirect object
LLD Question turns (n=56)	0% (0)
Answer turns to LLD Question turns (n=56)	2% (1)

Table 5.13 *Relative frequency of circumstantial adverbials in finite reporting clauses relative to number of question and answer turns, defined by speaker role (1978–1988)*

Turn types and speaker roles	Adverbials of Time	Adverbials of Space	Adverbials of Speech event	Adverbials of Respect	Adverbials of Manner	Total
MPs Question turns (n=275)	1% (2)	0 % (0)	0% (0)	0% (0)	0% (0)	1% (2)
Answer turns to MPs Question turns (n=275)	0% (1)	0 % (0)	0% (0)	0% (0)	0% (0)	0% (1)
LO Question turns (n=44)	2% (1)	2% (1)	0% (0)	0% (0)	0% (0)	5% (2)
Answer turns to LO Question turns (n=44)	0% (0)	0% (0)	0% (0)	0% (0)	0% (0)	0% (0)
Leader of the Lib/SDP Question turns (n=12)	0 % (0)	0% (0)	0% (0)	0% (0)	0% (0)	0% (0)
Answer turns to Lib/SDP Question turns (n=12)	0 % (0)	0% (0)	0% (0)	0% (0)	0% (0)	0% (0)

Table 5.15a *Relative frequency of circumstantial adverbials in finite reporting clauses across turn types and speaker roles (MPs, LOs, PMs, 2003–2013)*

Finite clauses	Time	Space	Speech event	Respect	Manner	Total
MP Question turns (n=828)	3.3% (27)	0.2% (2)	1.1% (9)	0.4% (3)	0% (0)	5% (41)
Answer turns to MP Question turns (n=828)	1.5% (12)	0.1% (1)	0% (0)	0% (0)	0.1% (1)	1.7% (14)
LO Question turns (n=275)	8.0% (22)	0.4% (1)	2.6% (7)	0,7% (2)	0.4% (1)	12.1% (33)
Answer turns to LO Question turns (n=275)	4.0% (11)	1.1% (3)	0.4% (1)	0% (0)	0% (0)	5.5% (15)

Table 5.15b *Relative frequency of circumstantial adverbials in finite reporting clauses in question–answer sequences between the Leader of the Liberal Democrats and the PM (2003–2010)*

Finite clauses	Time	Space	Speech event	Respect	Manner	Total
LibDem Question turns (n=56)	7.1% (4)	0% (0)	1.8% (1)	0% (0)	0% (0)	8.9%(5)
Answer turns to LibDem Question turns (n=56)	1.8% (1)	0% (0)	1.8% (1)	0% (0)	0% (0)	3.6%(2)

Table 5.17 *Frequency of candidates for formulaic constructions relative to number of question and answer turns, defined by speaker role (1978–1988)*

n=1	I SAID	WE SAY	WE SAID	HE SAYS	HE SAID	IT SAYS	IT SAID	THEY SAY	THEY SAID	Total
MPs Question turns (n=275)	0% (0)	0% (0)	0% (0)	0% (0)	0% (0)	0% (0)	0% (0)	0% (0)	0% (0)	0% (0)
Answer turns to MPs Question turns (n=275)	0% (1)	0% (0)	0% (0)	0% (0)	0% (0)	0% (0)	0% (0)	0% (0)	0% (0)	0% (1)
LO Question turns (n=44)	0% (0)	0% (0)	0% (0)	0% (0)	0% (0)	0% (0)	0% (0)	0% (0)	0% (0)	0% (0)
Answer turns to LO Question turns (n=44)	0% (0)	0% (0)	0% (0)	0% (0)	0% (0)	0% (0)	0% (0)	0% (0)	0% (0)	0% (0)
Leader of the Lib/SDP Question turns (n=12)	0% (0)	0% (0)	0% (0)	0% (0)	0% (0)	0% (0)	0% (0)	0% (0)	0% (0)	0% (0)
Answer turns to Lib/SDP Question turns (n=12)	0% (0)	0% (0)	0% (0)	0% (0)	0% (0)	0% (0)	0% (0)	0% (0)	0% (0)	0% (0)

Table 5.19a Relative frequencies of candidates for formulaic constructions across turn types and speaker roles (2003–2013)[2]

n=81	I SAID	WE SAY	WE SAID	HE SAYS	HE SAID	IT SAYS	IT SAID	THEY SAY	THEY SAID	Total
MPs Question turns (n=828)	0% (0)	0% (0)	0% (1)	0% (1)	1% (5)	0% (0)	0% (0)	0% (0)	0% (1)	1% (8)
Answer turns to MPs Question turns (n=828)	0% (0)	0% (0)	0% (0)	0% (3)	0% (2)	0% (0)	0% (1)	0% (0)	0% (1)	1% (7)
LO Question turns (n=275)	0% (1)	0% (0)	0% (0)	3% (8)	4% (11)	1% (2)	1% (1)	1% (3)	0% (0)	10% (26)
Answer turns to LO Question turns (n=275)	1% (2)	1% (2)	1% (3)	5% (14)	6% (15)	0% (1)	0% (0)	0% (0)	2% (5)	15% (42)

2 Tokens of I SAY were not included in the count because they are treated as metapragmatic markers (see Ex. 84 for an example). Due to the third-person address system at PMQs, there are no occurrences of YOU SAY/SAID.

Table 5.19b *Relative frequencies of candidates for formulaic constructions across turn types and speaker roles (2003–2013)*

n=4	I SAID	WE SAY	WE SAID	HE SAYS	HE SAID	IT SAYS	IT SAID	THEY SAY	THEY SAID	Total
Leader of the LibDems Question turns (n=56)	0% (0)	0% (0)	0% (0)	0% (0)	0% (0)	0% (0)	0% (0)	0% (0)	0% (0)	4% (2)
Answer turns to LibDems Question turns (n=56)	0% (0)	0% (0)	0% (0)	2% (1)	0% (0)	0% (0)	0% (0)	2% (1)	0% (0)	4% (2)

References

Aarts, F. G. A. M. (1971). On the distribution of noun phrase types in English clause structure. *Lingua*, 26: 281–293.

Aijmer, K. (2004). The interface between perception, evidentiality and discourse particle use – using a translation corpus to study the polysemy of see. *TRADTERM – Journal of the Interdepartmental Centre for Translation and Terminology of the FFLCH/USP*, 10: 249–277.

Aijmer, K. (2009). Seem and evidentiality. *Functions of Language*, 16 (1): 63–88.

Aikhenvald, A. Y. (2004). *Evidentiality*. Oxford: Oxford University Press.

Aikhenvald, A. Y. 2006. Evidentiality in grammar. In K. Brown, ed., *Encyclopaedia of Language and Linguistics*, Vol. 4, 2nd edn, Oxford: Elsevier, 320–325.

Anderson, L. B. (1986). Evidentials, paths of change, and mental maps: typologically regular asymmetries. In W. L. Chafe and J. Nichols, eds., *Evidentiality: The linguistic coding of epistemology*. Norwood, NJ: Ablex, 273–312.

Antaki, C. and Leudar, I. (2001). Recruiting the record: Using opponents' exact words in parliamentary argumentation. *Text*, 21 (4): 467–488.

Arendholz, J., Kirner, M. and Bublitz, W., eds. (2015). *Quoting Now and Then*. Leiden: Brill.

Atkinson, J. M. (1982). Understanding formality: Notes on the categorisation and production of 'formal' interaction. *British Journal of Sociology*, 33: 86–117.

Atkinson, M. (1984). *Our Masters' Voices: The language and body language of politics*. London and New York: Routledge.

Atkinson, J. M. and Drew, P. (1979). *Order in Court: The organisation of verbal interaction in judicial settings*. London: Macmillan.

Auer, P. (2000). On line-Syntax – oder: Was es bedeuten könnte, die Zeitlichkeit der mündlichen Sprache ernst zu nehmen. Special issue 'Die Medialität der Gesprochenen Sprache'. *Sprache und Literatur*, 85: 43–56.

Auer, P. (2005). Projection in interaction and projection in grammar. *Text*, 25 (1): 7–36.

Auer, P. (2015). The temporality of language in interaction: Projection and latency. In A. Deppermann and S. Günthner, eds., *Temporality in Interaction*. Amsterdam and Philadelphia: John Benjamins, 27–56.

Ås, B. (1978). Hersketeknikker [Master suppression techniques]. *Kjerringråd*, 3: 17–21.

Barth-Weingarten, D. (2006). Parallel-opposition-Konstruktionen: Zur Realisierung einer spezifischen Kontrastkonstruktion. In S. Günthner and W. Imo, eds., *Konstruktionen in der Interaktion*. Berlin: de Gruyter, 153–179.

Barth-Weingarten, D. (2009). Contrasting and turn transition: Prosodic projection with parallel-opposition constructions. *Journal of Pragmatics*, 41: 2271–2294.

Barth-Weingarten, D. (2014). Dialogism and the emergence of final particles: The case of *and*. In S. Günthner, W. Imo and J. Bücker, eds., *Grammar and Dialogism*. Berlin: de Gruyter, 335–366.

Barth-Weingarten, D. (2016). *Intonation units revisited: Cesuras in talk-in-interaction*. Amsterdam and Philadelphia: John Benjamins.

Barth-Weingarten, D. and Couper-Kuhlen, E. (2002). On the development of final *though*: A case of grammaticalisation? In I. Wischer and G. Diewald, eds., *New Perspectives on Grammaticalisation*. Amsterdam and Philadelphia: John Benjamins, 345–361.

Barth-Weingarten, D. and Couper-Kuhlen, E. (2011). Action, prosody and emergent constructions: The case of *and*. In P. Auer and S. Pfänder, eds., *Constructions: Emerging and emergent*. Berlin: de Gruyter, 236–292.

Bates, S. A., Kerr, P. Byrne, C. and Stanley, L. (2014). Questions to the Prime Minister: A comparative study of PMQs from Thatcher to Cameron. *Parliamentary Affairs*, 67: 253–280.

Beard, A. (2000). *The Language of Politics*. London and New York: Routledge.

Bednarek, M. (2006). Epistemological positioning and evidentiality in English news discourse: A text-driven approach. *Text & Talk*, 26 (6): 635–660.

Bergs, A. and Diewald, G. (2008). Introduction: Constructions and language change. In A. Bergs and G. Diewald, eds., *Constructions and Language Change*. Berlin and New York: De Gruyter Mouton, 1–22.

Biber, D. (1999). A register perspective on grammar and discourse: Variability in the form and use of English complement clauses. *Discourse Studies*, 1 (2): 131–150.

Biber, D. (2003). Compressed noun phrase structures in newspaper discourse: The competing demands of popularization vs. economy. In J. Aitchison and D. Lewis, eds., *New Media Language*. New York: Routledge, 169–181.

Biber, D., Johansson, S., Leech, G., Conrad, S. and Finegan, E. (1999). *The Longman Grammar of Spoken and Written English*. London: Longman.

Blackwell, N. L. and Tree, J. E. F. (2012). Social factors affect quotative choice. *Journal of Pragmatics*, 44: 1150–1162.

Blackwell, N. L., Perlman, M. and Tree, J. E. F. (2015). Quotation as a multimodal construction. *Journal of Pragmatics*, 81: 1–7.

Blum-Kulka, S., Blondheim, M. and Hacohen, G. (2002). Traditions of dispute: From negotiations of Talmudic texts to the arena of political discourse in the media. *Journal of Pragmatics*, 34: 1569–1594.

Blyth, C., Recktenwald, S. and Wang, J. (1990). I'm like, 'Say what ?!': A new quotative in American oral narrative. *American Speech*, 65: 215–227.

Boas, F. (1911a). Kwakiutl. In F. Boas, ed., *Handbook of American Indian Languages*. Washington: Government Printing Office, 423–557.

Boas, F. (1911b). Introduction. In F. Boas, ed., *Handbook of American Indian Languages*. Washington: Government Printing Office, 5–83.
Boye, K. (2010). Semantic maps and the identification of cross-linguistic generic categories: Evidentiality and its relation to epistemic modality. *Linguistic Discovery*, 8 (1): 4–22.
Bromley, C., Curtice, J. and Seyd, B. (2004). *Is Britain Facing a Crisis of Democracy?* Technical Report, Constitution Unit, School of Public Policy. London: University College London.
Buchstaller, I. 2002. *He goes* and *I'm like*: The new quotatives re-visited. *Internet Proceedings of the University of Edinburgh Postgraduate Conference*. Online. www.lel.ed.ac.uk/~pgc/archive/2002/proco2/buchstaller02.pdf
Buchstaller, I. (2014). *Quotatives: New trends and sociolinguistic implications*. Malden, MA: Wiley-Blackwell.
Buchstaller, I. (2017). Reported speech. In A. Barron, P. Grundy and G. Yueguo, eds., *The Routledge Handbook of Pragmatics*. Oxford: Routledge, 399–417.
Buchstaller, I. and van Alphen, I., eds. (2012). *Quotatives: Cross-linguistic and cross-disciplinary perspectives*. Amsterdam: John Benjamins.
Bull, P. and Fetzer, A. (2006). Who are *we* and who are *you*? The strategic use of forms of address in political interviews. *Text & Talk*, 26 (1): 3–37.
Bull, P. and Waddle, M. (2019). 'Let me now answer, very directly, Marie's question': The impact of quoting members of the public in Prime Minister's Questions. *Journal of Language Aggression and Conflict*, 7 (1): 56–78.
Bull, P. and P. Wells. (2012). Adversarial discourse in Prime Minister's Questions. *Journal of Language and Social Psychology*, 31 (1): 30–48.
Bybee, J. (2003). Mechanisms of change in grammaticalisation: The role of frequency. In B. D. Joseph and R. D. Janda, eds., *The Handbook of Historical Linguistics*. Malden, MA and Oxford: Blackwell, 602–623.
Bybee, J. (2006). From usage to grammar: The mind's response to repetition. *Language*, 82 (4): 711–733.
Bybee, J. (2011). Usage-based theory and grammaticalisation. In H. Narrog and B. Heine, eds., *The Oxford Handbook of Grammaticalisation*. Oxford: Oxford University Press, 69–78.
Bybee, J. L. (2013). Usage-based theory and exemplar representation. In T. Hoffmann and G. Trousdale, eds., *The Oxford Handbook of Construction Grammar*. Oxford: Oxford University Press, 49–69.
Bybee, J. and Eddington, D. (2006). A usage-based approach to Spanish verbs of 'becoming'. *Language*, 82 (2): 323–355.
Bybee, J. and Thompson, S. (1997). Three frequency effects in syntax. In *Proceedings of the Twenty-third Annual Meeting of the Berkeley Linguistics Society*. Berkeley, CA: Berkeley Linguistics Society, 378–388.
Bybee, J., Perkins, R. and Pagliuca, W. (1994). *The Evolution of Grammar: Tense, aspect and modality in the languages of the world*. Chicago, IL: University of Chicago Press.
Caffi, C. (2006). Metapragmatics. In K. Brown, ed., *Encyclopedia of Language and Linguistics*, 2nd edn, London: Elsevier, 82–88.

Cappelen, H. and Lepore, E. 1997. Varieties of quotation. *Mind*, 106: 429–450.
Charteris-Black, J. (2014). *Analysing Political Speeches*. Basingstoke: Palgrave Macmillan.
Chafe, W. (1982). Integration and involvement in speaking, writing, and oral literature. In D. Tannen, ed., *Spoken and Written Language: Exploring orality and literacy*. Norwood, NJ: Ablex, 35–53.
Chafe, W. (1986). Evidentiality in English conversation and academic writing. In W. L. Chafe and J. Nichols, eds., *Evidentiality: The linguistic coding of epistemology*. Norwood, NJ: Ablex, 261–312.
Chafe, W. L. and J. Nichols, eds. (1986). *Evidentiality: The linguistic coding of epistemology*. Norwood, NJ: Ablex.
Chilton, P. (2007). *Analysing Political Discourse: Theory and practice*. London: Routledge.
Clark, H. H. and Gerrig, R. J. (1990). Quotations as demonstrations. *Language*, 66, 764–805.
Clayman, S. E. (1992). Footing in the achievement of neutrality: The case of news interview discourse. In P. Drew and J. Heritage, eds., *Talk at Work*. Cambridge: Cambridge University Press, 163–198.
Clayman, S. E. (1993). Booing: The anatomy of a disaffilitive response. *American Sociological Review*, 58: 110–130.
Clayman, S. E. and Heritage, J. (2002a). Questioning presidents: Journalistic deference and adversarialness in the press conferences of Eisenhower and Reagan. *Journal of Communication*, 52: 749–777.
Clayman, S. E. and Heritage, J. (2002b). *The News Interview: Journalists and public figures on the air*. Cambridge: Cambridge University Press.
Clayman, S. E., Elliott, M. Heritage, J. and McDonald, L. L. (2006). Historical trends in questioning presidents 1953–2000. *Presidential Studies Quarterly*, 36: 561–583.
Clayman, S. E., Heritage, J., Elliot, M. and McDonald, L. (2007). When does the watchdog bark? Conditions of aggressive questioning in presidential news conferences. *American Sociological Review*, 72: 23–41.
Clift, R. (2006). Indexing stance: Reported speech as an interactional evidential. *Journal of Sociolinguistics*, 10 (5): 569–595.
Coe, J. and Kelly, R. (2009). *Prime Minister's Questions*, House of Commons Library.
Collins, P. (1995). The indirect object construction in English: An informational approach. *Linguistics*, 33: 35–49.
Comrie, B. (1985). *Tense*. Cambridge: Cambridge University Press.
Conboy, M. (2003). Parochialising the global language and the British tabloid press. In J. Aitchison and D. M. Lewis, eds., *New Media Language*. London: Routledge, 45–54.
Connal, L. R. (1996). Comparison. In Enos, T., ed., *Encyclopedia of Rhetoric and Composition: Communication from ancient times to the information age*. New York and London: Garland, 145–146.

Cornillie, B. (2009). Evidentiality an epistemic modality: On the close relationship between two different categories. *Functions of Language*, 16 (1): 44–62.
Couper-Kuhlen, E. (1986). *An Introduction to English Prosody*. Tübingen: Niemeyer.
Couper-Kuhlen, E. (1993). *English Speech Rhythm: Form and function in everyday verbal interaction*. Amsterdam: John Benjamins.
Couper-Kuhlen, E. (1999). Coherent voicing: On prosody in conversational reported speech. In W. Bublitz and U. Lenk, eds., *Coherence in Spoken and Written Discourse: How to create it and how to scribe it*. Amsterdam and Philadelphia: John Benjamins, 11–32.
Couper-Kuhlen, E. (2004). Prosody and sequence organisation: The case of new beginnings. In *Sound Patterns in Interaction*. E. Couper-Kuhlen and C. E. Ford, eds., Amsterdam and Philadelphia: John Benjamins, 335–376.
Couper-Kuhlen, E. (2007). Assessing and accounting. In E. Holt and R. Clift, eds., *Reporting Talk: Reported speech in interaction*. Cambridge: Cambridge University Press, 81–119.
Couper-Kuhlen, E. 2011. Grammaticalisation and conversation. In H. Narrog and B. Heine, eds., *The Oxford Handbook of Grammaticalisation*. Oxford: Oxford University Press, 424–437.
Couper-Kuhlen, E. and Barth-Weingarten, D. (2011). A system for transcribing talk-in-interaction: GAT 2 [An English translation and adaptation of Margaret Selting *et al.*: Gesprächsanalytisches Transkriptionssystem 2]. *Gesprächsforschung – Onlinezeitschrift zur verbalen Interaktion*, 12: 1–51.
Couper-Kuhlen, E. and Selting, M. (1996). Towards an interactional perspective on prosody and a prosodic perspective on interaction. In E. Couper-Kuhlen and M. Selting, eds., *Prosody in Conversation: Interactional studies*. Cambridge: Cambridge University Press, 11–56.
Couper-Kuhlen, E. and Selting, M. (2001). Introducing interactional linguistics. In M. Selting and E. Couper-Kuhlen, eds., *Studies in Interactional Linguistics*. Philadelphia and Amsterdam: John Benjamins, 1–22.
Couper-Kuhlen, E. and Selting, M. (2018). *Interactional Linguistics: Studying language in social interaction*. Cambridge: Cambridge University Press.
Couper-Kuhlen, E. and Thompson, S. A. (2006). 'You know it's funny': Eine Neubetrachtung der 'Extraposition' im Englischen. In S. Günthner and W. Imo, eds., *Konstruktionen in der Interaktion*. Berlin: de Gruyter, 23–58.
de Haan, F. (1999). Evidentiality and epistemic modality: Setting boundaries. *Southwest Journal of Linguistics*, 18: 83–101.
de Haan, F. (2012). Evidentiality and mirativity. In R. I. Binnick, ed., *The Oxford Handbook of Tense and Aspect*. Oxford: Oxford University Press, 1020–1046.
Dehé, N. (2009). Clausal parentheticals, intonational phrasing, and prosodic theory. *Journal of Linguistics*, 45 (3): 569–615.
Dehé, N. and Kavalova, Y. (2007). Parentheticals: An introduction. In N. Dehé and Y. Kavalova, eds., *Parentheticals*. Amsterdam and Philadelphia: John Benjamins, 1–22.

Dehé, N. and Wichmann, A. (2010). The multifunctionality of epistemic parentheticals in discourse: Prosodic cues to the semantic-pragmatic boundary. *Functions of Language*, 17 (1): 1–28.

Deutscher, G. (2011). The grammaticalisation of quotatives. In H. Narrog and B. Heine, eds., *The Oxford Handbook of Grammaticalisation*. New York: Oxford University Press, 646–655.

Dickerson, P. (1997). 'It's not just me who's saying this …': The deployment of cited others in televised political discourse. *British Journal of Social Psychology*, 36 (1): 33–48.

Diewald, G. (2011). Grammaticalisation and pragmaticalisation. In B. Heine and H. Narrog, eds., *Oxford Handbook of Grammaticalisation*. Oxford: Oxford University Press, 450–461.

Diewald, G. and Smirnova, E. (2010a). *Evidentiality in German: Linguistic realisation and regularities in grammaticalisation*. Berlin and New York: de Gruyter Mouton.

Diewald, G. and Smirnova, E., eds. (2010b). *Linguistic Realisation of Evidentiality in European Languages*. Berlin and New York: de Gruyter Mouton.

Du Bois, J. W. (1986). Self-evidence and ritual speech. In W. L. Chafe and J. Nichols, eds., *Evidentiality: The linguistic coding of epistemology*. Norwood, NJ: Ablex, 313–336.

Du Bois, J. W. (2007). The stance triangle. In *Stancetaking In Discourse: Subjectivity, evaluation, interaction*. In R. Englebretson, ed., Amsterdam and Philadelphia: John Benjamins, 139–182.

Eckert, P. (2006). Communities of practice. In K. Brown, ed., *Encyclopedia of Language and Linguistics*. New York: Elsevier, 683–685.

Eckert, P. and McConnell, S. (1992a). Think practically and look locally: Language and gender as community-based practice. *Annual Review of Anthropology*, 21, 461–490.

Eckert, P. and McConnell, S. (1992b). Communities of practice: Where language, gender, and power all live. In K. Hall, M. Bucholtz and B. Moonwomon, eds., *Locating Power. Proceedings of the 1992 Berkeley Women and Language Conference*. Berkeley, CA: Berkeley Women and Language Group, 89–99.

Eckert, P. and E. Wenger. (2005). Communities of practice in sociolinguistics. *Journal of Sociolinguistics*, 9 (4): 582–589.

Edwards, D. (2000). Extreme case formulations: Softeners, investment, and doing nonliteral. *Research on Language and Social Interaction*, 33 (4): 347–373.

Enfield, N. J. (2013). Reference in conversation. In J. Sidnell and T. Stivers, eds., *The Handbook of Conversation Analysis*. Malden, MA: Wiley-Blackwell, 433–454.

Erickson, F. (1992). They know all the lines: Rhythmic organisation and contextualisation in a conversational listing routine. In P. Auer and A. Di Luzio, eds., *The Contextualisation of Language*. Amsterdam and Philadelphia: John Benjamins, 365–397.

Erskine May. (1989). *Erskine May's Treatise on The Law, Privileges, Proceedings and Usage of Parliament*, 21st edn, C. J. Boulton, ed., London: Butterworths.

Ernst, T. (2009). Speaker-oriented adverbs. *Nat Lang Linguist Theory*, 27: 497–544.
Fairclough, N. (1992). *Discourse and Social Change*. Cambridge: Polity.
Fetzer, A. (2014a). Foregrounding evidentiality in (English) academic discourse: Patterned co-occurrences of the sensory perception verbs seem and appear. Special issue 'Evidentiality in Discourse'. *Intercultural Pragmatics*, 11 (3): 333–355.
Fetzer, A. (2014b). We and I, and you and them: people, power and solidarity. In H. Pishwa and R. Schulze, eds., *The Expression of Inequality in Interaction: Power, dominance and status*. Amsterdam: John Benjamins, 213–238.
Fetzer, A. (2014c). 'Judge us on what we do': The strategic use of collective *we* in political discourse. In T.-S. Pavlidou, ed., *Constructing Collectivity: 'We' across languages and contexts*. Amsterdam and Philadelphia: John Benjamins, 331–350.
Fetzer, A. (2014d). *I think, I mean* and *I believe* in political discourse. Collocates, functions and distribution. *Functions of Language*, 21 (1): 67–94.
Fetzer, A. (2015). 'When you came into office you said that your government would be different': Forms and functions of quotations in mediated political discourse. In A. Fetzer, E. Weizman and L. N. Berlin, eds., *Dynamics of Political Discourse: forms and functions of follow-ups*. Amsterdam and Philadelphia: John Benjamins, 245–273.
Fetzer, A. (2020). 'And I quote': Forms and functions of quotations in Prime Minister's questions. *Journal of Pragmatics*, 157: 89–100.
Fetzer, A. and Bull, P. (2012). Doing leadership in political speech: Semantic processes and pragmatic inferences. *Discourse and Society*, 23 (2): 127–144.
Fetzer, A. and P. Bull. (2019). Quoting ordinary people in Prime Minister's Questions 1. In A. Fetzer and E. Weizman, eds. *The Construction of 'Ordinariness' across Media Genres*. Amsterdam: John Benjamins: 73–101.
Fetzer, A. and E. Oishi, eds. (2014). Evidentiality in discourse. *Intercultural Pragmatics*, Special issue. 11 (3).
Fetzer, A. and Reber, E. (2015). Quoting in political discourse: Professional talk meets ordinary postings. In J. Arendholz, M. Kirner and W. Bublitz, eds., *Quoting Now and Then*. Berlin and Boston: de Gruyter Mouton, 97–124.
Fetzer, A. and Weizman, E. (2018). 'What I would say to John and everyone like John is ...': The construction of ordinariness through quotations in mediated political discourse. *Discourse & Society*, 29 (5): 1–19.
Fillmore, C. J., Kay, P. and O'Connor, M. C. (1988). Regularity and idiomaticity in grammatical constructions: The case of *let alone*. *Language*, 64 (3): 501–538.
Fischer, O. (2007). The development of English parentheticals: A case of grammaticalisation? In U. Smit, S. Dollinger, J. Hüttner, G. Kaltenböck and U. Lutzky, eds., *Tracing English through Time: Explorations in language variation*. Vienna: Braumüller, 99–114.
Ford, C. E. (2000). The treatment of contrasts in interaction. In B. Kortmann and E. Couper-Kuhlen, eds., *Cause, Condition, Concession and Contrast: Cognitive and discourse perspectives*. Berlin and New York: de Gruyter Mouton, 283–311.

Fox, B. (1987). *Discourse Structure and Anaphora*. Cambridge: Cambridge University Press.

Fox, B. A. (2001). Evidentiality: Authority, responsibility, and entitlement in English conversation. *Journal of Linguistic Anthropology*, 11 (2): 167–192.

Fox, B. A. and Thompson, S. A. (2007). Relative clauses in English conversation: Relativisers, frequency and the notion of construction. *Studies in Language*, 31: 293–326.

Fried, M. (2013). Principles of constructional change. In T. Hoffmann and G. Trousdale, eds., *The Oxford Handbook of Construction Grammar*. Oxford: Oxford University Press, 419–437.

Galatolo, R. (2007). Active voicing in court. In E. Holt and R. Clift, eds., *Reporting Talk: Reported speech in interaction*. Cambridge: Cambridge University Press, 195–220.

Garfinkel, H. (1956). Conditions of successful degradation ceremonies. *American Journal of Sociology*, 61(5): 420–424.

Gerhardt, C. (2006). Moving closer to the audience: Watching football on television. Special issue 'Linguistics and Media Discourse.' *Revista Alicantina de Estudios Ingleses*, 19: 125–148.

Gerhardt, C. and Reber, E. (2019). Embodied activities. In E. Reber and C. Gerhardt, eds., *Embodied Activities in Face-to-face and Mediated Settings: Social encounters in time and space*. Cham: Palgrave Macmillan, 3–27.

Giddings, P. and Irwin, H. (2005). Objects and questions. In P. Giddings, ed., *The Future of Parliament: Issues for a new century*. Basingstoke: Palgrave Macmillan, 72–73.

Givón, T. (1979). *On Understanding Grammar*. New York: Academic Press.

Goffman, E. (1979). Footing. *Semiotica*, 25(1/2): 1–29.

Good, J. S. (2015). Reported and enacted actions: Moving beyond reported speech and related concepts. *Discourse Studies*, 17: 663–681.

Goodwin, C. (2007). Interactive footing. In E. Holt and R. Clift, eds., *Reporting Talk: Reported speech in interaction*. Cambridge: Cambridge University Press, 16–46.

Goodwin, M. (1990). *He-Said-She-Said: Talk as social organisation among black children*. Bloomington, IN: Indiana University Press.

Gruber, H. (2001). Questions and strategic orientation in verbal conflict sequences. *Journal of Pragmatics*, 33: 1815–1857.

Günthner, S. (1997). Direkte und indirekte Rede in Alltagsgesprächen: Zur Interaktion von Syntax und Prosodie in der Redewiedergabe. In P. Schlobinski, ed., *Syntax des gesprochenen Deutsch*. Opladen: Westdeutscher Verlag, 227–263.

Günthner, S. (2000). Zwischen direkter und indirekter Rede. Formen der Redewiedergabe in Alltagsgesprächen. *Zeitschrift für Germanistische Linguistik*, 28 (1): 1–22.

Günthner, S. (2011a). Between emergence and sedimentation: Projecting constructions in German interactions. In P. Auer and S. Pfänder, eds., *Constructions: Emerging and emergent*. Berlin and New York: de Gruyter, 156–185.

Günthner, S. (2011b). *N be that*-constructions in everyday German conversation: A reanalysis of 'die Sache ist/das Ding ist' ('the thing is')-clauses as projector phrases. In R. Laury and R. Suzuki, eds., *Subordination in Conversation: A cross-linguistic perspective*. Amsterdam: John Benjamins, 11–36.

Günthner, S. (2011c). The construction of emotional involvement in everyday German narratives – interactive uses of 'dense constructions'. *Pragmatics*, 21 (4): 573–592.

Hall, E. T. (1969). *The Hidden Dimension*. New York: Anchor Books.

Hall-Lew, L., Friskney, R. and M. Scobbie, J. (2017). Accommodation or political identity: Scottish members of the UK Parliament. *Language Variation and Change*, 29 (3): 341–363.

Hanks, W. F. 2012. Evidentiality in social interaction. Special issue 'Evidentiality in Interaction.' *Pragmatics and Society*, 3 (2): 169–180.

Hara, Y. (2008). Evidentiality of discourse items and *because*-clauses. *Journal of Semantics*, 25: 229–268.

Harrington, J. (2006). An acoustic analysis of 'happy-tensing' in the Queen's Christmas broadcasts. *Journal of Phonetics*, 34: 439–457.

Harrington, J. (2007). Evidence for a relationship between synchronic variability and diachronic change in the Queen's annual Christmas broadcasts. In J. Cole and J. Hualde, eds., *Laboratory Phonology 9*. Berlin and Boston: de Gruyter Mouton, 125–143.

Harrington, J., Palethorpe, S. and Watson, C. (2000a). Does the Queen speak the Queen's English? *Nature*, 408: 927–928.

Harrington, J., Palethorpe, S. and Watson, C. (2000b). Monophthongal vowel changes in Received Pronunciation: An acoustic analysis of the Queen's Christmas broadcasts. *Journal of the International Phonetic Association*, 30 (1/2): 63–78.

Harrington, J., Palethorpe, S., and Watson, C. (2005). Deepening or lessening the divide between diphthongs? An analysis of the Queen's annual Christmas broadcasts. In W. J. Hardcastle and J. Beck, eds., *A Figure of Speech: Festschrift for John Laver*. London and Mahwah, NJ: Erlbaum, 227–261.

Harris, S. (2001). Being politically impolite: Extending politeness theory to adversarial political discourse. *Discourse and Society*, 12 (4): 451–472.

Heine, B. 2002. On the role of context in grammaticalisation. In I. Wischer and G. Diewald, eds., *New Reflections on Grammaticalisation*. Amsterdam and Philadelphia: Benjamins, 83–101.

Heritage, J. (1985). Analysing news interviews: Aspects of the production of talk for an 'overhearing' audience. In T. van Dijk, ed., *Handbook of Discourse Analysis*, Vol. 3. London: Academic Press, 95–117.

Heritage, J. (2013). Epistemics in conversation. In J. Sidnell and T. Stivers, eds., *Handbook of Conversation Analysis*. Boston: Wiley-Blackwell, 370–394.

Heritage, J. (2015). Well-prefaced turns in English conversation: A conversation analytic perspective. *Journal of Pragmatics*, 88: 88–104.

Heritage, J. and Clayman, S. E. (2013). The changing tenor of questioning over time: Tracking a question form across US presidential news conferences. 1953–2000. *Journalism Practice*, 7 (4): 481–501.

Heritage, J. and Greatbatch, D. (1986). Generating applause: A study of rhetoric and response at party political conferences. *American Journal of Sociology*, 92 (1): 110–157.

Heritage, J. and Raymond, G. (2005). The terms of agreement: Indexing epistemic authority and subordination in talk-in-interaction. *Social Psychology Quarterly*, 68 (1): 15–38.

Heritage, J. and Raymond, G. (2012). Navigating epistemic landscapes: Acquiescence, agency and resistance in responses to polar questions. In J. P. de Ruiter, ed., *Questions: Formal, functional and interactional perspectives*. Cambridge: Cambridge University Press, 179–192.

Heritage, J. and Sorjonen, M.-L. (1994). Constituting and maintaining activities across sequences: *And*-prefacing as a feature of question design. *Language in Society*, 23: 1–29.

Hjarvard, S. (2008). The mediatisation of society: A theory of the media as agents of social and cultural change. *Nordicom Review*, 29 (2): 105–134.

Holland, E., Wolf, E. B., Looser, C. and Cuddy, A. 2017. Visual attention to powerful postures: People avert their gaze from nonverbal dominance displays. *Journal of Experimental Social Psychology*, 68: 60–67.

Holly, W. (1989). Credibility and political language. In R. Wodak, ed., *Language, Power and Ideology: Studies in political discourse*. Amsterdam: John Benjamins, 115–135.

Holt, E. (1996). Reporting on talk: The use of direct reported speech in conversation. *Research on Language and Social Interaction*, 29 (3): 219–245.

Holt, E. (2009). Reported speech. In S. D'hondt, J.-O. Östman and J. Verschueren, eds., *The Pragmatics of Interaction*. Amsterdam and Philadelphia: John Benjamins, 190–205.

Holt, E. and R. Clift (2010). *Reporting Talk: Reported speech in interaction*. Cambridge: Cambridge University Press.

Hopper, P. (1987). Emergent grammar. *Berkeley Linguistic Society*, 13: 139–157.

Hopper, P. (1998). Emergent grammar. In M. Tomasello, ed., *The New Psychology of Language: Cognitive and functional approaches to linguistic structure*. Englewood Cliffs, NJ: Erlbaum, 154–175.

Hopper, P. J. (1991). On some principles of grammaticisation. In E. C. Traugott and B. Heine, eds., *Approaches to Grammaticalization*, Vol. I. Amsterdam and Philadelphia: John Benjamins, 17–35.

Hopper, P. (2001). Grammatical constructions and their discourse origins: prototype or family resemblance? In M. Pütz, S. Niemeier and R. Dirven, eds., *Applied Cognitive Linguistics I: Theory and language acquisition*. Berlin: de Gruyter Mouton, 109–129.

Hopper, P. and Thompson, S. A. (1980). Transitivity in grammar and discourse. *Language*, 56: 251–299.

House of Commons Information Office. (2010). *Broadcasting Proceedings of the House*, Parliamentary Copyright August 2010.
House of Commons Information Office. (2012). *Visitors to the Gallery*, Information leaflet, December 2012.
House of Commons Information Office. (2013). *Parliamentary Questions*, Parliamentary Copyright March 2013.
Hundt, M. and Mair, C. (1999). 'Agile' and 'uptight' genres: The corpus-based approach to language change in progress. *International Journal of Corpus Linguistics*, 4: 221–242.
Ilie, C. (2010a). Identity co-construction in parliamentary discourse practices. In C. Ilie, ed., *European Parliaments under Scrutiny: Discourse strategies and interaction practices*. Amsterdam: John Benjamins: 57–78.
Ilie, C. (2010b). Strategic uses of parliamentary forms of address: The case of the UK Parliament and the Swedish riksdag. *Journal of Pragmatics*, 42: 885–911.
Ilie, C. (2013). Gendering confrontational rhetoric: Discursive disorder in the British and Swedish parliaments. *Democratization*, 20 (3): 501–521.
Ilie, C. (2015). Follow-ups as multifunctional questioning and answering strategies in Prime Minister's Questions. In A. Fetzer, E. Weizman and L. N. Berlin, eds., *Dynamics of Political Discourse: Forms and functions of follow-ups*. Amsterdam: John Benjamins, 195–218.
Imo, W. (2007). *Construction Grammar und Gesprochene-Sprache-Forschung: Konstruktionen mit zehn matrixsatzfähigen Verben im gesprochenen Deutsch*. Tübingen: Niemeyer.
Imo, W. (2009). Inszenierungen eigener und fremder Rede durch Konstruktionen mit dem Verb sagen. In M. Buss, S. Habscheid, S. Jautz and F. Liedtke, eds., *Theatralität des sprachlichen Handelns*. Paderborn: Fink, 319–336.
Jakobson, R. (1990 [1957]). Shifters, verbal categories, and the Russian verb. In L. Waugh and M. Monville-Burston, eds., *On Language: Roman Jakobson*. Cambridge, MA: Harvard University Russian Language Project, 386–392.
Janney, R. (1999). The whole truth and nothing but the truth: Linguistic avoidance in the O.J. Simpson transcripts. In W. Falkner and H.-J. Schmid, eds., *Words, Lexemes, Concepts – Approaches to the Lexicon. Studies in honour of Leonhard Lipka*. Tübingen: Narr, 259–272.
Jansen, W., Gregory, M. L. and Brenier, J. M. (2001). Prosodic correlates of directly reported speech: Evidence from conversational speech. Conference paper. Prosody in Speech Recognition and Understanding. Red Bank, NJ, 22–24 October. Online. https://bit.ly/3uMTYq7
Jefferson, G. (1990). List construction as a task and interactional resource. In G. Psathas, ed., *Interactional Competence*. New York: University Press of America, 63–92.
Johnstone, B. (1987). 'He says ... so I said': Verb tense alternation and narrative depictions of authority in American English. *Linguistics*, 25, 33–52.

Jones, G. W. (1972/1973). The prime minister and parliamentary questions. *Parliamentary Affairs*, 26: 260–273.
Jucker, A. H. (1986). *News Interviews: A pragmalinguistic analysis*. Amsterdam: John Benjamins.
Jucker, A. H. (1992). *Social Stylistics: Syntactic variation in British newspapers*. Berlin and New York: de Gruyter Mouton.
Jucker, A. H. (1996). News actor labelling in British newspapers. *Text*, 16 (3): 373–390.
Jucker, A. H. and Kopaczyk, J. (2013). Communities of practice as a locus of language change. In J. Kopaczyk and A. H. Jucker, eds., *Communities of Practice in the History of English*. Amsterdam: John Benjamins: 1–16.
Jucker, A. H. and Landert, D. (2015). Historical pragmatics and early speech recordings: Diachronic developments in turn-taking and narrative structure in radio talk shows. *Journal of Pragmatics*, 79: 22–39.
Kärkkäinen, E. (2003). *Epistemic Stance in English Conversation: A description of its interactional functions, with a focus on I Think*. Amsterdam: John Benjamins.
Keevallik, L. (2008). Conjunction and sequenced actions: The Estonian complementizer and evidential particle *et*. In R. Laury, ed., *Crosslinguistic Studies of Clause Combining: The multifunctionality of conjunctions*. Amsterdam and Philadelphia: John Benjamins, 125–152.
Keevallik, L. (2010). Bodily quoting in dance correction. *Research on Language and Social Interaction*, 43 (4): 401–426.
Keevallik, L. (2013). The interdependence of bodily demonstrations and clausal syntax. *Research on Language and Social Interaction*, 46 (1): 1–21.
Klewitz, G. and Couper-Kuhlen, E. (1999). QUOTE – UNQUOTE? The role of prosody in the contextualisation of reported speech sequences. *Pragmatics*, 9 (4): 459–485.
Koch, P. and Oesterreicher, W. 2007. Schriftlichkeit und kommunikative Distanz. *Zeitschrift für germanistische Linguistik*, 35 (3): 346–375.
Komter, M. (2013). Conversation Analysis in the courtroom. In J. Sidnell and T. Stivers, eds, *The Handbook of Conversation Analysis*. Malden, MA: Blackwell: 612–629.
Labov, W. (1981). What can be learned about change in progress from synchronic description? In D. Sankoff and H. Cedergren, eds., *Variation Omnibus*. Edmonton, Alberta: Linguistic Research, 177–201.
Labov, W. (1994). *Principles of Linguistic Change*, Vol. 1: Internal Factors. Oxford: Basil Blackwell.
Lakoff, G. and Johnson, M. (2003). *Metaphors We Live By*. London: University of Chicago Press.
Lave, J. and Wenger, E. (1991). *Situated Learning: Legitimate peripheral participation*. Cambridge: Cambridge University Press.
Lawson, P. A., Citron, D. M., Tyrrell, K. L. and Finegold, S. M. (2016). Reclassification of *Clostridium difficile* as *Clostridioides difficile* (Hall and O'Toole 1935) Prévot 1938. *Anaerobe*, 40: 95–99.

Leech, Geoffrey. 2004. *Meaning and the English Verb*, 4th edn, Harlow: Pearson Longman.

Leech, G., Hundt, M., Mair, C. and Smith, N. (2009). *Change in Contemporary English: A grammatical study*. Cambridge: Cambridge University Press.

Levin, B. (1993). *English Verb Classes and Alternations: A preliminary investigation*. Chicago: University of Chicago Press.

Levinson, S. C. (2013). Action formation and ascription. In J. Sidnell and T. Stivers, eds., *The Handbook of Conversation Analysis*. Malden, MA: Wiley-Blackwell, 103–130.

Linell, P. (2005). *The Written Language Bias in Linguistics: Its nature, origins and transformations*. Abingdon and New York: Routledge.

Love, R., Dembry, C., Hardie, A., Brezina, V. and McEnery, T. (2017). The Spoken BNC2014: Designing and building a spoken corpus of everyday conversations. *International Journal of Corpus Linguistics*, 22 (3): 319–344.

Lovenduski, J. (2014a). Prime Minister's Questions underpins an expectation that politics is an activity best performed by men. *Democratic Audit*, 16 March. Online. http://bit.ly/3dYWaF7

Lovenduski, J. (2014b). The institutionalisation of sexism in politics. *Political Insight*, 5: 16–19.

Lyons, J. (1995). *Linguistic Semantics: An introduction*. Cambridge: Cambridge University Press.

Mair, C. (2006). *Twentieth-Century English: History, variation, and standardisation*. Cambridge: Cambridge University Press.

Mair, C. (2013). Using 'small' corpora of written and spoken English to document ongoing grammatical change: The case of specificational clefts in 20th century English. In M. Krug and J. Schlüter, eds., *Research Methods in Language Variation and Change*. Cambridge: Cambridge University Press, 181–194.

Mair, C. and Leech, G. (2006). Current change in English syntax. In B. Aarts and A. MacMahon, eds., *The Handbook of English Linguistics*. Oxford: Blackwell, 318–342.

Mann, W. C. and Thompson, S. A. (1988). Rhetorical structure theory: Towards a functional theory of text organisation. *Text*, 8 (3): 243–281.

Mathis, T. and Yule, G. (1994). Zero quotatives. *Discourse Processes*, 18 (1): 63–76.

Mayes, P. D. (1990). Quotation in spoken English. *Studies in Language*, 14: 325–363.

Mazeland, H. (2003). A politician's sociology: US Vice President Gore's categorisation of the participants in the Warsaw Uprising. In T. Ensink and C. Sauer, eds., *The Art of Commemoration: Fifty years after the Warsaw uprising*. Amsterdam and Philadelphia: John Benjamins, 95–115.

Mazeland, H. (2007). Parenthetical sequences. *Journal of Pragmatics*, 39 (10): 1816–1869.

Mollin, S. (2007). The Hansard hazard: Gauging the accuracy of British parliamentary transcripts. *Corpora*, 2 (2): 187–210.

Mondada, L. (2019a). Conventions for multimodal transcription. Version 3.0.1. www.lorenzamondada.net/multimodal-transcription

Mondada, L. (2019b). Practices for showing, looking, and videorecording: The interactional establishment of a common focus of attention. In E. Reber and C. Gerhardt, eds., *Embodied Activities in Face-to-face and Mediated Settings: Social encounters in time and space*. Cham: Palgrave Macmillan, 63–104.

Mulder, J. and Thompson, S. A. (2008). The grammaticalization of *but* as a final particle in English conversation. In R. Laury, ed., *Crosslinguistic Studies of Clause Combining: The multifunctionality of conjunctions*. Amsterdam: John Benjamins, 179–204.

Munro, P. (1982). On the transitivity of 'say' verbs. In P. Hopper and S. Thompson, eds., *Studies in Transitivity*. New York: Academic Press, 301–318.

Mushin, I. (2001). *Evidentiality and Epistemological Stance: Narrative retelling*. Amsterdam and Philadelphia: John Benjamins.

Niemelä, M. (2005). Voiced direct reported speech in conversational storytelling: Sequential patterns of stance taking. *SKY Journal of Linguistics*, 18: 197–221.

Noonan, M. (1985). Complementation. In T. Shopen, ed., *Language Typology and Syntactic Description*, Vol. II. Cambridge: Cambridge University Press, 42–139.

Norton, P. (1996). Calling time on questions. *Parliamentary Review*, June.

Nuckolls, J. and Michael, L., eds. (2012). Evidentiality in interaction. Special issue. *Pragmatics and Society*, 3 (2).

Nuyts, J. 2001. *Epistemic Modality, Language, and Conceptualisation: A cognitive-pragmatic perspective*. Amsterdam and Philadelphia: John Benjamins.

Palmer, F. R. 1986. *Mood and Modality*. Cambridge: Cambridge University Press.

Park, Y. (2009). Interaction between grammar and multimodal resources: Quoting different characters in Korean multiparty conversation. *Discourse Studies*, 11 (1): 79–104.

Pomerantz, A. (1986). Extreme case formulations: A way of legitimizing claims. *Human Studies*, 9 (2/3): 219–229.

Portner, P. (2009). *Modality*. Oxford: Oxford University Press.

Quirk, R., Greenbaum, S., Leech, G. and Svartvik, J. (1985). *A Comprehensive Grammar of the English Language*. London: Longman.

Raymond, G. (2000) The voice of authority: The local accomplishment of authoritative discourse in live news broadcasts. *Discourse Studies*, 2 (3): 354–379.

Raymond, G. (2003). Grammar and social organisation: Yes/no type interrogatives and the structure of responding. *American Sociological Review*, 68: 939–967.

Raymond, G. and J. Heritage (2006). The epistemics of social relationships: Owning grandchildren. *Language in Society*, 35 (5): 677–705.

Reber, E. (2012). Evidential positioning in follow-ups in news interviews. In A. Fetzer, E. Weizman and E. Reber, eds., *Proceedings of the EFS Strategic Workshop on Follow-ups across Discourse Domains: A cross-cultural exploration of their forms and functions, Würzburg (Germany), 31 May–2 June 2012*. Würzburg: Universität Würzburg, 205–220. URN: nbn:de:bvb:20-opus-71656

Reber, E. (2014a). Constructing evidence at Prime Minister's Question Time: An analysis of the grammar, semantics and pragmatics of the verb see. Special issue 'Evidentiality in Discourse'. *Intercultural Pragmatics*, 11 (3): 357–387.
Reber, E. (2014b). Follow-ups in parliamentary request sequences, Unpublished ms.
Reber, E. (2014c). Obama said it: Quoting as evidential strategy in online discussion forums. Special issue 'Certainty and Uncertainty in Dialogue' *Language and Dialogue*, 4 (1): 76–92.
Reber, E. (2019). Punch and Judy politics? Embodying challenging courses of action in parliament. In E. Reber and C. Gerhardt, eds., *Embodied Activities in Face-to-face and Mediated Settings: Social encounters in time and space*. Cham: Palgrave Macmillan, 255–297.
Reber, E. (2020a). Zur Rolle von Phonetik und Prosodie in CAN I X-, LE? ME X-, und LEMME X-Konstruktionen. In W. Imo and J. P. Lanwer, eds., *Prosodie und Konstruktionsgrammatik*. Berlin: de Gruyter, 135–165.
Reber, E. (2020b). Visuo-material performances: 'Literalised' quotations in Prime Minister's Questions. Special issue 'Linguistic recycling.' *AILA Review*, 33: 176–203.
Reber, E. (2021). Calibrating syntax, prosody and gaze in parliamentary questions. In M. Kupetz and F. Kern, eds., *Prosodie in der multimodalen Welt*. Heidelberg: Universitätsverlag Winter, 239-266.
Reynolds, E. (2011a). Epistemics in conflict: Enticing a challengeable in protest arguments. *Proceedings of the 106th American Sociological Association – Ethnomethodology and Conversation Analysis stream*.
Reynolds, E. (2011b). Enticing a challengeable in arguments: Sequence, epistemics and preference organisation. *Pragmatics*, 21 (3): 411–430.
Reynolds, E. (2013). Enticing a challengeable: Instituting social order as a practice of public conflict. PhD dissertation. University of Queensland.
Reynolds, E. (2015). How participants in arguments challenge the normative position of an opponent. *Discourse Studies*, 7 (3): 299–316.
Robles, J. S. (2011). Doing disagreement in the House of Lords: 'Talking around the issue' as a context-appropriate argumentative strategy. *Discourse and Communication*, 5 (2): 147–168.
Roth, A. L. (2005). 'Pop quizzes' on the campaign trail: Journalists, candidates, and the limits of questioning. *The International Journal of Press/Politics*, 10 (2): 28–46.
Rumsey, A. (1992). Wording, meaning, and linguistic ideology. *American Anthropologist*, 92: 346–361.
Sacks, H. and Schegloff, E. A. (2007 [1979]). Two preferences in the organization of reference to persons in conversation and their interaction. In N. J. Enfield and T. Stivers, eds., *Person Reference in Interaction: Linguistic, cultural and social perspectives*. Cambridge: Cambridge University Press, 23–28.
Sacks, H., Schegloff, E. A. and Jefferson, G. (1974). A simplest systematics for the organization of turn-taking for conversation. *Language*, 50: 696–735.
Sato, I. L. (2014). Social relations and institutional structures in modern American political campaigns, Dissertation. University of California, Santa Barbara.

Schegloff, E. A (1968). Sequencing in conversational openings. *American Anthropologist*, 70 (6): 1075–1095.
Schegloff, E. A. (1972). Notes on a conversational practice: Formulating place. In D. N. Sudnow, ed., *Studies in Social Interaction*. New York: MacMillan, The Free Press, 75–119.
Schegloff, E. A. (1996a). Some practices for referring to persons in talk-in-interaction: A partial sketch of a systematics. In B. Fox, ed., *Studies in Anaphora*. Amsterdam and Philadelphia: John Benjamins, 437–485.
Schegloff, E. A. (1996b). Turn organisation: One intersection of grammar and interaction. In E. Ochs, E. A. Schegloff and S. A. Thompson, eds., *Interaction and Grammar*. Cambridge: Cambridge University Press, 52–133.
Schegloff, E. A. (2007). *Sequence Organisation in Interaction: A primer in conversation analysis*. Cambridge: Cambridge University Press.
Schubiger, M. (1958). *English Intonation: Its form and function*. Tübingen: Niemeyer.
Sealey, A. and Bates, S. (2016). Prime ministerial self-reported actions in Prime Minister's Questions 1979–2010: A corpus-assisted analysis. *Journal of Pragmatics*, 104: 18–31.
Seggewiß, F. (2013). Current changes in the English modals: A corpus-based analysis of present-day spoken English. Doctoral dissertation. University of Freiburg.
Selting, M. (1994). Emphatic speech style: With special focus on the prosodic signalling of heightened emotive involvement in conversation. *Journal of Pragmatics*, 22: 375–408.
Selting, M. (2007). Lists as embedded structures and the prosody of list construction as an interactional resource. Special issue 'Diversity and continuity in conversation analysis.' *Journal of Pragmatics*, 39: 483–526.
Shaw, S. (2000). Language, gender and floor apportionment in political debates. *Discourse Society*, 11: 401–418.
Sidnell, J. (2006). Coordinating gesture, gaze and talk in re-enactments. *Research on Language and Social Interaction*, 39 (4): 377–409.
Sidnell, J. (2012). 'Who knows best?' Evidentiality and epistemic asymmetry in conversation. Special issue 'Evidentiality in interaction.' *Pragmatics and Society*, 3 (2): 294–320.
Sidnell, J. (2013). Basic conversation analytic methods. In J. Sidnell and T. Stivers, eds., *The Handbook of Conversation Analysis*. Malden, MA: Wiley-Blackwell, 77–99.
Sinclair, J. and Coulthard, M. (1975). *Towards an Analysis of Discourse*. Oxford: Oxford University Press.
Slembrouck, S. (1992). The parliamentary Hansard 'verbatim' report: The written construction of spoken discourse. *Language and Literature*, 1 (2): 101–119.
Stivers, T. (2011). Morality and question design: 'Of course' as contesting a presupposition of askability. In T. Stivers, L. Mondada and J. Steensig, eds., *The Morality of Knowing in Conversation*. Cambridge: Cambridge University Press, 82–106.

Stivers, T., Mondada, L. and Steensig, J. (2011). Knowledge, morality and affiliation in social interaction. In T. Stivers, L. Mondada and J. Steensig, eds. *The Morality of Knowing in Conversation*. Cambridge: Cambridge University Press, 3–24.

Stec, K, Huiskes, M. and Redeker, G. (2016). Multimodal quotation: Role shift practices in spoken narratives. *Journal of Pragmatics*, 104: 1–17.

Streeck, J. (1993). Gesture as communication I: Its coordination with gaze and speech. *Communication Monographs*, 60 (4): 275–299.

Streeck, J. (2008). Gesture in political communication: A case study of the Democratic presidential candidates during the 2004 primary campaign. *Research on Language and Social Interaction*, 41 (2): 154–186.

Tannen, D. 2007. *Talking Voices: Repetition, dialogue, and imagery in conversational discourse*, 2nd edn, Cambridge: Cambridge University Press.

Thompson, S. A. 2002. 'Object complements' and conversation towards a realistic account. *Studies in Language*, 26 (1): 125–164.

Thompson, S. A. and Hopper, P. J. (2001). Transitivity, clause structure, and argument structure: Evidence from conversation. In J. L. Bybee and P. J. Hopper, eds., *Frequency and the Emergence of Linguistic Structure*. Amsterdam and Philadelphia: John Benjamins, 27–60.

Thompson, S. A. and Koide, Y. (1987). Iconicity and 'indirect objects' in English. *Journal of Pragmatics*, 11: 399–406.

Thompson, S. A. and Mulac, A. (1991a). A quantitative perspective on the grammaticisation of epistemic parentheticals in English. In E. Traugott and B. Heine, eds, *Approaches to Grammaticalisation*, Vol. II. Amsterdam: John Benjamins, 313–339.

Thompson, S. A. and Mulac, A. 1991b. The discourse conditions for the use of the complementizer *that* in conversational English. *Journal of Pragmatics*, 15: 237–251.

Traugott, E. C. (2010). Grammaticalisation. In S. Luraghi and V. Bubenik, eds., *Continuum Companion to Historical Linguistics*. London: Continuum Press, 269–283.

Traugott, E. C. and Trousdale, G. (2010). Gradience, gradualness and grammaticalisation: How do they intersect? In E. C. Traugott and G. Trousdale, eds., *Gradience, Gradualness and Grammaticalization*. Amsterdam and Philadelphia: John Benjamins, 19–44.

Traugott, E. C., and Trousdale, G. (2013). *Constructionalization and Constructional Changes*. Oxford: Oxford University Press.

Travis, C. E. and Lindstrom, A. M. (2016). Different registers, different grammars? Subject expression in English conversation and narrative. *Language Variation and Change*, 28 (1): 103–128.

van Dijk, T. A. (2014). *Discourse and Knowledge: A sociocognitive approach*. Cambridge: Cambridge University Press.

Varantola, K. (1984). An aspect of term-formation in engineering English. In H. Ringbom and M. Rissanen, eds., *Proceedings from the Second Nordic*

Conference for English Studies. Hanasaari/Hanaholmen, Finland, 19–21 May 1983. Åbo: Åbo Akademie, 94–102.

Vice, J. and Farrell, S. (n.d). *The History of Hansard*, House of Lords: Hansard and the House of Lords Library.

Vincze, L., Bongelli, R., Riccioni I. and Zuczkowski, A. (2016). Ignorance-unmasking questions in the Royal-Sarkozy presidential debate: A resource to claim epistemic authority. *Discourse Studies*, 18 (4): 430–453.

Vološhinov, V. N. (1986). *Marxism and the Philosophy of Language*. Cambridge, MA: Harvard University Press.

Waddle, M. T., Bull, P. and Böhnke, J. R. (2019). 'He is just the nowhere man of British politics': Personal attacks in Prime Minister's Questions. *Journal of Language and Social Psychology*, 38 (1): 61–84.

Weinreich, U., Labov, W. and Herzog, M. (1968). Empirical foundations for a theory of language change. In W. P. Lehmann and Y. Malkiel, eds., *Directions for Historical Linguistics*. Austin, TX: University of Texas Press, 95–195.

Wenger, E. (1998). *Communities of Practice: Learning, meaning, and identity*. Cambridge: Cambridge University Press.

Whitt, R. J. (2010). *Evidentiality and Perception Verbs in English and German*. Oxford: Peter Lang.

Wilson, J. (1990). *Politically Speaking: The pragmatic analysis of political language*. Oxford: Blackwell.

Wooffitt, R. and Aliston, S. (2008). Participation, procedure and accountability: 'You said' speech markers in negotiating reports of ambiguous phenomena. *Discourse Studies*, 10 (3): 407–427.

Vandelanotte, L. and Davidse, K. (2009). The emergence and structure of *be like* and related quotatives: a constructional account. *Cognitive Linguistics*, 20 (4): 777–807.

For EU product safety concerns, contact us at Calle de José Abascal, 56–1°,
28003 Madrid, Spain or eugpsr@cambridge.org.

www.ingramcontent.com/pod-product-compliance
Ingram Content Group UK Ltd.
Pitfield, Milton Keynes, MK11 3LW, UK
UKHW030805150425
457293UK00016B/257